Indian Names For Girls

More than 20,500 Most Popular
Indian Baby Names with Meanings

Atina Amrahs

About the Book

It is a very difficult task for parents to keep children's name. They want their child's name to be unique and extraordinary. For this, they start preparing even before the baby is born. They try to find new names from many sources. But now you do not have to wander around here. This book contains all the names that you are looking for.

So what's the matter of late, find the simple, beautiful and best name for your child today.

—Author

Name Alphabets

Indian Names For Girls—A

Aab—water, shine
Aas—hope, asylum, acceptance, faith
Aau—span of life, age
Ababa—bloom, garden stuff, fruit
Abala—immovable, the earth
Abani—earth, ground, land
Abantika—city of ujjain, princess of ujjain
Abarajitha—roar
Abaranji—pretty, lovely, handsome, graceful name
Abarna—ornament, jewellery, ornamentation, adornment, figuration
Abayomi—pleasant meeting
Abbinnaya—pretty, lovely, handsome, graceful name
Abdhija—born in the sea, goddess lakshmi
Abeedha—permanent
Abeela—pretty, lovely, handsome, graceful name
Abha—beauty, splendour
Abha—brightness, lustre, shine
Abharana—ornament, jewellery, ornamentation, adornment
Abharan—jewellery, ornamentation, adornment, figuration
Abharantee—without error
Abhari—grateful
Abharika—the goddess
Abha—shine, luster, sun-rays, aura
Abha—the illumination, luminosity, radiance
Abhati—splendour, illumination, luminosity, radiance
Abhavya—signifies fear, goddess parvati
Abhaya—fearless, intrepid, nirbhay, unshrinking
Abhayankari—one who gives courage
Abhaya—one who is fearless
Abhaya—without fear, fearless
Abhera—a cowherd
Abheri—fearless, intrepid, unshrinking

Abhesha—goddess of will
Abhibha—fearless, fluttering
Abhibha—glittering
Abhichandrika—one who is like moon
Abhidha—literal meaning
Abhidhya—desire, aspiration, longing, longing
Abhidhya—word, name
Abhidya—of thought, desire, aspiration, longing, longing
Abhi—fearless
Abhi—fearless, surprise, very nice
Abhigeetha—praised
Abhigjna—wisdom
Abhigna—valuable, valued, rare, knowledgeable
Abhignya—wise one
Abhigoortee—chant of praise
Abhigya—wise one, expert
Abhijaata—well born
Abhijata—well born woman
Abhijaya—complete victory, victorious
Abhijaya—victory
Abhijina—skillful, clever, remembrance
Abhijishya—independent girl
Abhijita—conquered
Abhijita—victorious woman
Abhijitee—victory
Abhijitha—lakshmi
Abhijit—victory
Abhijiya—pretty, lovely, handsome, graceful name
Abhijna—expert
Abhijna—remembrance, recollection
Abhikanksha—longing for, ambition, intent, passion
Abhikhya—glory, beauty, splendour, fame
Abhilasa—ambition, intent, passion, desire, aspiration, longing
Abhilasa—desire, aspiration, longing, ambition, intent, passion

Abhilasha—ambition, intent, passion, desire, aspiration
Abhilasha—desire, aspiration, longing, ambition, intent, passion
Abhilash—desire, aspiration, longingngel
Abhilashini—full of ambition, intent, passion
Abhilashita—ambition, intent, passion, desire, aspiration, longed
Abhilipsa—first desire, aspiration, longing
Abhilipsha—aspire
Abhilisa—ambition, intent, passion
Abhimaanine—who possesses, self respect
Abhimanene—self respected woman
Abhimani—full of pride
Abhimanini—a woman who possesses self respect
Abhimanini—proud of herself
Abhimukhi—facing
Abhinanda—illumination, luminosity, radiance
Abhinandana—happiness, good desire, aspiration, longinges
Abhinandita—one who illumination, luminosity, radiances
Abhinandni—one who illumination, luminosity, radiances
Abhinavi—always new, rock star, creative
Abhinaya—actingctressction
Abhineta—perfect
Abhineti—one who achieve perfection
Abhinetri—actress
Abhinita—suitable, proper, excellent
Abhiniti—gesture, friendship
Abhinivesha—possessiveness
Abhinoor—listensngel
Abhioruchi—deep interest
Abhipreeti—full of love
Abhiprithi—full of love
Abhipriti—full of love
Abhipriya—the first amiable, pleasing, suave, interesting
Abhipsa—ambition, intent, passion

Abhipsha—desire, aspiration, longing, ambition, intent, passion
Abhira—cow-herd
Abhiraksa—one who protects
Abhiraksha—one who protects
Abhirami—goddess gouri, goddess parvati
Abhirathi—pleasure
Abhirati—pleasure
Abhirati—pleasure, illumination, luminosity, radiance
Abhiri—a ragini of indian music
Abhirka—wife of cowherd
Abhiroopa—luminosity, radianceful, beloved, pretty, lovely, handsome, graceful
Abhiruchi—pretty, lovely, handsome, graceful, taste, relish
Abhirupa—pretty, lovely, handsome, graceful woman
Abhirupa—handsome, favourite
Abhisaarikaa—fearless, goddess parvati
Abhisarika—a person who keeps trust of beloved
Abhisarikaa—the beloved one
Abhisarika—beloved
Abhisha—pleasant, consolation
Abhishikta—installed on a throne
Abhishree—illumination, luminosity, radiance
Abhishri—surrounded with glory
Abhishu—a ray of illumination, luminosity, radiance
Abhismita—perfectionist, pretty, lovely, handsome, graceful smile
Abhisneha—love, longing
Abhisri—surrounded by glory, shining
Abhista—one for whom you care
Abhitha—fearless, goddess parvati
Abhithi—fearlessness
Abhiti—fearlessness
Abhivadaka—a devotee
Abhivanadaka—respectful salute
Abhivandana—to salute
Abhivandya—respected
Abhivibha—illuminating
Abhivyakti—expressions

Abhja—water lily
Abhpri—gladdening, refreshing
Abhraganga—the celestial ganga
Abhramani—sun or moon
Abhramu—steady, clear
Abhranti—without error
Abhrayanti—forming clouds, bringing rain
Abhriruci—deep interest
Abhya—fearless
Abilasha—desire, aspiration, longing, ambition, intent, passion, goddess lakshmi
Abila—skilled expert
Abimola—born to be rich
Abina—born on a thursday, cute
Abinaya—god, pretty girl, lovely, sweet
Abirami—friendly, goddess lakshmi
Abiramsundari—pretty, lovely, handsome, graceful like a fairy
Abira—strong
Abisha—gift of god
Abishai—my father is a gift
Abishta—lady of the house
Abja—born in water
Abjini—bunch of lotus
Abjini—multitude of lotuses
Abla—perfectly formed bloom, garden stuff
Abmel—support, indoctrination, assurednessful
Abni—air, fire
Aboil—the bloom, garden stuff
Aboli—a bloom, garden stuff
Aboli—a bloom, garden stuff, bloom, garden stuff
Absara—moves in the rains in the clouds
Abudita—awakened
Acala—the immovable one
Acane—the bed of river
Acchal—shelter
Acchoda—with clear water river
Acchupta—in active
Achala—firm, constant
Achala—steady, mountain, river, constant

Achalatanya—daughter of the mountain
Achal—shelter, dwelling
Achal—steady, mountainous, constant
Acharat—astonishment
Acharati—astonishment
Acheri—little girl
Achhita—rice, whiteness
Achint—having no worry
Achintya—beyond thought
Achiraprabha—illumination, luminosity, radiance
Achira—to the point, one who is brief
Achira—very short, cold season
Achita—pay, filled
Achit—constant
Achitha—filled
Achi—whole
Achla—constant, earth, stable
Achu—can not destroy, brilliant, sagacious, gifted, wise, learnedly
Achyutha—immovable
Acira—brief, swift, fast
Adag—holy, sanctified, pious, solemn, chaste, sacred
Ada—graceful and noble, holy, sanctified, pious, solemn, chaste, noble
Adah—from the pretty, lovely, handsome, graceful scenery
Adakavalli—ideal, modelim
Adanna—father's loving daughter
Adanya—beginning, goddess parvati
Adarsha—ideal, model
Adarsh—ideal, model
Adarshi—ideal, model
Adarshini—ideal, moralistic
Adasi—free woman
Adatta—unmarried girl
Adbhutha—holy, sanctified, pious, solemn, chaste as marvel
Addhwara—pretty, lovely, handsome, graceful name
Addhya—worshipped
Addrija—mountain born
Adeity—devoted to god
Adeshini—ordering, commanding
Adhana—being first
Adhana—one without money

Adharshana—ideal, modelistic
Adhaya—brilliant, sagacious, gifted, wise, learned, brave
Adhaya—first power
Adhena—goddess of art
Adheni—nearest
Adhidevta—a deity
Adhideya—goddess
Adhika—more, greater
Adhiksha—pretty, lovely, handsome, graceful name
Adhikshitha—ultimate, absolute, highest, best god
Adhilakshmi—summer sun
Adhila—pretty, lovely, handsome, graceful name
Adhinanda—daughter of moon
Adhirai—a special star
Adhira—illumination, luminosity, radiance, jasmine, success
Adhira—restless, moon
Adhishree—superior, elevated
Adhisree—goddess lakshmi
Adhita—a scholar
Adhiya—full of sweetness, courageous
Adhiya—worship of goddess amba
Adhrika—mountain, goddess lakshmi
Adhrisha—truth, devotion, unique
Adhrushta—luck, one of the ten durgas
Adhrushtha—luck
Adhrysa—invincible
Adhuna—name of lord shiva
Adhvaithya—un-perishable
Adhvi—earth
Adhvika—unique
Adhya—beginning, first power,
Adhya—first power, lord ganesha
Adhya—goddess durga
Adhyashri—goddess durga
Adhyasree—goddess durga
Adhyatha—first preference
Adhyatmika—one who is very laborious
Adhyay—goddess durga
Adi—adornment, ornament, jewellery, ornamentation, adornment, figuration, the first

Adia—first one on earth, goddess durga
Adi—beginning, st, first
Adi—firstborn, beginning
Adija—goddess parvati
Adiksha—intention of education
Adilakshmi—the primal lakshmi
Adil—sincere, ultimate, absolute, highest, best being
Adimata—the primal mother
Adipta—pretty, lovely, handsome, graceful name
Adira—strong, noble, pretty, lovely, handsome, graceful, powerful
Adisakti—the primal energy
Adisha—pretty, lovely, handsome, graceful
Adishakti—first, original power
Adishakti—glorious, goddess parvati
Adisha—without direction, lakshmi deity
Adishree—superior, elevated
Adishree—superior, elevated, goddess lakshmi, parvati
Adishri—goddess lakshmi
Adishri—goddess lakshmi, superior, elevated, dignity
Adisree—superior, elevated
Adisri—mother of gods
Adita—first root, sun, beginning
Adita—from the beginning
Adita—the first root, the sun
Adita—the sun, from the beginning
Aditha—the first root
Adithi—freedom, safetybundance, guest
Adithya—sun god, son of adithi
Aditi—beginning, peak
Aditi—nature, the earth, creative, perfection
Aditi—the earth
Aditi—universal, boundless, limitless
Adit—peak, shade, bright
Aditri—goddess lakshmi
Aditri—highest honour, goddess lakshmi
Aditsha—ambition, intent, passion to talk

Aditya—the first, lord of the sun
Adiya—gods treasure
Adnah—eternal rest
Adna—pleasure, illumination, luminosity, radiance, in the bible
Adnya—instruction
Adona—serenity, calm, calmness, stillness, silence, joy
Adrija—daughter of mountain
Adrija—of the mountain
Adrika—a small mountain
Adrika—goddess lakshmi, mountain
Adrika—mountain, goddess lakshmi
Adrisa—mountain lord
Adrisha—perception
Adrisha—pretty, lovely, handsome, graceful name
Adrita—adorable
Adrithi—beloved, loved by everyone
Adriti—ornament, jewellery, ornamentation, adornment, figuration
Adriya—strong, noble, powerful
Adrsyanti—invisible
Adrushya—invisible
Adrustha—luck
Advaita—a unique woman
Advaita—non duality
Advaitavadini—propounder of the uniqueness
Advaitha—oneness, non duality
Advaiya—unique
Adveka—unique
Advika—unique
Advika—unique, matchless
Advita—unique, first one, number one
Adviteeya—unique, the first one, no second
Advitha—goddess lakshmi, eternal
Adwaita—one, united, unique
Adwika—unique
Adwita—unique
Adwiteeya—only one, no alternate
Adwiteya—matchless, unique
Adwitha—pretty, lovely, handsome, graceful name
Adwitiya—a unique woman
Adwitiya—matchless, the first
Adwrika—small mountain

Adyahi—always first
Adyanthi—beginning and the end within
Adya—one who is always first, best
Adyasha—the first support, indoctrination, assuredness
Adya—unparalleled, st preference
Aeesha—womanlive
Aeindri—the power of lord indra
Aeisha—pretty, lovely, handsome, graceful, obedient
Aekta—unity
Aelena—pretty, lovely, handsome, graceful name
Aesha—love, woman, lifelivewake
Aeshna—earth
Afashana—fiction
Afreen—encouragement, pretty, lovely, handsome, graceful
Afren—sweet, name of goddess durga
Afrin—happiness, praise, lucky, brave
Afsaana—storey
Afsana—fiction, amour, love, affection, storey
Afsara—angel
Afshana—fiction, storey
Aftab—the sun
Agaja—born of mountain
Agaja—mountainous
Agalya—amiable, pleasing, suave, interesting, illumination, luminosity
Agamani—descent of durga to earth
Agam—arrival, holy jain scripture
Agamya—knowledge, wisdom
Aganit—countless
Aganiya—uncommon
Aganya—born from fire, goddess lakshmi
Agaraja—elder sister
Agarthika—shine
Agasthi—a learned lady
Agasthya—a sage star
Agasti—name of a sage, pitcher-born
Agastya—destroyer of sins
Agasya—maharshi
Agatha—good-hearted, good
Agati—arrival, coming, return, origin
Aggrta—to move forward

Aghanashini—destroyer of sins
Aghna—holy, sanctified, pious, solemn, chaste, virginal
Aghnya—born from fire, goddess lakshmi
Agman—arrival, welcome
Agmaya—born from fire, knowledge
Agna—command
Agna—holy, sanctified, pious, solemn, chaste, virginal, kind, good
Agnajita—one who has conquered
Agnaya—born from fire, new fire
Agnayi—fiery
Agnayi—goddess of fire
Agnes—holy, sanctified, pious, solemn, chaste
Agneta—sacred, chaste, fire, holy, sanctified, pious, solemn, chaste
Agneye—daugther of fire
Agneyi—daughter of fire
Agnibha—shining like fire or gold
Agnidurga—leadership
Agni—fire
Agnije—daughter of fire
Agnijita—one who attain victory over fire
Agnika—belonging to fire
Agnimitra—agni's friend, friend of fire
Agnimukhi—fire faced
Agninayan—shiva
Agnisa—belongs to fire, part of fire
Agnisha—belongs to fire, part of fire
Agnishikha—flames of fire, arrow of fire
Agnivadhu—wife of fire
Agnivardhini—increasing fire
Agnivesha—the sun
Agnyasa—born from fire
Agraja—born first, elder daughter
Agraja—main, first born
Agraj—elder daughter
Agrani—best, number one
Agrasandhya—sunrise
Agrata—leadership
Agratha—leadership
Agraye—a wife of agni
Agrayi—primal wife of agni

Agreshi—god desire, aspiration, longing
Agrika—first
Agrima—coming first, stay on top
Agriya—first and best
Agya—order, permission
Ahad—pledge, commitment, delegation
Ahailya—wife of sage gautama
Ahaladita—happy, luminosity, radiance
Ahaldita—a woman who is happy
Ahalidita—happy woman
Ahalya—wife of rishi gautam
Ahana—dawn
Ahana—first ray of sunrise, chaht
Ahana—first rays of the sun
Ahankaara—indicates pride, goddess parvati
Ahanti—gift
Ahanya—richest of rich
Ahava—loved one, beloved, water
Aheli—grace, goddess lakshmi
Aheli—holy, sanctified, pious, solemn, chaste
Ahi—heaven and earth conjoined
Ahika—cute
Ahila—worldly, knowledgeable
Ahilya—a famous historical name
Ahilya—maiden, without any deformation
Ahimsa—nonviolent virtue
Ahira—brilliant, dazzling
Ahisma—no boundaries
Ahita—hostile, evil
Ahladini—in happy mood
Ahladita—happy, luminosity, radiance
Ahladita—in happy mood, illumination, luminosity, radiance
Ahladitha—illumination, luminosity, radiance
Ahladit—happy mood
Ahlad—joy
Ahna—live, exist, rise
Ahna—live, exist, rise, pretty, lovely, handsome, graceful, traditional
Ahobal—powerful
Ahria—spiritual, music

Ahrmshulla—pretty, lovely, handsome, graceful name
Ahsha—support, indoctrination, assuredness
Ahshika—joyful
Ahu—calling, invomonarch, ruler, prince, earl, bright
Ahuka—offerer, sacrificer
Ahuk—god gift
Ahuti—calling, offering
Ahuti—offering
Ahwaana—invitation
Ahwaintha—wanted
Aice—pretty, wonderful, kind
Aida—visiting, noble, nobility, reward
Aidha—power, splendour flame
Aiesha—womanlive, she who lives, life
Aifa—gift, gift of god
Aiksavaki—produced from sugar cane
Aikshvakee—very sweet
Aikya—unity, oneness
Ailiyah—a great one
Aimee—belovedmazing, talented
Aimiah—perfect
Aina—belonging to black doe
Aina—mirror, illumination, luminosity, radiance, pretty
Aina—mirror, reflection
Aindri—illumination, luminosity, eye, glimmers, the powerful
Aindrila—female star
Aine—spring bloom, garden stuff
Aingeene—agitated
Aingini—goddess durga
Aiouv—nature, gods, happiness
Aira—beloved jasmine, of the wind
Airavati—name of river
Airisha—serenity, calm, calmness, stillness, silence
Aisa—alive
Aisa—obedient, lively person
Aisha—pretty, lovely, handsome, graceful, obedient
Aisha—living, prosperous, lively
Aishani—another name of goddess durga
Aishani—goddess durga
Aishanya—pretty, lovely, handsome, graceful life
Aisheya—ocean
Aishi—being fond of poetry gift
Aishika—god's gift
Aishini—goddess lakshmi
Aishita—sweet
Aishna—ambition, intent, passion, desire, aspiration, longing
Aishu—enjoy life, lively
Aishvarya—luxury
Aishvarya—wealth, richness, goddess lakshmi
Aishvi—lakshmi
Aishvini—female horse
Aishwariya—wealth
Aishwarya—money, wealth
Aishwarya—wealthy, prosperity
Aishwini—angel, star
Aisiri—prosperous, wealth
Aissa—wonderful, grateful
Aisu—long life
Aiswaria—pretty, lovely, handsome, graceful name
Aiswariya—wealth
Aiswarya—wealth, good luck, intellectual
Aiushi—one with long life, live long
Aiyana—eternal blossom, eternal, everlasting beauty
Aiyanna—eternal blossom, innocent
Aiyushi—one with long life, live long
Aizel—one who brings luck and fortune
Aja—a female goat, not born
Ajaa—energy
Ajabu—rare
Ajaganda—daughter of aja
Ajagandha—daughter of aja
Aja—high priestess of mecca
Ajala—earth
Ajala—eternal, birth less
Ajala—the earth
Ajamukhi—daughter of sage kashyap
Ajane—noble birth
Ajani—he fights for what is his
Ajanta—a famous buddhist cave
Ajanta—famous buddhist cave

Ajantha—creative famous buddhist cave

Ajara—not wearing out, everlasting

Ajastha—young earth, earthy, trusting

Ajatha—one who has no enemies, lord shiva

Ajaya—invincible, unconquered

Ajay—unconquerable, god

Ajeenkya—ultimate, absolute, highest, best

Ajeeta—invincible, unconquerable

Ajeitha—a winner

Ajendra—monarch, ruler, prince, earl of mountains

Ajeya—one who cannot be conquered

Ajhati—a woman who possesses good character

Ajinkya—brilliant, invincible

Ajira—a winner

Ajisa—strong and proud

Ajita—always winning winner

Ajitha—winner, unbeatable

Ajit—invincible, victorious

Ajju—mother

Ajmal—pious

Ajooni—infinite

Akaanksha—desire, aspiration, longing or ambition, intent, passion

Akahaye—imperishable

Akaisha—the bloom, garden stuff

Akaksha—ambition, intent, passion

Akalanka—flawless

Akaligai—pretty, lovely, handsome, graceful name

Akalika—moon, illumination, luminosity, radiance

Akalikee—illumination, luminosity, radiance

Akaliki—illumination, luminosity, radianceining

Akalka—holy, sanctified, pious, solemn, chaste, moon illumination, luminosity, radiance

Akalmasha—holy, sanctified, pious, solemn, chaste

Akalya—desire, aspiration, longing

Akane—someone you cannot stop loving

Akangsha—ambition, intent, passion, desire, aspiration, longingmbition, support, indoctrination, assuredness

Akankasha—ambition, desire, aspiration, longing, intent, passion

Akanksha—ambition, desire, aspiration, longing, intent, passion

Akanksha—ambition, intent, passion

Akanksha—expectations, desire, aspiration, longing, ambition, intent, passion, support, indoctrination, assuredness

Akankshi—desirous, desire, aspiration, longing

Akankshya—ambition, intent, passion, desire, aspiration, longing

Akansha—amiable, pleasing, suave, interesting, desire, aspiration, longing, ambition, intent, passion

Akansha—desire, aspiration, longing, ambition, intent, passion

Akanshitha—ambition, intent, passion

Akara—chief deity

Akarsha—above everybody

Akarshaka—pleasing, favourite, charming

Akarshana—attraction

Akarshika—having pleasing, favourite, charming power

Akarshika—pleasing, favourite, charming

Akarshini—pleasing, favourite, charming

Akarshin—pleasing, favourite, charming

Akasadipa—a lamp in the sky

Akasaganga—the milky way

Akasa—open air, space

Akasha—open air, space, sky

Akashara—words

Akashini—women with pretty, lovely, handsome, graceful hair

Akashi—of the sky

Akashi—sky colour

Akashlena—star

Akashna—sky, heaven

Akashy—belongs to sky

Akasi—the atmosphere

Akasya—belongs to the sky
Akchaya—indestructible, goddess lakshmi
Akeelah—eagle
Akeen—devotion
Akeera—graceful vigour
Akhandita—unbroken
Akhandi—whole, entire
Akharnitha—pretty, lovely, handsome, graceful bloom, garden stuff
Akhi—eye, glimmers
Akhila—brilliant, beauty, complete
Akhila—entire
Akhil—all
Akhileswari—lalithamba's other name
Akhira—white lily
Akhshita—immortal
Akhya—fame, glory
Akhyati—famous
Akila—brilliant, sagacious, gifted, wise, learned, completetal
Akila—entire
Akilambigai—goddess parvathi
Akilandam—earth
Akina—spring bloom, garden stuff, relations
Akira—gentle bloom, garden stuff natural
Akiyatri—diagram
Akku—sweet and pretty, lovely, handsome, graceful
Aklima—the first step, pretty, lovely, handsome, graceful
Akranti—force
Akranti—power
Akrant—might, force, power
Akrati—figure, appearance, structure
Akrita—daughter
Akriti—figure, appearance, structure, diagram, form
Akriti—figure, appearance, structure, form, design
Akriti—figure, aspect
Akrodhini—wrathful, calm lady
Akruthi—figure, appearance, structure
Akruti—figure, appearance, structure
Aksamala—a rosary of rudrksa
Aksa—soul

Aksasutra—bearer of knowledge
Aksavali—a string of aksa
Aksaya—everlasting
Aksayini—everlasting
Akshadha—god's blessings
Aksha—god's blessing
Akshainie—goddess parvati
Akshaja—thunder
Akshamala—garland of rudraksh
Akshara—letter, indestructible
Akshata—holy rice, sacred rice of worship
Akshata—unmarried woman
Akshatha—no end, rice
Akshaya—earth
Akshaya—goddess lakshmi, special star
Akshaya—indestructible
Akshayakirti—eternal fame
Akshaya—pretty, lovely, handsome, graceful name
Akshayata—indestructible, unlimited
Akshaye—undeceiving
Akshayni—immortal
Akshe—eye, glimmers
Akshena—blessing of god
Akshera—goddess saraswati
Aksheti—victorious serenity, calm, calmness, stillness, silence
Akshi—eye, glimmers, very valuable, valued, rare, eye, glimmers
Akshika—one with pretty, lovely, handsome, graceful eye, glimmers
Akshi—live, exist, rise, being, entity
Akshima—goddess durga
Akshina—one who is not feeble
Akshini—eye, glimmers, not diminishing
Akshita—holy, sanctified, pious, solemn, chaste
Akshita—wonder, seen, wonderful
Akshitha—unlimited, permanent
Akshithi—victorious serenity, calm, calmness, stillness, silence
Akshiti—victorious serenity, calm, calmness, stillness, silence
Akshit—permanent
Akshobhya—immovable

Akshra—alphabet, letter
Akshta—showing regard towards older
Akshtia—showing regard towards older
Akshu—eye, glimmers
Akshyamati—immortal
Akshyani—immortal
Akshyata—one who does not perish, immortal
Aksima—limitless, eternal, everlasting
Aksithi—imperishably
Aksiti—imperishability
Akula—goddess parvati
Akupara—unbounded, free
Akuta—not of the earth
Akuti—ambition, intent, passion, intention
Akutila—simple
Akuti—princess
Akya—the only one
Alabhya—unique, difficult to acquire
Alagu—knowledge, world
Alaina—valuable, valuable, valued, rare, dear child
Alak—a lock of curly hair
Alaka—a girl with a lovely hair
Alaka—moon, illumination, luminosity, radiance
Alakananda—name of a river
Alakaravati—loving
Alakhnanada—a name of the river, a young girl
Alaknanda—a river in the himalayas
Alaknanda—the river ganga
Alaksha—uncared, unaimed
Alak—world, pretty, lovely, handsome, graceful tresses
Alambusa—a line not to be crossed
Alameda—grove of cottonwood, promenade
Alamela—extremely brilliant, sagacious, gifted, wise, learned
Alamelu—goddess, god balaji wife name
Alamu—god vishnu's wife
Alancrita—ornament, jewellery, ornamentation, adornment, figurationed, decorated
Alankaaram—a ornamentation, adornment, figuration
Alankara—ornament, jewellery, ornamentation, adornment
Alankrita—decorated
Alankrita—decorateduspicious touch
Alankritha—decorated lady, pretty, lovely, handsome, graceful girl
Alapini—a woman who sings, a songstress
Alapini—lute
Alataksi—fire eye, glimmers
Alaya—holy, sanctified, pious, solemn, chaste
Alaya—lofty, sublime
Alaysha—noble, kind, truthful
Alda—old but graceful, rich, old, wise
Aleahya—sunshine
Alekha—pretty, lovely, handsome, graceful name
Alekhya—which cannot be written, picture
Alekya—which cannot be written
Alena—torch of illumination, luminosity, radiance, dear
Alesa—serenity, calm, calmness, stillness, silence, pretty
Aleshane—one who plays all the time
Alesha—noble, nobility, noble sort
Aletrice—pretty, lovely, handsome, graceful name
Alfiya—sweet, one in thousand
Ali—pretty, lovely, handsome, graceful
Alia—superior, elevated, highest social standing
Alin—to soothe, bearer of the illumination, luminosity, radiance
Aliptha—protected
Alisa—kind type, god is salvation, sun
Alisha—a star, god gifted
Alisha—devotee
Alisha—truthful, noble
Alish—impressive, cute
Alishka—brilliant, sagacious, gifted, wise, learned
Alis—noble, kind, noble sort
Alissa—noble kind, nobility, rational

Aliya—high, tall, excellent
Aliyah—to ascend, high, lofty, sublime
Aliya—superior, elevated, sublime, superior, finer
Aliza—joyous, happiness, devotionful
Aliza—joyous, happiness, pious
Alka—pretty, lovely, handsome, graceful hair
Alka—diamond
Alla—an angel, name of truth, defender
Alli—long-tailed duck, noble, nobility
Allpana—expressive, versatile
Alma—caring, fostering, soul
Almas—valuable, valued, rare stone diamond
Almika—the sky
Almira—woman of nobility, princess
Aloka—faultless
Aloka—lustrous
Aloka—lustrous woman
Alokananda—creative, decisivettractive
Aloki—brightness, lustrous
Alokita—unseen
Alokshya—illumination, luminosity, radiance
Alok—sun illumination, luminosity, radiance, universe
Alokya—brightness, illumination, luminosity, radiance, incomparable
Alopa—faultless, without fault
Alopana—free from ambition, intent, passions
Alopa—without ambition, intent, passion
Alpa—little
Alpa—minute
Alpana—a highness, empress, queen
Alpana—decorative design, pretty, lovely, handsome, graceful
Alpini—miser
Alpita—miser
Alsia—grand, stately
Altthea—sincere
Alvy—bright, elf, magical being
Alya—from heaven, sky, loftiness

Amaal—support, indoctrination, desire, aspiration, longing
Amaanya—unmatchable, unacceptable
Amadalikri—appreciation
Amala—goddess lakshmi
Amala—the holy, sanctified, pious, solemn, chaste one, bird
Amaldeepti—camphor
Amalendu—holy, sanctified, pious, solemn, chaste like a moon, full moon
Amalia—industrious, work, striving
Amal—to have support, indoctrination, assuredness, bright,
Amalua—name of ganga river
Amanat—god's treasure, present or gift
Amandeep—illumination, luminosity, radiance of serenity
Aman—friendly disposition, affection
Amani—road, one who shows the path
Amani—spring season
Amanita—modesty, humility
Amanpreet—the protector of serenity, calm, calmness, stillness, silence
Aman—serenity, calm, calmness, stillness, silence
Amanthika—god
Amanya—stubborn
Amara—elegance, grass,
Amaraja—a sacred river,
Amarangana—celestial damsel, immortal beauty
Amarangani—angel
Amaraprabha—eternal shine
Amarata—immortality
Amaratatini—river of deathless
Amaravathi—river name
Amaravati—abode of the eternal, immortal
Amaravti—name of city
Amari—a miracle from god, special gift
Amari—eternal
Amaris—god has promised, child of the
Amarjaa—name of river, immortal
Amarja—goddess
Amarjyoti—eternal flame
Amar—one who lives forever

Amarprabha—eternal shine
Amarta—immortality
Amartha—immortal, everlasting
Amarthakala—pretty, lovely, handsome, graceful name
Amarthi—princess of ejipuran ancient
Amarthya—immortal
Amashu—illumination, luminosity, radiance way
Amati—beyond intellect
Amavashya—parvati
Amavasya—dwelling together
Amaya—goddess of nature, night's rain
Amaya—night rain
Amayra—princess
Amba—goddess durga, mother, wakeful
Ambala—mother, compassionate, scar
Ambalika—mother
Ambalika—mother, one who is sensitive
Ambali—mother
Ambali—sensitive, compassionate, loving
Amba—mother, goddess durga
Ambara—perfumembergris
Ambar—sky, gold-brown semivaluable, valued, rare stone
Ambaya—mother
Amber—gemstone, sky, from the stone
Amberleigh—the sky
Amberley—the sky
Amberlie—the sky
Ambhasa—goddess parvati
Ambhini—born of water
Ambhojini—an assemblage of lotuses
Ambika—goddess durga
Ambika—goddess parvati, durga
Ambikai—goddess durga
Ambi—mother
Ambruni—water
Ambuda—cloud
Ambudha—cloud
Ambudhi—ocean
Ambuja—born of a lotus, goddess lakshmi
Ambuja—cloud

Ambujakshi—lotus eye, glimmers
Ambujam—lotus
Ambumani—nectar
Ambumati—containing water
Ambupadma—lotus of the water
Ambur—name of a semivaluable, valued, rare stone
Ambuvahini—carrying water
Ambu—water, pretty, lovely, handsome, graceful
Ameeka—nectar, sweetness
Amee—sweetness, beloved
Ameeta—boundless, without limit
Ameya—boundless, devotional, devotion
Ameya—signifies beyond measure, goddess
Amidi—boundless, magnanimous
Amiee—mecter
Ami—my people, dearly loved, beauty
Amini—spring season
Aminta—protector, defender
Amira—princess, high-born, speech
Amirtha—elixir of life
Amisa—free from guile
Amisha—honest
Amisha—most pretty, lovely, handsome, graceful, sunshine, brave
Amishi—honest
Amishi—very sweet, holy, sanctified, pious, solemn, chaste
Amishta—fruit
Amishtha—fruit
Amita—egoist
Amita—eternal, everlasting, limitless, unlimited
Amit—friend, infinite, that which
Amitha—unique
Amithi—immeasurable, unique
Amiti—boundless
Amitjyoti—ever bright, limitless brightness
Amitrasudan—illumination, luminosity, rianceful
Amitusha—famous
Amixa—eye, glimmers water
Amiya—nectar

Amiya—nectar, illumination, luminosity, radianceful

Amlankusum—unfading bloom, garden stuff

Amla—the holy, sanctified, pious, solemn, chaste one, goddess of wealth

Amleshlata—goddess parvati

Amlika—tamerind

Amma—born on saturday

Amman—devotionful, trustworthy

Ammani—gem of a girl, pretty, lovely, handsome, graceful gem

Ammaponnu—one who is always ready for new

Ammu—happiness, the holy, sanctified, pious, solemn, chaste, innocent

Amna—serenity, calm, calmness, stillness, silence, softll

Amoda—happiness, joy, pleasure

Amodha—pleasure

Amodine—fragrance

Amodini—fragrance

Amodini—full of joy

Amodini—happy girl, joyful, pleasurable

Amodini—pleasureable

Amodita—happiness, illumination, luminosity, radiance

Amodita—happy, with strong fragrance

Amodita—to give pleasure

Amogha—fruitful

Amoghaksi—of unerring eye, glimmers

Amoghasiddhi—one who does not fail

Amolika—priceless

Amoli—priceless, valuable, valued, rare

Amol—priceless

Amonda—amiable, pleasing, suave, interesting

Amonghakshe—of unerring eye, glimmers

Amoolya—valuable, valued, rare

Amorata—beloved

Amrakali—mango bud

Amrakali—the bud of the mango bloom, garden stuff

Amrakuta—disciple of buddha

Amramanjari—bunch of mango bloom, garden stuffs

Amrapali—a bird

Amrapali—kind of mango, princess, famous

Amrapali—leaf of mango tree

Amrapallavi—leaf of mango tree

Amrapallavi—leaves of mango

Amratama—food obtained from the ocean of milk

Amrata—nectar

Amrat—god's nectar

Amrath—nectar

Amreeta—nectar

Amreet—god's nectar

Amrisha—truth, lucky

Amrita—beloved nectar, spiritual

Amrita—immortal

Amritalata—a nectar giving creeper

Amritamalini—eternally fresh garland

Amritambu—moon

Amritaya—the immortal, lord vishnu

Amrit—god's nectar, immortal, drink

Amritha—nectarrt, immortality

Amrithavarshini—the rain

Amritkala—nectarine art

Amritrashmi—moon illumination, luminosity, radiance

Amritvarshini—one who showers nectar

Amrtama—food obtained from the ocean

Amrusha—sudden, truly, unexpected

Amrush—taken aback

Amruta—immortalmbrosia, nectar

Amrutha—nectar

Amrutkiran—moon illumination, luminosity, radiance

Amrutmayi—full of nectar

Amrut—nectar

Amrutvarshini—one of the ragas of classical

Amsaveni—a ray of illumination, luminosity, radiance, fair

Amshamala—a garland of rudraksh

Amshula—sunny
Amshumala—the sun
Amshumati—brilliant, sagacious, gifted, wise, learned, river yamuna
Amshu—sunny
Amtheshwari—eternal god
Amudamozhi—sweet voice
Amukta—can't be touched, valuable, valued, rare
Amukta—shelter
Amuktha—non conquered
Amukti—liberation, final liberation
Amukulita—resilient
Amula—very expensive, rootless
Amulaya—priceless
Amuliya—valuable, valued, rare
Amulya—priceless
Amulya—priceless, valuable, valuable, valued, rare
Amursha—truth
Amutha—happines, lively
Amuthan—sweetness
Amuthavalli—pretty, lovely, handsome, graceful name
Amutheswari—a goddess
Amvi—a goddess
Amya—soft, night rain
Amy—beloved
Amy—beloved, dearly loved
Amyra—high-born, princess
Amyrah—princess, high-born
Anaamika—name of ring finger
Anaanya—different from others
Anaar—familiar with anaar
Anaarkali—without sin
Anaaya—exclusive, care, powerful
Anabhra—cloudless
Anabhra—without clouds
Anadi—always happy
Anadita—startless
Anadi—without beginning
Anadya—without beginning
Anaemia—without name
Ana—form of anna, gracious
Anaga—sinless
Anagha—sinless, soft, goddess parvati
Anagi—valuable
Anagya—goddess durga

Anahata—far of pain
Anahita—goddess of wisdom and fertility
Anahit—the immaculate one
Anaika—powerful and complete, goddess
Anais—grace, favour, holy, sanctified, pious, solemn, chaste
Anaisha—answered prayer, special
Anaiya—she who brings sunshine
Anajana—mother of god
Anaka—a holy cow
Anakha—sinless, goddess parvati, lakshmi
Anala—fiery
Anala—fiery, goddess of fire
Anala—goddess of fire
Analapriya—beloved of fire
Analilia—full of grace and lily
Anam—blessing, noble man with power
Anamica—without name, with no name
Anamikapal—goddess durga
Anamika—ring-finger
Anamika—the one without a name
Anamika—without a name
Anamitra—the sun
Anami—without name
Anamone—type of bloom, garden stuff
Anamra—humble, modest, propitious
Anamra—modest
Ananadini—joyful
Ananatdeve—eternal goddess
Ananaya—infinity, eternal, everlasting, matchless
Anan—clouds
Ananda—happy, joyful, bliss joy
Anandalahari—wave of happiness
Anandalakshmi—goddess of happiness
Anandamaye—blissful mother
Anandamaye—joy permeated
Anandamayi—full of joy
Anandana—woman who gives joy, happiness
Anandanayaki—joyful
Anandani—joyful

Anandaparna—one who spread happiness and joy
Anandaprabha—an apsara
Anandaprana—a woman of joy
Anandbhairavi—one of the ragas of classical
Anandhi—always merry and full of smiles
Anandhita—joyous girl
Anandi—a person who gives joy
Anandi—always happy
Anandi—always happy, joyful
Anandie—one who brings happiness
Anandi—happy, cherful
Anandika—happy person
Anandini—blissful, joyful
Anandini—full of joy
Anandini—giver of joy
Anandini—joyful, blissful, happy
Anandita—a happy person who spreads joy
Anandita—happy
Anandita—joy giver
Anandita—purveyor of joy
Anandmaye—full of happiness
Anandmayi—happy nature
Anandruna—eternal joy
Anandrupa—eternal joy
Anandya—happiness
Anan—face
Anangadeity—formless goddess, holy, pure, sanctified, pious, solemn
Anangalekha—a love letter
Anangalekha—letter written from heart
Anangamalini—god of love
Ananga—sinless, goddess lakshmi
Anangee—cupid's consort
Anangkiti—pretty, lovely, handsome, graceful name
Anangmalini—garland of lord kama
Anangu—human being
Anania—special, invaluable
Ananika—brave, fearless
Ananiya—unique, goddess parvati
Anannya—unique, goddess parvati, nothing
Ananparna—the wings of the joy

Ananshi—goddess parvati
Anantaa—eternal, infinite, joyful
Ananta—eternal, everlasting, prosperous, free
Anantashirsa—with an immortal mind
Anantashree—woman who has abundant money
Ananta—unlimited
Anant—eternal, everlasting, eternal
Anant—eternal, everlasting, galaxy, never ending
Anantha—eternal, everlasting, eternal
Ananthalakshmi—eternally fortunate
Ananthi—eternal, everlasting, infinite, lord shiva
Ananthika—eternal, everlasting, sharp
Ananthini—gift
Ananti—eternal, everlasting
Ananti—gift
Anantika—end-less
Anantika—eternal, everlasting
Anantya—eternal, everlasting
Anantya—eternal, everlasting, eternal
Ananya—inalienability, limitless feeling
Ananya—infinity, inalienability
Ananya—the only one
Ananya—unique, inalienability
Anapayina—eternal
Anara—shooting star
Anargha—valuable, valued, rare
Anarghya—valuable, valued, rare, priceless
Anarkali—name of a woman
Anarkali—pomegranate blossom
Anar—pomegranate, priceless, radiant
Anarta—belonging to stage, theatre
Anashree—food goddess
Anasooya—friend of shakuntala, wife of
Anasooya—not jealous, rishi atri's wife
Anasua—one who is not jealous of anybody
Anasuya—a star, rain, without spite or
Anaswara—one which can't be destroyed
Anata—a singer, not bentnswer

Anathi—modest, respectful, joyful
Anati—bent, bowing, salutation
Anatrika—prayer
Anavadya—faultless, goddess durga
Anave—humane
Anavi—kind
Anavi—one with a heart like ocean
Anavi—serenity, calm, calmness, stillness, silence loving, kind to people
Anaya—blessed with god, god gifted
Anaya—blessing of god, origin
Anaya—complete freedom, one who none can
Anayna—mirror, unique, matchless, goddess
Ana—young, food grain, most valuable, valued, rare
Anayra—happiness
Anaysua—with a short life
Anayta—exclusive, graceful
Anayusha—short life
Anbarasi—a kindful girl
Anbar—perfumembergris, barn or
Anbu—lovely, kindness
Anbumozhi—amiable, pleasing, suave, interesting
Anbuvizhiyal—shelter
Anchala—border, lap
Anchala—one end of saree which is free
Anchal—one end of saree which is free
Anchal—the decorative end of a sari, part
Anchika—something to worship
Anchita—honoured, worshipped, curved
Anchit—praised, worshipped
Andal—female saints
Andal—female saints name
Andika—elder sister
Andolika—type of raga
Anegha—pearl
Aneha—one love
Aneka—goddess durga, grace, favour, god
Anekavarna—person with multiple complexions
Aneksha—bringing happiness
Anekta—diversity
Anela—holy, sanctified, pious, solemn, chaste
Anela—windir
Anema—first of the eight siddhis
Anemone—type of bloom, garden stuff, wind, breath
Anenasya—free from sins
Aneri—uniquetally different
Anesa—friendly, of good company
Anes—friendly, of good company, inmate
Anesha—holy, sanctified, pious, solemn, chaste, chaste, kind and caring
Anesha—ultimate, absolute, highest, best
Anesha—victory, uninterrupted
Aneshka—lord vishnu
Aneta—grace, without guile, favour
Anet—awesome, smart, rare
Aneya—eternal, everlasting
Angaja—born of the body
Angaja—daughter of aja
Angaj—son, daughter, passion
Angalekha—a creeper
Angana—pretty, lovely, handsome, graceful
Angana—an suspicious or pretty, lovely, handsome, graceful woman
Anganaa—study, pretty, lovely, handsome, graceful woman
Angani—pleasing, favourite, charming girl
Angaravati—having fire
Angarika—a flame-coloured bloom, garden stuff, palash
Angarita—a luminous plant
Angel—fairy little messenger from
Angelia—angelic, holy, pure, sanctified, pious, solemn messenger
Angeli—gift, offering
Angelika—angelic, messenger from god, like
Angeni—angel, spirit
Angha—sinless, without any fault
Angi—one with pretty, lovely, handsome, graceful body, fire
Angira—celestial

Angira—mother of birhaspati
Angiri—mother of brihaspati
Angi—to decorate the body of jain god
Anglen—christ
Anglina—various name for angel
Angna—place front of home, house
Angoori—grape
Angoori—of the grapes
Anguri—finger ring
Anhadh—never stop
Anhad—no limits
Anha—representation of love
Anhatee—gift
Anhika—prayer of god
Anhitee—gift
Anhithi—gift, donation, loan
Anhiti—gift, donation
Ania—gracious, merciful
Anica—grace
Anichamalar—bloom, garden stuff
Anideepa—monarch, ruler, prince, earl
Anidipa—non illumination,
luminosity, radiance
Anidita—goddess durga
Aniha—indifferent, unwillingness
Anika—goddess durga, grace, favour
Anika—grace, favour, god is gracious
Aniketa—homeless
Aniksha—unobstructed
Anila—air, god of wind
Anila—breezeir, wind
Anilaja—related to god
Anil—cloud, immaculate being
Anima—the power of becoming
minute
Anima—the power of becoming
second
Anina—answer to my prayer, god has
Aninda—irreprochable
Anindina—one who does not speak ill
of others
Anindini—who does not speak ill of
others
Anindita—someone who is never
insulted
Aninditha—virtuous, venerated
Anindya—beyond fault
Anintika—immortal, never ending

Anirvinya—wife of lord vishnu
Anisa—joy and pleasure, friendly
Anisha—pretty, lovely, handsome,
graceful
Anisha—full of brightness
Anisha—holy, sanctified, pious,
solemn, chaste, grace, continuous, day
Anisha—one whose life has no
darkness
Anishi—bright and luminous
Anishka—an atom
Anishka—who has friends, no enemies
Anishma—pretty, lovely, handsome,
graceful name
Anish—pretty of love
Anishree—pretty, lovely, handsome,
graceful name
Anismita—friend of close friend
Anitabha—charming
Anita—grace
Anita—gracious, merciful, grace,
leader
Anitha—goddess, grace, favour
Anitika—elder sister
Anitra—gracious, grace, offering with
Anixa—unobstructed
Aniya—pretty, lovely, handsome,
graceful, grace
Aniya—searching, creative, gracious
Aniyora—place in braja, near
govardhan
Anjaani—illusion
Anjalai—modest, mark of respect
Anjala—perfect, god
Anjale—homage
Anjal—free flowing, wind, shine of
Anjali—handful
Anjalika—one of arjuna's arrows
Anjali—proposing, join hands, palms
Anjal—pleasing, favourite, charming
lady
Anjana—beauty, mother of lord
hanuman
Anjana—mother of hanuman, a
mountain
Anjane—adorn with sandalwood paste
Anjane—illusion
Anjanie—hotness

Anjani—illusion, maya, mother of lord
Anjasi—honest, deceit-less
Anji—a blessing
Anjika—blessed
Anjini—mother of hanuman
Anjish—sweet
Anjle—holy, pure, sanctified, pious, solemn offering
Anjli—holy, pure, sanctified, pious, solemn offering
Anjly—illumination, luminosity, radiance
Anjna—dusky, mother of lord hanuman
Anjna—mother of lord hanuman, dusky
Anjni—mother of lord hanuman
Anjori—shining illumination, luminosity, radiance
Anju—pretty, lovely, handsome, graceful
Anjugham—a signet
Anjuli—blessings, in conquerable, one who
Anjum—star tokenngel, meeting
Anjuna—pretty, lovely, handsome, graceful
Anju—one who lives in the heart
Anjushree—dear to one's heart, beloved
Anjushree—pretty, lovely, handsome, graceful woman
Anjushri—dear to one's heart, beloved
Ankal—whole
Ankamma—love
Ankamuthu—pretty, lovely, handsome, graceful name
Ankana—demarcated area mark
Ankareeda—night star, graceful, shining
Ankayarkanni—conquered signet, symbol
Ankey—beauty, talent, love
Ankhi—eye, glimmers
Ankita—spotted, marked, written
Ankitha—with auspicious marks, marked
Ankiti—pretty, lovely, handsome, graceful name
Ankolika—an embrace
Ankolika—personification of love and respect
Ankshika—fraction of the cosmos
Anktika—a lady name
Ankura—a sprout
Ankushe—excercising restrain
Anmisha—goddess
Anmolika—priceless
Anmol—priceless, valuable, valuable, valued, rare
Annada—giving, providing food, goddess
Annakamu—pretty, lovely, handsome, graceful name
Annakodi—tree on which the bird sits
Annalakshmi—who bestows grain
Annamal—lucky, wise, the one who provides
Annamayil—swan bird, peacock
Annan—goddess of grains
Annanta—who has no end, never ends
Annanya—unique
Annapoorna—goddess of grains, goddess lakshmi
Anna—present, graceful
Annapurani—goddess parvati
Annapurna—goddess of food, goddess parvati
Annapurneswari—goddess of food
Annasha—pretty, lovely, handsome, graceful name
Annaya—unique
Anne—grace, favour, god is gracious
Annel—pretty
Annesha—pretty, lovely, handsome, graceful, holy, sanctified
Annika—giving food
Annina—soldier, army, grace
Annisa—friendly
Annisha—unique girl
Annjaya—ocean of blood
Annona—roman goddess of the harvest
Annpoorni—one who provides food

Annpurna—generous with food, goddess
Annu—atom prefix, tiny part
Annusmriti—goddess durga, paravati
Annya—grace, favour, blossom
Anoha—princess
Anokhe—unique
Anokhi—unique, different, special
Anoma—illustrious
Anona—grace, grain harvest
Anoochana—well-behaved
Anooja—continuous
Anoona—portion, whole, entire
Anoopa—miracle, unequalled
Anoosha—illumination, luminosity, radiance, happy
Anora—illumination, luminosity, radiance, honour, grace
Anouka—spirit of god
Anouksha—fulfilment of desire, aspiration, longing
Anousha— eternal, everlasting, endless
Anoushka—a term of endearment, fulfilment
Anpurna—goddess of food
Ansana—love
Anshal—pretty, lovely, handsome, graceful name
Ansha—portion
Anshi—gift of god, whole
Anshi—god's gift
Anshika—a part
Anshika—part of body, part of parents
Anshini—star
Anshita—a part of tree
Ansh—portion
Ansh-saini—fire
Anshuka—ray of sun
Anshuka—silk cloth
Anshula—fiery
Anshula—sparkle, radiant, lustering, sunny
Anshumaala—garland of rays
Anshumala—garland of rays
Anshumala—garland of rays, illumination, luminosity, radiance
Anshumalinia—garland of rays

Anshumali—sun
Anshumi—every part or element of the earth
Anshumita—first ray of sun
Anshu—sun rays, sun, tolerance, durability, toleration, beam
Anshutha—illumination, luminosity, radiance, ray
Anshvae—part of things, part of body
Anshvi—portion, part of things
Ansika—pretty, lovely, handsome, graceful
Ansooya—learned
Ansruta—unique, unheard of
Ansumala—a garland of rays
Ansumati—wise, glorious, splendid
Ansuya—learned woman, sage atri's wife
Antali—pretty, lovely, handsome, graceful name
Antara—a note of music
Antara—who lives in one's heart
Antarbhuti—soul, life
Antariksha—space, sky
Anthahkarana—mercy
Antika—an elder sister plant fire
Antika—name of a star
Antima—the final, ultimate, ray of sun
Antine—one who lives in hermitage
Antini—living in a hermitage
Antram—lie
Antra—the second note in hindustani
Antriksha—space, sky
Antriksha—the sky
Anu—atom, silence, favour, grace
Anubama—holy, pure, sanctified, pious, solemn blessing
Anubam—experience
Anubha—illumination, luminosity, radiance, sunshine
Anubhi—pretty, lovely, handsome, graceful
Anubhoothi—realisation
Anubhuti—experience
Anubhuti—feelings, experience
Anuca—name of goddess
Anudeepthi—holy, pure, sanctified,

pious, solemn illumination, luminosity, radiance

Anudeepti—holy, pure, sanctified, pious, solemn brightness

Anudhya—monarch, ruler, prince, earl or desire, aspiration

Anu—full of pride, proud

Anuga—a companion

Anugathadeity—a friend wife

Anugraha—holy, pure, sanctified, pious, solemn blessing, favour, kindness

Anugya—permission

Anuhaya—little sister

Anuhya—different, beyond ones

Anuja—holy, sanctified, pious, solemn, chaste

Anuja—younger sister

Anujee—younger

Anujika—slowly

Anukampa—god's grace

Anukeertana—praising god's virtues

Anukirtana—praise of god's virtues

Anukriti—photograph

Anukrrish—pretty, lovely, handsome, graceful name

Anukruthi—photograph

Anuksha—every moment

Anukulika—pretty, lovely, handsome, graceful name

Anula—gentle

Anula—not wild, gentle

Anulata—one with very slim figure

Anulekha—born later

Anulekha—one who follows destiny

Anulika—happiness is the best

Anuloma—sequence

Anumathi—consent

Anumati—consent, permission

Anumati—permission

Anumaya—pretty, lovely, handsome, graceful name

Anumegha—following the rain

Anumeha—after the rain

Anumita—love and kindness

Anumitha—love and kindness

Anumlacha—agreeable

Anumloche—an apsara's name

Anunaya—unique, unparalleled

Anunayika—modest

Anuneta—respectable

Anunita—disciplined

Anunitha—courtesy

Anuniti—courtesy

Anupallavi—part of a song

Anupama—matchless, unique, unparalleled

Anupam—matchless, unique

Anupa—pond, unique

Anupma—pretty, lovely, handsome, graceful woman, incomparable

Anuprabha—brightness

Anuprama—atom god

Anupriya—beloved

Anupriya—like beloved, uncomparable

Anupsara—pretty, lovely, handsome, graceful woman

Anupurva—in order

Anuradha—like radha

Anuradha—name of a star, bright star

Anuraga—beloved

Anuragha—blessing, love

Anuragini—beloved

Anurag—red, love

Anura—knowledgeable, brilliant, sagacious, gifted, wise, learned, kind

Anurakthi—affection

Anurakti—loveffection

Anurama—goddess lakshmi

Anuranita—resonance, vibration

Anuranjana—consent, pleasing

Anurapa—suitable

Anurati—consent

Anurati—full of affection

Anuriddhi—good fortune

Anurima—lovely, attached

Anurithi—always fortunate, prosperous

Anuri—to flow after

Anurit—style, tradition

Anuroopa—extremely pretty, lovely, handsome, graceful, goddess

Anurupa—suitable, resembles of figure

Anurupika—pretty, lovely, handsome, graceful name

Anusara—full of ambition, intent, passion
Anusaya—learned, lord krishna
Anusha—pretty, lovely, handsome, graceful morning, the universe
Anushaka—a term of endearment
Anusha—the universe, pretty, lovely, handsome, graceful morning
Anushela—full of goodness
Anusheta—calm mind
Anushi—brave
Anushiya—name of hindu goddess
Anushka—pleasing, favourite, charming, bloom, garden stuffs, guardian
Anushma—without heat
Anushmita—always smiling
Anushree—goddess lakshmi
Anushreya—most pretty
Anushri—goddess, pretty, goddess
Anushruti—pretty, lovely, handsome, graceful silence
Anush—single, sweet
Anushtuti—praise
Anushya—holy, sanctified, pious, solemn, chaste
Anuska—grace
Anu—smallest
Anusmita—one who always smiles
Anusmriti—remembrance, cherished
Anusooya—goddess lakshmi, talented
Anusoya—pretty, lovely, handsome, graceful name
Anusree—pretty
Anusri—glorious, famous, happiness
Anusruti—silence beauty
Anusuya—learned woman
Anusuyasarkar—goddess lakshmi
Anusuya—wife of sage atri, non-jealous
Anutara—unanswered
Anuthi—unique
Anuttara—unanswered, ultimate, highest
Anuttma—best of all
Anuttra—without answer
Anuva—knowledge
Anuvidya—to gain knowledge

Anuvinda—discoverer
Anuvindha—one who receives
Anuvrinda—lord krishna's highness, empress
Anuya—follower
Anve—joyful gift
Anveksha—reflection, meditation, searching
Anve—one of deity's names
Anvesha—quest, curious search
Anveta—connected, following
Anvidha—pretty, lovely, handsome, graceful name
Anvie—goddess durga
Anvi—goddess lakshmi
Anvika—powerful and complete
Anviksha—to give
Anvisha—goddess, extraordinary beauty
Anvi—shine, goddess of nature
Anvita—connected, following
Anvita—one who bridges the gap
Anvitee—following
Anviti—followed after
Anviya—pretty, lovely, handsome, graceful name
Anvvidha—great achiever, goddess, clever
Anwayi—joined, with no fear
Anweeksha—extraordinary beauty
Anwesha—invention, quest, love, search
Anwesha—quest, curious, invention
Anwika—an atom
Anwika—powerful
Anwiksha—adored woman, extraordinary beauty
Anwita—goddess durga
Anwitha—goddess durga
Anwith—goddess durga
Anya—different, goddess durga, graceful
Anya—inexhaustible, gracious, graceful
Anyaka—different
Anyi—destiny
Aoka—lustrous, shining
Aolani—cloud from heaven

Aopsana—love
Apaara—infinite, knowledge
Apaksha—compare, expectations
Apala—an ancient learned woman
Apala—name of a learned woman
Apala—unguarded
Apanya—pretty, lovely, handsome, graceful name
Apara—another, the west
Apara—eternal, everlasting
Aparajita—unconquerable woman
Aparajita—unconquered, parvati, goddess
Aparajita—undefeated, unconquerable
Apara—knowledge, materialistic
Apara—materialistic knowledge
Aparamitha—boundless
Aparanji—holy, sanctified, pious, solemn, chaste gold, pretty
Aparijita—undefeated, bloom, garden stuff
Aparna—leafless, valuable, valued, rare gemstone, leaf
Aparoopa—extremely pretty, lovely, handsome, graceful
Aparupa—beauty, extremely pretty, lovely, handsome, graceful
Aparupa—special
Aparup—rare, pretty, lovely, handsome, graceful
Apaya—milkless
Apeksha—expectation
Apeksha—expectation, passion
Apeksha—support, indoctrination, assuredness, expected
Apekshita—ambition, intent, passion
Apekshita—desire, aspiration, longing, expected
Apexa—support, indoctrination, assuredness, ambition, intent, passion, expected
Apheksha—expectation
Apinaya—expressions in dance
Apoorane—one who fulfil ambition, intent, passion
Apoorva—unique, never before, special
Apoorva—very new, unprecedented

Apoorve—ultimate, absolute, highest, best soul
Appala—bright
Appara—knowledge
Apporva—rare, special
Appu—cute, sweet, valuable, valued, rare
Appurva—unique, different from everyone
Aprajita—undefeated bloom, garden stuff
Apra—top level of intelligence
Apraudha—powerful
Apra—western direction
Aprna—leafless, one who possess the
Apsara—pretty, lovely, handsome, graceful woman
Apsara—angel, beauty, celestial maiden
Apsha—pretty, lovely, handsome, graceful
Apta—angel, proximity
Aptee—fulfilment
Apt—friend, devotional, trustworthy
Apti—completion
Apti—completion, fulfilment
Apti—fortune
Apurba—never seen before
Apuroopa—valuable, valued, rare, rarest of the rare
Apurva—unique, valuable, valued, rare, different from
Apurva—valuable, valued, rare
Apurvi—unique, different from everyone
Apurwa—unique, valuable, valued, rare
Aqila—brilliant, sagacious, gifted, wise, learned
Aqsha—blessing of god
Arabhdha—tolerance, durability, toleration
Arabhi—musical, raga, famous note
Araceli—altar in the sky, gate of heaven
Arada—a name of goddess
Araddhya—to be worshipped

Aradhana—respectable, worship, prayer
Aradhana—worship
Aradhana—worship, prayer
Aradhana—worship, prayer, devoted effort
Aradha—worship
Aradhaya—able to worship, devotee of god
Aradhaya—to worship, ornament, jewellery, ornamentation, adornment, figuration
Aradhika—a woman who worship
Aradhika—worshipped
Aradhika—worshipper, devotee, worshipped
Aradhita—worshipped
Aradhita—worshipper, one who adores
Aradhiya—worshipped
Aradhna—worship
Aradhnya—pretty, lovely, handsome, graceful name
Aradhya—blessing of lord ganesha
Aradhya—devotee, worship, goddess
Aradhya—to devote, worship
Aradhya—worshipped, first, prayer
Aradhy—god's prey
Aradya—devotee, worship, goddess
Aradya—worshipped, holy, prayer
Aragi—detached, passionless, cool
Aragili—parrot
Araina—holy, sanctified, pious, solemn, chaste
Araiya—holy, pure, sanctified, pious, solemn, pretty, lovely, handsome, graceful
Araja—clean
Araj—fragrant
Aral—bloom, garden stuff
Aramalavika—charming maiden
Aram—righteous woman, high, superior, elevated
Aramya—who requires nothing from outside
Aranam—name of the ornament, jewellery, ornamentation, adornment, figuration
Arana—name of goddess lakshmi

Arane—remove the darkness
Arani—pretty, lovely, handsome, graceful
Aranya—forest, wood, jungle, bountiful forest, wood, jungle
Aranya—illumination, luminosity, radiance bringer, superior, elevated
Aranyane—goddess of food
Aranyani—goddess of forest, wood, jungle
Aranya—sunshine, forest, wood, jungle, green
Ara—ornament, jewellery, ornamentation, adornment, figuration, brings rain
Arashi—beautified by god, brilliant, sagacious, gifted, wise, learned
Arashi—first ray of sun
Aras—ornamentation, adornment, figuration
Arathi—worship god
Arati—hymns sang in praise of god
Arati—to worship
Arati—towards the highest love for god
Aratrika—bearer of illumination, luminosity, radiance, basil plant
Aratrika—dusk lamp below tulsi plant
Aratrikia—the dusk lamp beneath tulsi plant
Aravali—name of a hill
Arav—cute, serenity, calm, calmness, stillness, calm
Aravi—friend of the people
Arav—in high regard of, ray, support, indoctrination, assuredness
Aravinda—blue lotus
Aravindine—fragrant, a bunch of lotuses
Aravi—serenity, calm, calmness, stillness, silence
Araya—princess, goddess parvati, noble
Arayna—highness, empress, queen
Arayna—vivacious
Archana—prayer, worship
Archana—worship
Archan—worship

Archa—worship
Archie—genuine courage
Archika—worshipper
Archine—one who offers prayers, rituals
Archini—ray of illumination, luminosity, radiance
Archi—ray of illumination, luminosity, radiance, goddess lakshmirt
Archisha—a ray of illumination, luminosity, radiance
Archisha—ray of sun
Archisha—rays of illumination, luminosity, radiance
Archismita—brilliant, sagacious, gifted, wise, learned
Archi—sunrise, comic
Archita—one who is honoured
Archita—worshipping goddess, goddess
Architi—to offer prayers perform
Archna—prayer
Archy—wonderful, grace
Ardhangi—half, worship
Ardhra—wetness, green, the moist one
Ardhvika—a big heart, helpful
Ardhya—lover of pray, bank of knowledge
Ardra—mild, soft
Ardra—moisture, kind, a nakshatra
Ardrata—humidity
Areeka—pretty, lovely, handsome, graceful heart, eye, glimmers
Areekta—full, satisfied
Areeya—pretty, lovely, handsome, graceful name
Arghya—offering to the lord
Arha—beauty
Arhana—valuable
Arhana—worship, honour, giving happiness
Arhantika—one who left violence
Arhantika—one who worships nun
Aria—gentle music, brings rain
Aria—gentle music, brings rain, pledge
Arianna—holy one, holy, sanctified, pious, solemn, chaste

Ariba—brilliant, sagacious, gifted, wise, learned, skilful
Arien—man, pledge, enchanted
Arij—fragrance, sweet smell, pleasant
Arika—admired for looks
Ariktha—fulfilled
Arina—serenity, calm, calmness, stillness, silence
Arini—adventurous
Arin—mountain vigour
Ariona—bringer of life
Aripra—clean
Aripra—faultless, clear, holy, sanctified, pious, solemn, chaste
Arisha—mirror, reflection
Arisha—serenity, calm, calmness, stillness, silence
Arishi—first ray of the sun
Arishka—goddess of serenity, calm, calmness, stillness, silence
Arishta—pretty, lovely, handsome, graceful name
Arishta—secure
Arisina—turmeric
Arismiti—happiness, brave
Aritha—serenity, calm, calmness, stillness, softness, goddess lakshmi
Aritra—navigator
Aritra—one who shows the right path
Aritri—earth, goddess durga
Aritrika—dusk lamp beneath tulsi plant
Arivazhagu—brilliant, sagacious, gifted, wise, learned, beauty, smart
Arivuchudar—ray of intelligence
Ariya—blossom, purity
Ariyana—silver
Ariyan—of purity, blossom
Arja—princess, pretty, lovely, handsome, graceful
Arjav—honest, sincere
Arja—without dust
Arjita—acquired, gained
Arjita—earned
Arjita—one who has given away
Arjna—powerful
Arjoo—desire, aspiration, longing
Arju—desire, aspiration, longing

Arju—desire, aspiration, longing, mountain of vigour
Arjuni—dawn, white cow
Arka—flash of illumination, luminosity
Arkaja—born from sun, river yamuna
Arkashuta—daughter of the sun
Arkita—plentiful
Armana—ambition, intent, passion
Arman—desire, aspiration, longing, longing, ambition, intent, passion
Armita—ambition, intent, passion
Arna—ocean, wave, goddess lakshmi
Arna—ornament, jewellery, ornamentation, adornment
Arnavi—ocean, sea, luster of sun
Arnavi—starting of universe, bird
Arnav—lord vishnu, ocean
Arnika—goddess durga, wonderful
Arni—moon, sun
Arogyada—granter of good health
Arohe—pretty, lovely, handsome, graceful name
Arohi—ascending, musical note
Arohi—progress, pretty, lovely, handsome, graceful, evolving
Arohi—the first part of the musical sargam
Aroma—smell, fragrance distinctive
Aronya—forest, wood, jungle
Aroohi—daughter of god, progress
Aroohi—daughter of lord shiva
Arookshana—young, tender
Aroona—dawn
Aroopa—formless
Aroushi—first ray of sun
Aroushi—ray of sunshine
Arpanan—offering
Arpana—surrendered, offering
Arpan—god's special
Arpita—dedicated
Arpita—dedicated, awesome
Arpitha—devotee of god, daughter of god
Arppitha—render
Arrishta—pretty, lovely, handsome, graceful name
Arsha—prayer ceremony, great

Arshdeep—illumination, luminosity, radiance of universe
Arshe—holy, pure, sanctified, pious, solemn
Arsheya—holy, pure, sanctified, pious, solemn
Arshia—heavenly
Arshia—holy, pure, sanctified, pious, solemn, holy, heavenly
Arshika—success, love friendly
Arshi—mirror, heavenly, goddess durga
Arshini—god lakshmi, blessing
Arshi—pretty, lovely, handsome, graceful name
Arshita—dominion
Arshitha—blessed, heavenly, holy, pure, sanctified, pious, solemn
Arshiya—above of everything
Arshiya—belonging to throne, sky
Arshnoor—desire, aspiration, longing, sky illumination
Arsh—throne, power, dominion, crown
Arshu—pretty, lovely, handsome, graceful name
Arshvi—name of lord vishnu
Arsi—mirror, illumination, luminosity, radiance, shine, brightness
Artana—vanquisher of all foes
Artee—form of worship, prayer
Arthada—goddess lakshmi
Artha—meaningful, wealthy, purpose
Arthana—request
Arthikha—pretty, lovely, handsome, graceful name
Arthita—ambition, intent, passion, request, petition
Arthi—worship, gift for god, confidence
Arthna—request, entreaty
Arti—form of worship, prayer
Artika—a method of worshipping
Artika—an elder sister, goodness
Artika—elder sister
Arti—prayer ceremony, god worship
Arti—worship
Arudra—lord shiva, gentle
Aruhe—daughter of god

Aruhi—daughter of god
Aruhi—starting, related to music
Aruja—daughter of god sun, healthy
Aruja—daughter of sun
Arula—shining as the sun, brilliant
Arulmozhi—parrot
Arulvani—pretty, lovely, handsome, graceful name
Arunabha—red luster of the sun, life giving
Arunadeity—bright like rays of the sun, wife
Aruna—morning, the dawn
Arunamshu—reddish tint
Aruna—mythical charioteer of the sun
Aruna—sun
Arundhathi—fidelity, star, unrestricted
Arundhati—a star
Arundhati—a star, name of lord shiva
Aruneta—red coloured, bright like ray of
Aruni—dawn
Arunika—passionate, bright, life giving
Arunika—reddish
Arunima—morning redness in the sky
Arunima—pearly, luster of dawn, red luster
Aruni—sun, morning, dawn
Arunita—bright like rays of the sun, red
Arunya—first ray of the sun
Arunya—wife of lord sun
Arupa—pretty, lovely, handsome, graceful
Arup—goddess lakshmi
Arusha—first rays of morning sun, calm
Arusha—first rays of the morning sun
Arushi—first ray of sun, beauty, dawn
Arushi—first ray of the sun, careful
Arushika—victory
Arushka—goddess of serenity, calm, calmness, stillness, silence
Arushya—ray of rising sun, sunshine
Aru—soul
Aruvi—nature
Aruvi—water falls

Arva—from the seashore
Arvantee—mare
Arve—friends to all
Arve—serenity, calm, calmness, stillness, silence
Arvi—first ray of sun, serenity, calm, calmness, stillness, silence
Arvi—friends to all
Arvika—universal
Arvika—universal, lord ganesha
Arvinda—lotus
Arwa—female satisfied, pleasant, fresh
Arya—a noble lady, goddess durga
Aryadasi—goddess durga
Arya—goddess parvati, noble in
Aryahi—goddess durga
Aryakee—honoured
Aryaki—goddess durga
Aryama—the sun
Aryamba—start, mother of shri
Aryananda—the one who brings joy
Aryanandini—pretty, lovely, handsome, graceful name
Aryana—noble, utterly holy, sanctified, pious, solemn
Arya—noble, honoured, goddess paravati
Aryasri—gift of god
Arya—valuable, valued, rare, princess
Arythy—doughter of aarya
Arzoo—desire, aspiration, longing, ambition, intent, passion
Asaavari—name of a raga or melody
Asah—plant known for its greenness
Asalah—purity, nobility of descent
Asangine—not attached
Asa—support, indoctrination
Asavari—a melodious raga
Asavari—sprite of hevan, raga or
Asawaree—raga in hindustani classical music
Asawari—raga in hindustani classical
Aseema—limitless, protector, devotee
Aseena—pretty, lovely, handsome, graceful
Asees—bless
Asgari—devotee
Ashadeep—illumination, luminosity

Ashadha—name of a sacred brick,
Ashadhi—the day of full moon
Ashajyoti—illumination, luminosity
Ashaka—blessing
Ashakiran—ray of support,
indoctrination, assuredness
Ashakti—powerbility, might
Ashalata—creeper of support,
indoctrination, assuredness
Ashalata—creeper of support,
indoctrination, assuredness,
traditionally
Ashalatha—creeper of support,
indoctrination, assuredness
Ashana—daughter of bali, friend
Ashandika—born in the month of
ashadha
Ashani—illumination, luminosity,
thunder
Ashankita—doubtless
Ashankita—without doubt, full of
support, indoctrination, assuredness
Ashanya—easy, simple, desire,
aspiration, longing
Ashapurna—one who fulfils ambition,
intent, passions
Ashara—ash tree, good fortune, holy,
sanctified, pious, solemn, chaste
Asharika—the ray of support,
indoctrination, assuredness
Asha—support, indoctrination,
assuredness
Asha—support, indoctrination,
assuredness, devotion
Asha—support, indoctrination,
aspiration, longing, ambition, intent,
passion
Ashavari—name of a raga
Ashay—powerful, meaningful
Ashcharya—wonder
Ashelesha—to embrace
Ashesha—holy, sanctified, pious,
solemn, chaste
Ashiana—shelter, home, house
Ashia—place to live
Ashi—evening, night, reward, smile
Ashifa—courageous, princess

Ashika—amiable, pleasing, suave,
interesting
Ashika—beloved
Ashika—one without sorrow, mercury
Ashiki—amour, love, affection
Ashi—love, full smile, highness,
empress
Ashima—limitless
Ashima—one who is full of support,
indoctrination, assuredness
Ashimita—unlimited, limitless, no
limit
Ashini—illumination, luminosity
Ashinya—pretty, lovely, handsome,
graceful home
Ashiqa—sweet heart, beloved,
romantic
Ashira—wealthy
Ashirya—from the land of god
Ashish—greetings, benison, blessing
Ashisha—a woman who has been
blessed
Ashisha—a woman with blessings
Ashisha—blessings
Ashish—truthful, blessings
Ashita—blessings, support,
indoctrination
Ashita—one who is full of support,
indoctrination, assuredness
Ashitha—love
Ashiti—innocent
Ashivini—egoist
Ashiwarya—pretty, lovely, handsome,
graceful
Ashiyana—pretty, lovely, handsome,
graceful home
Ashiyana—pretty, lovely, handsome,
gracful
Ashiya—place to live, habitat
Ashiya—spirit of ash tree, spiritual
Ashka—blessings
Ashlesha—like a goddess star, hairs
Ashlesha—name of a nakshatra
Ashley—meadow of ash trees
Ashma—rock, mountain of rocks,
strong
Ashmatee—hard as rock, strong

Ashmeet—friendly with everyone, blessed
Ashmi—brightness, happy
Ashmika—dream
Ashmika—pretty, lovely, handsome, graceful name
Ashmira—heaven's bloom, garden stuff
Ashmitaa—pride
Ashmita—pride, bold, strong, rock born
Ashmitha—rock born, hard and strong
Ashnaa—daughter of monarch, ruler, prince
Ashna—friend, beloved, ambition, intent, passion
Ashna—support, indoctrination, assuredness, devoted to love, beloved
Ashner—sacred water or amrit
Ashni—a flash of illumination, luminosity, radiance
Ashni—illumination, luminosity, radiance
Ashnoor—like a diamond, pretty, lovely, handsome, graceful
Ashohini—pretty, lovely, handsome, graceful name
Ashoka—without grief
Ashooja—eternally happy, blessed
Ashra—happiness
Ashra—shelter
Ashraya—shelter, comfort
Ashree—not pretty, lovely, handsome, graceful, ill luck
Ashree—one of the name of goddess durga
Ashreya—shelter, protection
Ashrika—helping other
Ashrita—goddess lakshmi, parvati
Ashrita—helpfully, dependent, protected
Ashritha—another name of lord ganesha
Ashritha—helping nature
Ashriti—pretty, lovely, handsome, graceful name
Ashriya—pretty, lovely, handsome, graceful name
Ashrutha—pretty, lovely, handsome, graceful name
Ash—support, indoctrination, assuredness, expectation
Ashtamy—eight directions, beauties
Ashtha—devotion
Ashtu—serenity, calm, calmness, stillness
Ashu—quick, horse, fast
Ashu—support, indoctrination, strong, great
Ashvakine—as swift as horse
Ashvana—pretty, lovely, handsome, graceful name
Ashvandika—pretty, lovely, handsome, graceful name
Ashvattha—full moon in the month of ashvina
Ashveni—female horse
Ashve—victorious, goddess saraswati
Ashvi—pretty, lovely, handsome, graceful, mother of earth
Ashvi—goddess saraswati, blessed
Ashvika—little mare
Ashvini—female horse
Ashviny—female horse
Ashviqua—love, pride
Ashvitha—strong, bright
Ashwabha—illumination, luminosity
Ashwa—horse
Ashwathi—one of the star
Ashwathy—star, the angel
Ashwika—goddess santhoshi mata
Ashwika—goddess santoshi mother
Ashwina—child of the star
Ashwine—attached to heart, attractive
Ashwini—angel, attractive, good
Ashwini—pleasing, favourite, charming
Ashwita—successful
Ashya—long live
Ashyanah—nest
Asia—support, indoctrination, assuredness
Asika—goddess lakshmi
Asikne—the night
Asima—defender, protector, virtuous

Asin—holy, sanctified, pious, solemn, chaste
Asini—smile
Asis—love, blessing
Asita—river yamuna
Asita—the river yamuna, goddess durga
Asi—very pretty, lovely, handsome, graceful girl, mirror
Asiya—goodness
Aska—pious
Askini—daughter of prajapati virat
Aslesha—a star
Aslesha—name of star
Aslesha—star constellation of stars
Asli—sincere, original, holy, sanctified, pious, solemn, chaste, genuine
Asmaa—prestige
Asmaira—pretty, lovely, handsome, graceful name
Asma—sky, excellent, valuable, valued, rare, higher
Asma—valuable, valued, rare, excellent, sky
Asmee—self-confident
Asmi—I am present, nature, self
Asmi—I am soul
Asmika—beauty, pretty, lovely, handsome, graceful soul
Asmita—glories, love, identity, pride
Asmita—pride
Asmitha—pride
Asna—purity
Asra—anchor, support, shelter
Asra—generous, nobler
Asraya—shelter, comfort
As—support, indoctrination, devotion
Asta—ambassador, of the stars
Astabhuja—with eight hands
Asta—devotion, trust
Astee—live, exist, rise
Astesha—a star
Astha—belief, devotee of god, devotion
Astha—devotion
Astha—devotion, ambition, intent, passion to achieve

Astha—devotion, regard
Astha—devotion, trust, support, indoctrination, assuredness, devotion
Asthika—devotion
Asthika—with hastha nakshatra
Asthoola—not fat
Astika—one who has devotion in god
Astimati—possessed of property wealthy
Asti—presence, live, exist, rise
Astitve—pretty, lovely, handsome, graceful name
Astuti—prayer
Asura—demon, spiritual
Asvika—goddess parvati, little mare
Asvi—lord, lord shiva's wife
Asvitha—goddess parvati
Aswani—pretty, lovely, handsome, graceful, star
Aswathi—name of a horse
Aswathy—beginner star
Aswika—pretty, lovely, handsome, graceful
Aswini—healer of lords, name of a star
Aswita—pretty, lovely, handsome, graceful name
Aswitha—beauty of victory
Asya—place to live, grace, gracious
Asya—related to mouth, face
Ataksha—to bring from all sides
Atalaya—guard, watch tower
Atari—good person
Atashi—a blue bloom, garden stuff
Atasi—a blue bloom, garden stuff
Athalia—god is sublime, god is superior, elevated
Atharva—lord ganesha
Athasha—ultimate
Athashri—goddess lakshmi
Atheva—ultimate
Athika—generous, noble
Athilesha—lord of intelligence
Athimanthi—support, indoctrination, assuredness
Athira—a full moon night star
Athirai—red star
Athira—moon illumination, luminosity, radiance at day

Athi—sun, first
Athiya—donated substance
Athma—soul
Athmika—friendly, closest
Athmika—related to soul
Athmikha—a god
Athmiya—spiritual
Athulya—something valuable, unrivalled
Atifa—empathy, affectionate, sympathetic
Atikah—kind affectionate, gorgeous
Atika—kind affectionate
Atiksha—more desire, aspiration, longing
Atimoda—extremely, luminosity, radiance
Atirajni—a woman superior to a monarch, ruler, prince, earl
Atirakta—extremely red
Atira—pray
Atiriya—beloved, very dear
Atirupa—most pretty, lovely, handsome, graceful
Atisha—serenity, calm, calmness, stillness, silence, spiritual luminosity
Atishaya—superiority
Atish—fireworks
Atishi—a burning glass
Atishi—fiery, joyful, passionate
Atishri—prosperous
Atiya—gift
Atmadhika—dearer to heart
Atmaja—daughter
Atmaja—daughter of the mountain
Atmanandini—one who has conquered the soul
Atmika—belongs to the soul, soul
Atmika—illumination, luminosity, radiance
Atmikha—illumination, luminosity, radiance of god
Atrayi—pretty, lovely, handsome, graceful name
Atreye, glimmers—name of a river
Atreyi—container of glory
Atreyi—pride
Atri—name of a star

Attiya—gift
Atula—uncomparable
Atuli—incomparable
Atulya—matchless
Atulya—matchless, unequalled
Auchitee—appropriate
Auhna—passion
Aumika—from deityne sound aum
Aumnshi—from lord shiva's mantra
Aurav—roman goddess of dawn
Aurel—golden angel
Aurima—soft like lotus, bright like moon
Aushenaree—one who belongs to mountain
Aushi—knowledgeable, careful, long life
Aushima—illumination, luminosity, radiance
Ausi—goddess lakshmi
Ausija—renowned, bright as the dawn
Ava—a fulfilling sound, voice
Avaapya—achieving
Avadhika—belongs to ayodhya
Avajiti—triumph
Avali—a line get
Avandhika—pretty, lovely, handsome, graceful name
Avane—earth
Avane—the earth, a river
Avani—earth
Avanija—one born out of the earth
Avanika—the earth, powerful
Avanish—lord of the earth
Avanita—the earth
Avanji—daughter of earth
Avanshika—pretty, lovely, handsome, graceful name
Avansika—pretty, lovely, handsome, graceful name
Avanthi—illumination, luminosity, radiance, love, historical
Avanthika—princess, princess of ujjain
Avanti—eternal, everlasting
Avantikaa—princess of world, goddess
Avantika—people reside in avanti city
Avantika—princess of ujjain
Avantika—princess of ujjain, goddess

Avantika—very modest
Avanti—modest, old name of ujjain
Avanya—princess of world
Avapya—achieving
Avarna—shelter, cover
Avasa—independent
Avatansa—ornament, jewellery, ornamentation, adornment, figuration
Avathara—goddess in human reflection
Avaya—to arrive or to inform
Avedna—painless
Aveni—the earth
Aventika—lotus
Avesha—tolerance, durability, toleration, calm, gift of god
Avha—oxygen, breathe of life
Avi—pretty, lovely, handsome, graceful
Avighna—without any hindrance, ignorant
Avigna—without obstacles
Avihshka—altruism, advantage, virtue
Avika—beauty, earth, rays of sun
Avika—pretty, lovely, handsome, graceful name
Avi—kindly, the sun
Avila—bird, vigour, ambition, intent, passion, sun rays
Avilokita—earth, illuminated by sun rays
Avina—fire
Avinandita—pretty, lovely, handsome, graceful name
Avinashi—indestructible
Avinashika—indestructible
Avinashini—eternal
Avinashini—indestructible
Avinashne—one who cannot be destroyed
Avinoor—pretty, lovely, handsome, graceful
Avipsa—ambition, intent, passion, desire, aspiration, longing
Avira—brilliant, sagacious, gifted, wise, learned, introduced into
Aviral—continuous, ongoing

Avisha—gift of god, tolerance, durability, toleration, calm
Avishe—without poison, ocean
Avishi—earth, river, not poisonous
Avishka—to invent, god gifted, sun
Avishya—ambition, intent, passion, desire, aspiration, longing
Avisri—beauty
Avita—protected
Avitashri—long life
Avlenta—blessed by god, inventory
Avlisha—confidence, princess of world
Avlokita—illumination, luminosity, radiance
Avne—earth
Avnet—belongs to sky, kind
Avnika—powerful and completed, protected
Avnita—the earth
Avni—the earth
Avriti—repeat
Avshini—pretty, lovely, handsome, graceful name
Avya—god gift
Avya—god gift, first ray sun
Awanti—eternal, everlasting, ancient city of ujjain
Awantika—goddess, princess of ujjain
Awigha—pretty, lovely, handsome, graceful name
Awiyam—pretty, lovely, handsome, graceful fragrance
Awni—the earthssist help
Axali—power of holy, pure, sanctified, pious, solemn blessing
Axa—reflection
Axia—indestructible
Ayana—goddess saraswati
Ayana—pretty bloom, garden stuff
Ayan—gift of god
Ayanna—innocent, pretty, lovely, handsome, graceful bloom, garden stuff, royal
Ayanshi—lucky, nakshatra, rashi
Ayanshi—part of the sun
Ayantika—goddess of durga

Ayantika—mobile, move or travel to place
Ayanti—recognise
Ayatee—a descendant
Ayati—royal, god like
Ayaushi—long life
Ayeh—sign, distinct
Ayera—respectable
Ayesha—a popular name
Ayesha—obedient
Ayesha—woman, life, small one, simple
Ayessha—small one, successes, woman, life
Ayisha—pretty, lovely, handsome, graceful name
Ayisha—star, woman, life, lively woman
Ayita—first to dance, beloved
Ayna—mirror
Ayna—mirror, pretty, lovely, handsome, graceful eye, glimmers
Aynna—innocents
Ayodhika—serenity, calm, calmness, stillness, silence loving calm
Ayra—respectable person
Ayra—respectable, noble, vision filler
Aysa—obedient
Aysha—obedient
Aysha—woman, life
Ayshe—beauty
Ayshu—lively, enjoy life
Ayugoo—frieternal, everlasting
Ayukta—surya or sun
Ayumi—pace, walk
Ayurda—bestower of longevity
Ayurdha—goddess durga
Ayusha—life, life span
Ayushika—long life
Ayushi—long life
Ayushi—one with long life, live long
Ayushis—the blessed one
Ayushivi—long life, lord shiva
Ayushka—life
Ayush—lifege
Ayushmati—one who has a long life
Ayushmati—who has a long life, eternal one
Ayushna—blessed with eternal life
Ayushna—one with long life
Ayushree—age, span of life
Ayushree—long life, forever, pretty, lovely, handsome, graceful
Ayusi—one with long life
Ayu—span of life, age
Ayusri—good brilliant, sagacious, gifted, wise, learned
Ayuti—different, unique
Ayuti—illumination, luminosity, radiance, freedom, independence
Ayza—pretty, lovely, handsome, graceful name
Azeena—beauty, pretty, lovely, handsome, graceful

****

Indian Names For Girls—B

Babay—small kid
Babbu—pretty, lovely, handsome, graceful name
Babeeta—pleasant, pretty, lovely, handsome, graceful, polite
Babhravi—victorious, carrying, brown
Babhru—reddish brown cow
Babita—pretty, lovely, handsome, graceful, pleasant, polite, born
Babita—born in the quarter of an astrological day
Babitha—serenity, calm, calmness, stillness, born in the first
Babli—lovely, chubby
Baby—a child
Baby—infant
Bachendri—the sense of speech
Badarivasa—another name of durga
Badari—jujube tree
Badra—full moon, pretty, goddess durga
Badrika—source of river ganga
Badriya—resembling full moon, moor-like
Baduri—bravery
Bagavathideity—name of a raga
Bagavathi—mother of goddess
Bageshawaree—a raga, beauty
Bageshree—a raga
Bageshree—beauty
Bageshree—beauty, saraswati
Bageshri—name of a raga, good luck
Bageshvari—goddess durga, raga
Bageshwari—goddess
Bagula—crane
Bagula—white duck village
Bagya—luck, fortune
Bahara—brings the spring
Bahar—spring
Bahar—spring season, prime of life
Bahati—luck or be lucky, good fortune
Bahieh—boat to the sun
Bahina—sister

Bahi—pretty, lovely, handsome, graceful, elegant, graceful
Bahubhuja—a river's name
Bahuchara—name of goddess parvati
Bahudama—a star
Bahudanti—with many teeth
Bahuda—giving much
Bahugandha—one with lot of scent, bud
Bahula—a star, various forms, cow
Bahula—abundant
Bahule—full moon in the month of kartik
Bahulika—magnified
Bahulika—magnified, star
Bahuli—manifold
Bahuli—one who has many facets
Bahulya—ganga river
Bahulya—variety, manifoldness
Bahumathi—scholar
Bahumati—extremely knowledgeable, gift
Bahupushpa—bloom, garden stuffs
Bahuputrika—sita
Bahuputri—with many sons, durga
Bahuratna—rich in gems
Bahurupa—with many forms
Bahu—daughter-in-law
Baibhabi—goddess lakshmi
Baidehi—goddess sita, wife of lord rama
Baidehi—sita
Baijanti—name of bloom, garden stuff, flower
Baijayanthi—prize, garland of lord vishnu
Baijayanti—flag, prize, garland of lord
Baijjyanti—name of a bloom, garden stuff
Bairagi—independent
Bairavi—goddess durga
Baisakhi—of the month baishakh
Baisakhi—the month of baishakh

Baishakhi—pretty, lovely, handsome, graceful
Baishali—an ancient city of india
Baji—joyful
Bakavati—very attentive, patient
Baka—crane
Bakeruka—a small crane
Bakhirathi—maa ganga
Bakhiyam—explanation
Bakhiyavathi—bloom, garden stuff name
Bakhiya—lucky girl
Bakudi—small bowl
Bakulamala—necklace of bhakul bloom, garden stuffs
Bakulavali—string of bakula bloom, garden stuff, bird
Bakula—a bloom, garden stuff, nagakeshar bloom, garden stuff
Bakule—magnified
Bakulika—small bakula blossom
Bakuli—resembles a crane, blossom
Bakul—string, name of bloom, garden stuff
Balaja—a little goddess
Balaja—born of power, the earth
Balaji—lord venkatesh
Balakunda—a young bloom, garden stuff
Balamani—youthful, tender, small ornament, jewellery
Balammal—pretty, lovely, handsome, graceful name
Balanchita—carried by power
Balancita—pretty, lovely, handsome, graceful name
Balandhara—possessed by power
Balanteena—cute one, beloved
Balaprada—giver of vigour, goddess parvati
Balaprada—vigour giver
Balaprasoo—rohini, mother of balram
Balapuspika—the young blossom
Balasandhya—illumination, luminosity, radiance, dawn
Balavikarnika—a river, pretty woman, goddess
Balavinashtaka—destroyer of childhood
Bala—a girl, an ever year old girl young
Balchandrika—woman, pretty, lovely, handsome, graceful like moon
Baldev—the mighty god
Balendra—lord of illumination, luminosity, radiance
Bale—cute child
Balhini—pretty, lovely, handsome, graceful name
Balika—a girl, female child
Balika—daughter, little daughter, girl
Baline—powerful
Balini—powerful, strong, constellation of
Bali—earring, strong, sacrifice
Ballari—creeper, vine, ruler, prince, earl, quietly
Balotkata—creeper
Baltishna—powerful
Balwanti—brave
Bama—a old monk
Bambi—little, female baby, child
Bamini—pretty, lovely, handsome, graceful, glorious
Banamala—forest, wood, jungles
Banani—evergreen forest, wood, jungles
Banashankari—forest, wood, jungles
Banashree—beauty of forest, wood, jungle
Banasri—beauty of the forest, wood, jungle
Bandana—worship
Bandhavi—who loves friends and family
Bandhini—bound
Bandhne—bound
Bandhula—charming
Bandhula—charming, curved, pleasing, favourite, charming
Bandhura—pretty
Bandini—preserve
Bandna—prayer
Banhishikha—flame
Banhi—fire

Banht—strong, caring
Banita—a woman
Banita—brilliant, sagacious, gifted, wise, learned, woman
Bani—earth
Bani—goddess saraswati
Bani—speech
Banmala—a garland, bloom, garden stuffs
Banmala—forest, wood, jungles
Banni—maiden
Bansari—flute
Banshika—belongs to lord krishna
Banshri—flute
Bansika—flute, generation
Bansi—flute
Bansi—flute of lord krishna, whistle
Bansri—flute
Bansuri—flute
Banulatha—pretty, lovely, handsome, graceful name
Banumathi—sun and moon
Banupriya—wife of sun, holy, sanctified, pious, solemn, chaste
Banu—princess, lady, flute, instrument
Banvi—love
Barani—a star, nakshatra
Bargavi—goddess durga
Barhayita—pretty, lovely, handsome, graceful
Barhina—adorned with peacock feather
Barhisha—sacrificial grass
Barhismati—blazing, holy, sanctified, pious, solemn, chaste, pious
Barikha—rainy season
Barisha—rained, holy, sanctified, pious, solemn, chaste
Barishmati—a woman with a luster
Barkavi—god, good
Barkha—rain
Barnali—rainbow of colours
Barneta—good woman
Barsana—radha's birthplace
Barsha—rain
Baruna—wife of the lord of the sea
Baruni—of the ocean, goddess durga
Barvadakumari—goddess durga

Basabi—wife of lord indra
Basaira—shelter, roost
Basanta—cool climate
Basantika—goddess of spring
Basanti—of spring, spring season, yellow
Basanti—of the spring
Basanti—spring season, related to spring
Basant—spring alive
Baseema—smiling, spring
Bashina—sister
Bashira—joyful, predictor of good news
Basila—feminine of basil, brave
Basil—royal, monarch, ruler, prince, earlly, the great
Basistha—someone special
Basu—pretty, lovely, handsome, graceful name
Basveswari—pretty, lovely, handsome, graceful name
Bathiravathi—goddess parvati
Batika—a bloom, garden stuff garden, derivation from
Bati—the wick
Batuk—small
Baumathi—extremely knowledgeable, gift
Bavana—feeling, clear knowledge
Bavanya—goddess durga
Bavatarani—who can free one to world
Bavina—adventurous, confident
Bavisha—future
Bavishya—future
Bavita—person who knows future, oracle
Bavya—goddess parvati
Bawri—madness, loving like mad
Bayjayanti—a garland of lord vishnu
Bebi—baby, from swahili
Bebo—darling
Bebu—little cute girl, baby
Beejajarine—tamonarch, ruler, prince, earl away seed
Beejali—illumination, luminosity, radiance
Beeja—origin of soul

Beeja—seed
Beemla—without any spots
Beena—a musical instrument, seeing
Beena—intelligence, musical instrument
Beila—pretty, lovely, handsome, graceful name
Bekuri—an apsara
Bela—a bloom, garden stuff
Bela—evening time bloom, garden stuff, jasmine
Beli—a bloom, garden stuff-jasmine
Bella—promise of god, pretty, lovely, handsome, graceful
Belli—silver companion
Belma—husband
Bel—sacred wood apple tree
Benaka—name of lord ganesh
Benazir—grace, without like, unique
Benisha—flashing
Benita—blessed, good person
Beni—triveni sangam
Benu—flute
Berdina—glorious
Bethina—from the house of god's grace
Bhabani—goddess durga
Bhabiya—great
Bhadrabala—goddess, gentle, auspicious young woman
Bhadrakaali—one of the forms of goddess kali
Bhadrakali—auspicious kali
Bhadrakshi—pretty, lovely, handsome, graceful eye, glimmers
Bhadrakshi—one with pretty, lovely, handsome, graceful face
Bhadrale—beautiflu female friend
Bhadrali—pretty, lovely, handsome, graceful female companion
Bhadramallika—pretty, lovely, handsome, graceful
Bhadramukhi—pretty, lovely, handsome, graceful eye, glimmers
Bhadramurti—an embodiment of benevolence
Bhadraprana—a plant with pretty, lovely, handsome, graceful leaves

Bhadrapriya—auspicious, beloved
Bhadrapriya—lover
Bhadrashela—a woman with good character
Bhadrasvapna—seeing nice dream
Bhadravati—gentle woman
Bhadravati—goddess of welfare
Bhadrawathi—wife of monarch, ruler, prince, earl
Bhadra—gentle, blessed, prosperous
Bhadra—goodness
Bhadra—one of the name of river ganga
Bhadrika—pretty, lovely, handsome, graceful noble lady
Bhadrika—goog nature
Bhadrusha—the ganges
Bhagada—a lucky woman
Bhagada—bestow of happiness and wealth
Bhagananda—bestower of happiness
Bhagarekha—destinity
Bhagavanti—shareholder, fortunate
Bhagavathi—goddess durga, lakshmi
Bhagavath—knowledgeable, inspired
Bhagavati—nature and self conjoined, goddess
Bhagavti—goddess saraswati
Bhageerathe—of bhagiratha
Bhageerathi—name of an river
Bhageerathi—the ganga
Bhageshree—a raga
Bhageshwari—goddess of luck
Bhagini—mountain stream
Bhagirathe—name of ganges river
Bhagirathi—the ganga river
Bhagirathi—the river ganga, mother of bhishma
Bhagirati—god is grate
Bhagshri—lucky women
Bhagvanti—lucky, goddess
Bhagvatee—name of lakshmi and durga
Bhagvatee—the ganges
Bhagvati—another name of goddess lakshmi
Bhagvati—fortunate woman
Bhagwani—goddess

Bhagwanti—fortunate
Bhagwanti—lucky
Bhagwati—fortunate
Bhagwati—goddess durga
Bhagyajyothi—fortune
Bhagyajyoti—illumination, luminosity, radiance of good fortune
Bhagyalakshmee—illumination, luminosity, radiance of good fortune
Bhagyalakshmi—goddess lakshmi
Bhagyalakshmi—goddess lakshmi, wealth, luck
Bhagyalakshmi—goddess of good fortune, goddess
Bhagyarekha—goddess of wealth
Bhagyashree—fortunate, goddess lakshmi
Bhagyashree—goddess lakshmi
Bhagyashri—goddess lakshmi, fortunate
Bhagyasree—fortunate, goddess lakshmi
Bhagyasree—goddess lakshmi, fortunate
Bhagyasri—lucky
Bhagyatra—goddess lakshmi
Bhagyavati—fortunate
Bhagyavi—fortunate, luckyuspicious
Bhagyawati—fortunate, lucky, goddess lakshmi
Bhagyawati—lucky
Bhagya—fate, prosperity
Bhagya—luck, fortune, devotion, wealth
Bhagyeshree—fortunate, goddess lakshmi
Bhagyshe—fortunate, goddess lakshmi
Bhagyshri—fortunate, goddess lakshmi
Bhaina—not afraid
Bhairave—goddess durga, a raga in classical music
Bhairave—lucky
Bhairavi—a melody in classical music
Bhajnandini—goddess
Bhajna—praise
Bhajuna—sun illumination, luminosity, radiance

Bhaktigamya—devotee
Bhaktipriya—god lover
Bhaktivashya—devotee
Bhakti—devotion
Bhakti—worship, devotion, prayer
Bhaktja—religious by birth
Bhalchandra—goddess durga
Bhama—passionate woman
Bhama—prayer, passionate, famous, loving
Bhamine—pretty, lovely, handsome, graceful
Bhamine—pleasing, favourite, charming woman
Bhamini—glorious, woman, pretty, lovely, handsome, graceful
Bhamini—wife
Bhami—passionate woman
Bhanave—daughter of bhanu
Bhanavi—sacred, illuminating
Bhandhavi—friendship, relationship
Bhano—special
Bhanujaa—name of river yamuna
Bhanuja—daugther of sun
Bhanuja—river yamuna, goddess radhika
Bhanukiran—ray of sun
Bhanulata—pretty, lovely, handsome, graceful creeper
Bhanumatee—pretty, lovely, handsome, graceful woman
Bhanumathi—full of lustre
Bhanumati—pretty, lovely, handsome, graceful, skillful
Bhanumati—full of lustre, famous
Bhanumati—glorious, a highness, empress, queen
Bhanuni—charming woman
Bhanupriya—beloved of sun
Bhanupriya—beloved of the sun
Bhanushree—pretty, lovely, handsome, graceful woman
Bhanushree—brightness of the suns glorious
Bhanushri—brightness of the sun
Bhanusri—rays of lakshmi, deity
Bhanusuta—woman, daughter of the sun

Bhanuvi—the sun, fame
Bhanu—sun
Bhanu—sun, fame, illumination, luminosity, radiance, brightness
Bhanvaree—name of a woman
Bhanve—shining like sun
Bhanvi—daughter of sun, sun-rays
Bharagavi—knowledge, beauty of nature
Bharamane—lustrous
Bharani—one who fulfils nakshathra
Bharata—engrossed in pleasures
Bharatee—goddess of speech, belongs to india
Bharathi—goddess of knowledge and
Bharath—india
Bharati—female form of bharat, goddess
Bharati—goddess of knowledge and
Bharavi—radiant sun, tulsi
Bharda—mother of kartikaiya
Bhargavi—charming, daughter of bhanu
Bhargavi—goddess parvati
Bhargavi—knowledge, beauty of nature
Bharghavi—the world, goddess parvati
Bhargvi—grass, goddess durga
Bharni—a star
Bharshika—pretty, lovely, handsome, graceful name
Bharti—goddess of speech
Bharvi—holy basil plant
Bhasha—language
Bhashe—of the nature of illumination, luminosity, radiance, lustrous
Bhashini—talkative
Bhashita—spoken
Bhashvika—illumination, luminosity, radiance, sun
Bhashwini—meaningful
Bhasini—talkative
Bhaskari—sun, radiant like the sun
Bhasvara—origin of illumination, luminosity, radiance
Bhasvati—a old river
Bhasvati—luminous, splendid

Bhaswatee—pretty, lovely, handsome, graceful name
Bhaswati—bright, shining, sun, bright side
Bhati—luster, splendour, perception
Bhatri—goddess saraswati
Bhattarika—noble lady, sacred
Bhauma—belonging to earth
Bhaumika—associated with earth
Bhaumi—earth, goddess sita
Bhavaane—goddess parvati
Bhavada—giving life
Bhavada—nurturing
Bhavaghna—goddess durga
Bhavagna—name of goddess lalitha deity
Bhavagnya—one of name of goddess lalitha
Bhavaja—born of the heat
Bhavajna—a woman who knows the world
Bhavambee—mother of a noble woman
Bhavana—emotions, feelings, meditation
Bhavana—emotions, meditation
Bhavana—feeling
Bhavana—feelings, ambition, intent, passion
Bhavangi—noble lady
Bhavani—goddess durga
Bhavani—goddess parvati
Bhavani—goddess, the abode of the
Bhavanya—concentration, brave, meditation
Bhavaprita—loved by everyone in the universe
Bhavasri—pretty, lovely, handsome, graceful name
Bhavatharini—goddess name
Bhavati—outstanding, athletic
Bhavatu—outstanding, athletic
Bhavayami—imagine of god, morning
Bhava—ecstasy, beauty
Bhavda—giving life
Bhavdhi—land
Bhaveka—righteous, honest, cheerful
Bhavesha—emotion, future

Bhavesha—goddess
Bhaveshwari—lord of expression
Bhaviada—happy
Bhavika—lot of emotional, well-meaning
Bhavika—natural
Bhavikia—sentimental
Bhaviksha—emotions, devout, virtuous, well
Bhavina—full of emotions
Bhavini—pretty, lovely, handsome, graceful, illustrious
Bhavini—goddess parvati, emotional
Bhavini—the pretty, lovely, handsome, graceful woman, goddess
Bhavisana—holy, pure, sanctified, pious, solemn
Bhavisha—feeling, emotion, future
Bhavishya—feature, future
Bhavishya—future's of parent
Bhaviska—simple
Bhavisri—pretty
Bhavita—imagined
Bhaviya—great
Bhavi—emotional, brave, pretty, future
Bhavna—devotion, ambition, intent, passion
Bhavna—feelings, sentiments, emotions
Bhavna—spirit
Bhavnet—moral of the world
Bhavne—the moon, the sun
Bhavni—all upon god, emotion, goddess
Bhavnoor—out of this world
Bhavtu—holy, holy, pure, sanctified, pious, solemn
Bhavukta—emotions, filled with feelings
Bhavu—emotion
Bhavyanshika—bigger part, part of grand, big
Bhavyanshi—part of grand, splendid, big
Bhavyashree—splendid wealth
Bhavyashri—grand, big, goddess parvati,

Bhavyasri—grand, splendid, goddess parvati
Bhavyata—bigness, huge
Bhavya—goddess parvati
Bhavya—grand, splendid, big, goddess
Bhavya—represent to future
Bhavyshree—grand
Bhawana—feeling
Bhawani—illuminating, creator
Bhawna—feelings, emotions, sentiment
Bhayanashini—remover of fear
Bhayana—fearfull
Bhayanshini—remover of fear
Bhayharini—remover of fear
Bhayhari—remover of fear
Bha—god, sun, historic or religious
Bhedi—one who gives our secrets
Bhela—jasmin bloom, garden stuffssertive
Bhemai—serenity, calm, calmness, stillness, silenceful
Bhema—goddess durga, powerful
Bheni—wet
Bhervi—pretty, lovely, handsome, graceful name
Bhe—god
Bhilangana—a river
Bhimanshi—brilliant, sagacious, gifted, wise, learned, brave
Bhimarika—enemy of the terrible, powerful
Bhindu—drop of water, lover, loveable
Bhini—mild fragrance, humid
Bhinna—different kinds
Bhinu—wet
Bhiravi—goddess durga
Bhogavati—curving female serpent
Bhogaya—worthy of enjoyment
Bhogvati—one who gives the pleasure
Bhojana—food
Bholi—innocent
Bhomika—earth
Bhomira—originating from earth
Bhomi—earth, goddess durga
Bhoodeity—mother earth
Bhooma—earth
Bhoomija—daugther of the earth

Bhoomija—tolerant, ram's wife sita
Bhoomika—the earth, role, character
Bhoomi—earth, the earth
Bhoopali—a goddess
Bhoorik—the earth
Bhoorita—abundance
Bhooshani—ornament, jewellery, ornamentation, adornment,
Bhooshita—ornament, jewellery, ornamentation, adornment, decorated
Bhoosuta—sita
Bhoovika—pretty, lovely, handsome, graceful name
Bhoovi—heaven
Bhoo—earth
Bhovika—emotions
Bhragavi—pretty, lovely, handsome, graceful name
Bhramarika—wandering in all direction
Bhramari—dancing around
Bhramari—honey-bee
Bhramee—whirlpool
Bhrami—traveller
Bhrammani—sarswati
Bhramti—beauty
Bhrgavi—goddess lakshmi
Bhrigu—name of a saint
Bhringi—an attendent of lord shiva
Bhristee—rain
Bhrithi—vigourened, cherished
Bhriti—love for nation
Bhrringaree—as bright as fire
Bhruhanth—pretty, lovely, handsome, graceful name
Bhrungara—golden bloom, garden stuff
Bhrutika—earth
Bhruve—earth
Bhujwala—fire under the earth
Bhumanya—accepted by earth, ambition, intent, passion
Bhumayi—full of live, exist, rise, being, entity
Bhuma—goddess of earth, mother earth
Bhumeshvani—sympathetic, from the earth

Bhumeshvari—universe, goddess of galaxy
Bhumija—godddes sita, earth
Bhumika—earth, role, character
Bhumiksha—earth daughter
Bhumi—earth, strong, big heart
Bhupali—rag of music, ragini in indian
Bhurvi—loyal
Bhushandev—goddess of ornament, jewellery, ornamentation, adornment, figurations
Bhusita—ornament, jewellery, ornamentation, adornment
Bhuti—well being, live, exist, rise, being, entity
Bhuvainika—heaven
Bhuvanapaavani—makes the earth sacred
Bhuvana—the earth
Bhuvana—universe, the earth
Bhuvandeve—goddess of the world
Bhuvaneshane—mistress of earth
Bhuvanesha—earth, universe, abode of god
Bhuvaneshe—goddess of earth
Bhuvaneshwaree—earth mother
Bhuvaneshwari—goddess of earth
Bhuvaneshwari—goddess of world, the earth
Bhuvaneswari—goddess of earth
Bhuvanika—heaven
Bhuvanmati—owner of the world, earth
Bhuvanya—belongs to the earth, land
Bhuvika—heaven
Bhuviksha—belong to earth, land
Bhuvisha—heaven
Bhuvi—heaven, bliss, earth, land
Bhuvi—the earth
Bhuvneshwari—universe, the earth
Bhuwana—earth
Bhuwi—heaven
Bhvaneshwari—earth mother
Bhvatu—pretty, lovely, handsome, graceful name
Bhvya—grand, big
Bianca—the white one

Bibha—shine, ray, illumination, luminosity, radiance, radiance
Bibhuti—goddess lakshmi
Bibhu—lord vishnull pervading
Bibin—forest, wood, jungle
Bidhika—pretty, lovely, handsome, graceful name
Bidhisa—pretty, lovely, handsome, graceful name
Bidhya—knowledge
Bidisha—illumination, luminosity, radiance, knowledge, educated
Bidita—genius, brilliant, sagacious, gifted, wise, learned
Bidiya—strong
Bidula—name of a tree
Bidu—earth, calm
Bidya—knowledge
Bihula—pretty, lovely, handsome, graceful name
Bijali—illumination, luminosity, radiance
Bijal—illumination, luminosity, radiance, bright
Bijesha—belongs to lord shiva
Bijita—winner
Biji—willow tree
Bijjal—illumination, luminosity, radiance, bright
Bijli—illumination, luminosity, radiance, bright, electricity
Bijoli—illumination, luminosity, radiance
Bijori—a kind of a tree
Bijoya—victory
Bijuli—illumination, luminosity, radiance
Biju—great, powerful, awesome
Bikunja—a thicket bower place
Bilori—made of crystal glass
Bilpa—bloom, garden stuff
Bilvanilaya—reside under bilva tree
Bilvani—goddess saraswati
Bilva—auspicious fruit, bael sacred
Bilwasri—holy leaf offered to lord shiva
Bilwa—holy leaf offered to lord shiva

Bimala—holy, sanctified, pious, solemn, chaste
Bimba—image, mirror
Bimba—reflection
Bimbika—disc of the stars of satellite
Bimbika—round faced, mirror
Bimbi—as luminous as the sun
Bimbi—glorious, gold
Bimla—holy, sanctified, pious, solemn, chaste
Bimola—spotless
Binaisha—father's pride
Binaita—pretty, lovely, handsome, graceful name
Binaka—name of lord ganesha
Binaki—red decorative mark on forehead
Binal—princess
Binata—the wife of sage kashyap
Binatee—request
Bina—a musical instrument, melodious
Bina—a popular name
Bindadeity—name o a girl
Bindhiya—dew drop
Bindhushree—goddess lakshmi
Bindhu—drop of water, dot on the forehead
Bindia—beauty, small dot on forehead
Bindita—point, drop
Bindiyan—droplet
Bindiya—drop, point forehead ornamentation, adornment, figuration
Bindi—small round to wear on forehead
Bindulekha—name of woman
Bindumaalini—wearing a garland of pearls
Bindumalini—pearl garlanded
Bindumatee—pretty, lovely, handsome, graceful name
Bindumathi—learned
Bindumati—an anient learned woman
Bindumati—wise, illumined
Bindurekha—a line of dots verse
Bindushri—point
Bindusree—point
Bindusri—drop point

Bindu—a drop, point, goddess parvati
Bindu—drop, dot
Bindya—a droplet
Bindya—drop, point
Bindya—small red dot, bindi that married
Bineta—humble person
Binita—modest, the most amiable, pleasing, suave, interesting, humble
Bini—architec
Binjal—goddess
Binnaha—request
Binodine—joyous woman
Binodini—full of recreation
Binodini—handsome, pretty, lovely, handsome, graceful radha
Binoli—bloom, garden stuff
Binta—with god
Binti—request, daughter
Bintu—pretty, lovely, handsome, graceful one
Binu—entertainment
Bipasa—a river
Bipasha—a river, beas river in the
Bipsa—a river
Bipsha—pretty, lovely, handsome, graceful name
Bipula—plenty, strong
Birajini—lord shiva
Biranavy—pretty, lovely, handsome, graceful name
Birina—garden
Bironika—brave
Birva—leaf, love
Birwa—belief
Bisa—fibre of the water-lily, lotus
Bishakha—a star
Bishala—sprout, bud
Bishthi—rain
Bisini—a bunch of lotus
Bisini—lotus
Bisma—sliver, freshness and smile
Bisthi—vision
Bisu—pretty, lovely, handsome, graceful name
Biswajita—winner of the world, universe

Biswamber—pretty, lovely, handsome, graceful name
Bithika—path between trees
Bithi—bunch of bloom, garden stuff
Bitta—honest, helpful
Bitti—sweet, cute
Bittu—sweet, cute
Bivasa—bright illumination, luminosity, radiance of full moon
Bixita—developed
Biyanka—blessed with lord ganesha
Bobby—strange, bright famous one
Boby—bright fame
Bodhana—the illumination, luminosity, radiance, enlightenment
Bodhana—inspiring, expand
Bodhini—wise, illumination, luminosity, radiance, knowledge
Bodhi—awakened, illumination, luminosity, radiance
Bodhni—intellect, understanding
Bodhvati—learned woman
Bodh—perfume, scent
Bommi—a sweet person
Bonasri—flute, instrument played by lord
Boomika—playing role
Boond—drop
Booshani—a nakshatra
Boo—a desert plant
Borsha—rain
Bosky—herb
Boudhi—lesson
Bowshika—beauty
Brahanta—very strong, powerful
Brahan—big
Brahmacharini—seeker of brahma
Brahmalin—absorbed in devotion of lord
Brahmanibka—mother of brahmanda
Brahmani—wife of lord brahma, saraswathi
Brahmanjale—to pray with folded or cupped hands
Brahmattmika—daughter of brahma
Brahmavaadini—present everywhere, goddess
Brahmcharini—seeker of brahma

Brahmini—goddess
Brahmishtha—the highest form of absolute
Brahmistha—the highest form of absolute
Brahmi—goddess durga
Brahmi—holy, the shakti of brahma
Brahmnet—absorbed in gods love
Brahmputri—daughter of brahma
Branda—distilled wine
Branucika—pretty, lovely, handsome, graceful name
Bratati—creeper, vine
Breezsha—nature of wind
Brhamramba—goddess parvathi
Briduna—pretty, lovely, handsome, graceful name
Briella—pretty, god is my vigour
Brihanalla—character in mahabharata
Brijabala—daughter of nature
Brijal—loveable, goddess of wealth
Brijangana—woman of brija
Brija—seed
Brijbala—daughter of brija
Brijbala—radha
Brijesha—lord krishna
Brijlata—a creeper grows in brij
Brindadeity—goddess radha
Brindavanam—name of a place
Brinda—kind of princess, the basil plant
Brinda—name of a sacred plant, basil
Brindha—pretty, lovely, handsome, graceful
Brisha—smile, beloved
Brishi—a roll of twisted grass, cushion
Brishna—pretty, lovely, handsome, graceful name
Brishtee—rain
Brishti—rain, weather, sprinkle of
Brisi—a roll of twisted grass, cushion
Briti—vigour, bloom, garden stuff
Brrihadyuti—luminous
Brrihatee—heaven and earth
Brrinda—surrounded by many

Brundah—tulsi, the basil plant, radha
Brundashree—pretty, lovely, handsome, goddess
Brunda—pretty, lovely, handsome, graceful, goddess
Brundha—basil, tulasi tree
Bruthika—baseline
Bruvana—earth
Bryn—strong, vigilant, honoured, hill
Bubble—valuable, valued, rare, gorgeous
Bubby—my beloved
Budarika—one of the sources of the river
Buddhana—aware, illumination, luminosity, radiance one
Buddhideity—goddess of wisdom
Buddhikama—pretty, lovely, handsome, graceful name
Buddhikari—bestower of wisdom
Buddhimathi—brilliant, sagacious, gifted, wise, learned, wise
Buddhi—intelligence, wisdom
Buddhi—reason, intellectual
Budhana—illumination, luminosity, radiance
Budhikari—goddess saraswati
Budhita—awakened, illumination, luminosity, radiance one
Buji—a loving nick name
Bujji—small
Bukala—purity, innocence
Bula—a bird
Bulbuli—a songbird
Bulbul—name of a bird
Bulbul—singing bird, nightingale
Bumika—earth
Bunny—good, fair of face, charming, cute
Bushra—happy news, glad tiding, glad
Buthayna—of pretty, lovely, handsome, graceful and tender body
Buvana—goddess
Buvanisha—beauty

****

Indian Names For Girls—C

Calama—beauty, pen
Cala—fortress, lovely, most pretty, lovely, handsome, graceful
Camaksi—goddess parvati, goddess
Camerina—pretty, lovely, handsome, graceful name
Camunda—goddess
Candalika—goddess durga
Candamunda—pretty, lovely, handsome, graceful name
Candavata—pretty, lovely, handsome, graceful name
Candika—fierce goddess
Candi—clarity, whiteness
Candogra—pretty, lovely, handsome, graceful name
Candradara—river on the moon
Candrakala—artwork like moon
Candrali—pretty, lovely, handsome, graceful name
Candramasi—like moon
Candrama—full moon
Candrasita—moon illumination, luminosity, radiance
Candra—luminescent, moon, holy, sanctified, pious, solemn, chaste
Capala—swift, illumination, luminosity, radiance
Carcika—name of a god
Carma—garden or field of fruits, song
Carmem—garden
Carsani—daisy in a field of roses
Carudharar—diamond figure, appearance, structure, meet of river
Caruvi—instrument
Catalina—chaste, holy, sanctified, pious, solemn, chaste, proud, warlike
Catuskarni—pretty, lovely, handsome, graceful name
Catuspatha—pretty, lovely, handsome, graceful name
Cauvery—name of a river
Cavery—name of a river in india
Chabbi—picture

Chaddalika—pretty, lovely, handsome, graceful name
Chadna—love
Chagu—smart
Chahak—lover, voice of sweet bird
Chahal—loving
Chahana—love, ambition, intent, passionffection
Chahat—ambition, intent, passion, love
Chaha—ambition, intent, passion, desire, aspiration, longing, love
Chaheti—lovely, amiable, pleasing, suave, interesting for all
Chahna—ambition, intent, passion, love
Chahna—love, like
Chaina—serenity, calm, calmness, stillness, silence
Chainika—specially selected, chosen one
Chairavali—full moon of chaitra month
Chaitaale—born in chaitra month
Chaitale—girl born in month of chaitra
Chaitale—one who belongs to mind
Chaitali—born in the month of chaitra
Chaitali—memory
Chaitaly—name of an ancient city
Chaital—consciousness
Chaitana—consciousness
Chaitanya—consciousness
Chaithana—very active
Chaithra—first month of the year, spring
Chaiti—a musical form
Chaitna—conscience
Chaitna—sunbloom, garden stuff seed
Chaitrali—born in the month of chitra
Chaitrashree—pretty, lovely, handsome, graceful name
Chaitravi—born in month of chaitra
Chaitra—aries sign
Chaitree—born in spring

Chaitri—full moon day
Chaitya—concerning the mind
Chaitya—its a buddhist hindu shrine in
Chakkubai—pretty, lovely, handsome, graceful name
Chakku—knife
Chakorine—beloved of chakor
Chakori—alert bird enamoured of the
Chakori—name of a bird
Chakor—size of moon bird, pretty, lovely, handsome, graceful
Chakranhi—power of whel
Chakria—lakshmi
Chakrika—goddess lakshmi
Chakrila—goddess lakshmi
Chakrini—potter
Chakshendree—sense of sight
Chakshika—pretty, lovely, handsome, graceful eye, glimmers
Chakshine—soothing the eye, glimmers
Chakshita—pretty, lovely, handsome, graceful eye, glimmers
Chakshumatee—eye, glimmersight
Chakshu—eye, glimmers
Chaksushe—preceptor
Chalama—goddess parvati
Chala—earth
Chalisa—worship, prayers
Chalsia—pretty, lovely, handsome, graceful, graceful
Chaman—garden
Chama—a bloom, garden stuff
Chamba—name of a woman
Chamele—a creeper with bloom, garden stuffs
Chameli—jasmine creeper with bloom, garden stuffs
Chameli—jasmine, a bloom, garden stuff
Chamini—love like ocean
Chamisha—pretty, lovely, handsome, graceful name
Chamkee—shine-full
Champaavatee—angaraj's karna's capital
Champabati—the capital

Champakale—bud of yellow fragrant bloom, garden stuff
Champakali—pretty, lovely, handsome, graceful like bloom, garden stuff
Champakali—a bud of champa
Champakavathi—owner of champak trees
Champaka—a tree with yellow fragrant bloom, garden stuff
Champakmala—a garland made of champa bloom, garden stuffs
Champakmala—a garland of champa bloom, garden stuff
Champakpalavi—a creeper with bloom, garden stuffs
Champamalini—garland of champa bloom, garden stuff
Champavarne—complexion of a champak bloom, garden stuff
Champavarne—complexion of champa bloom, garden stuff
Champavati—everfragrant
Champavati—owner of champak tree
Champa—a bloom, garden stuff
Champa—a bloom, garden stuff, essence of sun, fragrant
Champikaa—pretty, lovely, handsome, graceful bloom, garden stuff called champa
Champika—little champa bloom, garden stuff
Chamudi—goddess durga, killer of demons
Chamunda—fierce form of durga
Chamunda—goddess parvati, goddess who
Chamundee—hindu goddess form of durga
Chanakshi—clever
Chanashay—illumination, luminosity, radiance
Chanasya—illumination, luminosity, radiance, pretty
Chana—famous, well-known
Chanchalakshi—restless, playful eye, glimmers

Chanchala—the goddess of wealth, unsteady
Chanchala—unsteadyctive, goddess lakshmi
Chanchal—active, spontaneous, lively
Chanchal—trembling, moving
Chanchari—bird, vortex of water
Chancy—goddess lakshmi
Chandalikaa—another name of durga
Chandalini—glorious
Chandan gandha—a fragrance of sandalwood
Chandana—of the sandal
Chandana—sandalwood, parrot
Chandane—moon, illumination, luminosity, radiance
Chandanika—a small sandal-wood tree
Chandanika—diminutive
Chandani—star river, moon, illumination, luminosity, radiance, silver
Chandan—sandlewood
Chandara—moon
Chandasri—holy, pure, sanctified, pious, solemn
Chanda—moon
Chanda—the moon
Chandee—name of a god
Chandhana—bird, sandalwood
Chandhini—moon illumination, luminosity, radiance
Chandhraka—moon
Chandika—like moon, diminutive of chandana
Chandika—name of durga
Chandila—wrathful
Chandima—moon illumination, luminosity, radiance
Chandini—star, moon, illumination, luminosity, radiance
Chandira—moon
Chandi—name of goddess kali, goddess
Chandna—sandalwood, dear to god, soothing
Chandne—illumination, luminosity, radiance of the moon
Chandni—moon, illumination, luminosity, radiance
Chandni—moon, illumination, luminosity, radiance, star, humble
Chandogra—one who is fierce and angry
Chandrabala—daughter of moon
Chandrabali—moonlit, krishna's devotee
Chandrabhaga—river chenab in india
Chandrabha—moon illumination, luminosity, radiance
Chandrabindu—crescent moon
Chandradipa—illumination, luminosity, radiance of moon
Chandrahasa—pretty, lovely, handsome, graceful smile
Chandraja—daughter of moon
Chandraja—daughter of moon, moon beam
Chandrajyoti—moon illumination, luminosity, radiance
Chandrakaantaa—as lovely as the moon
Chandrakala—beams of the moon, ray of the moon
Chandrakala—moon-rays
Chandrakali—progressive digit of the moon
Chandrakanta—beloved of the moon, moonstone
Chandrakanti—moon illumination, luminosity, radiance
Chandrakant—wife of moon
Chandrakin—a peacock
Chandrakiran—rays of moon
Chandrakishore—pleasing, favourite, charming man
Chandraki—peacock
Chandralekha—a ray of moon
Chandralekha—ray of moon
Chandralekha—the phase of moon two nights after
Chandraleksha—a ray of the moon
Chandrale—friend of moon
Chandramaala—garland of the moon
Chandramallika—a variety of jasmine bloom, garden stuff

Chandramallika—highness, empress, queen of the moon
Chandramallika—jasmine
Chandramani—moonstone
Chandramani—moonstone, ornament, jewellery, ornamentation, adornment, figuration
Chandramashe—moon
Chandramasi—pretty, lovely, handsome, graceful like moon
Chandramathi—as pretty, lovely, handsome, graceful as the moon
Chandramati—as pretty, lovely, handsome, graceful as the moon
Chandrama—moon
Chandramoli—one who wears the moon-figure, appearance, structured
Chandramukhe—as pretty, lovely, handsome, graceful as moon
Chandramukhi—a woman pretty, lovely, handsome, graceful like moon
Chandramukhi—face like moons pretty, lovely, handsome, graceful as
Chandrane—moon's wife
Chandrani—pretty, lovely, handsome, graceful as moon, wife of moon
Chandrani—wife of moon
Chandrani—wife of moon god
Chandranshu—a moon beam
Chandraprabha—star, moon illumination, luminosity, radiance
Chandraprabha—the moon lit
Chandrapushpa—star
Chandrarekha—ray of moon
Chandrasheda—soft, gentle
Chandrashree—holy, pure, sanctified, pious, solemn moon
Chandratara—the moon and the stars conjoined
Chandrateja—bright as moon
Chandravadane—moon faced
Chandravadane—moon like face
Chandravali—brindavan friend of radha
Chandravali—like moon
Chandravallabha—beloved of moon
Chandravallaree—moon creeper

Chandravathi—lit by the moon, illumination, luminosity, radiance of moon
Chandravati—a highness, empress, queen
Chandravati—lit by the moon, brilliant
Chandra—moon, glittering
Chandra—shining moon, moon
Chandree—moon-illumination, luminosity, radiance
Chandresha—from the moon
Chandreye, glimmers—moon's daughter
Chandria—moon, illumination, luminosity, radiance, candleillumination, luminosity, radiance
Chandrika—lustering moon, starillumination, luminosity
Chandrika—the moon lit
Chandrima—moon, illumination, luminosity, radiance night
Chandrima—of the moon
Chandrin—made of gold
Chandri—moon, illumination, luminosity, radiance, illuminating
Chand—moon
Chand—the moon
Chane—name of a god, dependability
Changla—a musical note
Changla—good
Changuna—a good woman
Chanki—clever
Channakka—pretty, lovely, handsome, graceful lady
Channaya—eminent
Channa—oldncient
Channi—motionful
Chantin—moon
Chanti—serenity, calm, calmness, stillness, silence, small one
Chantni—beloved
Chanvi—love, kindness
Chanyatha—pretty, lovely, handsome, graceful name
Chan—a clan name, moon, monday
Chapala—restless, illumination, luminosity, radiance, quick

Chapala—restless, unsteady
Chapla—goddess lakshmi
Charachrika—illumination, luminosity, radiance, happy
Charane—goddess saraswati
Charani—goddess saraswati
Charanvi—pretty, lovely, handsome, graceful
Charanya—good attitude
Chara—quiet and frisky, option
Charcha—discription
Charchikaa—a goddess name
Chardy—a burning fire that ambition, intent, passions love
Charisma—possessing an extraordinary
Charita—dear, past storey, history
Charita—of the good character
Charithattha—one having a clean character
Charitha—good, one having a very clean
Charithra—creates history
Charithya—good behaviour
Charitra—character, history
Charitrya—history, personality
Charla—from charlotte, little and
Charlie—free-woman, womanly
Charmaine—filled with illumination, luminosity, radiance, song
Charmi—pretty, lovely, handsome, graceful
Charmy—charming, lovely
Charnika—charming
Charrulochan—a woman with pretty, lovely, handsome, graceful eye, glimmers
Charru—pretty, lovely, handsome, graceful, body as the full moon
Charshane—moon, illumination, luminosity, radiance, active
Charu-mithra—lucky, talented
Charubala—pretty, lovely, handsome, graceful girl
Charubala—a pretty girl
Charubhashree—one who speaks pretty, lovely, handsome, gracefully

Charuchitra—pretty, lovely, handsome, graceful picture
Charudarshana—pretty, lovely, handsome, graceful to look
Charudarshina—one who appears to be pretty, lovely, handsome, graceful
Charudatta—very charming
Charudhara—indra's wife
Charuhi—pretty, lovely, handsome, graceful name
Charukeshe—one who has pretty, lovely, handsome, graceful hair
Charukeshini—one with pretty, lovely, handsome, graceful hair
Charukeshi—one with pretty, lovely, handsome, graceful hair
Charukeshi—with pretty, lovely, handsome, graceful hair
Charukesh—a woman with pretty, lovely, handsome, graceful hair
Charukesi—name of a raga of carnatic music
Charulata—pretty, lovely, handsome, graceful creeper
Charulata—pleasing, favourite, charming
Charula—pretty, lovely, handsome, graceful
Charulekha—pretty, lovely, handsome, graceful picture
Charuli—pretty, lovely, handsome, graceful
Charulochana—a woman with pretty, lovely, handsome, graceful eye, glimmers
Charul—lovely, pretty, lovely, handsome, graceful
Charumatee—pretty, lovely, handsome, graceful
Charumathi—pretty, lovely, handsome, graceful mind
Charumati—brilliant, sagacious, gifted, wise, learned woman
Charumati—brilliant, sagacious, gifted, wise, learned, wise pretty
Charumat—pretty, lovely, handsome, graceful name

Charuna—pretty, lovely, handsome, graceful name
Charunetra—one with pretty, lovely, handsome, graceful eye, glimmers
Charunetra—with pretty, lovely, handsome, graceful eye, glimmers
Charungi—pretty, lovely, handsome, graceful woman
Charunya—pleasing, favourite, charming, pretty, lovely, handsome, graceful
Charuprabha—pretty, lovely, handsome, graceful
Charuprabha—most pretty, lovely, handsome, graceful
Charuroopa—extremely pretty
Charushela—pretty, lovely, handsome, graceful ornament, jewellery
Charushila—diamond, pretty, lovely, handsome, graceful ornament
Charusila—pretty, lovely, handsome, graceful ornament
Charusmita—one with pretty, lovely, handsome, graceful smile
Charusri—pretty, lovely, handsome, gracefulttractive
Charuta—good, moon
Charuti—pretty, lovely, handsome, graceful
Charuvadane—a woman with pretty, lovely, handsome, graceful face
Charuvakee—name of a highness, empress, queen
Charuvakee—one who is soft spoken
Charuvardhana—woman whose beauty increases day by day
Charuveni—with pretty, lovely, handsome, graceful hair
Charuve—splendid
Charuvi—splendour
Charuvrata—pretty, lovely, handsome, graceful name
Charu—pretty, lovely, handsome, graceful
Charu—pretty, lovely, handsome, gracefulttractive, pleasing
Charu—beloved

Charu—lovely, pretty, lovely, handsome, graceful
Charvana—reflection
Charvangee—one who possess pretty, lovely, handsome, graceful body
Charvangee—pretty, lovely, handsome, graceful name
Charvanya—black forest, wood, jungle
Charve—lovely, pretty, lovely, handsome, graceful
Charvika—pretty, lovely, handsome, graceful
Charvi—pretty, lovely, handsome, graceful girl, sanskrit
Charvi—pretty, lovely, handsome, graceful lady
Charvi—pretty, lovely, handsome, graceful woman, lovely
Charvi—splendour
Charvy—pretty, lovely, handsome, graceful, pleasing, favourite, charming eye, glimmers
Chashmum—my eye, glimmers
Chaswitha—bright, permanent
Chatima—pretty, lovely, handsome, graceful
Chatrika—star
Chatura—clever
Chatura—clever, smart, wise
Chaturya—clever
Chaula—rice
Chaundra—little, moon
Chaunta—one who outshines the stars
Chavi—reflection, daughter, radiance
Chavya—a pulse
Chayana—moon
Chayanica—selection choose
Chayanika—the chosen one, leadership
Chayantika—the chosen one
Chayan—selection
Chaya—shade, shadow
Chaya—shadowlive, living, lustre
Chayla—fairy, chaya plus lea
Chayna—moon
Chaytanya—a holy illumination, luminosity, radiance
Chayu—showing awe, respect

Chea—healthy, well-being be well
Chehak—happiness
Chehal—joyful, happy
Chehek—lover, voice of sweet bird
Chehra—face
Chekriya—earth
Chelan—pretty, lovely, handsome, graceful lake
Chellamani—valuable, valued, rare gem
Chellamari—pretty, lovely, handsome, graceful name
Chellam—pampered
Chembi—name of wooden part
Chena—holy, sanctified, pious, solemn, chaste white marble
Chenbagam—bloom, garden stuff name
Chenbaga—bloom, garden stuff
Chenmayi—holy, sanctified, pious, solemn, chaste knowledge, blissful
Chen—morning, break of the day, dawn
Cheranya—supportive
Cherika—moon, cherry bloom, garden stuff
Cherry—fruit, cherry fruit, dear
Cheru—small, love
Chervishree—rear star
Cheshtaa—hard desire, aspiration, longing of heart
Cheshta—effort, trying, neds
Cheshta—try, joke
Cheshtha—to try
Chestaka—love
Chesta—ambition, intent, passion
Chestha—courage, effort, motion
Chetali—name o a woman
Chetal—coldngel, having life
Chetana—consciousness, sense
Chetana—full of spirit, consciousness
Chetanya—consciousness
Chetashree—pretty, lovely, handsome, graceful name
Chetasi—relating to mind, heart
Chetasvi—pretty, lovely, handsome, graceful name
Chetas—mind

Chetayitri—pretty, lovely, handsome, graceful name
Chethana—consciousness, lifective
Chetika—pretty, lovely, handsome, graceful name
Chetishta—goddess
Chetna—consciousness, power of intellect
Chetna—wisdom, consciousness
Chetobuh—love
Chetravi—pretty, lovely, handsome, graceful name
Chetuya—twinkle
Chetu—power of intellectlert
Chevi—ears
Cheye, glimmersnne—born dancer, firm, triballien
Chhabili—charming, pleasing, favourite, charming
Chhabi—picture, image, photo
Chhablu—reflection
Chhali—a kind of creeper
Chhamisma—pretty, lovely, handsome, graceful name
Chhamiya—one who tinkles, fashion
Chhanna—sweet sound
Chhavisha—image, picture
Chhavi—beauty, image
Chhavi—reflection, outlook, reflection
Chhavvi—image, radiance
Chhayanshi—pretty, lovely, handsome, graceful name
Chhaya—shade
Chhaya—shadow
Chhaya—shadow, name of goddess durga
Chhoti—pretty, lovely, handsome, graceful name
Chidiya—one of a bird
Chikitsa—medication
Chikku—sweet, fruit
Chikrisha—ambition, intent, passion to do something
Chimaye—wonderful, loved and blessed one
Chimayi—pretty, lovely, handsome, graceful, happy, blissful
Chimni—quiet bird

Chinar—maple tree
Chindamani—a literature
Chingaree—spark
Chingee—spark
Chinhita—identified
Chinitya—pretty, lovely, handsome, graceful name
Chini—sweet, sugar
Chinki—sweet, small, little
Chinmai—ultimate, absolute, highest, best consciousness
Chinmaye—blissful, live long life
Chinmaye—eye, glimmers, cute
Chinmayi—holy, sanctified, pious, solemn, chaste knowledge, intellect
Chinnambal—pretty, lovely, handsome, graceful name
Chinni—cute, sweet
Chinnu—nice, cute
Chintaamani—a gem
Chintal—deep thinmonarch, ruler, prince, earl, meditation
Chintamani—philosopher's stone
Chintana—meditation, deep thinmonarch, ruler, prince, earl
Chintanika—meditation
Chintani—meditation
Chintan—meditation
Chinta—worry
Chinthana—thinmonarch, ruler, prince, earl
Chipara—power of thinmonarch, ruler, prince, earl
Chippi—a pearl and something very very
Chiraiya—bird
Chiranjeeveni—long life
Chiranjeeveta—long life
Chiranjeevini—long livingn epithet of kamadev
Chiranjeevita—long living
Chiranjit—long life
Chirantana—immortal, long life
Chirashree—everlasting beauty
Chirayu—long life
Chirayu—long living
Chira—permanently
Chirkut—sweet voice as bird

Chistha—river tributary
Chitansee—knowledgeable
Chitashree—holy, pure, sanctified, pious, solemn beauty
Chither—chaitra month in hindu calendar
Chithira—star
Chithrangi—pretty, lovely, handsome, graceful body
Chithra—painting
Chitiksha—butterfly, mind
Chiti—little, love
Chiti—lovely, knowledge
Chitkala—knowledge
Chitrabala—young moon, painting
Chitradeity—a creeper
Chitragandha—a fragrant material
Chitrajyoti—wonderfully glorious
Chitrakala—arts of eternal knowledge
Chitrakeshe—pretty, lovely, handsome, graceful hair
Chitrakeshi—a woman with pretty, lovely, handsome, graceful hair
Chitrakesi—having wonderful hair
Chitrakshe—having beautifl eye, glimmers
Chitrakshi—a bird
Chitrakshi—colourful eye, glimmers
Chitralata—wonderfulvine
Chitralekha—as pretty, lovely, handsome, graceful as a picture
Chitralekha—pretty, lovely, handsome, graceful woman
Chitralekhe—pretty, lovely, handsome, graceful woman
Chitrale—pretty, lovely, handsome, graceful lady
Chitrali—a row of pictures, pretty, lovely, handsome, graceful lady
Chitrali—picture-full
Chitramala—name of a woman
Chitramala—series of pictures
Chitramaya—worldly illusion
Chitramayi—full of wonders
Chitramayi—like a portrait
Chitrambal—pretty, lovely, handsome, graceful name

Chitrangada—decorated with wonderful bracelets
Chitrangada—name of arjun's wife
Chitrangada—with pretty, lovely, handsome, graceful body
Chitrangdae—arjun's wife
Chitrangda—river ganga
Chitrangini—origin
Chitrangi—a woman with lovely body
Chitrangi—with a charming body
Chitrangi—with pretty, lovely, handsome, graceful body
Chitrani—the river ganga
Chitranjali—picture, image
Chitranksha—colourful eye, glimmers
Chitrapushpi—variegated blossom
Chitrarathe—with a bright chariot
Chitrarathi—with a bright chariot
Chitrarati—granter of a excellent gift
Chitrarekha—picture, goddess firstly started
Chitrasena—with a bright spear
Chitrashila—of strong character
Chitrashri—one with holy, pure, sanctified, pious, solemn beauty
Chitrasri—with holy, pure, sanctified, pious, solemn beauty
Chitrathi—a bright chariot
Chitravati—pretty, lovely, handsome, graceful woman
Chitra—drawing, picture star, name of
Chitra—name of a nakshtra
Chitrika—painted
Chitrika—spring
Chitrine—talented woman
Chitrini—pretty, lovely, handsome, graceful woman with artistic
Chitrita—picturesque, goddess durga
Chitrvati—decorated
Chitta—mind
Chitti—butterfly
Chiya—bird, pretty, lovely, handsome, graceful, birdy

Chloemay—green shoot, month of may
Chndraja—daughter of the moon
Cholakin—pretty, lovely, handsome, graceful name
Choska—chosen for fate, powerful
Choti—little, small
Chretheka—a star
Chrishna—pretty, lovely, handsome, graceful name
Chudaka—forming the crest
Chudamani—a ornament, jewellery, ornamentation, adornment
Chudamani—crest ornament, jewellery, ornamentation, adornment, figuration
Chuki—star
Chulin—crisp, calm, reserved
Chullaki—pretty, lovely, handsome, graceful name
Chulli—coomonarch, ruler, prince, earl fire
Chumban—kiss
Chumki—decorative star, sitara
Chunika—bringer of happiness
Chunmun—pretty, lovely, handsome, graceful name
Chunni—star
Chunta—a bird
Chunti—a small ruby
Chupunika—quite one
Chutki—little one, tiny girl
Cilji—lovely girl
Cinthana—always smiling
Ciroon—pretty
Citapara—pretty, lovely, handsome, graceful name
Citrangada—river ganga
Citrarathi—pretty, lovely, handsome, graceful name
Corian—modern, trendy emotion
Corona—crown town
Cristina—anointed, christian
Czaee—name of bloom, garden stuff

****

Indian Names For Girls—D

Dadhija—daughter of milk
Daevaki—wife of vasudeva,
Daevika—minor deity, goddess
Daevi—goddess, the deity
Dahi—curd, pretty, lovely, handsome, graceful
Daisha—pretty and friendly woman
Daityasena—one who has an army of demons
Daivanshi—belongs to god, part of holy, pure, sanctified, pious, solemn
Daivika—like an angel, little goddess
Daiviya—holy, pure, sanctified, pious, solemn
Daivi—pious soul, goddess, like an angel
Daizy—bloom, garden stuff, girl, eye, glimmers
Dajshi—glorious
Daka—to eat something
Daksakanya—an able daughter
Daksayani—goddess parvati
Dakshaja—goddess durga
Dakshakanya—goddess durga
Dakshana—sweet
Dakshatanya—an epithet of goddess durga
Dakshata—skill, cautions
Dakshayani—goddess parvati
Daksha—alert, clever, competent, skillful
Daksha—the earth, the skilled one
Dakshena—competent
Daksheyu—perfect, monarch, ruler, prince, earl
Dakshika—skilled
Dakshina—a donation to god or priest
Dakshina—donation to an officiation priest or teacher
Dakshini—from south direction
Dakshinya—goddess parvathi, modesty
Dakshita—pretty, lovely, handsome, graceful, fully skill person

Dakshitha—skill
Dakshiya—earth, skilled, fit
Dakshi—daughter of goddess parvati
Dakshi—the glorious
Dakshta—perfection, varsatile
Dakshyani—goddess durga
Dakshya—cleverness, honesty, brilliance
Daksina—goddess durga
Dalaja—nectar
Dalaja—produced, born from bloom, garden stuff petals
Dalakamal—a lotus
Daleshvari—pretty, lovely, handsome, graceful name
Dali—a bloom, garden stuff
Dalkosha—the jamine bloom, garden stuff
Daman—beauty, mysterious, innovative
Damarava—goddess
Damara—gentle girl, calf, bitter
Damaruki—sound of emotion
Damayanthi—wife of rishi
Damayanti—name of nal's wife
Damayanti—subjugating, name of princess
Damayant—pretty, lovely, handsome, graceful name
Dama—control of the senses
Damine—illumination, luminosity, radiance
Damini—illumination, luminosity, radiance
Damini—nature, illumination, luminosity, radiance
Damita—little princess
Damma—the soothing voice
Damyanti—pretty, lovely, handsome, graceful, source of energy
Danam—wealth, cash
Danavera—an extremely generous person
Danayusha—suppressed

Dandagauri—goddess durga
Dandine—brahmine
Daneshvari—the one who donates
Daneshwari—gift of god, goddess durga
Daneshwary—the one who donates
Danet—rich
Danika—morning star
Danika—morning star, god is my judge
Danisa—princess
Danisha—star
Danita—from denmark, god is my judge
Dani—illumination, luminosity, radiance green
Danna—god is my judge, form of dana
Danushika—pretty, lovely, handsome, graceful name
Danusiya—luster
Danu—a popular name
Danu—goddess earth
Danvika—bright
Danvi—goddess lakshmi
Danyata—satisfied
Darcy—dark one, from arcy dark, fortress
Darika—maiden, daughter
Daritree—luster, earth
Dariyana—brave
Darmine—happy
Darni—goddess durga
Darpana—a mirror
Darpanika—a small mirror
Darpan—reflection, mirror
Darpine—proud
Darpitaa—pretty, lovely, handsome, graceful name
Darpita—proud
Darsana—seeing, sight
Darsani—worth monarch, ruler, prince, earl at
Darsa—reflection, see, glimpse, goddess
Darshaka—vision, spectator
Darshaki—bless
Darshanaa—vision, seeing

Darshana—pretty, lovely, handsome, graceful, vision
Darshana—to see and behold, vision, seeing
Darshane—worth monarch, ruler, prince, earl at
Darshani—pretty, lovely, handsome, graceful
Darshanojjvala—fair to look at
Darshatashree—a beauty
Darsha—pretty, lovely, handsome, graceful
Darsha—grapes, perceive, vision, wine
Darsheta—seen, display, vision, sight
Darshe—blessings
Darshe—percieved
Darshika—viewer, brilliant, sagacious, gifted, wise, learned
Darshini—one who blesses
Darshini—one who blesses, lord krishna
Darshita—displayed
Darshita—sight, seen, vision, display
Darshitha—sight, vision, seen
Darshi—vision, moon, illumination, luminosity, radiance, see, lord
Darshna—worth of seeing, pray to god
Darshne—one who has vision
Darshni—the one who blesses
Darshvi—vision, moon, illumination, luminosity, radiance, see, seen
Darshwana—holy, sanctified, pious, solemn, chaste of heart
Darsika—viewer
Darsini—vision, see, one who blesses
Daru—alcohol, wine
Darvika—sacrificial spoon
Darvi—made of wood, tender
Darya—sea, river, possesses a lot
Dasa—devotee
Dashahara—river ganga
Dashamee—the tenth day of lunar month
Dashami—tenth day according to the hindu
Dasharna—a name of the river
Dashbhujangane—goddess durga, ten armed

Dashbhuja—one who has ten hands, goddess durga
Dasheya—satyawati
Dashmee—the tenth day of the lunar month
Dasrasu—the energy of shiva
Dathuya—loveable person
Datri—happiness, earth, bestowing
Dattadeve—goddess of boons
Dattee—gift
Daupadi—tolerate
Davana—bloom, garden stuff, fruit
Davarni—princess of the highness, empress, queen
Dave—goddess
Davita—beloved, feminine form of david
Davi—cherishedngel
Davya—water, beloved, dear
Dawa—medicine, born on monday
Daxa—clever, glorious, brave, god gift
Daxita—nice
Dayadee—daughter
Dayagauri—kindness of fair woman
Dayalu—kindness, mercy, pity
Dayamani—kindness
Dayamaya—full of compassion
Dayamaye—kind
Dayamayi—merciful
Dayananda—one who gets joy in compassion
Dayanidhi—lord shiva
Dayanidhi—lots of compassion
Dayanita—tender, merciful
Dayani—kind hearted
Dayashela—sympathy
Dayashree—masterful teacher
Dayavanti—kind woman
Dayavati—full of mercy
Dayawanti—goddess of kindness
Daya—hunted bird, kindness, mercy
Daya—kindness, mercy
Daya—mercy, kindly
Dayita—beloved
Daysha—gift from god
Dayve—pious soul, like an angel, goddess

Dayvi—goddess, pure, sanctified, pious, solemn
Daywa—pretty, lovely, handsome, graceful name
Daywi—goddess, pure, sanctified, pious, solemn
Deaarshi—goddess lakshmi
Dea—goddess, valley
Debangi—like a goddess, organ of god
Debanjali—daughter of god
Debanshi—deva ansh
Debarpita—render to the god
Debashis—beauty
Debashmita—one who can smile
Debasmita—sweet of god, smile like goddess
Debina—impressive, discreet, enrich
Debi—goddess
Debjani—god of travel
Debopriya—god's favourite
Deborah—from a bee swarm, bee
Debotri—submitted to three gods
Debprasad—gods gift
Dedeepya—always shining, illumination, luminosity, radiance
Deeana—holy, pure, sanctified, pious, solemn, valley
Deebasri—teacher of god
Deeba—silk, goddess lakshmi
Deehar—love
Deeher—shiva's vigour
Deekshana—soft nature, name of shiva
Deeksha—consecreation
Deeksha—initiation teach learner
Deeksha—to teach, initiation, consecration
Deekshita—initiation
Deekshitha—initiation, concentration
Deekshi—god
Deekshta—holy teaching, point of direction
Deekshya—initiation teach
Deenal—sweet girl
Deena—holy, pure, sanctified, pious, solemn, god like
Deena—one who is ned
Deepaali—collection of lamps
Deepabali—row of lamps

Deepada—giver of illumination, luminosity, radiance
Deepadhari—river ganga
Deepajothi—a lamp
Deepakala—evening time
Deepakshe—bright eye, glimmers
Deepakshi—steady lamp, shine
Deepale—giving
Deepalika—flame of illumination, luminosity, radiance
Deepali—collection of lamps, illumination, luminosity, radiance
Deepali—row of lamps
Deepal—illumination, luminosity, radiance
Deepamala—row of lamps
Deepamale—river ganga
Deepana—illuminating
Deepana—illuminating, goddess lakshmi
Deepangana—love
Deepanjali—illumination, luminosity, radiance
Deepansha—illumination, luminosity
Deepanshi—brightness, illumination, luminosity, radiance, bright
Deepanshu—bright
Deepanvita—diwali festival
Deepanwita—lit by lamp, diwali
Deepanya—illuminating, illumination, luminosity, radiance, lamp
Deeparani—lit by lamps
Deeparathi—a ritual done with lamps
Deeparpita—illumination, luminosity, radiance
Deepasha—lamp
Deepashri—lamp, illumination, luminosity, radiance
Deepati—bright illumination, luminosity, radiance
Deepavali—rows of illumination, luminosity, radiances
Deepavati—a ragini
Deepavna—dedication pledge lamp
Deepa—illumination, luminosity, radiancefull
Deepa—lamp, dedication pledge

Deepeksha—a desire, aspiration, longing of candle
Deepika—a lamp of illumination, luminosity, radiance
Deepika—illumination, luminosity, radiance, pretty
Deepini—illumination, luminosity, radiance
Deepita—illuminated
Deepitha—illuminated
Deepi—beauty, gorgeous, illumination, luminosity, radiance
Deepjyoti—the illumination, luminosity, radiance of the lamp
Deepmala—row of lamps
Deepmalni—garland of illumination, luminosity, radiance
Deepmani—jewellery, ornamentation, adornment, figuration
Deepshika—illumination, luminosity, fire, lamp
Deepshikha—flame
Deepshikha—lamp's flame
Deepshita—full of illumination, luminosity, radiance, brightness
Deepshi—flame, illumination, luminosity, radiance, brightness
Deepsikha—illumination, luminosity, radiance of ray, flame, fire
Deepta—bright woman
Deepta—shining
Deeptha—illumination, luminosity, radiance candle
Deepthi—luster, shine, illumination, luminosity, radiance, bright
Deeptikana—a beam of illumination, luminosity, radiance
Deeptika—a lamp
Deepti—flame, lustre, luster, shine, nice
Deepti—splendour, brightness
Deepu—illumination, luminosity, radiance
Deep—luminosity, radiance, lamp, candle
Deeran—sacrifice
Deergha—long
Deergha—one with long life, goddess

Deerghika—tall
Deesha—direction
Deeshma—pretty, lovely, handsome, graceful name
Deeshna—offering, gift
Deeta—a name for goddess lakshmi
Deethya—goddess lakshmi
Deetika—thoughtful
Deetya—answer of prayers, goddess lakshmi
Deevanshi—one who is endowed of all beauties
Deeva—sacred lamp
Deevena—blessing
Deevitha—holy, pure, sanctified, pious, solemn power, god
Deevi—a lamp
Deevyanshi—part of holy, pure, sanctified, pious, solemn power
Deeya—a illumination, luminosity, radiance lamp
Dee—fear
Dehini—of the body
Dehisha—part of body
Deivamagan—luster, shine, flame
Deivanai—lord kartikeya's wife devasena
Deivayanai—lord murugan wife
Deiva—lustrous
Dekshna—great see
Delakshi—fortune
Delena—good monarch, ruler, prince, earl, dear
Delina—graceful, noble, kind, dear, small
Delisha—gives pleasure, illumination, luminosity, radiance
Delisha—the one who gives pleasure
Demira—devotee of lord krishna
Denali—great, high one
Densi—creative, people who give
Depanshi—bright lamp
Deprietta—dark skin
Depshika—row of illumination, luminosity, radiances
Deshana—direction
Deshapali—row of lamps
Deshika—viewing

Deshnaa—gift
Deshna—gift, present, god gift
Deshna—present
Deshne—from the country
Deshtree—indicator
Desiha—happy, lemon
Desna—offering, gift
Despina—lady-like, mistress, young lady
Des—ambition, intent, passion, indian, country
Devaangana—lord
Devaanshi—part of god, illumination, luminosity, radiance
Devaarti—aarti of god
Devacharnine—one who describes god
Devadeity—goddess of god
Devadhara—gods, jewellery, ornamentation, adornment, figuration
Devadrita—holy, pure, sanctified, pious, solemn respected, sun
Devadutta—given by the gods
Devaganika—a nymph
Devagarbha—the womb of the gods
Devaga—a form of shakti
Devagiri—holy, pure, sanctified, pious, solemn knowledge
Devagni—holy fire
Devagni—holy, sanctified, pious, solemn, chaste, holy fire
Devagnya—lakshmi
Devago—a form of shaktee
Devaharsha—goddess of joy
Devahootee—invocation of the gods
Devahuti—daughter of manu
Devahuti—mother of maharshi kapila
Devajaya—wife of the gods
Devaja—born from god
Devajna—one who knows about the god
Devajuti—attached to the gods
Devakali—name of a indian music ragini
Devakanta—beloved of the gods
Devakanya—celestial maiden
Devaka—goddess
Devakee—mother of lord krishna
Devakiree—tongue of the god

Devakiri—name of a ragini
Devakirti—with heavenly fame
Devaki—holy, pure, sanctified, pious, solemn, wife of vasudev
Devak—holy, pure, sanctified, pious, solemn
Devalata—a kind of jasmine bloom, garden stuff
Devalatha—holy, pure, sanctified, pious, solemn wine
Devala—a goddess
Devala—mother of krishna
Devala—woman attendant of idol of god
Devalekha—celestial beauty
Devalina—beloved of the gods
Devamani—pretty, lovely, handsome, graceful name
Devamata—goddess parvati
Devamati—godly minded, virtuous
Devamatri—mother of god
Devamatrri—mother of god
Devamatr—a goddess
Devamaya—a companion of god
Devamayi—holy, pure, sanctified, pious, solemn illusion
Devananda—daughter of gods
Devanandha—holy, pure, sanctified, pious, solemn pleasing
Devana—holy, pure, sanctified, pious, solemn
Devane—holy, pure, sanctified, pious, solemn
Devangana—a celestial female
Devangana—celestial maiden
Devangi—like a goddess
Devangshi—power of god
Devanika—celestial ones
Devanisha—pretty, lovely, handsome, graceful name
Devani—shining celestial goddess
Devanjana—eye, glimmers of god
Devanja—a lady who has knowledge of god
Devansha—eternal part of god
Devanshita—holy, pure, sanctified, pious, solemn

Devanshi—holy, pure, sanctified, pious, solemn, part of godngel
Devanshu—a part of god
Devansi—holy, pure, sanctified, pious, solemn, part of godngel
Devansri—holy, pure, sanctified, pious, solemn goddess
Devantika—holy, pure, sanctified, pious, solemn, worshipper of the god
Devanya—goddess lakshmi, illumination, luminosity, radiance
Devaprabha—holy, pure, sanctified, pious, solemn illumination, luminosity, radiance
Devapriya—national treasure, dear to gods
Devapushpa—bloom, garden stuff of the gods
Devarakshita—protected by god
Devarati—celestial woman
Devarsha—teacher of gods, gods gift
Devarshini—teacher of gods, sage of the devas
Devasena—one who is serving god
Devashree—goddess lakshmi
Devashree—holy, pure, sanctified, pious, solemn beauty
Devashri—goddess lakshmi, yagya
Devashya—like a god, lord
Devasmita—with a holy, pure, sanctified, pious, solemn smile
Devasmitha—with a deityne smile
Devasree—holy, pure, sanctified, pious, solemn beauty
Devasri—daksha's daughter, holy, pure, sanctified, pious, solemn goddess
Devaswi—goddess durga
Devatha—goddess
Devavachana—holy, pure, sanctified, pious, solemn speech
Devavamini—daughter of bharadwaj
Devavane—holy, pure, sanctified, pious, solemn voice
Devavani—holy, pure, sanctified, pious, solemn voice
Devavathi—a gandharva's daughter
Devavati—owned by the gods
Devavi—a devotee of god

Devayani—daughter of the guru shukracharya
Devayani—the gift given by god
Deva—deity, god, celestial spirit
Devdhani—holy, pure, sanctified, pious, solemn abode
Devena—luky person
Deven—holy, pure, sanctified, pious, solemn, like a god
Devesha—like a goddess
Deveshe—goddess parvati
Deveshi—goddess durga
Devesi—koushthub the gem worn by lord
Deveveti—enjoyment for god
Devhiti—holy, pure, sanctified, pious, solemn
Devi-priya—beloved of goddess
Deviani—like a goddess
Devianshi—illumination, luminosity, radiance
Devibala—goddess
Devikadeity—invested with holy, pure, sanctified, pious, solemn quantities
Devikala—goddess
Devikarani—highness, empress, queen of goddess
Devika—goddess of all, like an angel
Devila—attached to the gods
Devina—looks like a goddess
Devina—resembling a goddess
Devipriya—dearer to goddess
Devisa—like a goddess
Devisha—like goddess
Devishi—chief of the goddesses
Devishree—goddess
Devishri—dearest goddess
Devish—pretty, lovely, handsome, graceful name
Devisi—chief of the goddesses
Devisri—dearest goddess
Devithya—god
Deviyahini—chief of the goddesses
Deviyani—like a goddess
Deviya—holy, pure, sanctified, pious, solemn, god gift
Devi—a goddess
Devi—goddess, kindness, bright

Devkanchan—holy, pure, sanctified, pious, solemn gold
Devkanya—holy, pure, sanctified, pious, solemn damsel
Devkia—minor deity, minor goddess
Devkirti—with heavenly fame
Devki—lord krishna's mother
Devkriti—creation of god
Devkulya—holy, pure, sanctified, pious, solemn, belonging to god
Devkumari—daughter of god
Devkusum—holy, pure, sanctified, pious, solemn bloom, garden stuffs
Devkuver—goddess of wealth
Devlakshmi—wealth of gods
Devlekha—holy, pure, sanctified, pious, solemn, celestial beauty
Devlena—absorbed in god
Devmani—holy, pure, sanctified, pious, solemn, gift
Devmaya—holy, pure, sanctified, pious, solemn, illusion
Devmayi—holy, pure, sanctified, pious, solemn, illusion
Devmitra—a friend of the gods
Devna—godly, holy, pure, sanctified, pious, solemn
Devoshri—the diamond of kohinoor
Devpadnami—lords bloom, garden stuff
Devpriya—dear to god, beloved of lord
Devpriya—dear to the god
Devrajni—holy, pure, sanctified, pious, solemn night, highness, empress
Devrati—illumination, luminosity, radiance of the gods
Devraz—monarch, ruler, prince, earl of god
Devroopa—holy, pure, sanctified, pious, solemn form
Devrupa—of holy, pure, sanctified, pious, solemn form,n apsara
Devsena—gods army
Devshree—goddess
Devsmit—with a holy, pure, sanctified, pious, solemn smile
Devta—holy, pure, sanctified, pious, solemn damsel

Devu—lord shiva
Devyana—part of holy, pure, sanctified, pious, solemn, like a goddess
Devyane—lord krishna's mother
Devyani—daughter of sukracharya
Devyani—like a goddess
Devyanshi—illumination, luminosity, radiance
Devya—god gift, holy, pure, sanctified, pious, solemn power
Dewangi—like a goddess
Dewanshi—holy, pure, sanctified, pious, solemn
Dewi—goddess
Dexa—to teach
Deyanshi—part of illumination, luminosity, radiance
Dhagavi—pretty, lovely, handsome, graceful name
Dhairavi—firmly luster like sun, smart
Dhairyabala—a woman with courage
Dhairya—tolerance, durability, toleration, courage
Dhairyya—tolerance, durability, toleration
Dhakshaya—the earth, wife of lord shiva
Dhakshika—pretty, lovely, handsome, graceful name
Dhakshita—skill
Dhakshitha—rich and skill
Dhamadhama—mamonarch, ruler, prince, earl a noise
Dhamagani—believes in religion
Dhamini—illumination, luminosity, radiance or storm, focus
Dhamvati—damyanti
Dhanada—bestows treasures
Dhanada—goddess of wealth
Dhanadeepa—lord of wealth
Dhanaisha—richness, wealthy
Dhanajyoti—illumination, luminosity, radiance of wealth
Dhanali—the one who brings wealth
Dhananda—goddess lakshmi
Dhananjaya—victory over wealth
Dhanapriya—loved by wealth
Dhanashree—beauty
Dhanashree—goddess of wealth
Dhanashri—a raga, goddess lakshmi
Dhanashvi—wealthy, goddess lakshmi
Dhanasree—prosperity
Dhanasri—glory of wearlth
Dhanasri—richness, wealthy
Dhanasvi—money, goddess lakshmi
Dhanavidya—wealth of knwoledge
Dhanavi—lord of lakshmi
Dhana—wealthy, goddess lakshmi
Dhanesha—wealthy
Dhaneshi—having knowledge of the subject
Dhaneshwari—goddess of wealth
Dhanesh—wealthy, richness
Dhanesvari—goddess durga raga
Dhangauri—goddess of wealth
Dhanika—goddess lakshmi, wealthfull
Dhaniksha—rich and powerful
Dhanisha—wealth support, indoctrination, assuredness
Dhanishta—a star, the richest one
Dhanishtha—a star
Dhaniska—wealthy
Dhanista—one of the star, gopi
Dhanita—endowed with wealth
Dhanitha—kindness
Dhaniya—goddess of forest, wood, jungle
Dhani—illumination, luminosity
Dhani—rich, wealthy
Dhankeshri—lakshmi
Dhanlakshmi—wealthy, goddess lakshmi
Dhano—special
Dhanshika—highness, empress, queen of wealth
Dhanshka—wealthy
Dhanshree—goddess of prosperous, wealth
Dhanshri—goddess lakshmi
Dhansika—rich
Dhansya—pretty, lovely, handsome, graceful name
Dhanuhasta—archer, with a bow in hand
Dhanuja—arjuna's bow

Dhanurjaya—charm of wealth
Dhanusa—bow
Dhanusha—goddess lakshmirrow tip
Dhanushka—wealth
Dhanushri—lucky, holy cow
Dhanushwi—pretty, lovely, handsome, graceful name
Dhanushya—lord rama's bow
Dhanuska—wealth, rich, goddess lakshmi
Dhanusri—goddess
Dhanu—a bow, zodiacal sign
Dhanvanti—holding wealth
Dhanvanya—treasurer of the jungle
Dhanvati—containing wealth
Dhanvati—rich
Dhanvika—goddess annapurna, lakshmi
Dhanvitha—rich in knowledge
Dhanvi—money, wealth, name of goddess
Dhanyasa—wealthy, rich
Dhanyasri—wealthy, goddess lakshmi
Dhanyata—success, fulfilment
Dhanyatha—satisfied, thankful
Dhanyavi—rich
Dhanya—blessed
Dhanya—giver of wealth
Dhanya—great, grateful, blessed
Dhanyta—success, fulfilment
Dhan—wealth, goddess lakshmi
Dharabai—constant flow
Dharamani—pretty, lovely, handsome, graceful
Dharam—justice, morality
Dharanaa—concentration
Dharana—non violence movement, catch
Dharana—supporting act
Dharani—earth
Dharani—earth, success, bearing, the earth
Dharani—ruler of earth
Dharathi—earth
Dharati—earth
Dhara—constant flow, the earth
Dhara—current of water
Dhara—stream of water

Dhara—the earth
Dhara—the earth, constant flow
Dharika—sun, morning sun
Dharine—earth
Dharine—like a goddess
Dharine—possessing
Dharini—earth
Dharita—earth
Dharithri—earth
Dharitree—earth
Dharitri—the earth
Dhariya—having tolerance, durability, toleration
Dharmaja—mother of dharma
Dharmavrata—act according to one's religion
Dharma—firm law, decree, custom
Dharmika—devotion, religious, completeness
Dharmine—religious lady
Dharmini—religious
Dharmishta—devotion in religion
Dharmista—devotion in religion, lord in dharma
Dharmi—religious
Dharna—earth, pretty, lovely, handsome, graceful
Dharna—encompass
Dharna—to accept
Dharnika—wealth
Dharnitha—earth
Dharni—earth
Dharni—the earth
Dharpon—pretty, lovely, handsome, graceful, reflection, mirror
Dharshini—bright and happy one
Dharshni—vision, seeing, sight
Dharsika—earth
Dharti—earth
Dharuna—supporting
Dharunika—pretty, lovely, handsome, graceful name
Dharuni—to get aim quickly
Dharvika—turmeric
Dharvi—goddess parvati
Dhathri—earth
Dhatree—impulsive
Dhatrisri—goddess lakshmi

Dhatri—a nurse
Dhatri—earth, goddess lakshmi
Dhatri—mother, earth
Dhaula—holy, sanctified, pious, solemn, chaste white
Dhaumya—name of goddess ambe, durga
Dhavala—fair complextion
Dhavala—white, bright
Dhavala—white, holy, sanctified, pious, solemn, chaste
Dhaval—white, earth
Dhavana—holy leafy herb with fragrance
Dhavani—fire
Dhavani—voice, sound
Dhavina—adored, loved one
Dhavita—purified and clean
Dhavi—name of goddess gayatri
Dhavni—music, cruel against sound, noise
Dhayana—concentration, meditation
Dha—earth
Dheksha—religious pledge
Dhena—humble
Dhena—milch cow
Dhenuka—milch cow
Dhenumati—river gomati
Dhenumati—river gomti
Dhenu—a cow, goddess durga
Dheptha—goddess lakshmi
Dheraj—tolerance, durability, toleration
Dherata—courage
Dheravi—one who is courageous
Dhera—control of senses
Dhera—courageous, patient
Dheshana—knowlegeable
Dheshika—bright future, brilliant
Dheva—pretty, lovely, handsome, graceful name
Dheyanshi—god of meditation
Dhhruhi—daughter
Dhilsha—monarch, ruler, prince, earl of heart
Dhimahe—word from hindu mantra sloka
Dhimahi—wisdom

Dhinisha—pretty, lovely, handsome, graceful name
Dhiraj—tolerance, durability, toleration
Dhira—luck
Dhiriti—earth
Dhirshti—vision, sight
Dhitee—thought
Dhitha—daughter
Dhithi—thought, idea
Dhitika—thoughtful, wise
Dhitya—goddess lakshmi, parvati
Dhivani—pretty, lovely, handsome, graceful name
Dhivisha—born in heaven
Dhivya—holy, pure, sanctified, pious, solemn
Dhiyana—meditation
Dhiya—lamp, luminosity, radiance
Dhiyoni—word of mantra sloka
Dhlriti—courage, morale
Dhnushree—holy cow, lucky
Dhnya—blessed, grateful
Dhoolika—river gomathi's
Dhoollika—pollen of bloom, garden stuffs
Dhoomine—smoky
Dhoondra—smoky
Dhooni—shamonarch, ruler, prince, earlgitating
Dhoon—tune, music
Dhrasika—goddess
Dhravya—lord krishna
Dhra—earth, mother earth
Dhrina—pretty, lovely, handsome, graceful name
Dhrisha—goddess lakshmi, money
Dhrishta—sight
Dhrishti—sight
Dhristi—vision, sight, viewing
Dhrita—tolerance, durability, toleration
Dhrithi—visualise, eye, glimmers
Dhrithri—earth, mother earth
Dhritika—earth, supporting, steadfastness
Dhriti—courage, morale, tolerance, durability, toleration

Dhriya—tolerance, durability, toleration
Dhrritathe—full of water
Dhrritee—resolution
Dhrtimati—steadfast, resolute
Dhrti—earth, will, resolution, courage
Dhruamna—a woman with firmenss
Dhrumana—firm mind
Dhrumi—god of gift, holy, pure, sanctified, pious, solemn
Dhrupal—brilliant, sagacious, gifted, wise, learned
Dhrushika—pretty, lovely, handsome, graceful name
Dhrushma—pretty, lovely, handsome
Dhrutee—soften
Dhrutika—fixed destiny
Dhruti—firmness, boldness, motion
Dhruvadeve—a princess
Dhruva—brave girl
Dhruva—star, the polar star, constant
Dhruvena—blessings of dhruva
Dhruvika—firmly fixed, devotionful
Dhruvisha—part of star
Dhruvi—star, centre point of globe earth
Dhruvti—courageous
Dhruvty—pretty, lovely, handsome, graceful name
Dhuagni—part of fire
Dhulika—pollen of bloom, garden stuffs
Dhuli—dust
Dhumorna—buttermilk
Dhumra—vaporous daughter of daksa
Dhuna—pretty, obsession, tune
Dhundhale—childless
Dhunisha—pretty, lovely, handsome, graceful name
Dhunn—music, tune
Dhunrika—smoky cheked
Dhunu—pretty, lovely, handsome, graceful name
Dhun—music, tune
Dhupini—fragrance, sweet smell, simplicity
Dhurita—kind of bloom, garden stuff
Dhurjati—firm

Dhurvi—pretty, lovely, handsome, graceful name
Dhushitha—brave
Dhuthi—splendour, lustre
Dhuti—splendour, illumination, luminosity, radiance
Dhuti—splendour, shining
Dhuvaraga—safety god, lord krishna's city
Dhuvitha—water tap
Dhvanika—sound
Dhvani—sound stages, sound, voice
Dhvija—a name
Dhvisha—born in heaven, holy, pure
Dhviti—fairness, bright
Dhvni—speed
Dhwaja—flag, leadership
Dhwane—sound, melody, voice
Dhwani—voice, melody, music, sound
Dhwiti—mirror of lord krishna
Dhwity—holy, pure, sanctified, pious, solemn, name of lord krishna
Dhyana—meditation, meditate, conscious
Dhyane—goddess of meditation
Dhyanvi—thought, meditation
Dhyara—gift from the holy, pure, sanctified, pious, solemn
Dhyatri—one who reflects upon thinker
Dhya—thought, meditation
Dhyeya—aim, ideal, model
Dhyuthi—luster, illumination, luminosity, radiance, splendour
Dhyuti—full of splendour, lord krishna
Dhyuti—radiance
Diani—divinity
Dia—lamp, holy, pure, sanctified, pious, solemn
Dibya—brightness, holy, pure
Dichha—direction
Didhiti—firm, stable, devotion
Digambari—goddess durga
Digambera—without clothes
Digamberee—clotheless
Digangana—onefourth of the sky identified as young virgin
Digisha—regent of a direction

Digvijayi—to conquer the world
Digvi—high, god
Dihaer—brave
Diha—gift by god, hermit
Dikashya—pretty, lovely, handsome, graceful name
Dikhsha—holy teaching, gift by the god
Diki—healthy and wealthy
Dikshavi—gift by the god, lord
Diksha—gift by the god, holy teaching
Diksha—initiation
Diksheka—very silent, simple
Dikshika—blessing giver, gold
Dikshita—expert, the initiated
Dikshitha—the initiated
Dikshi—holy teaching, point of direction
Dikshya—initiation, consecration
Diksitha—solid like rock, imperishable
Diku—daughter
Dilani—lustering, iridescent
Dilavya—heart touched
Dilber—lover
Dildeep—lamps of heart
Diljot—illumination, luminosity, radiance of the heart
Dilna—heart, good heart
Dilsa—wrestling goddess
Dilshad—joyful, happy, initiation
Dilvi—mind, heart
Dimpal—cute, dimple on face
Dimpil—dimples
Dimpi—on who has dimple
Dimples—cute
Dimple—a small, natural hollow on the cheks
Dimpu—power like a god, sweet, beauty
Dimpy—cute, one who has dimple
Dinal—great chief, name of bloom, garden stuff
Dina—love, god has judged, dinah
Dinika—rising sun
Dinisha—bright, welcome, big, rising sun
Dinku—small
Dinosha—hearty welcome in bangoli

Dinu—kindness
Dipakshi—bright eye, glimmers
Dipali—lamps line of lamps
Dipal—burning lamps, illumination, luminosity, radiance
Dipanjali—like a simple angel
Dipanwita—illumination, luminosity, radiance, night of diwali
Dipasha—luminosity, radiance
Dipashri—lamp
Dipati—full of happiness
Dipa—luminosity, radiance
Dipesha—lamp, illuminating, lustrous
Dipeshi—sun, illumination, luminosity, radiance
Dipika—lamp, little illumination, pretty, lovely, handsome, graceful
Dipisha—lamp
Dipkala—evening time
Dipla—illumination, luminosity, like candle, small lamp
Diplen—the holy, pure, sanctified, pious, solemn candle
Dipsana—pretty, lovely, handsome, graceful name
Dipsha—river
Dipshika—the flame of a lamp
Dipshikha—the flame of a lamp
Dipshi—illumination, luminosity, radiance
Dipshri—small illumination, luminosity, radiance, candle, lamp
Dipsikha—fire, flame, illumination, luminosity, radiance of ray
Dipsi—a illumination, luminosity, radiance
Dips—dimple
Diptagni—like a small candle, mashal
Dipta—goddess lakshmi, illumination, luminosity, radiance
Diptee—illumination, luminosity, radiance
Dipti—brightness, illumination, luminosity
Dipty—lamp
Dipu—flame, illumination, luminosity, radiance

Dip—small illumination, luminosity, radiance like candle

Dirghayu—long life

Dirgha—long life

Dirsana—illumination, luminosity, radiance, lamp

Dishali—pretty, lovely, handsome, graceful name

Dishal—apropos illumination, luminosity, radiance, fuel

Dishana—instructor of sacred knowledge

Dishani—highness, empress, queen of all four directions

Dishant—end of directions

Dishari—who shows way

Disha—direction

Disha—direction, princess of the family

Dishika—direction

Dishita—focus, test

Dishitha—focussed, who knows direction

Dishi—gift of god, direction

Dishta—directed, fixed

Dishti—direction, good fortune

Dishti—fortunate

Dishu—direction

Ditee—pretty, lovely, handsome, graceful name

Ditika—thoughtful

Ditiksha—all over the world

Diti—sage kashyap's wife

Diti—wife of the sage kashyaprohi

Ditvi—holy, pure, sanctified, pious, solemn good

Ditya—goddess durga, lakshmi

Ditya—goddess lakshmi

Diu—tender, gentle, mellow

Divahini—goddess parvati

Divani—madly in love

Divanshi—holy, pure, sanctified, pious, solemn

Divansi—holy, pure, sanctified, pious, solemn

Divashini—shine among the day and all

Diva—holy, pure, sanctified, pious, solemn

Divena—blessing

Divia—friend, focus

Divija—born in heaven

Divika—holy, pure, sanctified, pious, solemn, heavenly

Divisha—holy, pure, sanctified, pious, solemn desire, aspiration, longing

Divita—full of shine

Divita—illumination, luminosity, radiance, chamak

Diviya—holy, pure, sanctified, pious, solemn power, lovely

Divi—holy, pure, sanctified, pious, solemn, the heaven, goodness

Divnsha—pretty, lovely, handsome, graceful name

Divu—a small lamp

Divvanshi—holy, pure, sanctified, pious, solemn

Divvy—very bright, sun like luster

Divyadeity—holy, pure, sanctified, pious, solemn goddess

Divyagna—holy, pure, sanctified, pious, solemn woman

Divyakanta—pretty, lovely, handsome, graceful woman

Divyakshi—solemn eye, glimmers, heavenly eye, glimmers

Divyakshu—holy, pure, sanctified, pious, solemn eye, glimmers

Divyambaree—heavenly dressed woman

Divyana—holy, pure, sanctified, pious, solemn

Divyane—praise, like a goddess, heavenly

Divyanga—heavenly, brilliant

Divyangi—daughter of god

Divyani—heavenly, heart of avi

Divyanka—holy, pure, sanctified, chaste, name of goddess

Divyanki—pretty, lovely, handsome, graceful name

Divyansha—holy, pure, sanctified, pious, solemn power

Divyanshi—part of holy, pure, sanctified, pious, solemn power ansh
Divyansi—illumination, luminosity, radiance, part of god
Divyante—divoted to holy one, pure, sanctified, pious
Divyanti—devoted to holy, pure, sanctified, pious, solemn, heavenly
Divyarani—heaven highness, empress, queen
Divyaroop—holy, pure, sanctified, pious, solemn vigour
Divyashi—holy, pure, sanctified, pious, solemn blessings
Divyashree—holy, pure, sanctified, pious, solemn woman
Divyasree—heavenly, holy, pure, sanctified, pious, solemn
Divyasri—kind, helpful human, pretty, lovely, handsome, graceful
Divyastree—holy, pure, sanctified, pious, solemn woman
Divyaswaroopini—holy, pure, sanctified, pious, solemn look
Divyata—holy, pure, sanctified, pious
Divyathi—white
Divya—holy, sanctified, pious, solemn, chaste, holy
Divya—shining, holy, pure, sanctified, pious, solemn
Divya—the highness, empress, queen of the universal
Divyesha—holy, pure, sanctified, pious, solemn
Diwale—the festival of illumination, luminosity, radiance
Diwali—bright illumination, luminosity, radiance
Diwita—a popular name
Dixa—god gift
Dixcha—gift by the god, holy teaching
Dixita—expert, splendour, name of parvati
Dixitha—expert
Dixi—good gift
Diyajal—illumination, luminosity, radiance

Diyanjal—make a bless with illumination, luminosity, radiance
Diyanshi—part of illumination, luminosity, radiance, dazzling
Diyansi—part of the candle, lamp
Diyara—bright siden island
Diyasri—radiance lamp
Diya—lamp, illumination, luminosity, radiance, dazzling personality
Diya—star, bright, lamp, pretty, lovely, handsome, graceful
Diyu—bright, star, lamp
Diyya—candle
Dnyanada—brilliant, sagacious, gifted, wise, learned
Dnya—power
Dodahi—lamp
Dodiya—asong bird
Doe—a gift of god female deer
Doha—god's grace, forenoon
Doiboki—names of krishna mother
Dolaki—music
Dola—crown
Dolika—doll
Doli—pretty, lovely, handsome, graceful like a doll
Dolly—cute baby
Doll—a gift of god
Dolma—honesty, holy, sanctified, pious, solemn, chaste
Doly—like as pretty, lovely, handsome, graceful doll
Doma—holy book of buddhists
Donabel—pretty, lovely, handsome, graceful lady
Dona—lady, world mighty
Doonica—respected women
Doorepashya—far sighted
Doorva—celestial grass
Doorva—panic
Dora—kind gift, gift of god, honesty
Dori—adored, gift from god, generation
Dorothy—gift of god, gift
Dor—generation, habitation
Doyal—a song bird
Doyel—singing bird songbird
Drashtaa—one who can perceive

Drashta—an onlooker
Drashti—sight, eye, glimmersight, vision of eye, glimmers
Drashty—vision, sight
Drashvi—vision, moon, illumination, luminosity, radiance, see, seen
Drasya—vision
Draupadee—wife of five pandavas
Draupadee—wife of pandavs
Draupadi—born from fire, wife of pandavas
Dravie—brave
Dravita—pretty, lovely, handsome, graceful name
Dravya—like lakshmi
Dreshni—happy
Dridha—firm
Dridiksha—ambition, intent, passion, desire, aspiration, longing to see
Drisana—daughter of the sun
Drishani—daughter of the sun
Drishika—pretty, lovely, handsome, graceful of nature, pretty
Drishna—daughter of sun
Drishne—vision, sight, seeing
Drishni—vision, sight, seeing
Drishthi—vision, pretty, lovely, handsome, graceful eye, glimmers
Drishti—vision, sight
Drishty—illumination, luminosity, radiance
Drishvi—sight, vision
Drishyana—daughter of the sun
Drishya—sight, scenery, visible, seen
Drishy—sight
Drisna—daughter of the sun
Dristi—eye, glimmers sight
Dristi—vision, eye, glimmersight, opinion
Dristy—eye, glimmers, vision, eye, glimmersight
Drithi—courage, morale, tolerance, durability, toleration
Driti—courage and morale
Drona—teacher of warrior arjuna
Dronika—seance of guru drone
Droni—name of a river
Dron—teacher of arjun in hindu epic mahabharata
Drrigbhoo—eye, glimmers-ball
Drsadvati—sight
Drshika—viewer
Druhiti—daughter of sun
Druhi—daughter
Drumi—derived from drum tree
Drupti—pretty, lovely, handsome, graceful name
Drushni—a ray of illumination, luminosity, radiance
Drusilla—strong woman, form of drew
Drusthi—monarch, ruler, prince, earl
Druthi—softened
Druti—motion, softened
Druvika—firm, goddess lakshmi
Druvi—firm, the polar star, constant
Duggu—doll
Duhita—daughter
Duiksha—two whel
Duladeity—name of goddess
Dularee—amiable, pleasing, suave, interesting
Dulari—dear one, beloved
Dulari—lovely
Dula—shamonarch, ruler, prince, earl
Dulhan—bridal
Dulhari—beloved
Dumati—with bright intellect
Duma—silence, resemblance
Durba—holy grass
Durba—sacred grass
Durgaasri—richness, goddess durga, loyal
Durgaini—the goddess
Durgai—god
Durgashi—goddess durga
Durga—goddess durga
Durga—goddess parvati
Durgee—absorbed, devotee of goddess
Durgeshnandini—daughter of lord shiva
Durgesh—goddess durga
Durge—one who live in fort
Durgila—fire, god durga
Durgila—one who owns fort
Durgi—one who lives in a fort

Durjara—a shining creeper
Durooktee—harsh speech
Durriya—expensive pearl
Duru—draupadi, wife of the pandavas
Durvakshe—ruining grass
Durvanshi—one who lives very far
Durva—goddess, sacred grass
Durvisha—pretty, lovely, handsome, graceful name
Durvi—star
Durwa—sacred grass, goddess
Dusana—a spirit soul vices
Dushala—a princess
Dushita—polluted
Dushya—destroyer of evil
Dussala—difficult to shake
Duti—idea, goddess lakshmi, wealth
Duti—shine
Dut—console
Dvipa—belonging to island, elephant
Dvita—live, exist, riseing in two forms, spiritual
Dvithi—another name of lord krishna
Dviti—bright, dual
Dviya—a brahman
Dwabha—twiillumination, luminosity, radiance
Dwani—nice voice, sound
Dwapara—a friend of kali
Dwaraka—gateway, capital of lord krishna's kingdom

Dwarika—lord krishna's monarch, ruler, prince
Dweepa—she elephant
Dwija—second, goddess lakshmi, fairy
Dwipadee—with two legs
Dwipavati—a river
Dwipa—female elephant
Dwip—island
Dwiti—dual, second, name of lord krishna
Dyamayi—kind lady
Dyani—deer
Dyanvi—pretty, lovely, handsome, graceful name
Dyoomaye—full of splendour
Dyotana—illuminating
Dyotine—splendour
Dyudhuni—heavenly ganga
Dyuksha—heaven
Dyumanhuti—invocation, inspired
Dyumani—shining gem
Dyumayi—full of brightness
Dyumna—glorious
Dyuthi—brightness, ray of illumination, luminosity, radiance, heaven
Dyuti—brightness, beauty
Dyuti—illumination, luminosity, lovely, handsome, graceful, kind hearted

****

Indian Names For Girls—E

Eaksha—rational
Eana—affection
Eashanai—illumination, luminosity, radiance
Eashana—glorious
Eashani—goddess parvathi
Eashanye—the hindu deity
Easha—ambition, intent, passion, durga
Easha—goddess parvati, ambition, intent, passion, desire, aspiration, longing
Eashita—one who ambition, intent, passions
Eashtadevata—favourite deity
Eashta—another name of goddess durga
Eashwari—goddess parvati
Easmatara—friend
Easwaranayaki—wife of lord shiva, wanted
Easwari—vigour
Ebbani—ambition, intent, passion
Eccha—goddess parvati
Ecchita—dew drop
Ecchumati—name of river
Edha—sacred
Edhitha—progressed, increased
Eekshita—the sight
Eelachelvi—eelam
Eelakili—parakeet from eelam, pretty, lovely, handsome, graceful
Eelampirai—young crescent
Eenakshi—whose eye, glimmers look like deer
Eeraja—wwind born
Eeravati—name of river
Eeshani—goddess parvati
Eeshavarkanta—name of durga
Eesha—purity, goddess parvati
Eeshika—gift of god, good
Eeshita—greatness, goddess lakshmi
Eeshta—beloved
Eeswari—another name of lalithamba

Eetra—fragrance
Eevan—love, beauty
Efrona—feminine of efron, songbird
Egatala—the nonaryan tutelary goddess of chennai
Ehani—song
Ehimaya—an all pervading intellect
Ehshanya—the roller of the direction
Eiesha—illumination, luminosity, radiance, pleasure, ambition, intent, passion
Eila—the earth, daughter of manu
Eilin—torch, bright illumination, luminosity, radiance
Eiravathi—river
Eiravati—illumination, luminosity, radiance, ravi river
Eirawati—a river
Eisha—pleasure, ambition, intent, passion, pious
Eishita—goddess lakshmi, beloved, ambition, intent, passion
Eisu—ambition, intent, passion, purity, pleasure
Eiti—ending and the new beginning
Eiyasree—pretty, lovely, handsome, graceful name
Ekaagra—one-pointed, with one attention
Ekaakine—goddess durga
Ekaa—goddess durga
Ekacharine—loyal
Ekacharine—single man's woman
Ekadashi—name of hindu day
Ekadeva—one god, word of god
Ekadhana—a portion of wealth
Ekadhsee—the eleventh day of the fortnight
Ekaja—the only child
Ekakine—one who is alone
Ekakitaa—loneliness
Ekakita—loneliness
Ekala—only child lake
Ekamati—single minded

Ekam—only one, united in one
Ekananga—lover
Ekanansha—new moon
Ekanayana—having one eye, glimmers
Ekangana—lover
Ekangika—dear to gods
Ekani—one
Ekansha—undivided
Ekanshi—quite
Ekanta—devoted girl
Ekanta—lonely, devoted to one
Ekantha—lovely
Ekanthika—devoted to one aim
Ekantika—devoted to one aim
Ekantika—one aim, singly focused
Ekapada—lord shiva
Ekaparana—wife of himalaya
Ekaparna—singly focussed
Ekaparnika—goddess durga
Ekaparnika—goddess parvati
Ekapatala—goddess parvati's sister
Ekarishi—first rishi
Ekastaka—collection of
Ekata—unity
Ekata—unity, harmony
Ekatha—unity
Ekavali—single-string, necklace
Ekavali—string of pearls
Ekavira—the bravest
Eka—matchlesslone, first child
Eka—unity
Ekda—one time
Ekikarana—pretty, lovely, handsome, graceful name
Ekine—one who is alone
Ekisha—one goddess
Ekiya—the only one person, love
Eki—a single string necklace
Ekkavali—single string of pearl
Ekmati—in concentration
Ekodara—sister
Ekodara—sister, born from same womb
Ekoparna—sister of parvathi, wife of a sage
Ekparna—wife of himalaya
Ekshan—philosophy
Eksha—rational

Eksha—visiting, monarch, ruler, prince, earl
Ekshika—eye, glimmers
Ekshita—beheld, regarded
Ektaa—unity, beauty
Ekta—unity, union, one in all
Ekvali—a string of pearl
Ekvera—lord shiva's daughter
Ekvira—highness, empress, queen fish
Eladeity—brave
Elakshi—a woman with bright eye, glimmers
Elamathi—young brain
Elamma—god name
Elampirai—young crescent
Elaro—beauty
Elavali—earth
Elavarasi—youthful, princess
Ela—god is my oath, stonell
Elika—pelican of god, earth
Elilammal—pretty, lovely, handsome, graceful girl
Elilarasi—pretty, lovely, handsome, graceful
Elili—pretty, lovely, handsome, graceful
Elilkani—pretty, lovely, handsome, graceful and as sweet as a fruit
Elilmani—pretty, lovely, handsome, graceful gem
Elilvili—pretty, lovely, handsome, graceful eye, glimmers
Elil—beauty
Elina—woman with intelligence, holy, sanctified, pious, solemn, chaste
Elisa—god is my oath promise
Elisha—my god is salvation
Ellaiyamma—boundary deity
Ellamaal—pretty, lovely, handsome, graceful name
Ellamma—the south indian goddess
Ella—sympathy, compassion, illumination, luminosity, radiance
Elokeshe—eye, glimmers like ela creeper
Elvisa—feminine of elvis
Emani—devotion, believer
Enaakshe—eye, glimmers like deer

Enajina—meaningful
Enakshe—doe-eye, glimmers
Enakshi—deer-eye, glimmers
Enayat—goddess
Enaya—forgiveness, pretty, lovely, handsome, graceful
Endiyah—pretty, lovely, handsome, graceful bloom, garden stuff or fountain
Endizhai—pretty, lovely, handsome, graceful name
Engita—signal
Enjal—god's gift
Eona—female version of ian
Epshita—in a sastra
Eravati—name of a river
Eravati—name of goddess
Era—breeze, long period of time, wind
Erisha—speech
Eshal—the name of bloom, garden stuff in the heaven
Eshanadeity—name of woman
Eshana—ambition, intent, passion
Eshana—bloom, garden stuff, pleasure, search, life
Eshane—a name of durga
Eshane—deity durga
Eshani—close to god, goddess parvati
Eshanka—goddess parvati, lord shiva's wife
Eshanvi—name of goddess saraswati
Eshanya—east
Eshan—blessed by god
Eshawari—goddess parvati
Esha—of the god
Esha—purity, pleasure, ambition, intent, passion
Eshikaa—dartn arrow
Eshika—an arrow, dart
Eshika—the eye, glimmers
Eshita—blessed, one who ambition, intent, passions

Eshma—honey, lucky
Eshmita—smiling, smile, ever smiling lady
Eshna—desire, aspiration, longing, strong ambition, intent, passion
Eshni—name of goddess durga
Eshtartha—ambition, intent, passion
Eshu—purity, ambition, intent, passion
Eshvari—a goddess
Eshvarya—ultimate, absolute, highest, best god, master, lord shiva
Eshwara—part of lord shiva
Eshwari—ultimate, absolute, highest, best goddess, powerful
Eshwarya—lord shiva
Eshwitha—goddess parvati
Esita—ambition, intent, passion, one who ambition, intent, passions
Esma—kind defender, loved, emerald
Eswari—hindu goddess name
Etasa—one who ambition, intent, passions
Etasha—shining
Etash—luminous
Ethaha—shining
Etiksha—who fulfil desire, aspiration, longinges of all
Etisha—beginning after endssets
Eti—arrival, star
Etrika—two souls
Euphrata—from the river euphrates
Euxina—from the euxine, black sea
Evandne—fortunate
Evanshi—similarity
Eva—living and breathing, life
Eyan—kind, find
Ezhilarasi—highness, empress, queen of beauty
Ezhili—beauty, gods blessed
Ezhil—pretty, lovely, handsome, gracefulzhagu

****

Indian Names For Girls—F

Fadhela—virtuous, outstanding, superior
Fagun—holy month in spring
Fahamitha—pretty, lovely, handsome, graceful name
Faina—fairy, crown or garland, shining
Faisha—pretty, lovely, handsome, graceful name
Faiza—gain, victorious, winner
Fajyaz—artistic
Falak—star, sky, heaven, orbit, space
Falan—pretty, lovely, handsome, graceful
Falasha—ambition, intent, passion, landless ones, jews
Falesha—indian tulip
Falgune—day of full moon
Falguni—pretty, lovely, handsome, graceful, grater bloom, garden stuff
Falguni—name of a hindu month
Falgun—a month in the hindu calendar
Falgu—pretty, lovely, handsome, graceful
Falgu—falgun month
Falini—bearing fruit species of plant
Falisha—happiness, lucky
Falita—a menstruous woman
Faloni—in charge
Falvi—amiable, pleasing, suave, interesting, cute
Fancy—pleasing, favourite, charming
Fanendra—pretty, lovely, handsome, graceful
Faneshwari—highness, empress, queen of serpents
Fane—serpent
Fannah—getting destroyed in love, fun
Fanya—young deer
Faqeeri—saintly
Farahan—cherfully
Farahat—liveliness
Fara—level measure, pretty, lovely, handsome, graceful, lovely

Fareeda—unique, matchless, valuable, valued, rare pearl
Fareena—happiness
Farha—happiness
Farhina—happiness
Faria—a caravan, pretty, lovely, handsome, graceful
Farida—turquoise, unique, love, proud
Fariishta—angel
Farishta—angel, messenger
Farjana—you are kind, home-loving
Farzana—intelligence, wise, illumination, luminosity, radiance, shy
Fasika—happiness
Faten—tempting
Fatina—captivating
Fawiza—successful
Fazeela—devotionful
Feeoni—violin—yellow bloom, garden stuff
Felicy—happiness
Fenal—pretty, lovely, handsome, gracefulngel of beauty
Fenil—name of a french bloom, garden stuff
Feni—sweet
Fenna—scented bloom, garden stuff
Fenny—smart
Feral—wild, untameable
Ferika—free
Ferin—unknown, stranger, gift
Fiona—white, fair, pale, blond
Fione—pretty, lovely, handsome, graceful name
Firaki—fragrance
Firoja—bloom, garden stuff, pretty, lovely, handsome, graceful, precious stone
Firoza—turquoise, pretty, lovely, handsome, graceful
Fiyanshi—pretty, lovely, handsome, graceful angel
Fiyanshu—great angel
Fiya—powerful

Fiza—breeze, nature
Foolan—bloom, garden stuffing
Foolmala—garland
Foolwati—delicate as a bloom, garden stuff
Foolwati—full of bloom, garden stuff
Foram—fragrance, pleasant smell
Forum—stage, platform, fragrance
Freena—delicate as a bloom, garden stuff

Freyal—name
Freya—goddess of love
Friya—wife of methodologists
Fuli—to bloom like a bloom, garden stuff
Fulki—spark
Fullan—blooming
Fullara—wife of kalketu
Fulloo—of the bloom, garden stuffs
Fulmala—garland

****

Indian Names For Girls—G

Gaganasri—highness, empress, maharani, sky

Gagana—the sky, extreme

Gagandeep—illumination, luminosity, radiance of the sky

Gagini—goddess

Gahana—ornament, jewellery, ornamentation, adornment, figurations, deep

Gajal—song, love

Gajara—garland of bloom, garden stuffs

Gajara—wreath of bloom, garden stuffs

Gajdant—lord ganesha

Gajendra—valuable, valued, rare, elephant monarch, ruler, prince, earl

Gajgamini—pretty, lovely, handsome, graceful name

Gajra—a string of bloom, garden stuffs

Gajshri—pretty, lovely, handsome, graceful name

Gamani—golden, diamond

Gamati—with a flexible mind

Gambhera—depth, river

Gambhera—serious

Gambherika—name of a river

Gambhiri—noble

Gamini—goddess parvati, walk run

Gamya—pretty, lovely, handsome, graceful destiny

Ganakee—an astrological prediction

Ganakshi—ambition, intent, passion or want

Gananya—pretty, lovely, handsome, graceful name

Ganavati—name of parvati

Ganavika—happiness

Ganavi—knowledge

Ganavi—raga

Ganda—knot

Gandhaharika—perfumed lady

Gandhalata—a creeper with fragrance

Gandhale—a sweet smelling woman

Gandhali—fragrance of bloom, garden stuff

Gandhamalince—strong scented

Gandhamalini—garland of sweet smell

Gandhara—fragrance

Gandharee—name of the highness, empress, queen of hastinapur

Gandharika—a person who prepares perfumes

Gandhari—highness, empress, queen, who was mother of kauravas

Gandharvakanya—a virgin woman

Gandharvapada—a gandharva girl

Gandharva—durga

Gandharve—a woman musician from the heaven

Gandharvi—a name of durga

Gandharvi—the army of gandharvas

Gandhashekhara—musk

Gandhasoma—white water lily

Gandhavadhu—a perfume

Gandhavajra—a goddess

Gandhavallari—a fragrant creeper

Gandhavalli—the earth

Gandhavati—the earth

Gandha—fragrant

Gandha—good smelled

Gandhini—fragrant

Gandhlata—a name of the creeper

Ganesa—good luck

Ganesha—lord ganesha

Ganeshika—part of lord ganesha

Ganeshi—lord shiva son, lord ganesha

Ganeta—regarded, maths, calculative

Ganev—priceless wealth

Gangaa—name of holy river in india

Gangabhai—friendly

Gangadeity—river ganga

Gangamata—great devotee of the lord

Gangangne—daughter of ganga

Ganga—sacred river of india

Ganga—the river ganga

Gangey—of ganga

Ganghari—girl from gandhar

Ganghavalleri—a creeper with sweet smell
Gangika—river ganga
Gangi—goddess durga
Gangotri—a place from where ganga originates
Gangotri—sacred river of india
Ganhakali—goddess kali
Ganika—an astrologer
Ganika—bloom, garden stuff
Ganika—who sings melodiously
Ganisha—healthy, lord ganesha
Ganisha—healty
Ganishkha—goddess parvathi
Ganita—regarded
Ganitha—regarded
Ganit—calculative, defender, mathematics
Ganjan—exceeding
Gannika—pretty, lovely, handsome, graceful name
Ganvika—independent
Ganvitha—independent
Ganya—garden of the lord
Gaouri—goddess parvati
Garati—virtuous woman
Gargee—ancient scholar
Gargee—inspires to think
Gargi—an ancient scholar
Gargi—daughter of sage garg
Gariana—truthful
Garima—respect, greatness
Garima—warmth, proud, dignity, prowess
Garjana—loud cry
Garjita—sound of thunder
Garuda—eagle
Garvari—warmth
Garvika—having respect
Garvisha—devotion of god
Garvita—full of pride be proud of
Garvita—proud woman
Garvi—pride, love
Gatha—lovely storey
Gatha—story
Gatha—sublime songs
Gathika—song
Gatik—speed, fast

Gatima—a river
Gatita—a river
Gati—life
Gauarangee—goddess parvati
Gauhar—a pearl
Gauraja—pleasing, favourite, charming
Gaurangana—fair complexioned
Gaurange—wife of lord shiva
Gaurangi—pretty, lovely, handsome, graceful, coloured like a cow
Gauranshi—a sacred part of goddess parvati
Gauravangana—proud woman
Gauravi—famous
Gauravi—honour, pride, goddess durga
Gaura—a fair woman, goddess parvati
Gaura—goddess parvati
Gaurika—a young girl, pretty, little gauri
Gaurika—virgin
Gaurinath—husband of gauri
Gaurisha—pretty, lovely, handsome, graceful goddess parvati
Gaurish—lord shiva
Gaurita—hindu goddess parvati
Gauri—fair, white, golden complexioned
Gauri—goddess parvati
Gaurshi—goddess parvati
Gaurushi—pretty, lovely, handsome, graceful name
Gauryai—another name of goddess durga
Gauryanvi—who makes proud
Gautamee—river godavari, wife a sage gautam
Gautami—wife a sage gautam, river godavari
Gauthami—river godavari
Gavana—a garment worn by woman on the upper part
Gaveshna—search
Gavina—white hawk
Gavithra—goddess of garba and dance
Gawakshi—like cows eye, glimmers

Gayana—singingg, singing, knowledge

Gayantee—wife of monarch, ruler, prince, earl gaya

Gayantika—singing

Gayan—river godavari

Gayathri—good charactern valuable, valued, rare angel

Gayatree—name of a very sacred mantra

Gayatree—sacred verse goddess

Gayatrine—one who sings vedic mantra

Gayatri—goddess durga

Gayatri—singer, mantra

Gaya—a holy city of india

Gaya—a name of the hindu pilgrimage

Gaytri—goddess gayatri

Gazala—a deer

Gazal—singing song

Geashna—victory

Geena—silvery

Geena—silvery, farm worker

Geerna—fame

Geerne—celebrity

Geetadeity—the soul of holy book bhagwat

Geetai—version of geeta rahasya

Geetakshi—holy book geeta

Geetanshi—goddess

Geeta—a holy book of hindus

Geeta—the holy book of the hinduism

Geetha—holy book of the hindus

Geethika—a song little song

Geethu—a smile, pretty, lovely, handsome, graceful

Geetika—a little song, music

Geetika—a short song

Geeti—a song, melody

Geeti—singing, a song

Geetmalini—a string of handful of poem

Geetsudha—sweet music

Geetu—a smile, pretty, lovely, handsome, graceful, very special

Geet—song, melody

Gehena—ornament, jewellery, ornamentation, adornment, figurationlery

Gehine—gold

Gehini—housewife

Gehna—ornament, jewellery, ornamentation, adornment

Gemine—third sign of zodiac, twins

Gemini—third sign of zodiac, twins

Genelia—charming

Geneliya—charming

Genisha—pretty, lovely, handsome, graceful name

Geshna—singer

Gesma—silent pretty, lovely, handsome, graceful and sacred

Geyata—melody

Ghada—pretty, lovely, handsome, graceful small song

Ghaena—ornament, jewellery, ornamentation, adornment, figuration

Ghaliya—fragrant, which can be sung

Ghanajani—a lover of nature

Ghanakshari—cloud

Ghanali—a group of cloud

Ghananjane—with collyrium, dark as could

Ghananjani—a dark cloud

Ghanavalli—creeper of the cloud

Ghanavi—singing star

Ghana—knowledge

Ghanika—pretty, lovely, handsome, graceful bloom, garden stuff

Ghani—richest

Ghantaka—pretty, lovely, handsome, graceful name

Ghantali—a string of small bells

Ghantika—a small bell

Ghantika—bell ringer, dahtura plant

Ghanya—bunch, singing

Ghasi—one type of ryms to kasi

Ghatala—pretty, lovely, handsome, graceful

Ghatari—pretty, lovely, handsome, graceful name

Ghata—clouds

Ghauree—bullet

Ghena—ornament, jewellery, ornamentation, adornment, figurationlery
Ghewri—name of a sweet
Ghnamika—pretty, lovely, handsome, graceful name
Ghnanika—brilliant, sagacious, gifted, wise, learned
Ghoshali—a musical instrument
Ghoshana—declaration
Ghoshanin—famed
Ghoshavati—vena, lute
Ghosha—loud noise
Ghoshine—proclaimed
Ghoshinin—proclamation
Ghoshna—declaration
Ghrani—a ray of illumination, luminosity, radiance
Ghrishma—warmth
Ghritachi—name of saraswati
Ghritavati—name of river
Ghughari—a ornament, jewellery, ornamentation, adornment, figuration
Ghunghari—bracelet with jingling bells
Ghungroo—dancer's wear for feet
Giaa—sweet heart, life
Gian—knowledge
Gia—life piece of heart
Giinni—valuable, valued, rare gold coin
Gina—well born, race of women
Ginisha—idol of gold, silver
Gini—gold coin, parrot
Ginni—valuable, valued, rare gold coin
Giradeity—valuable, valued, rare gold coin
Giraja—goddess parvati
Giral—pretty, lovely, handsome, graceful name
Gira—language
Gira—speech
Gireesha—goddess parvati
Giribala—daughter of mountain
Giribala—goddess parvati
Giriganga—name of the river
Girijatanya—daughter of parvati

Girija—consort of lord shiva
Girija—goddess parvati
Girika—summit of a mountain, lord shiva
Girika—summit of mountain
Girinandani—ganga, parvati
Giriraj—mountain monarch, ruler, prince, earl
Girisha—goddess parvati
Girisha—wife of a mountain
Giritanya—daughter of mountain
Girita—graceful
Giri—hill, mountain
Girja—goddess parvati
Gisele—pledge, hostage, oath
Gitale—one who loves songs
Gitali—lover of song
Gitanjali—poem by tagore, an anthology of poems
Gitanshi—part of bhagwat geeta
Gitansh—part of geeta
Gitashri—the bhagvat gita
Gitasri—pure, sanctified, pious, solemn, pious gita, holy
Gitasudha—sweet music
Gita—hindu holy text, holy book of hindus
Githika—a small song
Gitihika—a small song
Gitika—small song
Gitisha—seven sound of song
Gitu—pretty, lovely, handsome, graceful name
Giva—hill
Glara—heart
Gnanadha—goddess saraswati
Gnanalia—strong, independent
Gnanam—the bhagvat gita
Gnanasri—valuable knowledge
Gnana—cleverer, good knowledge
Gnanita—one who knows scared knowledge
Gnani—good knowledge, knows everything
Gnansika—the creator
Gnanvati—absorbed in knowledge
Gnapika—brilliant, sagacious, gifted, wise, learned

81 Indian Names For Girls

Gnatha—knowing everything
Gobikaa—woman of gokulam
Gobindi—krishna's concert
Godavari—a river
Godavari—sacred river of india
Godavri—a river
Goda—goddess, giver of cows
Goddess—devi, illumination, luminosity, radianceful, goddess
Godhika—lizard of sita
Godhuli—dust of the earth raised by cows
Godwini—best friend
Gokama—river godavari
Gokanya—maid who looks after cows
Gokila—monarch, ruler, prince, earl of the world
Gokuli—the one who is from lord krishna's
Gokul—pretty, lovely, handsome, graceful name
Gola—a river
Gold—pretty, lovely, handsome, graceful name
Goli—round figure, appearance, structured, tablet
Gomadhi—wealthy in cows
Gomatee—a river
Gomathi—holy, sanctified, pious, solemn, chaste, true
Gomathy—monarch, ruler, prince, earl of beauty
Gomati—a river
Gomati—name of a river
Gomattie—tributary of river ganga
Gomini—owner of cattle
Gomti—a river
Gomti—name of a river
Gomyasri—pretty, lovely, handsome, graceful name
Gomya—nice and graceful
Goohari—parakramam
Gool—a bloom, garden stuff
Goonjan—humming of a bee
Goonj—sound
Goorti—praise
Gopabala—daughter of a cow herd
Gopali—an epithet of krishna

Gopa—gautama's wife
Gopee—milkmaid
Gopika—beloved to krishna
Gopika—girls who loves lord krishna
Gopila—krishna's friend
Gopini—girlfriends of lord krishna
Gopi—woman who loves cows, cow-herd
Gopu—lord krishna, gopal
Goral—the fair girl
Gorandee—fair complextion
Gori—fair, white, goddess parvati
Gorma—gauri, fair
Gorma—goddess parvati
Gormi—goddess parvati
Gorochana—yellow pigment
Gorvi—pretty, lovely, handsome, graceful name
Goshthi—conservation
Goshti—conversation
Gotamee—ahilaya, gautam rishi's wife
Gourangi—fair, complexioned
Gouravi—proud, honour, respect, pride
Goura—goddess parvati
Goure—goddess parvati fair woman
Gouri—bright, fair, most pretty, lovely, handsome, graceful
Gourvi—honour, proud, pride, respect
Gourya—lord shiva's wife
Goutami—river godavari, devoted to lord
Gouthami—river godavari life
Govindi—a devotee of lord krishna
Gowrangi—fair complexioned
Gowri—goddess parvati, bright, fair
Gowsalya—a place where cows are kept
Gowthami—river of india
Grahita—accepted
Grahi—accepting
Gramakali—goddess kali of the village
Granthika—composer
Granthi—relation
Granth—religious books
Greashma—summer
Grecy—loves god, graceful, goodwill
Greema—sweet

Greeshma—warm, summer season, hot season
Greeshmi—a kind of season
Greeshu—love
Greeva—with sweet voice, neck
Greha—planet
Gresha—cute, with wise
Greshy—loves god, graceful
Grhitha—understood and accepted
Grihalakshmi—the lakshmi of the house
Grihastini—house wife
Grihini—house wife
Grihita—understood
Grimi—variant form of garima
Grisha—watchful, goddess parvati, beloved
Grishika—pretty, lovely, handsome, graceful name
Grishma—summer
Grishma—warmth, summer season
Grisma—season
Gritika—good voice
Grittika—good voice, powerful
Griva—girls who has pretty, lovely, handsome, graceful singing
Gruhi—pretty, lovely, handsome, graceful charming
Gudakesha—victory over sleep
Guddi—doll
Guddu—small baby
Guddy—doll
Gudia—doll, excellence
Gudiya—doll
Gudi—sweet, doll
Guhasri—lord murugan
Guhika—voice of birds
Gulabi—colour name, rose-coloured
Gulabi—rosy
Gulab—rose, beloved's tears
Gulab—rose, bloom, garden stuff
Gulal—crown of the head
Gulal—reddish powder
Gulika—ballnything round pearl
Gulista—bloom, garden stuff garden
Guljaan—pretty, lovely, handsome, graceful bloom, garden stuff
Gullika—pearl

Gull—god
Gulshan—garden of roses, garden
Gulshita—the rose bloom, garden stuff
Gul—bloom, garden stuff, rose, bouquet
Gunaja—daughter of virtue
Gunakali—possessing virtues
Gunakshi—kind, one who is good by nature
Gunasree—good behaviour
Gunasundri—the ultimate, absolute, highest, best being
Gunavanti—a virtuous woman
Gunavara—better in qualities, virtuous
Gunavatee—a virtuous woman
Gunavati—virtuous
Gunavi—pretty, lovely, handsome, graceful name
Guna—good character
Guncha—bloom, garden stuff buds
Gunesha—one with good character
Gungun—singing, humming, soft and warmth
Gunika—star, pearl
Gunisha—goddess of talent
Gunita—victory, virtuous
Gunita—virtuous
Gunitha—proficient
Guniyal—a virtuous woman
Gunjana—a woman who knows how to admire virtues
Gunjana—buzzing, humming of bee
Gunjan—humming, buzzing of a bee
Gunjan—musical sound
Gunja—inset sweet sound
Gunja—singing girl
Gunjika—humming
Gunjita—humming of bee
Gunjot—illumination, luminosity, radiance of excellence
Gunj—the sound, the echo
Gunmala—bestowed with qualities
Gunnidhi—virtuous
Gunnika—garland
Gunnikka—well-woven
Gunsaki—treasure of guru's thoughts
Gunvanti—virtuous virtues
Gunvara—full of qualities and virtues

Gunvati—bestowed with qualities
Gunwanti—virtuous
Gunwant—talent
Gunwati—good quality
Gupil—garland
Gupti—preserving, protecting
Gurbani—sikhs religious prayer
Gurdeep—blessings of the guru
Gurdev—god, lord of guru, master
Guri—cub, young, youthful lion, god
Gurjari—a raga
Gurjot—a illumination, luminosity, radiance of god
Gurpreet—guru's favourite
Gurpreet—lover of god, guru's love
Gursharn—getting shelter where god lives
Gurshen—guru's pride, reflection of guru
Gurti—approval, praise
Gurumita—friend of the guru
Guruvachan—words of the guru

Guruvayi—a raga
Guru—teacher
Gurve—beloved by teacher
Gurvisha—pretty, lovely, handsome, graceful name
Gutika—pearl
Gyami—life is dream
Gyanada—goddess saraswati
Gyana—full of knowledge deity name
Gyana—knowledge, goddess parvati
Gyanda—knowledgeable
Gyandeity—sarasvati
Gyaneshwari—wise
Gyanisha—superior, elevated, holy, pure, sanctified, pious, solemn
Gyanprabha—illumination, luminosity, radiance of knowledge
Gyanshi—full of knowledge
Gyanshi—having bright knowledge
Gyata—who knows everything
Gyati—full of knowledge
Gyna—silvery

****

Indian Names For Girls—H

Hadara—bedecked in beauty, glory
Hadiya—guide to righteousness
Haeksha—love and affection
Hailley—friendly, friend
Haimantika—growing in winter
Haimavathi—goddess lakshmi
Haimavati—goddess parvati
Haima—snow, winter, gold, singer
Haimini—golden, winter, cold
Haimi—golden, goddess parvati, snow
Haishika—laugh love
Haitakshi—well desire, aspiration, longinger
Haith—good for everyone
Haituka—well desire, aspiration, longinger
Haiya—heart
Hala—halo around the moon, plough
Halema—gentle, patient, sympathetic
Hamaya—greatness
Hameen—god
Haminagni—pretty, lovely, handsome, graceful name
Hami—golden
Hamsavahini—who rides a swan
Hamsavalli—very pretty, lovely, handsome, graceful
Hamsaveni—swan
Hamsa—bird, swan hamsavahini
Hamshika—goddess saraswathi
Hamshi—wonder
Hamsika—pretty, lovely, handsome, graceful swan, goddess saraswati
Hamsini—one who rides a swan
Hamuda—desirable
Hananthika—pretty, lovely, handsome, graceful, good knowledge
Hananya—blessful
Hanasvi—god gift
Hanaya—every time new, florist, eye, glimmers
Hanesha—gift of god
Hanesh—lord shiva, cool, sweet

Hanifa—true believer, holy, sanctified, pious, solemn, chaste
Hanika—swan, graceful like swan
Hanima—a wave
Hanisha—pretty, lovely, handsome, graceful night, sweetest
Hanishi—swan
Hanishree—pretty, lovely, handsome, graceful name
Hanita—one who rides a swan
Hanitiya—pretty, lovely, handsome, graceful parrot
Haniya—pleased, happy, encampment
Hani—droplet, pleasant, illumination, luminosity, radiance
Hanmayasri—god of given
Hannah—gracious, grace, grace of god
Hansadhwani—swan, sound
Hansagamine—woman with graceful gait like a swan
Hansagamini—as graceful as swan
Hansagauri—fair woman like a swan
Hansali—grace, power
Hansamala—a line or row of swans
Hansanadini—chattering like a swan
Hansanandine—a woman with slender waist
Hansanandini—daughter of a swan
Hansavati—pretty, lovely, handsome, graceful woman
Hansaveni—another name of goddess saraswati
Hansa—a swan
Hansa—swan
Hansdhwani—vocal sound of swan
Hansee—a female swan
Hansgamini—walk like swan
Hanshika—swan or pretty, lovely, handsome, graceful lady
Hanshini—holy, sanctified, pious, solemn, chaste, swan
Hanshita—swan
Hanshitha—swan, gorgeous
Hanshu—happiness

Hansika—little swan
Hansika—swan, love, baby of swan
Hansini—swan
Hansini—swan and pretty, lovely,
handsome, graceful lady
Hansitha—like a swan, peceful mind
Hansja—river yamuna
Hansmukhi—smiling face
Hansnandni—with slender waist
Hansuja—goddess lakshmi
Hansveni—goddess saraswati, swan
Hansvi—god gift, swan
Hanswi—drinmonarch, ruler, prince,
earl milk
Hansy—gift of god, beauty
Hanumatee—name of a woman
Hanumathi—lord hanuman
Hanu—happy and new, lord hanuman
Hanvidha—pretty, lovely, handsome,
graceful, goddess durga
Hanvika—goddess lakshmi, sarasvati
Hanvitha—bridge of relations
Hanvi—beauty of mind
Happy—cherful, joyful
Hapy—full of laughter
Harabala—daughter of lord shiva
Haral—after sunset timing
Harani—pretty, lovely, handsome,
graceful name
Harapriya—beloved of lord shiva
Harathi—illumination, luminosity,
radiance, holy
Haravali—string of pearls
Hara—princess, seizer
Harda—lake
Hardeep—lamp of god
Hardika—affectionate
Hardika—wonderful, similar to hardik
Hardikya—hearty
Hardini—near of hart
Hardipa—lamp of god
Hardit—given by god
Hardi—from the heart
Hareesha—happy
Harhsa—joy, illumination, luminosity,
radiance
Hari-priya—favourite of lord vishnu
Haribala—daughter of lord vishnu

Haribala—god girl
Hariganga—ganga of vishnu
Hariharan—lord vishnu and lord shiva
Harihini—daughter of lord vishnu
Harijata—fair haired, fire haired
Harijatha—fair haired
Harija—goddess parvati, loveable
Harikanta—dear to visnu
Harika—lord vishnu, beloved by indra
Harika—wreath, beloved of indra
Harikiran—rays of gods
Harimani—ornament, jewellery,
ornamentation, adornment, figuration
Harimanti—born in the season of
hemanta
Harinaakshi—doe eye, glimmers
Harinakshi—doe eye, glimmers
Harinakshi—doe eye, glimmers, one
with eye, glimmers like deer
Harinanakshu—doe eye, glimmers
Harinandana—happiness, joy of the
lord, god
Harina—deer, lord hari
Harine—experience, deer, goddess
lakshmi
Harine—she deer
Harinika—goddess of vasu
Harininakshi—eye, glimmers like a
doe
Harininayna—doe eye, glimmers
Harini—pretty, lovely, handsome,
graceful like deer
Harinmani—green gem
Hariprita—beloved of vishnu
Haripriya—beloved of lord vishnu
Haripriya—consort of lord vishnu
Harirameshwari—pretty, lovely,
handsome, graceful
Harisha—happiness, rain
Harishika—pretty, lovely, handsome,
graceful name
Harishini—happiness
Harishitha—happiness
Harishrava—praising hari
Harishree—pretty, lovely, handsome,
gracefully golden
Harishri—god
Harish—lord shiva, grace

Harisitha—happiness
Harismita—one with eye, glimmers like deer
Harita—pretty, lovely, handsome, graceful woman
Harita—green, nature's friend
Haritee—greenery
Haritha—green, lovely, pretty, lovely, handsome, graceful princess
Harithi—god of love, green
Harithra—lord shiva's daughter
Haritika—happy, joyful
Haritima—greenery
Hariti—green, goddess
Haritra—the one belonging to god
Harivallabha—goddess lakshmi
Hari—a colour, joy, happiness
Harlena—thinmonarch, ruler, prince, earl of god at all times
Harlen—from the hare's meadow
Harley—from the hare's meadow
Harle—meadow of the hare
Harman—beloved soldier, beloved person
Harmaty—all agree
Harmeen—beauty, fish of god
Harmi—cute, lovely
Harmya—palace
Harnisya—one with good nature
Harnoor—gods illumination, luminosity, radiance, gift
Harper—pretty, harp player, maker
Harpita—dedicated
Harsa—happiness, pleasure joy
Harseerat—god's wisdom
Harshadayini—one who increases joy
Harshada—joyful
Harshada—one who brings happiness
Harshala—glad
Harshalika—happiness, joyful
Harshali—full of joy, happiness
Harshali—happinesslways happy
Harshal—gladlways happy
Harshanaa—bringer of happiness, joyful
Harshana—happiness, pleasure joy
Harshangane—one who spreads joy
Harshanjali—tears of happiness

Harshaprabha—joyous
Harshaprada—happiness, joy giver
Harsharani—highness, empress, queen of joy, smiling in happiness
Harshara—laughing lady
Harshashri—happiness
Harshata—happiness
Harshavardhini—highness, empress, queen of happiness, goddess
Harshavarthini—one who increases happiness
Harsha—happiness, golden, pleasure
Harsha—joyful
Harshda—happiness, giver of happiness
Harshdeep—candle of happiness
Harshen—happiness and joy illumination, luminosity, radiance
Harshe—joyous
Harshida—giver of happiness, giver of joy
Harshida—giver of joy
Harshika—happinesslways smiling, laugh
Harshikha—pretty, lovely, handsome, graceful name
Harshili—always happy, happiness
Harshine—happiness
Harshinika—the most happiest girl
Harshini—cherful
Harshini—happiness, joyous, happy, amiable, pleasing, suave, interesting
Harshita—full of joy
Harshita—one who bring happiness, joyful
Harshitha—happiness joy
Harshiya—future
Harshi—joyous
Harshmati—full of joy
Harshmita—friend of happiness
Harshna—happiness
Harshne—pleasant woman
Harshni—joyful, happiness
Harshprabha—full of joy
Harshprada—joy giver
Harshul—cherful
Harshu—happiness
Harshvena—musical instrument

Harshvina—a lute that illumination, luminosity, radiances
Harshwika—joyful
Harsh—happiness, happy
Harsida—giver of happiness, joy
Harsika—joyous, beauty
Harsita—always smile happiness
Harsitha—giver of happiness, joy
Harsmitha—friend of happiness
Harthika—blessing, good
Hartika—blessing
Haruni—messenger-ship
Harusha—happy, joy
Harvika—daughter of lord vishnu
Harvina—pretty, lovely, handsome, graceful name
Harvitha—lord shiva
Harvi—battle worthy, fine
Harwati—love of life
Haryka—wonderful
Hasanmukhi—full of laughter
Hasanthi—one that illumination, luminosity, radiances
Hasanth—one that illumination, luminosity, radiances
Hasas—happy
Haseena—smile, pretty, lovely, handsome, graceful, pretty
Hashica—smiling
Hashika—pretty, lovely, handsome, graceful name
Hashini—happiness, joyful
Hashmita—always happy
Hashrat—desire, aspiration, longing
Hashree—joyful
Hashti—live, exist, rise, being, entity, smiling, laughing
Hashwitha—pretty, lovely, handsome, graceful name
Hasia—smile, laughter
Hasida—sage
Hasika—smiling
Hasina—good, cherful, pretty, lovely, handsome, graceful, pretty
Hasini—always smiling
Hasini—happy, joyfuln atom, pretty
Hasin—pretty, lovely, handsome, graceful, elegant

Hasita—full of laughter, smiling, happy
Hasita—happiness
Hasitha—always smiling
Hasi—laugh, smile
Hasmita—always happylways smiling
Hasmitha—always happy, smiling face
Hasna—pretty, lovely, handsome, graceful, laughing, pretty
Hasni—always happy
Hasrat—grief, ambition, intent, passion
Hasri—always happy, joyful
Hassini—happiness
Hassi—laughter, smiling, smile
Hassu—strong, happy, smile, laugh
Hasti—laughing, happy, live, exist, rise, being, entity
Hasumati—happy
Hasumati—smiley, happy
Hasu—laugh
Hasvika—happy
Hasvitha—being happy happiness
Hasvi—laughter
Hasya—smile
Hatakamaya—one with smiling face
Hatakiya—pretty, lovely, handsome, graceful name
Hathavilasini—one who enjoys
Hatisha—with no ambition, intent, passion
Havina—safety
Havintha—bridge of relations, goddess durga
Havirbhoo—place of sacrifice
Havisa—goddess lakshmi
Havisha—goddess lakshmi
Havismati—lucky
Haviya—sun, moon, lord of sun, lord shiva
Havu—snake
Havya—pretty, lovely, handsome, graceful, hobby, goddess parvati
Hawa—air, longing, ambition, intent, passion, eve
Hayana—eye, glimmers
Hayan—alive, life, shine
Hayatee—flame

Hayathi—my life, presence
Hayati—my life, presence
Haya—modesty, decency, shyness, shame
Haye—ambition, intent, passion
Hea—grace
Heemali—bringer of wealth, gold, golden
Heema—gold, goddess parvati
Heenal—goddess of beauty and wealth
Heenaya—shine, bright, fairy
Heena—henna, myrtle
Heenita—grace
Heeral—lustrous, wealthy, diamond, rain
Heerani—highness, empress, queen of beauty
Heera—diamond
Heera—diamonds valuable, valued, rare as diamond
Heerdeity—of the diamond
Heerkani—small diamond
Heervita—mountain bird
Heer—diamond, generous
Heesha—hasmukh, beauty, happy
Heeteshi—desire, aspiration, kindly
Heetisha—well desire, aspiration, longinger
Heetva—desire, aspiration, love
Heeva—pretty, lovely, handsome, graceful eye, glimmers
Heeya—heart, voice from heart
Heiu—heart, mind, soul
Hejal—god blessing, fruit
Helan—torch, sun ray, shining illumination, luminosity, radiance
Hela—moon, illumination, luminosity, radiance, goddess of the
Hemaani—full of snow, river
Hemaa—gold, golden
Hemachandra—golden moon
Hemadaree—golden mountain
Hemadauta—a celestial damsel
Hemadri—golden hills
Hemagiri—golden mountain, peak
Hemagna—golden knowledge
Hemagni—golden body, goddess parvati

Hemakalasa—golden hills
Hemakamala—golden lotus
Hemakanti—golden charm, glitter of gold
Hemaketki—the ketki plant
Hemakshi—golden eye, glimmers
Hemalata—golden
Hemalata—golden creeper
Hemalatha—golden
Hemala—golden eye, glimmers
Hemali—from mountain, gold, golden
Hemal—golden
Hemamaalini—golden
Hemamala—consort of yama
Hemamalini—garlanded with gold
Hemamalini—golden bloom, garden stuffs
Hemamali—gold, golden
Hemamaya—covered with full of gold
Hemamrutha—cold vision
Hemanga—golden-bodied
Hemangee—woman having a shining body
Hemangini—girl with golden body
Hemangi—golden body
Hemangi—holy, sanctified, pious, solemn, chaste, like gold
Hemangni—golden body
Hemanika—goddess parvati
Hemani—goddess parvati
Hemanshi—golden night, goddess saraswati
Hemantanila—goddess parvati
Hemanta—winter
Hemantee—of the winter
Hemantee—winter
Hemanthi—lot's of love
Hemantika—of the winter season
Hemantika—princess, tolerance, durability, toleration, doll
Hemanti—early winter
Hemanti—shining like gold
Hemanya—golden bodied
Heman—golden-coloured
Hemaprabha—golden illumination, luminosity, radiance
Hemaprabha—golden lustre

Hemapriya—early winter, with golden body
Hemapushpa—early winter, golden bloom, garden stuff
Hemapushpa—golden bloom, garden stuff
Hemaraja—lord of gold
Hemarani—golden highness, empress, queen
Hemashankar—lord shiva
Hemashree—one with golden body, princess
Hemashri—one with golden body
Hemasita—golden bloom, garden stuff
Hemasri—one with golden body
Hematara—golden star
Hemavala—love of kind
Hemavalli—golden creeper
Hemavani—golden words
Hemavaran—golden complexion
Hemavaran—golden dressed
Hemavarna—golden complexioned
Hemavarshini—goddess of rain, golden
Hemavathi—name of a river
Hemavati—goddess parvati
Hemavijaya—cute, victory person
Hemaxiba—golden body, joyful
Hema—a kind of plant, golden
Hema—gold, golden
Hemika—golden
Hemina—moon's rays
Hemisha—happiness, golden
Hemish—lord of the earth
Hemita—covered with gold
Hemitha—pretty, lovely, handsome, graceful name
Hemitra—lord vishnu
Hemi—golden
Hemkanta—golden girl
Hemkesh—golden, with gold hair
Hemkunver—gold, closeness
Hemlata—gold-creeper
Hemlata—golden creeper, golden tree
Hemlta—goddess durga
Hemna—musical note
Hemshikha—peak of gold
Hemshree—goddess durga

Hemshri—pretty, lovely, handsome, graceful name
Hemsuta—goddess parvati
Hemvati—goddess parvati
Hemyutika—gold woven
Hem—gold
Henal—god of beauty and wealth
Hena—on who is polite bloom, garden stuff
Hency—gift of god
Henel—twinkling
Henika—pretty, lovely, handsome, graceful name
Henishi—love
Henna—golden creeper, home ruler
Hensi—cuteness
Heral—wealthy
Hera—highness, empress, queen of gods, protector, heroine
Heroni—actress, pretty, lovely, handsome, graceful lady
Hershivi—happiness
Hesha—pleasure, ambition, intent, passion, goddess parvati
Heshini—golden bloom, garden stuff
Heshvini—lovely eye, glimmers
Hessa—destiny
Hetaa—female version of het
Hetali—friendly, love, cherful
Hetal—friendly, love, cherful
Hetani—strong
Hetanshi—aanandi part of love
Hetarthi—synonym of love
Hetasvi—pretty, lovely, handsome, graceful name
Hetavi—amiable, pleasing, suave, interesting
Heta—love, battle
Hethal—good
Hethanshri—a part of love
Hethika—sun rays
Hethvika—loveffection
Hetika—sun rays
Heti—sun ray, bright
Hetpari—angel of love
Hetshree—love of god, amiable, pleasing, suave, interesting

Hetsi—amiable, pleasing, suave, interesting
Hetuka—directions
Hetu—noble
Hetve—love, well desire, aspiration, longinger
Hetvika—love, desire, aspiration, lord shiva
Hetvi—love, well desire, aspiration, longinger
Hetwika—love, well desire, aspiration, longinger
Het—love
Heya—sweet, lovely
Hezal—the colour of rising sun nut
Hianu—love
Hiba—gift, present, gift from god
Hida—present, gift, warrior, friendly
Hidhanshi—hearty
Hidhyanshi—heartly
Hihikara—sinless, the holy, sanctified, pious, solemn, chaste one
Hiladine—illumination, luminosity, radiance
Hila—praise or appreciation
Hilla—timid
Hima-gowri—goddess parvati
Himaadri—snow mounted
Himaa—snow, gold, golden, haven
Himabindu—drop of a snow
Himadree—river ganga
Himadri—peak of snow
Himadri—the mountain himalaya
Himaghna—timid
Himagouri—goddess parvati
Himaja—goddess parvati, born from gold
Himakshi—saviour of snow
Himalini—goddess parvati
Himali—ice, goddess parvati, mountainous
Himanani—mass of snow
Himana—snow, membrane
Himangini—made of snow
Himani—goddess parvati, snow
Himani—of the snow
Himank—nature
Himanni—sweet, kind

Himanshi—pretty, lovely, handsome, graceful, part of ice, snow
Himanshi—lord shiva
Himanshu—baraf ka tukda, valuable, valued, rare
Himansi—cool
Himanya—cool, ice bodied
Himarashmi—full of snow, cool rayed
Himarsha—from the mountains
Himasailaja—parvati
Himashweta—as white as snow
Himasri—white rays, pretty, lovely, handsome, graceful snow
Himasvi—snow, ice, cold
Himavarsha—snow rain
Himavarshini—snow falling, ice raining
Hima—ice, snow, cold, moon
Himendri—snow, winter, ice, goddess parvati
Himgouri—goddess parvati
Himika—made of snow
Himma—snow, winter, ice
Himsuta—parvati
Himtanya—daughter of himalaya, goddess parvati
Himu—snow
Hinali—henna
Hinal—goddess of beauty and wealth
Hinaya—shine, bright, pretty, lovely, handsome, graceful, fairy
Hina—henna shrub, fragrance
Hindavi—hindu
Hinda—female deer, doe
Hindola—a raga, swing
Hindusri—goddess of prosperity
Hindvi—of hindu
Hind—proper name, india, land of hindus
Hinu—fragrance
Hiradeity—a swing
Hiradha—lake
Hirakani—a small diamond
Hiralakshmi—goddess of diamond
Hirali—pretty, lovely, handsome, graceful name
Hiral—highness, empress, queen, lustrous, wealthy, diamond

Hiramani—of the diamond
Hirananda—pretty, lovely, handsome, graceful name
Hiranayada—giving gold
Hiranga—wealthy
Hirani—gold
Hirani—like a deer
Hirankshi—eye, glimmers like deer
Hiranmai—golden, made of gold
Hiranmaye—golden
Hiranmaye—name of goddess lakshmi, golden
Hiranmayi—golden girl, golden appearance
Hiranyadha—giving gold
Hiranyaka—gold
Hiranyaksha—a woman with golden eye, glimmers
Hiranyakshi—one having golden eye, glimmers
Hiranyamaye—golden
Hiranyashri—gold, golden valuable, valued, rare metal
Hiranya—gold, golden
Hiran—deer
Hirarama—pretty, lovely, handsome, graceful name
Hirava—blessing
Hira—diamond, name for lakshmi
Hirbai—valuable, valued, rare diamond
Hirkani—small diamond
Hirni—deer
Hiroka—a small diamind
Hirsha—saintly
Hirva—blessing
Hirwa—diamond
Hir—diamond, ranjha's lover
Hisha—pretty, lovely, handsome, graceful
Hishetha—wonder
Hissa—star, proud
Hissna—love
Hitaishi—well desire, aspiration, longinger
Hitaisshi—well desire, aspiration, longinger

Hitakshi—desire, aspiration, longinger, eye, glimmers
Hitali—favourable
Hitanshi—desire, aspiration, helper
Hitansi—well desire, aspiration, longinger
Hitarshi—well desire, aspiration, longinger
Hitarthe—one who always do well to others
Hitarthe—desire, aspiration, benevolence
Hitarthi—well desire, aspiration, longinger
Hitasa—another name of fire
Hitashi—well desire, aspiration, longinger
Hitashri—one who thinks good for everyone
Hitasini—goddess gayatri, parvathi
Hitasshi—well desire, aspiration, longinger
Hitaxi—desire, aspiration, friend, amiable, pleasing, suave, interesting, eye, glimmers
Hita—golden, beneficial, lovabl
Hitee—love and care
Hiteksha—well desire, aspiration, longinger
Hiten—holy, sanctified, pious, solemn, chaste, friendly, helping others
Hitesha—well desire, aspiration, longinger
Hiteshi—desire, aspiration, kindly
Hiteshree—well desire, aspiration, longinger
Hitexa—well desire, aspiration, longinger
Hithaishi—well-desire, aspiration, longinger
Hithaisree—well desire, aspiration, longinger
Hithaisri—well desire, aspiration, longinger
Hitha—one who want to do good for every
Hithisha—dare
Hithisri—blessing

Hithyashini—gold
Hitika—well desire, aspiration, longinger
Hitisha—well desire, aspiration, longinger
Hitishini—well-desire, aspiration, longinger
Hitixa—desire, aspiration, golden bloom, garden stuff
Hiti—well-desire, aspiration, longinger
Hitlata—well desire, aspiration, longinger
Hittu—innovation, god
Hitul—well desire, aspiration, longinger
Hitu—well desire, aspiration, longinger
Hitvi—love
Hityshi—well desire, aspiration, longingers
Hiva—song, gros bisous
Hiyansh—a piece of heart
Hiyashri—pretty, lovely, handsome, graceful name
Hiyashvi—happiness
Hiyasvi—full of happiness
Hiya—heart or mind
Hiza—lucky, fortunate
Hladini—gives joy to everyone
Holika—comparison
Holika—sister of hiranyakush
Homakala—the art of home
Homakashti—goddess of lord shivanganga
Homali—jasamine
Homashala—responsible, stable nature
Homa—a mythical bird
Homiya—angel
Honey—sweet as honey, sweetheart, honey
Honnesha—rich person, goddess lakshmi
Honnu—golden, gold
Hoor—a celestical, virgin of paradise
Hoshika—space, star
Hotravahana—a celestial beauty
Hotriya—heart throb

Houghai—pretty, lovely, handsome, graceful name
Houmesha—the ray of gold
Hoyala—holy
Hrada—pond
Hradha—lake
Hradine—very happy
Hradini—illumination, luminosity, radiance
Hreeta—green
Hridayashwari—wife, beloved
Hridaya—heart
Hridayesh—god of the heart
Hriday—heart
Hrida—holy, sanctified, pious, solemn, chaste
Hriddha—heart touching
Hriddhima—full of love and prosperity
Hriddhismita—determine to achieve the goal
Hridhavika—pretty, lovely, handsome, graceful name
Hridha—heart, heart touching
Hridhika—part of heart
Hridhvika—one with great heart
Hridhya—hearty
Hridika—of heart
Hridisha—directed towards heart
Hridita—of heart
Hridya—heart, amiable, pleasing, suave, interesting, cute
Hridyesa—heart
Hridyesha—heart
Hrikita—the one who give everything
Hrisha—saintly
Hrishika—the village of birth
Hrishita—always smiling, joyful
Hrishitha—one who bring happiness, joyful
Hrishka—one who is knowledgeable
Hrishmitha—happy
Hritesi—desire, aspiration, friend
Hrithika—heart, truthful, honest, joy
Hrithiksha—from the heart, pretty, lovely, handsome, graceful
Hritika—truthful, kind hearted
Hrittika—all stars power in favour of
Hritvika—scene of green plants, kind

Hritvi—season
Hriya—pretty, lovely, handsome, graceful name
Hrsita—happiness
Hrudai—heart
Hrudanshi—close to heart
Hrudavi—part of heart
Hrudhaini—heart
Hrudhani—flash of illumination, luminosity, radiance
Hrudvi—part of heart
Hrugvedi—type of a veda
Hrushikesha—pretty, lovely, handsome, graceful name
Hruthika—lord of heart, kind
Hruti—love
Hrutva—speech
Hrutvika—pretty, lovely, handsome, graceful name
Hrutvi—name of an angel, season
Hrutvy—angel, season
Huemisha—goddess saraswati, brilliant, sagacious, gifted, wise, learned

Humaila—golden necklace
Humaithi—god
Huma—bird of paradise
Humisha—goddess saraswati
Humpy—pretty, lovely, handsome, graceful name
Humshika—goddess saraswati
Humsiha—goddess saraswati, luckiest girl
Hunar—skill, skill talent
Huna—golden necklace
Huralopa—helpful
Husna—pretty, lovely, handsome, graceful belle
Hussey—smile
Huvishka—promise, godly qualities
Hymavathi—goddess lakshmi, parvati
Hymavati—pretty, lovely, handsome, graceful
Hyma—goddess parvati
Hyndavi—woman, goddess of hindus, durga
Hyndhavi—goddess durga

****

Indian Names For Girls—I

Iaza—pretty, lovely, handsome, graceful name
Ibbani—mist, fog, honey dew
Ibha—support, indoctrination, assuredness
Iccha—desire, aspiration, longing, ambition, intent, passion
Ichchani—pretty, lovely, handsome, graceful name
Ichcha—desire, aspiration, longing, ambition, intent, passion
Ichchha—ambition, intent, passion ambition
Ichha—desire, aspiration, longing, ambition, intent, passion
Idai—awakening, love
Idaya—the beauty of world, heart
Ida—prosperous, happy, work, labour
Ida—speech
Idhayakani—insight
Idhaya—heart
Idha—insight
Idhika—wife of lord shiv, goddess parvati
Idhitri—one who praises
Idika—the earth
Iditri—complimentary
Idris—powerful, wealthy
Iha—the earth, desire, aspiration, longing
Ihina—enthusiasm
Ihita—ambition, intent, passion, goddess durga, fighter
Ihitha—ambition, intent, passion
Iierathi—enthusiasm
Ijaya—sacrifice
Ijya—sacrifice, image
Ijya—sacrifice, offer
Ikka—pretty, lovely, handsome, graceful name
Ikkhata—sacrifice
Ikshana—sight, pretty
Ikshan—sight
Iksha—sight

Ikshenya—one who deserve to be seen
Ikshika—a glance
Ikshita—desirable
Ikshita—visible
Ikshitha—visible, cute, brilliant
Ikshuda—name of the river
Ikshula—holy river
Ikshumaaline—sugarcane
Ikshumalini—name of the river
Ikshumalin—a florist, river
Ikshumatee—possessor of sugarcane
Ikshumati—river in kurushetra
Ikshu—sugarcane
Ikshu—sweetness
Ikshwaaku—holy river
Iksura—fragrant grass
Iladeity—goddess of the earth
Ilakhumi—earth, daughter of manu
Ilakkiya—wisdom classic
Ilamathi—young moon
Ilampirai—young crescent
Ilangani—selected, chosen
Ilanguil—young little sparrow
Ilarasi—world princes
Ilavalagi—young and pretty, lovely, handsome, graceful
Ilavarasi—princess
Ilavenil—spring, youthful
Ila—speech, fish
Ila—woman from earth, earth
Ilesha—goddess, lord of the earth
Ilesha—lord of the earth
Ileshi—wife of monarch, ruler, prince, earl, highness, empress, queen
Ilhana—happiness, excellent
Ilina—highness, empress, queen
Ilina—very brilliant, sagacious, gifted, wise, learned
Ilisha—earth highness, empress, queen
Ilisha—highness, empress, queen of the earth, ruthful
Illa—tree
Illika—of earth

Illisha—highness, empress, queen of earth
Illisha—one who creates illusion
Ilma—resolute protector, strong helmet
Ilya—noble, high class
Imani—devotionful person, trustworthy
Imple—monarch, ruler, prince, earl, stronglways smiles
Inaam—act of kindness, benefaction
Inaki—warmth feeling
Inaksha—mother
Inakshe—sharp eye, glimmers
Inari—place name
Inas—capable, sociability, sweet voice
Inaxi—name of star
Inayat—blessing of god, kindness
Inaya—pretty, lovely, handsome, graceful, concern, solicitude
Ina—mother
Ina—strong, illuminate, illumination, luminosity, radiance up
Inbamozhi—kindness
Inbam—capable, sociability
Inbanayaki—highness, empress, queen of happiness
Inbavalli—happy girl
Inbha—happiness
Inchara—sweet voice, nature
Indale—to be powerful
Indaliai—sea-feather
Indali—powerful
Indarupini—name of god gayatri
Indhumathy—full moon
India—river, country
Indiradeity—trustworthy
Indirani—goddess of the sky
Indira—goddess lakshmi
Indira—goddess of wealth, lakshmi
Indivaraksha—lotus eye, glimmers
Indivaraprabha—beauty of blue lotus
Indivara—blue lotus, tree of devalokam
Indivarini—a group of blue lotus
Indivarini—collection of blue lotuses
Indivarne—a bunch of blue lotus
Indiya—knowledgeable
Indi—born in india, indian
Indrabala—indra's daughter
Indrabala—indra's daughter
Indrabhagini—sister of indra
Indraja—born of indra
Indraja—jupiter, daughter of lord indra
Indrakanta—goddess indrani, shachi
Indrakshe—eye, glimmers like indra
Indrakshi—pretty, lovely, handsome, graceful eye, glimmers
Indrakshi—one with pretty, lovely, handsome, graceful eye, glimmers
Indraksi—eye, glimmers like indra
Indranela—sapphire
Indranel—one with pretty, lovely, handsome, graceful eye, glimmers
Indrane—wife of indra
Indranilika—as blue as indra, sapphire
Indrani—wife of indra
Indrani—wife of indra, goddess of rage
Indrapushpa—name of a medicinal plant
Indrasena—daughter of monarch, ruler, prince, earl nala
Indratha—power and dignity of lord indra
Indrayani—name of sacred river, holy river
Indra—god of the sky, rain, thunder
Indra—wife of indra
Indrina—deep
Indubala—daughter of indu
Indubha—illumination, luminosity, radiance of the moon, water-lily
Indubha—name of the constellation, river
Induja—daughter of indra, river narmada
Induja—narmada river
Indukaksha—the orbit of the moon
Indukala—moon, illumination, luminosity, radiance
Indukanta—daughter of the moon
Indukanta—wife of moon, night
Indukiran—moon-rays
Indulala—moon illumination, luminosity, radiance

Indulekha—moon
Indulekha—the moon
Induleksh—the moon
Indumala—garland of the moon
Indumala—the blossom of white lotus
Indumalini—moon
Indumani—gem of the moon, moon stone
Indumatee—full moon
Indumathi—full phase of mooon, bright drop
Indumati—full moon
Indumati—the full moon
Indumauli—moon crested
Induma—glory of moon
Induma—moon
Indumukhi—moon like face
Induprabha—moon rays
Induprabha—the illumination, luminosity, radiance of the moon
Indurekha—full moon
Indurekha—the rays of the moon-illumination, luminosity, radiance
Indusekhara—shiva
Indushekhara—moon
Indushetala—cool like the moon
Indushree—moon illumination, luminosity, radiance
Induyasas—god of moon
Indu—illumination, luminosity, radiance descent, moon, lord chandra
Indu—moon, illumination, luminosity, radiance, the moon
Ineisha—the sparkling lady
Ingita—gesture, intention
Inia—body of water
Inika—energetic, vigourous, glorious
Inika—little earth
Iniyal—sweet
Iniyamozhi—small earth, sweet language
Iniyaval—sweet
Iniya—kind, sweet, happy
Inka—hero's daughter, lover of horses
Inka—little earth
Inkitham—manners
Inkurali—sweet voice

Inmozhiyan—sweet voice, sweet language
Innah—good will
Insuvai—sweet
Inu—pleasing, favourite, charming
Ipsa—ambition, ambition, intent, passion
Ipsha—desire, aspiration, longing
Ipshita—ambition, intent, passion, goddess lakshmi
Ipsita—ambition, intent, passion
Ipsita—ambition, intent, passion, love of life, desire, aspiration, longed for
Iraivi—goddess saraswati, earth
Iraja—daughter of wind
Iravatee—ambition, intent, passion
Iravati—a river
Iravati—ravi river in india
Ira—earth, goddess saraswati
Ira—the earth
Ireejaya—victorious wind
Ireeka—a diminutive of the earth
Ireen—serenity, calm, calmness, stillness, silence
Ireshi—highness, empress, queen
Irfath—pretty, lovely, handsome, graceful name
Irijaya—victorious wind
Irija—daughter of wind
Irika—the earth
Irit—daffodil
Irshita—goddess saraswati
Iruvantika—wind's daughter
Isaiarasi—parkishit's wife
Isai—of gods, music
Isa—promise of god promise
Ishalya—temple of rich
Ishanavi—goddess parvati
Ishana—goddess durga
Ishana—prosperous, rich, goddess durga
Ishane—one who protects, faculty, power
Ishanika—belonging to the north east
Ishani—goddess durga, parvati
Ishani—parvati
Ishani—the ruling goddess
Ishanni—goddess parvati

Ishanvi—goddess of knowledge
Ishanvi—goddess parvati
Ishanya—north east
Ishareet—pretty, lovely, handsome, graceful name
Ishat—goddess of fire
Ishavari—same as god
Ishaya—one who protects
Isha—energy, goddess durga
Isha—one who protects
Isha—the goddess
Isheshwari—chief goddess
Isheta—superior
Ishika—sacred, sacred paint brush
Ishiqa—sacred, the highness, empress, queen of the water
Ishita—mastery, wealth superior, bright
Ishita—prosperity, the goddess
Ishitha—mastery, wealth, superior
Ishivita—highly qualified
Ishi—goddess durga
Ishi—goddess durgarrow, rock
Ishka—love
Ishmita—individuality
Ishmit—lover of god
Ishq—love
Ishrat—desire, aspiration, longingffection, enjoyment
Ishra—related to god
Ishrita—owner, lord
Ishtaa—name of goddess lakshmi
Ishtani—loveffection
Ishtara—one who is dear
Ishta—another name for lord vishnu
Ishti—gods sister
Ishudhi—quiver
Ishuka—arrow
Ishuya—omnipotent
Ishu—arrow
Ishu—god, jesus, desire, aspiration, longing, ambition, intent, passion
Ishvari—the best among the holy, pure, sanctified, pious, solemn
Ishvarya—lord shiva, master
Ishva—a spiritual teacher
Ishwarakant—durga
Ishwari—goddess

Ishwari—goddess, god gift, lover of god
Ishwarpreet—god's beloved
Ishwarya—god's prosperity
Ishyana—goddess durga
Ishya—spring season
Isika—brush, sacred pen
Isiri—wealth
Isita—ambition, intent, passion, greatness
Isla—island
Ismita—individuality
Isshu—jesus
Istuti—praises, prayer
Isvari—the best, the goddess
Iswarya—gold, scene, powerful
Itakshi—pretty, lovely, handsome, graceful name
Itara—another
Itcha—pretty, lovely, handsome, graceful, ambition, intent, passion
Itihasa—history
Itika—eternal, everlasting, single goddess
Itiksha—fire
Itishree—the end
Itixa—fire
Iti—end, last, start, respected
Itkila—fragrant
Itkila—perfumed
Itrika—fragrant
Ivanshika—grace of god
Ivy—climber, ivy plant
Iyalisai—music
Iyana—god is gracious, mirror, princess
Iya—pervading
Iyesha—form of iesha
Iyla—moon, illumination, luminosity, radiance
Iysha—living, prosperous, lively, woman
Iyuna—lover
Iyushi—long life
Iyyamani—pretty, lovely, handsome, graceful name
Izana—powerful woman

Izhaiamudu—pretty, lovely, handsome, graceful name
Izhainayaki—a creeper

Izna—illumination, luminosity, radiance
Izumi—water spring, fountain

****

Indian Names For Girls—J

Jaanvi—river ganga, valuable, valued, rare
Jaan—life
Jaba—love, hibiscus
Jabeene—intelligence
Jabeen—forehead, river ganga
Jabhen—forehead
Jabili—moon, full moon
Jaboah—deepak, illumination, luminosity, radiance
Jacinta—hyacinth bloom, garden stuff, purple bloom
Jafit—pretty, lovely, handsome, graceful
Jagadambal—forehead
Jagadamba—mother of the universe
Jagadambika—goddess durga
Jagada—world wide
Jagadeeshwari—goddess of the world
Jagadeity—goddess durga
Jagamata—mother of the world, goddess durga
Jagamohini—one who attracts the world
Jagamohini—one who captivates the universe
Jaganamatri—mother of the world
Jaganmata—mother of the world
Jaganmaye—goddess lakshmi
Jaganmohini—goddess durga
Jagatee—earth
Jagatee—mother of the world
Jagatha—world, universe
Jagathi—of the universe
Jagati—bestowed with speed
Jagavi—born of the world
Jagdamba—goddess
Jagdambika—goddess durga
Jageshri—world richness
Jagmohini—mahamaya, durga
Jagori—awake
Jagpreet—love for world
Jagrati—awakening
Jagriti—awakeness
Jagriti—awakening, motivate for truth
Jagriti—illumination, luminosity, radiance
Jagruthi—awakening
Jagruthi—awareness, creator
Jagruti—awarenesswakening, vigilance
Jagvi—worldly
Jahaira—ornament, jewellery, ornamentation, adornment, figuration, dignified
Jahal—goddess of power
Jahanara—highness, empress, queen of the world, universe
Jahanvi—moon illumination, luminosity, radiance
Jahanvi—river ganga
Jahan—the world
Jahel—lake
Jahnave—river ganga
Jahnavi—water, river ganga
Jahnkar—murmur
Jahnukanya—ganga
Jahnu—fire, flame, lord vishnu
Jahnve—river ganga
Jahnvika—river ganga
Jahnvi—another name for river ganga
Jaidhwani—shout of victory
Jaihasini—victory of happiness
Jaika—conqueror
Jaikirti—glory of victory
Jailekha—a record of victory
Jaimala—garland of victory
Jaimal—garland of victory
Jaiman—victorious
Jaimathi—victorious mind
Jaimati—victorious mind
Jaimini—victory
Jaimi—devotee
Jaimni—a gem
Jaimol—beloved girl
Jaina—the lord is gracious
Jainika—pretty, lovely, handsome, graceful name

Jainisha—god of jains, find
Jaini—name from god vishnu
Jainy—gift from god
Jaipriya—beloved of victory
Jairekha—pretty, lovely, handsome, graceful
Jaishila—character of victory
Jaishnavi—goddess of victory
Jaishna—clarity
Jaishree—goddess of victory
Jaishree—honour of victory
Jaishri—goddess of victory, victorious
Jaishwari—god winner
Jaisnavi—goddess of victory
Jaisri—honour
Jaisudha—nectar of victory
Jaisvi—victory, happiness
Jaiswee—victory of goddess
Jaisya—victory
Jaitali—pretty, lovely, handsome, graceful, name of goddess, happy
Jaitashri—name of a music raga
Jaithika—bloom, garden stuff
Jaiti—welcome, winning
Jaivanti—long lived, being victorious
Jaivati—bearer of victory
Jaivika—holy, pure, sanctified, pious, solemn
Jaiwanti—victory
Jai—bloom, garden stuff, victorious, jasmine
Jaji—the sea
Jajwalya—brightness of flames from yagna
Jakshani—god name
Jalabala—daughter of a river
Jalabala—name of river
Jalabalika—daughter of the waters
Jalabalika—illumination, luminosity, radiance
Jaladhara—stream of water
Jaladhija—water, goddess lakshmi
Jaladhi—ocean, treasure of water, sea
Jalahasini—smile of water
Jalajaa—water
Jalajakshi—jasmine, lotus eye, glimmers
Jalajakshi—lotus eye, glimmers

Jalaja—lotus
Jalaja—water, lotus
Jalaj—lotus
Jalakandeswari—lotus
Jalak—instant appearance
Jalandhara—goddess lakshmi, water bearer
Jalandhara—net
Jalaneli—moss
Jalanhili—as blue as water
Jalapa—discussion
Jala—elucidation, special one, charity
Jalbala—lotus bloom, garden stuff
Jalbala—wife of bhima
Jaldhi—sea
Jalebi—indian sweat
Jalela—goddess of water
Jalini—one who lives in water
Jalini—spider, goddess of water
Jalita—flow like water
Jalpana—river, joyful
Jalpa—discussion, short form of jalpari
Jalpoorna—full of water
Jalsa—celebration
Jalvi—name of river may, sacrifice
Jambavati—monarch, ruler, prince, earl of the bears
Jameela—pretty, lovely, handsome, graceful, pretty, elegant
Jamie—supplanter, feminine of james, one
Jamila—gorgeous woman, pretty, lovely, handsome, graceful
Jamina—pretty, lovely, handsome, graceful, graceful, elegant
Jaminie—bloom, garden stuff
Jamini—night
Jamirah—pretty, lovely, handsome, graceful one
Jamkudi—highness, empress, queen
Jamna—indian river
Jamunadeity—celebration
Jamunarani—river
Jamuna—holy river in india
Jamuna—the river yamuna
Janakideity—night
Janaki—wife of lord rama

Janaknandini—daughter of monarch, ruler, prince, king janak daughter, goddess
Janaksutta—daughter of janak
Janaktanaya—janak's daughter
Janam—incarnation
Janane—the mother
Janani—mother
Janani—mother, tenderness, goddess
Janapadi—an apsara
Janata—public, people
Janatha—lord of people
Janave—epithet of the river ganga
Janavika—name of a river
Janavi—lovely, name of river
Janavi—mother, genga
Jana—harvest gift, gift from
Jandi—flag
Janesa—gracious
Janesha—pretty, lovely, handsome, graceful name
Janeshtha—ambition, intent, passion by men
Janhavi—river ganga
Janhavi—the river ganga
Janhita—one who thinks of the welfare of the people
Janhvi—ganga, originated from the lap
Janic—god gift
Janika—generating
Janisha—di-speller of ignorance
Janitha—bloom, garden stuffs, born
Janitra—birthplace
Janki—another name of goddess sita
Janki—lord rama's wife, sita
Jankruiti—made of music, musical
Janmita—borned
Janmohini—charming
Jannat—heaven, garden, paradise
Janpti—brilliant, sagacious, gifted, wise, learned
Jansci—brave, victory highness, empress, queen
Janshi—the brave, victory, highness, empress, queen
Jansi—life-like
Jantananda—pretty, lovely, handsome, graceful name

Januja—daughter
Janu—sweet heart, loved once
Janvika—another name of goddess saraswati
Janvi—another name of river ganga, name
Janwi—name of kalika
Janya—born life
Japa—recitation
Japjit—love respective
Japya—name of goddess, who's name can be
Jarak—something special
Jaral—water fairy
Jarana—lake, small river
Jarita—old, decayed, female offspring
Jarna—lake, spring water small stream
Jarn—luster
Jarshika—god gift
Jarul—female, offspring, bloom, garden stuff, highness, empress, queen
Jasavi—reserved, pretty, lovely, handsome, graceful
Jashangeet—celebration song
Jashika—loveable, cute, life is pretty, lovely, handsome, graceful
Jashiktha—goddess lakshmi, gorgeous princess
Jashkitha—goddess lakshmi
Jashmina—bloom, garden stuff
Jashmir—strong, scents of the forest, wood, jungle
Jashmitha—smiley
Jashoda—mother of god krishna
Jashu—brainy
Jashvanti—the one who gets credit
Jashvica—clear victory, responsible
Jashvika—responsible, pretty, lovely, handsome, graceful
Jashvi—one who gets credit
Jashwanthi—one who gets credit
Jashwanti—one who gets credit
Jashwika—goddess santoshi
Jashwi—to be proud of self
Jasika—warrior, rich grace
Jasima—pretty, lovely, handsome, graceful
Jaslen—in the name of god, successful

Jasmeet—famed, helpful, glorious friend
Jasmeh—absorbed in praising god
Jasmika—fragrance
Jasminder—lord's glory
Jasmine—fragrant bloom, garden stuff, bloom, garden stuff of
Jasmin—a bloom, garden stuff name gift
Jasmira—ocean of fame, money, scents of
Jasmitha—smiles, smile like jasmine
Jasmit—famed
Jasmi—jasmine bloom, garden stuff, reserved
Jasna—pretty, lovely, handsome, graceful
Jasnen—pretty, lovely, handsome, graceful name
Jasoda—mother of lord krishna
Jasodhara—lord buddha's mother
Jasodhara—wife of lord buddha
Jasrani—highness, empress, queen of fame
Jasritha—name of goddess lakshmi
Jassika—pretty, lovely, handsome, graceful and cute
Jassi—special angel, beauty, jasmine
Jassu—amiable, pleasing, suave, interesting
Jasumati—brainy
Jasum—hibiscus, a plant
Jasu—brainy
Jasvandi—hibiscus bloom, garden stuff
Jasvanti—one who gets credit, brainy
Jasve—joy
Jasvika—pretty, lovely, handsome, graceful name
Jaswanthi—victorious
Jaswanti—famous
Jaswanti—famous woman
Jasweer—victorious
Jaswinder—thunderbolt of indra
Jaswitha—smile
Jatalika—with twisted hair
Jatini—female ascetic, one having culted

Javali—song type of dance
Javeria—name of deity
Jawala—flame, fire
Jaya-lakshmi—goddess lakshmi
Jayabala—victorious
Jayabala—victory
Jayabanu—pretty, lovely, handsome, graceful name
Jayabheri—victory drum
Jayachitra—pretty, lovely, handsome, graceful name
Jayada—victory giver
Jayadeity—victorious goddess
Jayadeve—goddess of victory
Jayadurga—name of durga
Jayagauri—victory of fair women, victorious
Jayakala—success of lord jagannath
Jayakirthi—winning
Jayalakshmee—goddess of victory
Jayalakshmi—goddess lakshmi representing
Jayalakshmi—goddess of victory
Jayalaksmi—goddess lakshmi representing
Jayalalita—goddess of victory
Jayalalita—victorious goddess durga
Jayalalitha—goddess durga
Jayalalitha—goddess of love, victory
Jayamala—garland of victory
Jayamangala—auspicious victory
Jayamma—mother is god
Jayamogini—garland of victory
Jayam—victory
Jayanisha—gold
Jayani—vigour of lord ganesha
Jayantee—garland of victory
Jayanthisri—victorious
Jayanthi—victorylways win, profit
Jayantika—goddess durga, parvati
Jayanti—goddess parvati
Jayanti—goddess parvati, victorious, flag
Jayan—victory
Jayaporna—final victory
Jayaprabhavathi—victorious
Jayaprabha—illumination, luminosity, radiance of victory

Jayaprada—giver of victory
Jayapradha—giver of victory
Jayapriya—giver of victory
Jayarani—victorious lakshmi
Jayasanthi—winning with piecefull
Jayashree—the goddess of victory, victorious
Jayashri—goddess of victory
Jayashwika—goddess durga, santoshi, victory
Jayasmita—victorious smile
Jayasri—goddess of victory
Jayasudha—nectar of victory
Jayasvi—pretty, lovely, handsome, graceful name
Jayaswamine—goddess durga
Jayata—victorious
Jayathi—victorious
Jayati—victorious
Jayatri—victorious
Jayavanti—being victorious
Jayavanti—victorious
Jayavardhini—goddess who increases victory
Jayavarsha—rain of success
Jaya—goddess durga
Jaya—victory, victorious, respect
Jayesha—stars
Jayeshtha—chief, first
Jayeta—one who is successful
Jayeta—winner
Jayita—victorious
Jayitri—victorious
Jaymini—an ancient philosopher
Jayna—gracious, the lord has been
Jayne—the lord is gracious, has shown
Jayne—vigour of lord ganesha
Jaynika—victorious
Jayshree—goddess of victory
Jayshri—goddess of victory, victorious
Jaysree—victorious, goddess of victory
Jaysri—goddess of victory
Jayvantika—in praise of goddess of victory
Jayvanti—daughter of lord indra
Jebisha—prayerful
Jeel—silent lake

Jeenal—lord vishnu
Jeenam—river
Jeena—life, god is gracious
Jeenisha—long live
Jeep—seemonarch, ruler, prince, earl
Jeeteshi—goddess of victory
Jeetesh—goddess of victory
Jeethika—winer
Jeet—victory
Jeevajothi—victorious
Jeeval—full of life
Jeevana—life
Jeevani—life
Jeevanjyoti—illumination, luminosity, radiance of life
Jeevankala—art of life
Jeevanlata—creeper of life
Jeevanshi—part of soul
Jeevanteeku—bloom, garden stuff
Jeevanti—a creeper
Jeevarani—art of life
Jeeva—life
Jeeva—life, water, the earth
Jeevika—life, water
Jeevisha—desire, aspiration, longing to life
Jeevita—life
Jeevitha—lifelive
Jeevi—alive, life
Jeevne—auto biography
Jeevprabha—splendour of life
Jeewanjyoti—illumination, luminosity, radiance of life
Jeeya—life, sweetheart
Jegasri—goddess lakshmi, radiance
Jegatha—truth of the world
Jehannaz—pride of universe
Jeiya—sweet heart live
Jelakshmi—victory, star
Jema—gem
Jemini—a gem
Jemisha—highness, empress, queen of night
Jenali—joined
Jency—wave, smart, amiable, pleasing, suave, interesting person
Jenika—god's gracious gift
Jenisa—preety girl

Jenisha—preety girl
Jenita—white wave, god is gracious
Jeni—white wave
Jenma—new born
Jennisha—lord is gracious
Jenny—white wave
Jensi—god is gracious, massage
Jenya—noble by birth, true
Jenysa—preety girl
Jeroo—thunder
Jerusha—married, possession
Jesal—water
Jeshma—mother of warrior
Jeshna—victory
Jeshri—victory
Jeshvika—responsible, practical
Jesica—he sees, the lord beholds
Jesicca—the lord beholds, foresighted
Jesika—warrior, he beholds, rich
Jesita—cool
Jeslin—wonderful, victorious, life
Jesmitha—meaning of life
Jesri—victory, jayasri
Jessica—warrior, he beholds, rich
Jessina—victory
Jessy—a bloom, garden stuff, clever
Jesvica—responsible, practical
Jeswanth—brilliant
Jeswika—goddess santoshi, one who gets
Jeswitha—mother of goddess lakshmi
Jetal—winner
Jetashri—a raga
Jevaria—name of bloom, garden stuff
Jeyarani—highness, empress, queen of victory
Jhalak—glimpse, spark, sudden motion
Jhanak—melody
Jhanavika—ganges
Jhanavi—river ganga
Jhana—stream of water, life
Jhani—glimpse, spark, sudden motion
Jhankaar—pretty, lovely, handsome, graceful sound to listen, voice
Jhankarine—murmur
Jhankari—jingling
Jhankar—murmur

Jhankar—sound
Jhansi—victory, the brave, highness, empress, queen
Jhanu—pretty, lovely, handsome, graceful and cute girl, darling
Jhanvika—river ganga
Jhanvi—river ganga, educated and a right
Jharana—flowing water, lake
Jharapata—removed leaves on the ground
Jhara—women of heaven, princess, highness, empress, queen
Jharna—a stream, water falls, spring
Jharna—water-fall
Jha—pretty, lovely, handsome, graceful, lake, waterfall
Jhelika—the sun illumination, luminosity, radiance
Jhel—a lake
Jhel—lake
Jhilmil—shining
Jhilmil—sparkling, rain drop
Jhil—lake, waterfall, female
Jhinuk—oyster
Jhoomer—ornament, jewellery, ornamentation, adornment, figurations
Jhoomer—sparkling
Jhovitha—joyful, pretty, lovely, handsome, graceful
Jhrna—lake
Jhui—pretty, lovely, handsome, graceful name
Jhumki—earring
Jiaan—most powerful
Jiana—life, god is gracious
Jianshi—part of heart
Jiara—heart
Jia—sweet heart, lively, pretty, lovely, handsome, graceful
Jibon—life
Jidnyasa—curiosity
Jiera—pretty, lovely, handsome, graceful one, life piece of
Jiganasha—art of life, curiosity
Jigayasha—to known about something
Jigeesha—required victory
Jiggyasa—curiosity

Jighyasa—ambition, intent, passion to know
Jigisha—ambition, intent, passion to know lord, superior
Jigi—goddess lakshmi
Jignasa—academic curiosity
Jignasha—curiosity
Jigna—intellectual curiosity
Jigruksha—the support, indoctrination, assuredness for knowledge
Jigu—earth
Jigyasa—curiosity, curiosity to know
Jigyasha—curiosity to know
Jigya—curiosity to know
Jiivitha—life
Jiiya—life, near heart
Jijabai—victorious woman, chatrapati
Jija—mother of lord shivaji maharaj
Jiksa—perfect
Jilav—sweet, cute
Jill—youthful, girl
Jilpa—life giving
Jimi—modern female version of jimmy
Jinali—great, grateful, blessed
Jinal—pretty, lovely, handsome, graceful, brainy
Jincy—cute
Jindal—steel monarch, ruler, prince, earl
Jinesha—preety girl
Jinisha—superior person
Jinita—daughter of mahavir jain
Jinkal—very innocent, sweet voice
Jinnat—glamour
Jinny—white wave, variant of jenny which
Jisha—the person having the highest
Jishna—associated with lord vishnu
Jishni—pretty, lovely, handsome, graceful name
Jisni—pretty, lovely, handsome, graceful, special, one of a kind
Jissy—god live, exist, rises
Jital—winter
Jithya—victorious
Jitika—pretty, lovely, handsome, graceful name

Jitya—victorious
Jiu—small bloom, garden stuff
Jivani—the one who gives life, holy, pure, sanctified, pious, solemn
Jivanshi—pretty, lovely, handsome, graceful name
Jivanta—to give life
Jivantika—one who gives life
Jivasha—life, source of life
Jiva—a living beinglive, life
Jiveka—alive, humble
Jiven—life
Jivepreeya—one who loves the life
Jivesha—source of life
Jivetha—sweet heartngel
Jivika—life, source of life
Jivinta—life
Jivisha—desire, aspiration, longing to life
Jivita—alive, life, lively, spirited
Jivitva—life, pran
Jiviya—life
Jivi—live, life
Jivsha—source of life, courageous, desire, aspiration, longing
Jivya—livelihood
Jiwa—soul, spiritlive
Jiyana—reborn, name of moon
Jiyancy—part of heart
Jiyanshi—part of heart, goddess
Jiyansi—part of heart
Jiyan—reborn, moon
Jiyara—heart
Jiyara—pretty, lovely, handsome, graceful name
Jiya—sweet heart, life, lucky piece
Jiyera—heart
Jiza—shivaji's mother
Jnanada—aupreme knowledge
Jnanada—women
Jnanameru—utmost knowledge, absolute, highest, best
Jnanavi—knowledge
Jnanika—having knowledge
Jnanitha—one filled with knowledge
Jnatanandana—son of the jnata family
Jnateya—pretty, lovely, handsome, graceful name

Jnatri—successful life
Jnnanvitha—having knowledge
Jnya—life, new born
Jodha—princess, warrior
Joel—god prophet in the bible
Joeshni—intelligence
Jogendra—union with god
Jogeshwari—devotee of lord shiva
Jogindar—with god
Joginder—union with god
Jogini—saintly
Johanna—god is grace, the lord is merciful
Johnsi—love in life
Joita—victorious, winner
Jokumari—always lovely
Jolly—happiness
Jonaki—jugnu
Joncy—brave
Joogamba—god
Joshika—bud
Joshika—young maiden, elder
Joshila—filled with enthusiasm
Joshini—brilliant, sagacious, gifted, wise, learned, loveable
Joshita—a woman
Joshita—pleased, joyful
Joshitha—pleased
Joshna—happiness
Joshnika—cupid or follower of lord shiva
Joshvika—god gift, goddess durga
Joshya—brilliant, sagacious, gifted, wise, learned, happiness, god
Josh—excitement
Josita—pleased, joyful
Jositha—pleased
Josmitha—brave, brilliant, sagacious, gifted, wise, learned
Josna—moon illumination, luminosity, radiance, brave, lotus
Josnika—happiness, follower of lord shiva
Josya—illumination, luminosity, radianceful
Jothi-lakshmi—brightness of goddess lakshmi

Jothika—illumination, luminosity, radiance, candle
Jothinandhini—goddess
Jothirani—young maiden
Jothisorubini—pleased
Jothisri—bright
Jothisudha—lamp, nectar
Jothi—illumination, luminosity, radiance, bright
Jotika—a flame, illumination, luminosity, radiance
Joti—illumination, luminosity, radiance of the lamp
Joufi—joyful
Jovita—joy, happy, god is salvation
Jovitha—joy
Jowaki—a firefly
Joyatri—illumination, luminosity, radiance
Joya—rejoicing, joy, cute, happiness
Joyeta—victorious
Joyita—winner, happiness
Joy—rejoicing, joy, jubilation, ornament, jewellery
Juabai—pretty, lovely, handsome, graceful name
Juana—gift from god, bloom, garden stuff
Judzea—simla
Jue—generosity
Juhena—fragrance, jasmine
Juhitha—jasmine
Juhi—a bloom, garden stuff
Juhi—jasmine bloom, garden stuff, strong
Juh—bloom, garden stuff
Juily—bloom, garden stuff jasmine bloom, garden stuff
Jui—a bloom, garden stuff
Jule—nice one
Julie—youthful
Juli—youthful, child, youth
Jully—name of a month
Juma—friday, holy day
Jumna—having food
Juniali—moon illumination, luminosity, radiance

Juthika—illumination, luminosity, radiance
Jvala—blaze
Jvesha—pretty, lovely, handsome, graceful name
Jwala—fire, bravery, flame
Jwala—the flame
Jwalitha—fire
Jyanavi—having knowledge, intellect, wise
Jyanshi—part of heart, goddess
Jyena—princess
Jyeshta—eldest daughter nakshatra
Jyestha—elder
Jyoshika—happy, joyful
Jyoshikha—a bud
Jyoshnasree—pretty, lovely, handsome, graceful name
Jyoshna—moon illumination, luminosity, radiance
Jyoshnika—pretty, lovely, handsome, graceful name
Jyostana—moon illumination, luminosity, radiance
Jyostna—radiant like flames, moon, illumination, luminosity, radiance
Jyothi-sre—illumination, luminosity, radiance of goddess durga
Jyothika—flame, illumination, luminosity, radiance
Jyothirmayi—illumination, luminosity, radiance
Jyothishmathi—goddess durga
Jyothisree—illumination, luminosity, radiance of wealthy
Jyothsna—moon illumination, luminosity, radiance
Jyotibala—splendour
Jyotibala—woman of flame
Jyotika—full of illumination, luminosity, radiance

Jyotika—illumination, luminosity, radiance flame
Jyotikiran—agni, flame
Jyotila—flame, lamp, candle
Jyotiprobha—head of candle flame
Jyotirmayi—lustrous
Jyotirmoye—bloom, garden stuff, goddess durga
Jyotisha—astrology
Jyotisha—knowledge of illumination, luminosity, radiance
Jyotishikha—flame of illumination, luminosity, radiance
Jyotishmatee—flame, lamp
Jyotishmati—illumination, luminosity, radiance
Jyotishmati—luminous, bright, lustering
Jyotishna—illumination, luminosity, radiance
Jyoti—flame, lamp, head of candle
Jyoti—illumination, luminosity, radiance
Jyotsana-sre—goddess durga
Jyotsana—radiant like flames, goddess
Jyotshana—moon illumination, luminosity, radiance
Jyotshna—smiling face, moon illumination, radiance
Jyotsinalata—creeper of moon-illumination, luminosity
Jyotsna—moon, illumination, luminosity, radiance
Jyotsna—smiling face, moon, illumination, luminosity, radiance
Jyotsne—moon, illumination, luminosity, radiance
Jyotsnika—moon
Jyotsnika—moon-illumination, luminosity, radiance

****

Indian Names For Girls—K

Kaberi—full of water
Kabita—poem
Kachnar—a bloom, garden stuff
Kadale—daughter of moon
Kadambari—bloom, garden stuff of kadamb
Kadambari—goddess, goddess saraswati
Kadambini—an array of clouds
Kadambini—name of a lady
Kadambi—cloud, orange bloom, garden stuff
Kadambri—name of a bloom, garden stuff
Kadhiroli—brilliant, sagacious, gifted, wise, learned, brilliant like a ray
Kaetki—bloom, garden stuff, holy, sanctified, pious
Kahalin—bloom, garden stuff
Kahali—strong
Kahini—storey, young
Kahini—young woman
Kahita—saying
Kahlima—the goddess form kali ma
Kahnsi—a treasure, holy, sanctified, pious, solemn, chaste
Kahr—colour, disaster
Kahta—holy, sanctified, pious, solemn, chaste
Kaia—chaste, stability, ocean or sea
Kaikeye, glimmers—wife of monarch, ruler, prince, earl dasharatha
Kailashi—name of a himalayan peak
Kailash—abode of lord shiva himalayan peak
Kailas—a himalayan peak
Kairavi—full moon, moon, illumination, luminosity, radiance
Kairavi—moon illumination, luminosity, radiance
Kairav—white lotus, serenity, calm, calmness, stillness, silence
Kaira—sweet, serenity, calm, calmness, pious, solemn, chaste

Kairravini—lotus plant
Kaishori—the adolescent, goddess parvati
Kaivalya—absoluteloneness
Kaivya—knowledge of poet
Kaiya—forgiving, creativity
Kajali—collyrium
Kajalsri—eye, glimmers liner
Kajal—black, eye, glimmers-liner
Kajal—collyrium, soot
Kajal—mascara, surma
Kajamukhi—lord vinayaka
Kajari—a woman with black eye, glimmers
Kajel—beauty
Kajjali—eye, glimmers liner
Kajol—eye, glimmers liner, mascara
Kajol—with pretty, lovely, handsome, graceful figure
Kajori—goddess parvati
Kajri—cloud like
Kakale—luster of lamp
Kakale—sweet
Kakali—chipping of birds, lady
Kakarav—voice of bird
Kakoli—chirping of birds at dawn
Kakon—insect, caterpillar
Kakoodine—daughter of mountain
Kaksha—white bloom, garden stuff, white rose
Kaksi—perfume
Kalabai—eye, glimmers-liner
Kalabharathi—traditional
Kalabjari—parvati
Kaladeity—goddess durga
Kalaiamudha—art
Kalaiarasi—topmost
Kalaimagal—highness, empress, queen of arts, goddess saraswati
Kalaimani—gem of arts
Kalaipoonga—possessing many artistic skills
Kalaiselvi—an art work, goddess saraswati

Kalaivani—goddess saraswathi, goddess of
Kalai—wrist
Kalakarni—goddess lakshmi, one with black ears
Kalaka—blue
Kalaka—pupil of the eye, glimmers, goddess durga
Kalandhika—bestower of art
Kalanidhi—treasure of art
Kalanidhi—treasure of art, moon
Kalanjari—parvati
Kalapini—peacock, night
Kalapi—peacock, nightingale
Kalapriya—lover of art
Kalarani—the highness, empress, queen of art
Kalashree—art's treasure
Kalash—a water pot, pitcher
Kalasi—pitcher
Kalavanti—artist, goddess parvati
Kalavathi—artist
Kalavati—artistrtistic, goddess parvati
Kalawanti—artist, goddess parvati
Kalawati—a woman with knowledge of arts
Kalawati—artist, goddess parvati
Kalayani—blessed, prospered
Kalayansundari—imagined
Kala— skill, ability, talent, art
Kala—the fine artsrt, miracle
Kalena—bloom, garden stuff name, place name
Kaleswari—chirpping of birds
Kalgi—feathers on a peacock's head
Kaliappa—pretty, lovely, handsome, graceful name
Kaligambal—a goddess
Kaliga—name of a place
Kalikaa—lustrous
Kalika—bud, deity durga
Kalika—group of clouds
Kalika—name of a goddess kalli small
Kalima—speaker, mouthpiece, blackness
Kalina—bloom, garden stuff name, place name
Kalinda—the sea

Kalindi—river yamuna
Kalindi—yamuna river
Kalini—bloom, garden stuff
Kalipada—goddess durga
Kaliyah—tender heart
Kaliyamma—blackish
Kali—goddess durga
Kali—graceful, pretty, lovely, handsome, graceful
Kalka—goddess durga
Kalka—pupil if the eye, glimmers, goddess durga
Kallie—most pretty, lovely, handsome, graceful
Kalli—most pretty, lovely, handsome, graceful, lark, singing
Kallole—full of joy
Kallole—one who is happy
Kalloline—surging waves
Kalloline—yamuna riverlways happy
Kallol—large wave of water
Kallol—large waves, gurgling of water
Kalmashi—river yamuna
Kalmeshika—variegated
Kalnisha—eve of diwali
Kalollini—stream
Kalol—chirp of birds
Kalpaka—imagine
Kalpalata—determination, secret desire, aspiration, longing
Kalpanalahri—idea, imagination, fancy
Kalpanarani—large waves
Kalpana—imagination
Kalpana—imagination, idea, fancy, imagine
Kalpavalli—bloom, garden stuff, durga
Kalpa—thoughtble, fit
Kalpika—proper, dream
Kalpini—night
Kalpita—imaginative
Kalpita—imagined
Kalpitha—imagination, creative, imagined
Kalpna—imagination
Kalvinka—a sparrow

Kalyani—pretty, lovely, handsome, gracefuluspicious, blessed
Kalyani—well-desire, aspiration, longinger
Kalya—praise
Kalynda—the sun
Kamada—granting ambition, intent, passions
Kamadha—granting ambition, intent, passions
Kamakashi—durga
Kamakhya—sincere, goddess durga
Kamakshe—goddess parvathi
Kamakshi—goddess durga
Kamakshi—one with loving eye, glimmers, goddess
Kamakya—goddess durga, granter of desire, aspiration, longinges
Kamakya—granter of desire, aspiration, longinges, goddess durga
Kamalaja—born of the lotus
Kamalakshi—pretty, lovely, handsome, graceful eye, glimmers
Kamalakshi—eye, glimmers like lotus
Kamalakumari—lotus
Kamalalaya—blissful, pretty, lovely, handsome, graceful
Kamalalochna—eye, glimmers like lotus
Kamalamanjari—one of krishna's maidservant
Kamalambal—lord of lakshmi
Kamalam—one with lotus like eye, glimmers
Kamalanayane—lotus eye, glimmers
Kamalapriya—goddess lakshmi
Kamalarani—goddess lakshmi
Kamalashree—lotus bloom, garden stuff, goddess maha lakshmi
Kamalasundari—pretty, lovely, handsome, garden stuff
Kamalatchi—pretty, lovely, handsome, graceful name
Kamalaval—pretty, lovely, handsome, graceful name
Kamalavarna—lotus eye, glimmers
Kamalavati—lotus-like
Kamalaveni—mother of lotus

Kamala—bloom, garden stuff, goddess, lotus
Kamala—goddess lakshmi
Kamalesh—goddess of lutus
Kamalika—lotus, goddess lakshmi
Kamaline—a lotus plant
Kamalini—lotus
Kamalini—lotus plant
Kamalin—lotus
Kamali—spirit guide, protector
Kamalkali—the bud of a lotus
Kamalnayan—lotus-eye, glimmers
Kamalvathi—lotus
Kamal—lotus
Kamana—ambition, intent, passion
Kamana—desire, aspiration, longing, ambition, intent, passion
Kamania—well figure, appearance, structured, pretty, lovely
Kamaniyam—pretty, lovely, handsome, graceful
Kamatchideity—lotus
Kamatchi—goddess parvati, lakshmi
Kamavarthini—one with lotus like eye, glimmers
Kamayani—an epic
Kamayani—desire, aspiration, longing, ambition, intent
Kamayani—shradha, ambition, intent, passion
Kama—the golden one, love
Kameelah—perfect
Kameel—pretty, lovely, handsome, graceful
Kameesha—pretty, lovely, handsome, graceful name
Kameshvari—goddess parvati
Kameshwari—goddess durga
Kameshwary—goddess lakshmi
Kamesh—lord of ambition, intent, passion
Kameswari—another name of parvati
Kamika—pretty, lovely, handsome, graceful, ambition, intent, passion
Kamile—highness, empress, queen
Kamil—perfect
Kaminia—shy

Kamini—desirable, pretty, lovely, handsome, graceful woman
Kamini—pretty, lovely, handsome, graceful woman
Kamini—worthy love pretty, lovely, handsome, graceful
Kamisha—silent
Kamitha—ambition, intent, passion
Kamiya—sweetheart
Kamla—lotus, goddess lakshmi
Kamla—perfect
Kamlesh—goddess lakshmi
Kamlesh—goddess of lutus
Kamlika—belongs to lotus bloom, garden stuff
Kamli—lotus
Kamli—lotus, goddess saraswati
Kamna—ambition, intent, passion, expectation, desire, aspiration, longing
Kamneva—desirable
Kamnika—pretty, lovely, handsome, graceful
Kamniva—pretty, lovely, handsome, graceful
Kamodee—that which excite
Kamod—pretty, lovely, handsome, graceful angel of love
Kamolika—soft, tender, little lotus
Kampana—unsteady
Kamryn—auspicious
Kamsa—happiness
Kamuka—ambition, intent, passion
Kamu—a woman
Kamyarshi—pretty, lovely, handsome, graceful
Kamya—lucky, pretty, lovely, handsome, graceful
Kanagadeity—one with lotus like face
Kanagadhara—ambition, intent, passion
Kanagamalai—an atom
Kanagamuni—pretty, lovely, handsome, graceful name
Kanagam—capable
Kanagavathi—pretty, lovely, handsome, graceful name
Kanaga—gold
Kanai—contentment

Kanakabati—a fairy-tale
Kanakakali—an ornament, jewellery, ornamentation, adornment, figuration
Kanakali—an ornament, jewellery, ornamentation, adornment
Kanakambri—woman wearing gold ornament, jewellery, ornamentation
Kanakapriya—one who loves gold
Kanakavalli—golden creeper
Kanakavathi—possessing gold
Kanaka—a bloom, garden stuff, gold
Kanaka—gold
Kanaklata—golden creeper
Kanakpriya—lover of gold
Kanakvi—small kite
Kanak—gold, wheat, shining like gold
Kanana—a garden
Kananbala—nymph of the forest, wood, jungle
Kanan—garden, dark forest, wood, jungle
Kanasu—dream
Kanav—a great rishi beauty
Kana—an atom, powerful
Kanchal—golden
Kanchanadeity—lord sri krishna
Kanchanamala—the nymph of the forest, wood, jungle, garland
Kanchana—gold
Kanchanprabha—golden illumination, luminosity, radiance
Kanchan—gold
Kanchita—pretty, lovely, handsome, graceful name
Kanchi—a waistband, clear like mirror
Kanchi—golden, waist band
Kanchi—waist-band
Kanchmala—gold necklace
Kanchruchi—shining as gold
Kanchuka—disquise
Kancy—honest
Kandapushpa—bloom, garden stuff
Kanda—darling, root knot
Kandhal—pleasing, favourite, charming
Kandhara—lute
Kandiri—the sensitive plant
Kandi—lustering

Kaneshka—black beauty
Kangana—bangles bracelet
Kangana—bracelet
Kangan—bangle
Kangavalli—brave
Kangkana—a young girl wearing
bangle
Kangna—bangles
Kangsha—ambition, intent, passion,
desire, aspiration, longing, want
Kanhsi—like lord krishna treasure
Kanikasri—pretty, lovely, handsome,
graceful name
Kanika—an atom
Kanika—smalltom, black, molecule,
seed
Kaniksha—gold, little finger, small,
indian
Kanimoli—speaks with a gentle tone
Kanimozhi—sweet language
Kanira—grain
Kanisa—nice, pretty, lovely,
handsome, graceful church
Kanisha—one with pretty, lovely,
handsome, graceful eye, glimmers
Kanisha—one with pretty, lovely,
handsome, graceful eye, glimmers,
diamond
Kanishiya—pretty, lovely, handsome,
graceful eye, glimmers
Kanishkaa—pretty, lovely, handsome,
graceful blue diamond, gold
Kanishka—gold, daughter of monarch,
ruler, prince, earl kanishq
Kanishka—pretty, lovely, handsome,
graceful name
Kanishkha—gold
Kanishk—name of a famous monarch,
ruler, prince, earl
Kanishna—cute
Kanishthaka—little finger
Kanishtha—the youngest daughter
Kanishthika—small finger
Kanish—diamond
Kaniska—gold
Kaniskka—a gold
Kanitha—iris of the eye, glimmers
Kaniya—young girl, virgin

Kanizah—young girl
Kani—sound, pretty, lovely,
handsome, graceful girl
Kanjani—goddess of love
Kanjari—a bird
Kanjri—bird
Kankalini—one with necklace of
bones
Kankana—a bracelet
Kankana—the one who has the power
on music
Kankane—a small bell
Kankangi—gold
Kankasha—ambition, intent, passion
Kankatika—a comb
Kanka—scent of the lotus
Kanksha—ambition, intent, passion,
desire, aspiration, longing
Kanmani—eye, valuable, glimmers
Kannagi—treasonable women
Kannaki—devoted and virtuous wife
Kannambal—grain
Kannathal—a goddess
Kanneswari—bird
Kanniyammal—the apple of one eye,
glimmers's
Kannmalar—pretty, lovely, handsome,
graceful name
Kannmani—one who is liked the most
Kannu—name of a god
Kansate—pretty, lovely, handsome,
graceful name
Kansha—ambition, intent, passion
Kanshika—gold, moon, nil
Kansiyanila—pretty, lovely,
handsome, graceful name
Kansiya—holy, sanctified, pious,
solemn, chaste
Kantagauri—pretty, lovely, handsome,
graceful fair women, radiant
Kantapushpa—bloom, garden stuff
row on the neck
Kanta—earth, pleasing, favourite,
charming woman
Kanta—gorgeous pretty, lovely,
handsome, graceful, radiant
Kanteli—irresistible
Kanthan—name of lord muruga

Kantharani—beauty
Kantha—name of a god, radiant, pretty, lovely, handsome, graceful
Kanthika—a single spring
Kanthi—spiritual mala, necklace, lustre
Kantikara—pretty, lovely, handsome, graceful name
Kantimalika—a woman's girdle
Kanti—desire, aspiration, longing, ambition, intent, passion
Kanti—lustre, illumination, luminosity, radiance, brightness, sings
Kanttadhara—holder of lord shiva's neck
Kanuja—lowell warmth
Kanupritha—lover of kanha (radha)
Kanupriya—beloved of krishna
Kanupriya—beloved of lord krishna, goddess
Kanushi—beloved
Kanush—beloved
Kanu—name of lord krishna
Kanvi—flute, name of radha, bansuri
Kanwal—lotus
Kanyaka—goddess durga, the youngest girl
Kanyaka—virgin
Kanyakumari—the eternal virgin, maiden
Kanyal—stern
Kanyana—maiden
Kanya—lustre
Kanya—woman with youth, daughter
Kapaline—goddess durga
Kapalini—another name of goddess durga
Kapalini—durga
Kapardika—shell
Kapardini—a goddess
Kapardini—durga, goddess parvati
Kapatamalini—goddess durga
Kapila—name of the celestial cow
Kapila—simple woman
Kapile—with tawny waves
Kapinjala—a river
Kapoori—whitest beauty

Kapotakshi—eye, glimmers like a pigeon's
Kapotvaran—pigeon complexion
Karabi—a bloom, garden stuff
Karala—opening wide, tearing, goddess
Karalika—that which tears
Karalika—that which tears, goddess durga
Karane—action
Karan—holy, sanctified, pious, solemn, chaste, sweet melody, life
Kara—legend, graceful, pretty, lovely, handsome
Kardami—full moon
Kareena—holy, sanctified, pious, solemn, chaste white, bloom, garden stuff
Karenumati—like a female elephant
Karen—chaste, holy, sanctified, pious, solemn
Karida—untouched, virginal
Karigai—a woman
Karika—actress
Karina—blessed, chaste, holy, sanctified, pious
Karina—bloom, garden stuff, chaste, holy
Karini—elephant
Karisha—charcoal
Karishma—miracle
Karishma—strange, wonder
Karishna—honest
Karishvi—good person
Karish—pleasing, favourite, charming
Karisma—favour, gift, miracle
Karismhma—miracle
Karissa—grace, kindness, very dear
Karka—crab
Karla—peasant, farmer, strong, little
Karmanasa—a river which destroys one's evil
Karma—a starction, fate, destiny
Karmistha—extremely diligent
Karnapriya—sweet to the ears
Karne—with ears
Karnikaa—creeper, heart of lotus
Karnika—a name of creeper, earring

Karnika—gold, heart of the lotus, earrings
Karona—merciful, forgiving
Karpagambal—nakul's wife
Karpagam—richness
Karpagapriya—miracle
Karpagaveni—pretty, lovely, handsome, graceful name
Karpardini—goddess durga
Karpukarasi—pretty, lovely, handsome, graceful name
Kartavya—duty
Kartheswari—goddess born on kirthigai
Karthiaeini—indian goddess name
Karthiayini—indian goddess name
Karthica—a god's daughter
Karthic—strong, brave, son of lord shiva
Karthiga—simple, pretty, lovely, handsome, graceful
Karthika—lamp, character of angel, illumination, luminosity, radiance
Karthika—sun rice
Karthik—a hindu month, one who bestows
Karthi—love and affection
Kartika—pretty, lovely, handsome, graceful
Kartiki—strong, brave, bestowing courage
Kartikka—illumination, luminosity, radiance
Kartisha—lovely, handsome, graceful, bloom, garden stuff
Kartiyani—name of goddess durga
Karuka—heavenly piece of art
Karuli—innocent
Karunamaye—full of pity for others
Karunamayi—merciful compassion
Karunambal—goddess of mercy
Karunambigai—heavenly piece of art
Karunasindhu—ocean of mercy
Karuna—sympathy, compassion, mercy
Karuna—tender, pity
Karuneshwari—goddess of mercy
Karungurali—innocent

Karunika—compassion, caring
Karunya—compassionate
Karunya—compassionate, goddess lakshmi
Karunya—compassionate, merciful, goddess
Karvari—a name of the goddess durga
Karvira—cow
Kasak—test
Kashamaya—merciful
Kasha—perhaps, pretty, lovely, handsome
Kashikanya—pretty, lovely, handsome, graceful name
Kashika—name of a place, kaashi, banaras
Kashika—the shiny one
Kashini—bloom, garden stuff, goddess lakshmi
Kashin—compassionate, brightness
Kashish—an attraction
Kashi—the holy city, luminous, radiant
Kashmira—from kashmir, the holy city
Kashmir—heaven
Kashni—special
Kashta—direction
Kashta—luminous, pilgrimage spot
Kashti—a canoe
Kashvini—star
Kashvi—bright shining star
Kashvi—shining, blooming, goddess of luck
Kashwini—star
Kashwi—unique
Kashyapee—earth
Kashyapi—earth
Kasis—attraction
Kasivisalatchi—red, kumkum, goddess with big eye, glimmers
Kasiyammbal—shining
Kasi—holy city, blossoming
Kasmika—lotus
Kasmira—from kashmir, calm, calmness, stillness, silence
Kasni—bloom, garden stuff
Kasthuri—deer

Kastor—fragrance, love
Kasturba—a valuable, valued, rare stone
Kasturika—musk of deer
Kasturi—musk
Kasturi—musk fragrant material, earth
Kastur—fragrance of love
Kasu—gold coin, money
Kasu—luster
Kasvi—bright, brightness, shining
Kasyapa—name of a sage
Katelyn—chaste, holy, sanctified, pious, solemn, chaste
Kathakali—a dance form
Kathambari—holy, sanctified, pious, solemn, chaste, clean, happy
Kathan—storey teller
Katha—distress, form of catherine, holy, sanctified, pious, solemn, chaste
Kathiksha—beginnings
Kathinya—musk fragrant material
Kathyayani—goddess parvati
Kathyayini—goddess of power
Katikee—holy, the full moon, illumination, luminosity, month of kartik
Katrina—chaste, holy, sanctified
Kattyayani—goddess parvati
Katyayane—moon illumination, luminosity, radiance
Katyayani—sage katyanan worships this name
Katyayine—goddess parvati
Katyayini—one of name of goddess
Kaudambi—the full moon, illumination, luminosity, radiance
Kaumaari—adolescent, goddess parvati
Kaumadee—the moon, illumination, luminosity
Kaumari—the virgin
Kaumudee—moon, illumination, luminosity, radiance
Kaumudini—lotus
Kaumudi—illumination, luminosity, radiance of the moon
Kaumudi—moon, illumination, luminosity, radiance

Kausalya—mother of rama
Kausar—lake of paradise
Kaushaliya—lord ram's mother
Kaushali—skillful
Kaushalya—mother of rama
Kausha—silken
Kaushbi—pretty, lovely, handsome, graceful name
Kaushey—silken
Kaushika—a cup
Kaushika—friend of universe, silk
Kaushikee—hidden
Kaushikee—moon, illumination, luminosity, radiance
Kaushiki—river, enveloped with silk
Kausthuba—lord vishnu's gem
Kaustubhi—stone in lord vishnu's necklace
Kaustuki—goddess lakshmi, yoga of devotion
Kautirya—one who resides in a hut, goddess
Kautki—full of curiosity
Kautukee—one who is curious
Kavale—bracelet
Kavana—poem
Kavarya—moon
Kavera—goddess durga
Kaveri—a holy river
Kaveri—name of a river
Kaveri—name of a river in india
Kaver—name of love, river
Kaver—saffron
Kavia—full of imagination poetic
Kavia—lotus
Kavika—poetess
Kavikuil—pretty, lovely, handsome, graceful singer, sweet voice
Kavimalar—lord rama's mother
Kavinaya—poet, good girl
Kavindra—mighty poet
Kavinisha—pretty, lovely, handsome, graceful name
Kavini—composes pretty, lovely, handsome, graceful poems
Kavinya—poet
Kavin—handsome, pretty, lovely, handsome, graceful

Kavipriya—a river
Kavisha—poet, poetry
Kavishree—prosperous poet
Kavishri—goddess lakshmi, poetess
Kavisri—goddess lakshmi
Kavitanjali—a collection of poems
Kavita—poetic, poem
Kavita—poetry
Kavitha—wise, poetry, poem, poet, poem
Kaviya—poem, beauty of love
Kavi—cute
Kavi—poem, poet wise person
Kavni—a small poem
Kavrinthika—shining star
Kavri—pretty, lovely, handsome, graceful name
Kavsir—goddess lakshmi
Kavya-shri—poem
Kavyanjali—a poet of kadambari, offering of
Kavyapriya—pretty, lovely, handsome, graceful name
Kavyashree—lord sarasvati's name
Kavyasri—pretty, lovely, handsome, graceful name
Kavyatree—poetess
Kavya—famous poem
Kavya—poem, poetry in motion poetic
Kavya—poetry in motion
Kayalvili—fish-like pretty, lovely, handsome, graceful eye, glimmers
Kayal—name of a fish, lovely eye, glimmers
Kayashree—poem
Kayashta—a caste, holy, pure, sanctified, pious, solemn
Kayayine—goddess parvati
Kaya—body structure, nature goddess
Kayna—gold
Kayomi—love
Kayra—princess, unique
Kazanna—treasure
Kazhmir—place
Keasha—brilliant, northern star
Kedareshwari—lord of lord shiva
Kedarnatha—lord shiva
Kedma—towards the east

Keemaya—miracle
Keerataniya—one who is worthy of praise
Keera—lady, dark, black, feminine form
Keeritika—famous
Keerrtana—holy, sanctified, pious, solemn, chaste form of worship
Keertana—hymn song in praise of god
Keertan—worship
Keerthana—poem, music, singing, song
Keerthika—glory
Keerthisha—reputation, fame
Keerthi—fame, eternal flame, proud, winner
Keertida—one who is famous
Keertika—glory, fame
Keertimalini—garlanded with fame
Keertimati—goddess saraswati
Keerti—fame
Keerti—glory, fame
Keesha—life, woman, great joy
Keetal—pretty, lovely, handsome, graceful
Kehani—pretty, lovely, handsome, graceful girl
Keiarah—serenity, calm, calmness, stillness, sweet
Keisha—cassia tree, her life, woman
Keiyona—morning star
Kejal—eye, glimmersliner, kohl
Kekaa—sound of peacock, voice of a
Kekala—hymn song in praise of god
Kekavala—devotional song
Kekavalli—the cry of peacock
Kelikamala—shukracharya's daughter
Kelika—fame, sport amusement
Kelila—crowned, crown of laurel
Keli—strife, war, energy, dark goddess
Kena—pretty, lovely, handsome
Kendra—understanding, knowledge, family
Kenga—river
Kenisha—a person with pretty, lovely, handsome, graceful life
Kenum—brave
Keny—bright

Keosha—lovely
Kerani—sacred bells
Kera—holy, sanctified, pious, solemn, chaste, dusky, dark, black-haired
Keren—a ray of support, indoctrination, assuredness
Kesaree—saffron coloured
Kesari—saffron
Kesari—saffron lion
Kesar—saffron, pollen, lion
Kesavalli—style of pretty, lovely, handsome, graceful hair
Kesavi—wife of lord vishnu
Keshane—pretty, lovely, handsome, graceful hair
Keshavi—beloved of lord krishna, radha
Kesha—hair, stays awake, watches over me
Kesheka—pretty, lovely, handsome, graceful long hair
Keshika—a woman with pretty, lovely, handsome, graceful hair
Keshine—long-haired
Keshini—a woman with pretty, lovely, handsome, graceful hair
Keshin—saffron, lion
Keshitha—star
Keshi—a woman with pretty, lovely, handsome, graceful hair
Keshni—girl with long hair
Keshni—with pretty, lovely, handsome, graceful hair
Keshori—young cream coloured bloom, garden stuff
Keshvi—one with long pretty, lovely, handsome, graceful hair
Keshwati—a women with pretty, lovely, handsome, graceful hairs
Kesini—one with pretty, lovely, handsome, graceful hair
Kesvi—lord krishnattachment, one with
Ketaa—a flag
Ketakee—a cream coloured bloom, garden stuff
Ketaki—a bloom, garden stuff

Ketaki—a cream coloured bloom, garden stuff monsoon
Ketal—at the top
Ketana—home, dare, enjoy
Ketika—talented girl
Ketki—holy, sanctified, pious, solemn
Ketumala—pretty, lovely, handsome, graceful name
Ketu—one with pretty, lovely, handsome, graceful hair
Kevala—whole, holy, sanctified, pious, solemn, chaste
Kevali—holy, pure, sanctified, pious, solemn one
Keval—vishnu, holy, sanctified, pious, solemn, chaste, only
Keva—pretty, lovely, handsome, graceful child
Kevika—bloom, garden stuff
Keya—a monsoon bloom, garden stuff
Keyura—ornament, jewellery, ornamentation
Keyuri—armlet
Khadgini—goddess durga
Khailash—abode of lord shiva
Khaivya—lucky, bloom, garden stuff
Khamoshe—serenity, calm, calmness, stillness, silence
Khanak—sweet sound, sound of the bangles
Khandana—smiling, happiness
Khandine—the earth
Khanija—mother earth
Khanika—noble character
Khanish—pretty, lovely, handsome, graceful, loving
Khanjan—dimples
Khank—sweet sound
Khasindu—moon
Khasphatika—the moon gem
Khastane—the earth
Khavia—dream
Khavya—poem
Khayale—imagination
Khayal—thought, thinmonarch, ruler, prince, earl, imagination
Khayati—fame
Khayati—goodwill

Khel-priya—one who loves sports
Kheranshi—sweet
Khevna—desire, aspiration, longing, ambition, intent, passion
Kheyali—imaginative
Khia—boat
Khili—blooming
Khilna—blooming
Khilti—bloom, growing
Khira—ray of illumination, luminosity, radiance
Khivani—joy
Khoobi—characteristics, quality
Khooshi—happiness
Khragni—fire
Khrisha—lord krishna, holy, pure, sanctified, pious, solemn
Khuabpreet—full of dreams
Khuhshi—happiness
Khusali—happiness
Khusboo—fragrance
Khusbu—sweet smell, fragrance
Khuseema—more happiness
Khushali—happiness
Khushali—prosperity,—happiness
Khushboo—pretty, lovely, handsome, graceful fragrance, nice smell
Khushbu—fragrantromatic, sweet
Khushe—happiness
Khushie—happiness
Khushika—happiness
Khushi—happiness, joylways smile
Khushmita—happiness
Khushvika—reason for happiness
Khushvi—happiness
Khusi—happiness, pleasure, feelings
Khusmita—happy
Khusnuma—happiness forever
Khwahish—desire, aspiration, longing
Khwaish—ambition, intent, passion
Khyata—famous, known, one having
Khyatee—fame, reputation, popularity
Khyathi—fame, reputation, popularity
Khyath—famous, popular
Khyatika—having goodwill, famous, known
Khyati—fame
Khyati—fame, reputation, popularity

Khyati—knowledge, celebrity, idea, praise
Khyat—famous
Kiaasha—pretty, lovely, handsome, graceful name
Kianaa—holy, pure, sanctified, pious, solemn, princess
Kiansh—modern name of lord shiva
Kiara—dark, little dark one, clear
Kiarra—bright, famous, princess, dark
Kiasa—pretty, lovely, handsome, graceful name
Kichadh—dirt
Kichu—loveable, sweet heart
Kiki—wolf, she-wolf, favourite, from
Kilimoli—pleasing voice, parrot's speech
Kilimozhiyal—bloom, garden stuff
Kimatra—pretty, lovely, handsome, graceful
Kimaya—miracle, magic, holy, pure, sanctified, pious, solemn
Kimorna—moon
Kimti—valuable
Kimya—silent
Kim—from the royal fortress meadow
Kinaari—shore
Kinari—shore
Kinaya—complete
Kina—smaller, little one, bold
Kinchita—not a little bit
Kinisha—the one who remove darkness
Kinishka—little princess
Kinjala—brook
Kinjalika—pollen of bloom, garden stuff
Kinjal—river bank, emotional, filament
Kinju—calm river
Kinnari—demi god
Kinnari—musical instrument, goddess
Kinnary—goddess of wealth
Kinnera—red eye, glimmers, ray
Kintuben—pretty, lovely, handsome, graceful athlete
Kinu—a fruit like orange

Kirali—pretty, lovely, handsome, graceful name
Kirana—a ray of illumination, luminosity, radiance
Kiranila—love forever
Kiranjit—luminosity, radiance, holy, pure, sanctified
Kiranmala—a garland of illumination, luminosity, radiance
Kiranmayi—full of rays, radiant
Kiranmoyi—bright girl
Kiranpal—protector of rays
Kiranpreet—sun rays, love, love of rays
Kiranyasri—goddess lakshmi, money, lucky
Kiranya—rays of illumination, luminosity, radiance
Kiran—luminosity, radiance, holy, pure, sanctified
Kiran—rays
Kirath—pretty, lovely, handsome, graceful, goddess
Kirati—fame
Kirati—goddess durga the heavenly
Kirati—goddess parvati
Kireeti—another name for arjun
Kiren—radiance, luminosity, radiance
Kiriba—pretty, lovely, handsome, graceful name
Kirina—ray of illumination, luminosity, radiance
Kirishika—have love and kindness
Kirithika—a beam of illumination, luminosity, radiance
Kirit—crown
Kiri—luminosity, radiance, logical, mountain
Kirra—sun, throne leaf, dark lady
Kirsi—anointed, follower of christ
Kirtana—praise
Kirthana—devotional song, song
Kirthanya—a form of worship, songs of
Kirthigaiselvi—goddess durga
Kirthika—achiever, famous action
Kirthisha—pretty, lovely, handsome, graceful name

Kirthi—eternal flame
Kirtibala—fame, glory
Kirtika—sister of kartikey, a deity
Kirti—fame, glory
Kirti—fame, glory, reputation
Kirtmalini—garlanded with fame
Kirubavathi—goddess
Kiruba—grace, grace of god
Kisa—lord krishna, sun, illumination, luminosity, radiance
Kishala—a germinated seed
Kishmish—sweet as grapes
Kishnati—respect
Kishnita—lovely, respectful, caring
Kishoree—young girl
Kishore—young one
Kishori—a young girl, teenage
Kishori—young girl
Kishu—illumination, luminosity, radiance, lustre, lusterous
Kismat—luck
Kisori—youthful
Kisva—pretty, lovely, handsome, graceful name
Kittu—amiable, pleasing, suave, interesting
Kitu—singer
Kiva—pretty, lovely, handsome, graceful, lotus, protected
Kiyana—illumination, luminosity, radiance, deity
Kiyara—sweet
Kiya—the cooing of a bird, jovial lady
Kiyra—little dark one, princess
Kiyushka—brave
Knnikadeity—fame
Knnika—cristle
Knyashia—princess
Kodainayaki—leader
Kodeswari—beauty, rich
Kodhai—pretty, lovely, handsome, graceful girl
Kodialli—pretty, lovely, handsome, graceful name
Kodimalar—a young and slim girl
Kodimani—pretty, lovely, handsome, graceful name
Koel—a bird river in punjab, india

Kohala—kashish
Kohana—little bloom, garden stuff
Kohinoor—valuable, valued, rare diamond, ornament
Kohinur—valuable, valued, rare diamond, the bird
Kohlasa—fine
Kojagara—pretty, lovely, handsome, graceful name
Kokaha—bloom, garden stuff
Kokilaka—pretty, lovely, handsome, graceful name
Kokilam—feels of god
Kokilarani—cuckoo, nightingale
Kokilavaani—goddess saraswathi
Kokila—cuckoo, nightingale
Kokila—the cuckoo bird
Kokil—a bird
Kolamayil—peacock
Kolambee—shiva's lute
Kolambi—the flute of lord shiva
Komaari—pretty, lovely, handsome, graceful adolescent, goddess
Komalagita—soft song
Komalanga—tender
Komalangi—tender body
Komalata—calm
Komala—delicate
Komala—tender, soft
Komalika—tender, sensitive
Komali—tender
Komal—smooth, soft, delicate
Komal—soft, tender, sweet
Komatha—gods cow
Komilla—soft, pretty, lovely, handsome, graceful
Komlangi—sensitive
Kommona—pretty, lovely, handsome, graceful name
Komonika—valuable, valued, rare, sensitive
Kompali—bud
Kompal—bud
Komya—quick thinker
Konalaka—pretty, lovely, handsome, graceful name
Konali—tender

Konavadin—pretty, lovely, handsome, graceful name
Kona—angle, corner of a room
Konika—horn
Konika—related to bird koyal
Konva—corner
Koolvati—pretty, lovely, handsome, graceful name
Kootharasi—happy
Koothayi—pretty, lovely, handsome, graceful name
Kopal—a rose bud, gulab ki kali, new leaf
Kopanaka—pretty, lovely, handsome, graceful name
Kopisha—intelligence, wise
Koraka—name of the river
Korenia—pretty, lovely, handsome, graceful name
Kosha—cashier, origin, treasure
Koshin—bud, the mango tree
Koshna—active
Kosika—a river in north india river
Kosi—a river in north india
Koski—sweet
Kotapa—word
Kotavi—fun
Koteeswari—very rich
Kothai—goddess
Kotihoma—angel
Kotijit—conquering millions
Kotilakshakshi—goddess parvati's daughter name
Kotilinga—river name
Kotira—wonder
Kotishree—goddess of million
Koti—extreme corner, edge
Koumudi—full moon
Koundini—pretty, lovely, handsome, graceful name
Koundinya—name of a sage
Kour—princess
Kousaki—half moon
Koushaki—pretty, lovely, handsome, graceful name
Koushalya—mother of lord rama
Koushani—a nice place

Koushan—pretty, lovely, handsome, graceful name
Koushika—goddess of earth, pretty, lovely, handsome, graceful girl
Koushikha—sweet hearted, nice
Koushiki—goddess durga
Kousmita—good nature
Kousthubha—prayer
Kousumi—like a bloom, garden stuff
Koutuk—to pamper
Kovalum—silicate, valuable, valued, rare
Kovidh—wise
Kovisha—pretty, lovely, handsome, graceful name
Kowsika—happiness
Koyal—a bird
Koyal—a bird, voice of bird
Koyel—the cuckoo, bird
Koyna—the cuckoo
Koysha—pretty, lovely, handsome, graceful name
Kramani—pretty, lovely, handsome, graceful name
Krami—action, fate, destiny
Kranadasi—the sky and the earth
Krandasi—the sky and the earth
Krantee—revolution
Kranti—revolution
Kratajna—pretty, lovely, handsome, graceful name
Kratika—creation of star singer
Krati—creator, rachna
Kreemy—delicious
Kreena—holy, sanctified, pious, solemn, chaste, lord krishna
Kreesha—fame, blessing, holy, pure, sanctified, pious, solemn
Kreetika—name of bright star
Kreeti—pretty, lovely, handsome, graceful name
Kresha—holy, pure, sanctified, pious, solemn, blessing, fame
Kreshni—devotee of lord krishna
Kriday—lord krishna
Kridha—a goddess of purity, devotion
Krinal—brave

Krina—helpful, holy, sanctified, pious, solemn, chaste
Krinshi—cute
Kripacharya—drona's brother in law
Kripal—merciful
Kripasagar—full of kindness
Kripa—favour
Kripa—mercy, kind, blessing
Kripee—sister of kripa
Kripita—pretty, lovely, handsome, graceful
Kripi—pretty, lovely, handsome, graceful, wife of aacharya dron
Krippi—wife of guru
Krisanya—devotee of lord krishna, goddess
Krisa—holy, pure, sanctified, pious, solemn, fame, kind
Krishana—draupadi
Krishanga—slender
Krishang—lord shiva
Krishankanta—lord krishna
Krishanu—fire
Krishanya—devotee of lord krishna, goddess
Krishavi—pretty, lovely, handsome, graceful name
Krisha—holy, pure, sanctified, pious, solemn, blessing, fame
Krisha—holy, pure, sanctified, pious, solemn, kind, blessing, fame
Krishendu—lord krishna
Krishieka—grower, prosperity
Krishika—agriculture, name of god krishna
Krishita—powerful, illumination, luminosity, radiance, saintly woman
Krishitha—symbolising prosperity and nature
Krishi—agriculture, farming, princess
Krishma—strange, wonder
Krishma—sun rays
Krishmita—kind of season, miracle
Krishmitha—pretty, lovely, handsome, graceful name
Krishmit—pretty, lovely, handsome, graceful name

Krishna-priya—beloved of lord krishna
Krishna-veni—music of lord krishna
Krishnaa—love, serenity, calm, calmness, stillness, harmony
Krishnachand—lord krishna
Krishnadeva—lord krishna
Krishnakali—a bloom, garden stuff
Krishnakali—revolution, bloom, garden stuff
Krishnakanta—beloved of krishna
Krishnakumari—pretty, lovely, handsome, graceful
Krishnala—holy, pure, sanctified, pious, solemn
Krishnal—lord krishna
Krishnamala—draupadi
Krishnamurari—lord krishna
Krishnamurthy—lord krishna
Krishnan—lord krishna
Krishnapriya—lord krishna's favourite, ambition, intent, passion
Krishnaroop—lord krishna's copy
Krishnavale—black tulsi plant
Krishnaveni—a braid of black hair
Krishnavi—lord krishna
Krishna—draupadi
Krishne—admirable, devoted to lord krishna
Krishne—dropadi the wife of the five pandavas
Krishne—favour
Krishnika—belongs to krishna
Krishnika—blackness
Krishti—culture
Krishty—culture
Krishva—lord krishna, lord shiva
Krishvi—lord krishna
Krishwa—lord krishna
Krishya—tensity of purpose
Krish—sculpture, knowledge, victory
Krisma—strong, miracle
Krismita—pretty, lovely, handsome, graceful name
Krisshia—lord krishna and lord shiva
Krissi—lord krishna
Kristi—christiannointed, follower of
Kristy—mindnointed, follower of

Krisu—dearest one, lord krishna
Krisvi—pretty, lovely, handsome, graceful name
Kritagya—a grateful person
Kritant—lord vishnu
Kritanu—skillful, clever
Kritanya—angel of clever, lord vishnu
Kritarthi—satisfied, being happy
Kritashala—abode of action
Krita—perfection, created
Kriteshni—pretty, lovely, handsome, graceful name
Kriteyu—immortal
Krithiga—star
Krithika—admirable, star
Krithiksha—goddess parvathi granted
Krithinidhi—fame and wealth
Krithi—creation of god, work of art
Krithya—action
Kritika—a star
Kritika—one star, formation of stars
Kritiksha—pretty, lovely, handsome, graceful name
Kritiman—creator, sculpture
Kritisha—lord krishna work of art
Kritivarma—krishna's friend
Kritivi—accomplished
Kriti—a work of art, workchievement
Kriti—creation
Kritsnavidh—omniscient
Krittika—a holy star, the plaids,
Krittika—the god of war, the third of twenty seven lunar mansion
Krittishna—pretty, lovely, handsome, graceful name
Kritu—mercifulness
Kritve—accomplished
Kritvi—accomplished
Kritya—actionchievement
Kriva—unique, gift from god
Kriyanshi—performance
Kriya—performance
Kriya—performance, action
Krizuh—pretty, lovely, handsome, graceful name
Kroopa—kindness, grace, favour, blessing
Krounch—a bird

Krroora—brutal, goddess parvati
Krshane—dark night, beloved of lord krishna
Krshnavi—sweetest
Krudhaya—pretty, lovely, handsome, graceful name
Krunali—beauty of gold
Krupali—kind, who always forgives, ruler
Krupal—unparalleled kindness
Krupasankari—god who helps
Krupavathi—grace, serenity, calm, calmness, stillness, silence
Krupa—blessing, grace, favour, kindness
Krushangi—farmer
Krusha—delicate
Krushika—one shining pearl
Krushitha—legend, hard workerchiever
Krushi—agriculture, hard work
Krushmika—pretty, lovely, handsome, graceful name
Krushnali—belongs to lord krishna
Krushnaveni—lord krishna's flute
Krushna—pretty, lovely, handsome, graceful, darkness
Krushnika—lord krishna
Krutaghna—pretty, lovely, handsome, graceful name
Krutee—art, figure, appearance, structure
Krute—worn
Kruthika—name of a star
Kruthi—creative, one of goddess lakshmi
Krutica—image, creature
Krutika—image, creaturertificial
Kruti—recipe, creation
Kruttika—peacock
Krystal—ice monarch, ruler, prince, earl clear, brilliant
Ksema—safety, security, welfare
Kshamashel—who forgives
Kshama—forgiveness, tolerance, durability
Kshamita—serenity, calm, calmness, stillness

Kshamya—earth
Kshanaprabha—illumination, luminosity, radiance
Kshanika—electricity
Kshanika—momentary
Kshanprabha—electric
Kshanprabha—illumination, luminosity, radiance
Kshantee—tolerance
Kshantu—patient, enduring
Kshapa—night
Kshaunish—monarch, ruler, prince, earl
Ksha—cultivated earth
Kshemaa—a prosperous woman
Kshemalata—creeper of welfare
Kshemandhar—name of a manu in jain mythology
Kshema—serenity, calm, calmness, stillness, tranquil, goddess durga
Kshema—wealthy, prosperous
Kshemenkari—creation
Kshemya—goddess durga
Kshemya—goddess of welfare, goddess durga
Ksherja—goddess of wealth, lakshmi
Kshetra—place
Kshipa—night
Kshipra—fast, swift
Kshipra—name of a river in india
Kshipra—speedily
Kshipva—elasticized
Kshiraja—goddess lakshmi
Kshiraj—nectar, pearl
Kshirin—bloom, garden stuff, milky
Kshirja—goddess lakshmi
Kshirsa—goddess lakshmi
Kshitaditee—born from the earth
Kshitha—visible
Kshithija—earth
Kshithi—earth
Kshitija—earth, cute, horizon, highness, empress, queen
Kshitija—wife of shree ram
Kshitij—the lord of the earth
Kshitika—daughter of the earth
Kshitika—earth
Kshitipal—monarch, ruler, prince, earl

Kshiti—earth
Kshiti—the earth, a home
Kshma—goddess durga, pardon
Kshonhi—immovable
Kshoni—the earth
Kshubha—the ministery of the sun
Kshunu—fire
Kshyamarani—highness, empress, queen of pardon
Kuberchand—god of wealth
Kuber—god of wealth
Kudana—holy, sanctified, pious, solemn, chaste, gold, sparkling
Kudrat—nature
Kugapriya—elasticized
Kugha—pretty, lovely, handsome, graceful name
Kuhaneshwary—lord
Kuhan—man who offered service to lord
Kuhuk—sound of koyalia (bird)
Kuhu—the sweet note of the bird
Kuili—the earth
Kuja—goddess durga, drama
Kujitha—a jumper
Kukshija—born from the womb
Kukur—bloom, garden stuff
Kulagna—descended from noble family
Kulakeerthi—fame of the family
Kulakodi—the banner of community
Kulamani—ornament, jewellery, ornamentation, adornment
Kulangna—a woman from noble family
Kulapavai—goddess durga
Kulavardhini—developer of the race
Kuldeepa—the earth
Kulenvanshika—from the noble family
Kulshrestha—a woman from noble family
Kulvanti—noble, gentle
Kulwinder—ornament, jewellery, ornamentation, adornment
Kumaaril—pretty, lovely, handsome, graceful name
Kumari—unmarried girl or daughter
Kumari—unmarried lady

Kuma—illumination, luminosity, radiance of the family
Kumbha—earthen pot
Kumbhine—figure, appearance, structured like jar
Kumdwathi—river
Kumkum—vermilion
Kumkum—vermilion, saffron, red colour
Kumudani—a lotus
Kumudavanitta—loved woman
Kumuda—pleasure of the earth, lotus
Kumuda—red lotus
Kumudbala—lotus bloom, garden stuff
Kumudchandrika—lotus in moon-illumination, luminosity, radiance
Kumudha—pleasure of the earth
Kumudika—lotus of water lilies
Kumudini—a lotus, type of bloom, garden stuff
Kumudini—lotus
Kumudni—white lotus
Kumudprabha—water lily in moon, illumination, luminosity, radiance
Kumudvatee—lotus plant
Kumudwati—sacred powder, red
Kumud—lotus
Kumutha—loveable heart
Kunamalai—lotus
Kundaline—lotus pond
Kundana—pretty, lovely, handsome, graceful
Kundane—bunch of jasmine
Kundanika—creeper of jasmine
Kundanika—name of bloom, garden stuff, golden bloom, garden stuff
Kundan—gold, holy, sanctified, pious, solemn, chaste diamond
Kunda—jasmine blossom, bloom, garden stuff
Kundhavai—thanjavur monarch, ruler, prince, earl's sister name
Kundhavi—name of a bloom, garden stuff
Kundhimadeity—gold
Kundhi—siting
Kundini—an assemblage of jasmines
Kunhi—a soft bud of a plant

Kunica—bloom, garden stuff
Kunika—bloom, garden stuff
Kunika—pupil of the eye, glimmers
Kunisha—rosebud, hushed
Kunitala—woman with long hair, lock of hair
Kunjalata—cuckoo
Kunjalata—forest, wood, jungle creeper
Kunjala—koel
Kunjala—living in shrubs
Kunjal—cuckoo, nightingale
Kunjamma—god's name
Kunjana—forest, wood, jungle girl
Kunjani—one with sweet voice
Kunjan—name of a girl
Kunjan—waves of sounds
Kunja—grove of trees
Kunjika—born from the grove
Kunjilata—a creeper in grove
Kunjutham—pretty, lovely, handsome, graceful name
Kunju—like a little bird
Kunj—little one, lord krishna
Kunshita—pretty, lovely, handsome, graceful name
Kunshi—shining
Kuntala—a woman with luxurious hair
Kuntala—lady with pretty, lovely, handsome, graceful hair
Kuntal—hair
Kuntee—mother of pandavas
Kunthi—motherly
Kunti—a bee, mother of pandavas of mahabharata
Kunti—spear, the mother of the pandavas
Kupara—hair
Kupaya—please, request
Kurangi—a deer
Kurangi—deer
Kurinji—special, bloom, garden stuff which blooms once
Kuruvilla—unconquerable, invincible
Kusala—safe
Kusalini—bloom, garden stuff
Kushada—straightforward
Kushaja—pandavas' mother

Kushali—clever girl
Kushal—expert
Kushbu—fragrance
Kushika—happy
Kushira—happiest, capable artistic
Kushita—an adjective to happy as happiest
Kushivaani—lord shiva, good news
Kushi—happy, happiness
Kushka—pretty, lovely, handsome, graceful name
Kushmanda—ash guard, pumpkin
Kushmandini—born from a pumpkin
Kushmita—happy
Kushvitha—happy, goddess lakshmi
Kusmitha—blossomed, bloom, garden stuffs in bloom
Kusumanjali—an offering of bloom, garden stuffs
Kusumavati—bloom, garden stuffing
Kusuma—bloom, garden stuff
Kusumbala—bloom, garden stuff
Kusumgeet—bloom, garden stuff
Kusumita—blossomed
Kusumita—like a bloom, garden stuff, blossomed
Kusumlata—bloom, garden stuffing creeper
Kusumlata—bloom, garden stuffing, creeper
Kusummanjari—friend of goddess parvati's mother
Kusummodini—fragrance
Kusumrekha—bloom, garden stuffing
Kusum—a bloom, garden stuff pretty, lovely
Kusum—bloom, garden stuff
Kutaja—good
Kutaka—song of a bloom, garden stuff
Kuta—from where
Kuthodaree—wealthy
Kutila—curved
Kuvalai—bloom, garden stuff
Kuvalaya—lotus, world
Kuvalayine—plenty of water lilies
Kuvalayita—decorated with water lilies
Kuvam—sun

Kuvera—fighter of earth
Kuvira—courageous woman
Kuvrani—princess
Kuwayesha—cute, pretty, pretty, lovely, handsome, graceful
Kuyilsai—sweet voice like a cuckoo bird
Kuyil—cuckoo bird, sweet voice
Kuzhali—petal of a bloom, garden stuff

Kwaish—desire, aspiration, longing
Kyara—famous, little, dark
Kyathi—fame, prestigious
Kyivreeti—intelligence, tolerance, durability, toleration, beauty
Kyna—intelligence, wise, love
Kyra—little dark, princess, like the
Kyvalya—god name, heaven

****

Indian Names For Girls—L

Labangalata—sun, bloom, garden stuff, creeper
Labanya—pretty, lovely, handsome, graceful, beauty
Labdhi—heavenly power
Labham—profit, gain
Labhanshi—profitable
Labha—profit
Labhu—good, pleasure
Labonita—graceful, pretty, lovely, handsome, graceful one
Laboni—graceful
Labuki—musical instrument
Lacchu—sweet
Ladhi—sangeet
Ladli—loved one, the dearest one
Lado—god of marriage, mirth, pleasure
Lado—sweet, god gifted
Lagan—dedication
Laghima—goddess parvati
Laghuvi—tender
Laghu—blood, small
Lahanvi—goddess lakshmi
Lahari—waves, tender
Lahar—the wave
Lahek—pretty, lovely, handsome, graceful name
Laher—wave, flow
Lahita—smooth
Lahkshmi—goddess of wealth
Laiba—most prettiest angel of heaven
Laila—sweetheart, night beauty
Laina—form of alaina, path, roadway
Lairya—hindu goddess
Lajaka—modest
Lajita—modest
Lajjaamaye—full of modesty
Lajjaka—modest, a bashful woman
Lajjashela—one with modest character
Lajjashel—modest woman
Lajjavatee—full of modesty
Lajjawati—a sensitive plant, modest woman
Lajjawati—modest woman
Lajja—modesty
Lajjetta—a shameful woman
Lajjini—shy, modest
Lajjita—modesty, shy
Lajli—shy, blushing
Lajni—shy
Lajo—full of modesty
Lajvanti—shy
Lajvati—shy, shyness
Lajwantee—shyness
Lajwantie—god of illumination, luminosity, radiance
Lajwanti—sweet sensitive plant, modest
Lajwati—modest
Laj—modesty
Laj—shyness, honour, respect
Lakashya—pretty, lovely, handsome, graceful name
Lakha—writer
Lakhini—one who gives and takes
Lakhi—bronze colour
Lakhi—goddess lakshmi
Lakhmi—goddess of fortune, luck
Lakhshmi—goddess of fortune
Lakhsman—quality of mind
Lakhvinder—modesty
Laksayasri—respect toward target
Laksena—beauty, goddess lakshmi
Lakshakee—made of lac
Lakshaki—goddess sita
Lakshana—qualities
Lakshana—symbol, duryodhana's daughter
Lakshanya—the one who achieves in life
Lakshan—symptom
Lakshaya—aim, destination
Laksha—aim, white rose
Laksha—one which is made from wax
Laksha—white rose
Laksheta—distinguished
Lakshetha—distinguished

Lakshe—goddess of riches
Lakshika—aim, distinguished
Lakshita—recognised, seen
Lakshita—who has some aims
Lakshitha—aim, destination, goddess lakshmi
Lakshi—goddess lakshmi
Lakshmi-priya—beauty, wealth, goddess lakshmi
Lakshmibai—goddess lakshmi, goddess of
Lakshmibala—goddess lakshmi
Lakshmibanta—duryodhana's daghter name
Lakshmideity—goddess name and money
Lakshmideity—one who achieves woman
Lakshmikanta—distinguished
Lakshmika—goddess lakshmi
Lakshmikumari—wife of vishnu
Lakshminanda—prospirity
Lakshmipriya—beloved of goddess lakshmi
Lakshmisaraswati—lakshmi and saraswati
Lakshmishree—fortunate, goddess lakshmi
Lakshmitha—goddess lakshmi
Lakshmi—goddess of wealth
Lakshmi—goddess, goddess of wealth, wife
Lakshmi—observing, goddess of wealth
Lakshna—characteristics, character
Lakshna—symbol
Lakshyadeep—target, candleim
Lakshya—aim
Lakshya—aim, destination
Laksmi—goddess, wife of lord vishnu
Laladitya—red sun
Lalamani—ruby
Lalana—pretty, lovely, handsome, graceful lady
Lalana—pretty, lovely, handsome, graceful woman
Lalanika—caress

Lalantika—an ornament, jewellery, ornamentation, adornment
Lalan—nurturing
Lalasa—ambition, intent, passion
Lalasa—love
Lalasa—prayer
Lala—tulip, well-spoken, well spoken
Lalenthika—goddess lakshmi
Lalika—a slender, graceful woman
Lalima—beauty, wife of vishnu, redness
Lalima—blushing, reddish tint
Lalitaka—favourite darughter
Lalitakshi—one with playful eye, glimmers
Lalitalochan—a woman with pretty, lovely, handsome, graceful eye, glimmers
Lalitanga—one with pretty, lovely, handsome, graceful body
Lalitangee—a woman who possesses pretty, lovely, handsome, graceful body
Lalitangee—one with pretty, lovely, handsome, graceful body
Lalita—pretty, lovely, handsome, graceful woman, variety, beauty
Lalita—pleasing, favourite, charming, pretty, lovely, handsome, graceful
Lalithabai—ardent ambition, intent, passion
Lalithadeity—darling
Lalithakumari—wife of vishnu
Lalithamani—variety, beauty
Lalithambigai—fine arts
Lalithamohini—pretty, lovely, handsome, gracefulttractive
Lalitha—pretty, lovely, handsome, graceful woman woman form
Lalithkala—fine arts
Lalitkala—nurturing
Lalitochana—a woman with playful eye, glimmers
Lalitya—goddess durga, charm, loveliness
Lalitya—loveliness
Lali—a girl
Lali—blushing, darling, song girls

Lalli—blush, radiance, prestige
Lalsa—ardent, ambition, intent, passion
Lalsa—greedy
Lalsa—want, ambition, intent, passion
Laltesh—love
Lambane—hanging down
Lamees—soft touch, holy, sanctified, pious, solemn, chaste
Lamha—time
Lamika—goddess lakshmi, lucky
Lamisa—new born bloom, garden stuff, soft to touch
Lamita—slim girl creeper
Lamiyah—lustrous
Lamya—sweet lips, dark-lipped, of dark
Lani—heavenly womanngel from above
Lanka—island
Lapaya—diamond
Lapita—voice
Laranda—holy, pure, sanctified, pious, solemn
Laranya—graceful, goddess lakshmi
Larathana—pretty, lovely, handsome, graceful goddess
Larika—information, pretty, lovely, handsome, graceful
Larina—affection, soul, sea gull
Larisa—cherful, pretty, lovely, handsome, graceful
Larmika—a name of goddess lakshmi
Lasaki—sita, made of lac
Lashya—happiness
Lasika—highness, empress, queen of horizon, injection
Lasik—tender heart
Lasritha—always laughing
Lasyavi—smile of goddess lalita
Lasya—graceful, dance performed by
Lasya—graceful, happy, dance performed
Latacharya—pretty, lovely, handsome, graceful name
Latakara—mass of creepers
Latakastureeka—musk creeper
Lataka—body style

Latamani—a small creeper
Latangi—slim girl
Latangi—slim girl creeper
Latanji—a creeper
Latavya—one having creeper like body
Lata—a creeper
Lata—vine plant, creeper, vine
Lateesha—love
Lathambal—pretty, lovely, handsome, graceful name
Latha—holy, pure, sanctified, pious, solemn, wine
Lathika—elegant, happiest person small
Lathiksha—welcome
Lathisha—good
Latikara—mass of creepers
Latika—pretty, lovely, handsome, graceful, pleasing, favourite, charming
Latika—tendril, climber delicate tree
Latik—coconut syrup
Latyayana—slim girl
Laugheye, glimmers—copper coloured
Lauhitya—a river
Lavalika—a small creeper
Lavali—a creeper
Lavali—close, clove
Lavanaa—mineral
Lavanakshi—pretty, lovely, handsome, graceful eye, glimmers
Lavanamayi—one who is endowed with beauty and charm
Lavana—lustrous, pretty, lovely, handsome, graceful, salt
Lavana—lustrous, shiny
Lavana—the brightness
Lavanet—full of love, amiable, pleasing, suave, interesting
Lavangalata—clove creeper
Lavanga—clove
Lavangee—clove plant
Lavangee—with fragmented body
Lavangi—an angel, clove plant
Lavangi—name of a apsara
Lavanglata—clove vine
Lavanglata—pretty, lovely, handsome, graceful creeper

Lavanika—pretty, lovely, handsome, graceful
Lavanika—talkative, small creeper
Lavani—grace
Lavani—the graceful woman
Lavanny—pretty, lovely, handsome, graceful
Lavanshi—greenery
Lavanyag—grace
Lavanyakumari—delicate, creeper of clove
Lavanyalata—clove
Lavanyamayi—full of beauty
Lavanya—grace
Lavanya—grace, shiny
Lavanya—gracefulness, pretty, beauty
Lavelen—cool
Lavena—pretty, lovely, handsome, graceful
Lavenet—soccer
Lavenia—pretty, lovely, handsome, graceful name
Lavenia—purified
Lavika—grace
Lavina—mother of the romans, woman of
Lavisha—charming, pretty, lovely, handsome, graceful, love of god
Lavishka—lovely and lavish
Lavi—amiable, pleasing, suave, interesting, brave, lioness
Lavlen—absorbed
Lavli—loveable
Lavnya—attraction, grace, honest, beauty
Lavya—renowned for her devotion to her
Lavy—love
Laxita—famous, lucky
Laxsha—goddess lakshmi, pretty, lovely, handsome, graceful loving
Laxy—target
Layaki—ability
Layana—lives by the lane
Laya—musical rhythm
Laylah—night beauty
Layla—dark beauty, wine, intoxication
Layra—beauty

Laysa—dance
Laysa—worshipper, dance performed by
Leana—pledge, noble, nobility, sun, illumination, luminosity, radiance
Ledari—sweet
Leekshitha—written
Leelabai—miraculous, magician
Leelamaye—playful
Leelarani—goddess durga
Leelavathi—playful, goddess durga
Leelavathy—pretty, lovely, handsome, graceful name
Leelavati—goddess durga
Leelavati—playful, goddess durga
Leelawati—goddess durga, playful
Leela—holy, pure, sanctified, pious, solemn drama, play, amusement
Leela—play of god
Leelima—lovely
Leelu—a form of sugar, sugar cane
Leemanshi—strong character
Leenakshi—having eye, glimmers of devotion
Leenata—humility
Leenatha—humility
Leenavati—devoted, goddess of devotion
Leena—a devoted one, tender, illumination, luminosity, radiance, free
Leena—devoted
Leenulenu—tender
Leepaakshi—girl with peacock eye, glimmers
Leepakshi—painted eye, glimmers
Leepa—to spread
Leesha—fortunate, happy
Leeya—to take
Lehak—a illumination, luminosity, radiance, shines very bright
Lehar—wave, flow
Leher—wave
Lehitha—pretty, lovely, handsome, graceful
Leica—loved one
Leisha—happiness, pretty, lovely, handsome, graceful angel
Leivina—dragnet

Lekhana—power, pen, written poem, painting
Lekha—play, sport
Lekha—writing, picture
Lekhitha—writer
Lekhna—writing picture
Lekhya—mathematician, beauty, world
Lekisha—life, woman, cherful
Lekshana—pretty, lovely, handsome, graceful
Lelayamana—playful
Lela—black beauty, born at night
Lema—eye, glimmers, the beauty of an eye, glimmers
Lena—illumination, luminosity, radiance, pledge, bright one
Lenisha—pretty, lovely, handsome, graceful
Leora—illumination, luminosity, radiance
Lepakshi—with painted eye, glimmers
Letchumi—goddess of wealth
Levana—white, moon, shining white one
Levinika—infinite
Leysha—brilliant, sagacious, gifted, wise, learned, brilliant
Leyshya—colour
Libhiya—princess
Libni—manuscripts of god
Libuja—a creeper
Libuji—a creeper
Ligu—writing, picture
Ligy—bloom, garden stuff of angel
Lijina—energetic
Likha—written
Likhita—writing, lord saraswati, studious
Likhitha—writing, studious
Likhitri—pretty, lovely, handsome, graceful, goddess durga
Likita—writing
Likitha—writer, writing, goddess sarswathi
Likshita—pretty, lovely, handsome, graceful name
Lilavanti—god's will, purity, pleasure

Lilavati—god's will, playful, goddess durga
Lilawati—playful will, goddess durga
Lilawatti—to write
Lila—good, night, feminine of lyle
Lillian—blend of lily and ann
Lilly—lily, the bloom, garden stuff lily is a symbol
Liluma—pretty, lovely, handsome, graceful name
Lily—a bloom, garden stuff
Lily—lily, form of lillian, manuscripts
Limisha—twinkling of an eye, glimmers
Limna—special, the one, most knowledge
Limpa—leaf, bloom, garden stuff
Linasha—pretty, lovely, handsome, graceful
Lina—alive, pledge, noble, nobility
Lincy—a lake place of linden, garden
Lineysha—brilliant, sagacious, gifted, wise, learned
Lingadeha—pretty, lovely, handsome, graceful name
Lingadharini—wearing a badge of lord shiva
Lingammal—goddess parvati
Lingamurti—a bloom, garden stuff, lord shiva
Lingasarna—pretty, lovely, handsome, graceful name
Lingastha—lord shiva, birth from linga
Linga—part of lord shiva, gender
Lingin—long life
Linika—dedicated
Linisha—brilliant, sagacious, gifted, wise, learned
Linnet—idol small bird, little lake
Linu—illumination, luminosity, radiance, bright
Lipika—a short letter
Lipika—writing, litterslphabets, short
Lipi—script
Lipi—script, manuscripts of god
Lipsa—desire, aspiration, longing get more, ambition, intent, passion
Lipsika—smile, lipstick

Lira—love
Lirisha—truth, pretty, lovely, handsome, graceful angel
Lisbei—creative and brilliant, sagacious, gifted, wise, learned girl
Lisha—fortunate woman mystery
Lishika—cute, pretty, lovely, handsome, graceful, talented
Lishita—gold rice, good, cute
Lishitha—good, gold rice
Lithika—cute and perfect
Lithikkaa—pretty, lovely, handsome, graceful name
Lithiksha—brilliant, sagacious, gifted, wise, learned, beauty, cute
Lithisha—happiness
Litisha—happiness
Litvya—angel
Lityati—pretty, lovely, handsome, graceful name
Litya—happy
Livana—greece goddess, white
Liya—pretty, lovely, handsome, graceful, brilliant, sagacious, gifted, wise
Liza—consecrated to god, variation of
Locakasha—pretty, lovely, handsome, graceful name
Locana—universe, world
Locava—manuscripts of god
Lochana—a woman with pretty eyes, lovely, handsome, graceful
Lochana—bright eye, glimmers
Lochan—bright eye, glimmers
Lochan—the eye, glimmers
Logambal—goddess parvati
Loganayagi—leader of world
Loganayaki—goddess parvati, rulers of world
Logapriya—love of world
Logaratchagi—bright eye, glimmers
Logasundari—eye, glimmers
Logavani—miracle women
Logeshwari—ruler of the world
Logita—sweet
Logitha—beauty
Lohavara—pretty, lovely, handsome, graceful name
Lohinika—iron lady
Lohini—red skinned, red
Lohitaka—pretty, lovely, handsome, graceful name
Lohitakshe—red eye, glimmers
Lohita—red, ruby, lilli, sun, illumination, luminosity, radiance, copper
Lohita—ruby, red
Lohitha—goddess lakshmi in the form of
Lohitika—the ruby
Lohitiya—rice
Lohitya—rice
Lokaishana—pretty, lovely, handsome, graceful name
Lokajanani—mother of the world, goddess lakshmi
Lokakanta—thorn for the world
Lokakshi—eye, glimmers of universe, goddess lalita
Lokamatri—mother of the universe, goddess
Lokamaya—a form of goddess durga
Lokaniya—pretty, lovely, handsome, graceful name
Lokanksha—one who loves world
Lokanuraga—one who loves world
Lokapalini—one who rules the world, world
Lokapati—lord shiva
Lokesha—lord of monarch, ruler, prince, earl, water
Lokeshwari—pretty, lovely, handsome, graceful name
Lokhi—goddess lakshmi
Lokini—goddess who cares all
Lokitha—the illumination, luminosity, radiance one
Lokshani—pretty, lovely, handsome, graceful name
Loksha—pretty, lovely, handsome, graceful
Lokshita—pray for world
Lokshitha—pray for world
Lokya—goddess lakshmi group of people
Lolaksi—vigour of lord ganesha

Lola—lady of sorrows, strong woman
Lolika—love
Lolita—full of sorrows, ruby
Lolita—person who is roving
Lolithya—pretty, lovely, handsome, graceful name
Lolo—wealth
Lomaa—laxami maa
Lona—bliss, solitary one, lioness
Loneka—one who is aloof
Lonika—goddess lakshmi
Lopamudra—agastya rishi's wife
Lopamudra—wife of saint agastya, learned
Lopa—wife of sage, weaver, name of
Lopika—sweetness
Lord—pretty, lovely, handsome, graceful name
Lorena—crowned with laurels, sweet bay
Loshana—combination of rose and anna
Loshini—love, pretty, lovely, handsome, graceful and pleasing, favourite, charming
Loshitha—name of bloom, garden stuff
Loshtadeva—ruby
Lotica—give illumination, luminosity, radiance to others
Lotika—sorrel
Lotika—sorrel, illumination, luminosity, radiance reddish-brown
Loukya—goddess lakshmi, worldly wise
Loukyini—no
Lovanya—attraction
Loveiska—pretty, lovely, handsome, graceful name
Lovelen—loved one
Lovely—pleasing, favourite, charming, pretty, lovely

Lovenet—love
Lovisha—love
Lovya—piece of love
Lovy—love
Loxi—a rose with pink stem, sweet
Lubaba—the innermost essence, beauty
Lubaina—the innermost essence
Lubdhaka—hunter
Lubhawni—one who illumination, luminosity, radiance all
Lucia—bringer of illumination, luminosity, radiance
Luckyta—to be lucky
Lucky—luckiest
Lukasni—god of illumination, luminosity, radiance
Lukeshwari—highness, empress, queen of the empire
Lulaya—learned
Lumbika—a musical instrument
Lumbini—grove, place name
Lunasha—beauty and brightness of bloom, garden stuffs
Luna—moon, purity, lovely, bloom, garden stuff
Lunthanadi—pretty, lovely, handsome, graceful name
Luntha—pretty, lovely, handsome, graceful name
Luptika—who can hide easily, star
Lusi—fame, loud
Lussi—bright
Luta—pretty, lovely, handsome, graceful, pretty
Luttaka—pretty, lovely, handsome, graceful name
Luvlen—imbued, infusedbsorbed in love
Luxmi—goddess of money, goddess lakshmi

****

Indian Names For Girls—M

Macayla—unique
Machakanni—happiness
Madalsaa—honoured
Madana—goddess of love
Madanika—aroused, excited
Madayanika—a kind of jasmine
Madayanitika—exciting
Madhabee—as sweet as honey
Madhari—sweety
Madhavaselvi—goddess durga
Madhaveshta—ideal, model, idea
Madhave—goddess
Madhavika—creeper
Madhavilata—spring creeper
Madhavi—sweet, honeycreeper with
Madhevi—sweet
Madhi—moon, brilliant
Madhoolika—nectar
Madhubala—sister of madhubhala
Madhubala—sweet girl
Madhubhala—honey spear
Madhuchanda—pleasing metrical
composition
Madhuchhanda—sweet rhythm,
pleasing metrical
Madhuja—made of honey
Madhuja—the earth
Madhukanta—a creeper with fragrant
bloom, garden stuffs
Madhukartika—enormous
Madhuksara—one who showers honey
Madhulata—sweet creeper, lovely vine
Madhulatha—sweet creeper
Madhula—sugar, sweet
Madhulekha—pretty, lovely,
handsome, graceful
Madhulekha—a girl as sweet as honey
Madhulika—nectar, honey
Madhulika—sweet and pungent
Madhuli—mango tree
Madhulla—pomegranate
Madhul—sweet
Madhumalati—bloom, garden stuffing
creeper

Madhumalti—a creeping plant
Madhumani—pretty, lovely,
handsome, graceful name
Madhumanjari—sweet sprout
Madhumathi—illumination,
luminosity, radiance moon
Madhumati—full of honey
Madhumeeta—sweet friend
Madhumeet—friend of honey
Madhumita—honey
Madhumita—sweet honey, charming
Madhumitha—sweet, honey, sweet
person
Madhunika—sweetness of honey
Madhunisha—night full of pleasure
Madhunisha—pleasant night
Madhuparna—sun, tulsi leaf
Madhupriya—fond of honey, lover of
honey
Madhup—black bee
Madhurakshe—a person with pretty,
lovely, handsome, graceful eye,
glimmers
Madhurani—highness, empress, queen
of bees
Madhurasa—a bunch of grapes
Madhura—honey, sweet, pleasant,
sugar
Madhureema—honey
Madhureeta—sweetness
Madhuree—sweet
Madhuree—sweet, like sugar
Madhurideity—sweet girl
Madhurima—pretty, lovely,
handsome, graceful, sweetness
Madhurima—sweet girl, nectar, honey
Madhuri—honey, sweet, charming,
sweetness
Madhuri—sweetened girl
Madhurjya—sweatiness
Madhurya—pleasant night
Madhurya—sweetness
Madhur—melodious, sweet
Madhur—sweet

Madhusha—beauty
Madhushmita—one with sweet smile
Madhushree—beauty, of spring
Madhushree—the spring
Madhushri—beauty of spring
Madhusmita—sweet love, smile, honey
Madhusri—enchantment of spring season
Madhuswabhavine—sweet behaviour
Madhuvanthi—sweet, who is sweet like honey
Madhuyamine—enchanted night
Madhuyamine—sweet girl
Madhu—honey
Madhu—honey, sweet, beauty girl, sharp
Madhve—sweet drink made from honey
Madhvika—one who collects honey
Madhvi—jasmin, wife of madhav
Madhvi—spring
Madina—land of beauty, from the high
Madirakshana—with intoxicating eye, glimmers
Madiraksha—a woman with intoxicating eye, glimmers
Madirakshe—a damsel with intoxicating eye, glimmers
Madirakshi—woman with intoxicating eye, glimmers
Madiralochana—with intoxicating eye, glimmers
Madiranayani—a woman with intoxicating eye, glimmers
Madira—intoxicate, goddess of wine
Madira—nectar, wine
Madirekeshana—a woman with intoxicating eye, glimmers
Madnashini—she who destroys pride
Madree—princess of madra
Madreya—son of madri
Madri—name of the second wife of the pandu
Madri—wife of pandu
Madura—a bird
Madyanti—a bloom, garden stuff tree
Madyanti—pretty, lovely, handsome, graceful name
Maetri—friendship
Magadhe—name of daughter of magadh monarch
Magadhi—beauty, bloom, garden stuff
Magana—engrossed, ravenous
Magan—engrossed
Magarajothi—a lady with intoxicating eye, glimmers
Magathi—great
Mageshwari—name of a goddess
Maghi—giving gifts
Maghna—river gangas
Maghya—born in the month of magh
Magshri—pretty, lovely, handsome, graceful name
Maha-lakshmi—goddess lakshmi
Mahabala—vigour
Mahabhadra—ganga river
Mahabir—illustrious hero, lord hanuman
Mahadeity—goddess durga
Mahadeity—parvati
Mahaganga—the great ganga
Mahagauri—goddess durga
Mahagauri—goddess parvati
Mahajabeen—pretty, lovely, handsome, graceful
Mahakali—goddess durga
Mahakangee—one who smelled sweet
Mahakanta—earth
Mahak—fragrance
Mahalakshmee—jasmine, goddess lakshmi
Mahalakshmi—goddess lakshmi
Mahalaksmi—pretty, lovely, handsome, graceful name
Mahalasa—goddess mohini
Mahalika—a female attendant
Mahalsa—goddess parvati
Mahalya—pretty, lovely, handsome, graceful name
Mahamaaya—goddess of parvathi, bloom, garden stuff
Mahamathy—big moon, full moon
Mahamaya—goddess durga

Mahamya—bloom, garden stuff, goddess of parvati
Mahananda—name of the river
Mahanika—the great, proud one
Mahanisha—the greatest of night
Mahaniya—goddess lakshmi, praise worthy
Mahanthi—goddess
Mahanya—great progress, goddess
Mahanyu—lord shiva
Maharani—goddess narayani, great highness, empress, queen
Maharithi—best chariot
Mahashree—goddess lakshmi
Mahashweta—holy, sanctified, pious, solemn, chaste white
Mahashweta—perfectly white, goddess saraswati
Mahasmriti—pretty, lovely, handsome, graceful
Mahasri—goddess lakshmi
Mahasweta—goddess saraswati
Mahaswetha—goddess saraswati
Mahathi—lord rama wife name
Mahati—great power, name of narada
Mahatmika—great soul
Mahavidya—great knowledge
Mahek—fragrance, goog, pleasant smell
Mahelika—goddess durga
Mahema—greatness, glorious, fame
Mahendi—a paste of leaves
Mahera—highly skilled, expert
Maher—gift
Mahesa—lord shiva
Mahesha—the world
Maheshika—empresses, highness, empress, queen
Maheshi—goddess parvati
Maheshmati—god of love, lord shiva great
Maheshvari—power of lord shiva, goddess
Maheshwari—goddess durga
Maheshwati—goddess durga
Maheswara—goddess saraswati
Maheswari—consort of lord shiva, goddess

Maheswree—goddess durga
Maheya—goddess durga
Mahe—the world, the other name of earth
Mahia—love, special one, friend, lover
Mahiii—pretty, lovely, handsome, graceful name
Mahijuba—a hostess
Mahikaa—earth
Mahika—earth
Mahika—friend, frost, the earth
Mahika—the earth
Mahilini—pretty, lovely, handsome, graceful name
Mahima—greatness
Mahima—greatness, glorious, miracle, fame
Mahinam—pretty, lovely, handsome, graceful name
Mahiram—lovers
Mahira—superemely talented, gifted
Mahira—ultimate, absolute, highest, bestly talented
Mahir—heaven
Mahisaa—lord of the earth, goddess durga
Mahisa—goddess durga
Mahisha—the world, similar to mahi
Mahishe—a woman belonging to high family and rank
Mahishi—wife
Mahishka—the world, lord of the earth
Mahismathi—lord shiva great ruler
Mahita—flowing on earth
Mahita—greatness river
Mahitha—worshipped, greatness, quite
Mahithi—information
Mahitra—friend
Mahiya—happiness
Mahiya—lover, someone whom you love, joy
Mahi—pretty, lovely, handsome, graceful, love, river, attractive
Mahi—the earth
Mahi—the world, great earth
Mahna—a bloom, garden stuff
Mahodari—big-bellied
Mahua—a bloom, garden stuff

Mahua—an intoxicating bloom, garden stuff,
Mahubala—sweet
Mahuya—name of pretty, lovely, handsome, graceful bloom, garden stuff
Mahval—butter
Mahvash—moon-like beauty artist
Mahya—life
Maika—pretty, lovely, handsome, graceful name
Mainakee—goddess parvati
Mainak—love of god
Mainali—place
Mainavi—intellectual, singing bird
Maina—a bird
Maisha—grace, desirable as the moon
Maiteryi—wise woman
Maithali—pretty, lovely, handsome, graceful name
Maithali—sita
Maithile—sita
Maithili—goddess sita
Maithili—sita
Maithra—friendly
Maithri—friendship
Maitraiye—friendship
Maitraye—wise woman
Maitra—friendly
Maitree—friendship, dosti
Maitrevi—a learned woman
Maitreya—the sage, friendly
Maitreye, glimmers—a learned woman
Maitreye, glimmers—the illumination, luminosity, radiance of braveness bird
Maitreyi—name of a woman scholar, learned
Maitrin—the loving one
Maitri—friendship
Maitryi—friendship, good relation
Maitry—friendship and joy
Maiya—mother
Majeera—an ornament, jewellery, ornamentation, adornment, figuration for foot
Majhi—boat
Majushree—pretty, lovely, handsome, graceful goddess of wealth

Makali—the moon
Makanda—the mango tree
Makarandika—nectar like
Makara—born under capricorn, january
Makayla—pretty, lovely, handsome, graceful, who is like god
Makeswari—half of shiva, money
Makisha—honeybee
Makshe—honeybee
Makshika—honeybee
Makshita—honey
Makshi—honeybee
Malabika—pretty, lovely, handsome, graceful bloom, garden stuff
Malaiarasi—pretty, lovely, handsome, graceful name
Malaika—angel, small child
Malaimagal—goddess parvati, daughter of the
Malairani—pretty, lovely, handsome, graceful name
Malaiyarasi—hill highness, empress, queen
Malai—garland of bloom, garden stuffs
Malala—melancholic, pretty, lovely, handsome, graceful
Malarkodi—necklace, garland
Malarkuzhali—jasmine
Malarvili—pretty, lovely, handsome, graceful eye, glimmers like a bloom, garden stuff
Malarvizhi—cute eye, glimmers
Malar—bloom, garden stuff, pretty, lovely, handsome, graceful
Malasa—lakshmi deity
Malashree—pretty, lovely, handsome, graceful garland
Malashree—an early evening melody
Malathi—who loves to help, kind, good
Malathy—a bloom, garden stuff, sweet smelling
Malati—a variety of jasmine
Malati—jasmine bloom, garden stuff creeper with

Malavika—princess of malawa, most pretty, lovely, handsome, graceful
Malavya—loveable
Malav—the earth
Malayagandhne—perfumed with sandal wood
Malayavasine—a woman who dwell on malay mountain
Malayavati—very fragnant
Malaya—a creeper, forest, wood, jungle, fragrant
Malaya—name of a mountain
Mala—garland
Mala—pendant, necklace, garland, row
Maleha—gift, charming, pretty, lovely, handsome, graceful, salty
Maleswari—highness, empress, queen of rose, fragrance
Malhar—a classical raga, a musical note
Malha—highness, empress, queen
Maliha—strong, pretty, lovely, handsome, graceful, pleasant
Malika—a garland, bloom, garden stuff, industrious
Malika—garaland
Malikka—a creeper
Malina—follower of saint columbawer
Malinishri—pretty, lovely, handsome, graceful name
Malini—a florist
Malini—aromatic, sweet, fragrant
Malishka—fish
Maliya—good
Mali—wealth, riches, industrious
Maljumana—pretty, lovely, handsome, graceful
Malka—highness, empress, queen, princess blessed by god
Malkin—owner, powerful, princess
Malligavathi—dark
Malliga—jasmine
Malligeswari—florist river
Mallika—highness, empress, queen, jasmine
Malli—jasmine bloom, garden stuff, bloom, garden stuff
Malti—a bloom, garden stuffy creeper

Malti—small fragrant bloom, garden stuff, moon, illumination, luminosity, radiance
Malu—bloom, garden stuff, forgiven, bud
Malvika—of malava
Malvika—one who lived in malva
Mamata—love, affection, ture, motherly
Mamatha—love, affectionate regard
Mamathi—pretty
Mamta—affective, love
Mamta—mother's love, love, motherly
Mamtha—love
Manaara—illumination, luminosity, radiance house, guiding illumination, luminosity, radiance
Manada—giving honour digit of the moon
Manadha—giving honour
Manah—mind, goddess parvati
Manaka—according to the mind
Manaki—upper position
Manale—a friend of mind
Manalika—pretty, lovely, handsome, graceful
Manali—a name of the bird
Manali—cute, pretty bird, pretty, lovely, handsome, graceful
Manal—a bird
Manami—ocean, loving, pretty, lovely, handsome, graceful
Manana—meditation
Mananya—deserving praises
Manapriya—dear to heart
Manarika—who controls own mind
Manasavi—life, brilliant, sagacious, gifted, wise, learned
Manasa—mind
Manasa—name of the goddess, heart born
Manasa—river in himalaya, lake
Manasee—humanbeing, goddess of wisdom
Manashvi—brilliant, sagacious, gifted, wise, learned
Manashwini—brilliant, sagacious, gifted, wise, learned

Manasie—voice of heart
Manasika—of mind
Manasi—a complete woman lady, noble
Manasi—with a sound mind, with a
Manasmita—beauty, one who make you smile
Manasve—brilliant, sagacious, gifted, wise, learned, life
Manasve—intelligence
Manasvika—pretty, lovely, handsome, graceful name
Manasvine—a wise woman
Manasvini—proud, good, goddess durga
Manasvi—brilliant, sagacious, gifted, wise, learned, innocent, high
Manaswini—own thinmonarch, ruler, prince, earl, high minded, goddess
Manaswi—motherly love, energetic sprit
Manas—mind, lord shiva
Manat—a prayer, sweet desire, aspiration, longing, brilliant, sagacious, gifted, wise, learned
Manavazhagi—bird
Manavi—humanity, daughter of man
Manav—human
Manayi—wife of manu
Mana—supernatural power, lovelike
Mandagini—gentle wind
Mandagni—part of fire
Mandahasa—a lady
Mandakine—a name of river ganga
Mandakini—an indian river
Mandakini—name of a river
Mandakranta—a sanskrit metre
Mandana—cherful
Mandana—cherful, princess
Mandara—a smile
Mandara—mythical tree, large, firm
Mandarmalika—a river, garland of celestial
Mandave—name of the wife of the bharat
Mandavika—administration
Mandavi—wife of bharat
Manda—a name of the river, slow

Manda—name of a river, battle maid
Mandeepa—illumination, luminosity, radiance of heart, lamp
Mandeep—a illumination, luminosity, radiance of the soul
Mandeep—illumination, luminosity, radiance of the mind, heart
Mandhodari—wife of ravana, one who can digest
Mandira—a dwelling
Mandira—temple, brilliant, sagacious, gifted, wise, learned, helpful
Manditha—adorned
Manditree—that which adorns
Mandodari—with narrow abdomen, ravan wife
Mandodri—name of ravana's wife
Mandovi—a smile
Mandra—pleasant
Mandra—sober
Mandva—mandap
Mandvi—pretty, lovely, handsome, graceful name
Mandyanti—goddess durga
Manesha—ambition, intent, passion, intellect, goddess of desire, aspiration, longing
Maneshi—pretty, lovely, handsome, graceful eye, glimmers
Mangai—cultured lady
Mangalakumari—melody
Mangalam—prayer bless
Mangalanayagi—bharatha's wife name
Mangalavalli—auspicious, bliss
Mangalay—good time, before morning
Mangala—blissfull
Mangala—good song, auspicious, bliss
Mangalya—pious, holy, sanctified, pious, solemn, auspicious
Mangamma—a god name
Mangayarkarasi—goddess parvati
Manglagauri—before morning, fair women
Mangla—before morning
Mangla—goddess parvati
Mangu—pretty, lovely, handsome, graceful name
Manha—gift of god, gift of god

Manhitha—goodwill of people

Manhitha—together

Manibhu—a valuable, valued, rare ornament, jewellery, ornamentation, adornment, figuration

Manickam—pretty, lovely, handsome, graceful name

Manideepa—a lamp of valuable, valued, rare stones

Manideep—gem

Manikamohini—pretty, lovely, handsome, graceful damsel with ornament, jewellery, ornamentation, adornment, figuration

Manikanchan—an ornament, jewellery, ornamentation, adornment, figuration with gold and ornament

Manikarnika—name of rani lakshmibai, earring

Manika—a stone

Manika—money, honoured, gems, valuable, valued, rare

Manika—of ornament, jewellery, ornamentation, adornment, figurations

Manika—ruby

Manikkodi—flag of valuable, valued, rare stones

Manikuntala—a lamp of valuable, valued, rare stones

Manikya—a ornament, jewellery, ornamentation, adornment, figuration

Manikya—bead like lamp, ruby, wisdom

Manik—gem

Manik—valuable, valued, rare ruby stone

Manimaala—beads ornament, jewellery, ornamentation, adornment, figuration of an ear

Manimalai—pretty, lovely, handsome, graceful name

Manimalar—a woman whose hair is like gems

Manimala—a string of ornament, jewellery, ornamentation, adornment, figuration

Manimala—a string of pearls

Manimegalai—happy, highness, empress, queen of sounds

Manimekhala—a string of beads, girdle of gems

Manimozhi—collection of beads

Maninagai—nice

Manindra—diamond

Manine—resolute

Maninga—treasure of ornament, jewellery, ornamentation, adornment, figuration

Maninghosha—sweet acclamation

Manini—a proud woman

Manini—self respected lady, noble

Maniprabha—a string of beads, splendour

Maniratna—diamond

Manisa—goddess of desire, aspiration, longing, goddess of mind

Manisha—brilliant, sagacious, gifted, wise, learned woman

Manisha—brilliant, sagacious, gifted, wise, learned, wise

Manisha—wise, goddess of desire, aspiration, longing

Manishe—ambition, intent, passion by heart

Manishika—ambition, intent, passion, desire, aspiration, longing of mind

Manishika—intelligence, understanding

Manishita—wisdom

Manishi—ambition, intent, passion by heart, wisdom

Manisila—a ornament, jewellery, ornamentation, adornment, figuration led stone

Manisita—wisdom

Manisitha—wisdom

Manisi—ambition, intent, passion by heart

Manisvine—virtuous woman

Manita—honoured

Manitha—honoured

Manit—pretty, lovely, handsome, graceful name

Maniya—a glass bead

Maniya—glass bead

Mani—gem diamond ornament, jewellery, ornamentation, adornment, figuration, mantra
Mani—gem, a ornament, jewellery, ornamentation, adornment, figuration
Manjali—feel of love
Manjarika—a bud of small bloom, garden stuff
Manjarika—bud
Manjari—bunch of bloom, garden stuff, the sacred basil
Manjari—pearl, new tendril
Manjeet—one who wins her own heart
Manjika—sweet
Manjima—beauty with brains
Manjini—highness, empress, queen, beauty
Manjira—ankle-bells
Manjira—anklet
Manjiri—small bloom, garden stuff of common basil, god
Manjista—extremely
Manjistha—extremely
Manjit—one who wins her own heart
Manjoosha—a chest, box
Manjot—illumination, luminosity, radiance the heart
Manjri—the sacred basil, blossom
Manjubala—pretty, lovely, handsome, graceful girl sweet girl
Manjubarkavi—a bunch
Manjubhargavi—goddess lakshmi
Manjubhasha—goddess of mind, ambition, intent, passion
Manjukeshe—one with pretty, lovely, handsome, graceful hair
Manjukeshin—a woman with pretty, lovely, handsome, graceful hair
Manjulabai—very bright red colour
Manjuladeity—snow, dew drops
Manjula—pretty, lovely, handsome, graceful, charming
Manjula—lovely, soft, charming, melodious
Manjulika—pretty, lovely, handsome, graceful, charming damsel
Manjulika—a sweet girl
Manjuli—sweet natured

Manjul—sacred, lovely, sweet
Manjusha—a box
Manjusha—treasure chest box, with a
Manjushree—pleasant
Manjushree—sweet lustre
Manjushri—goddess lakshmi, sweet lustre
Manjusree—saraswati
Manjusri—saraswati, holy, pure, sanctified, pious, solemn beauty
Manjuvidhya—a box
Manju—lovely, charming
Manju—pleasant, snow, dew drops, sweet
Manjyot—illumination, luminosity, radiance of heart
Manjyot—illumination, luminosity, radiance of the mind
Mankalam—saraswati
Mankalasundari—saraswati
Mankalyam—pretty, lovely, handsome, graceful name
Mankamma—woman who strays from husband
Manka—a wooden pearl
Mankirat—work of heart
Manmatha—god of love, cupid
Manmathpriya—consort of kamdeva
Manmat—sweet
Manmayi—jealous, goddess radha
Manmeet—friend of mind
Mannati—desire, aspiration, longing, ambition, intent, passion
Mannatt—desire, aspiration, longing
Mannat—desire, aspiration, longing, petition to god, special
Manna—heavenly
Mannvizhi—deer eye, glimmers
Mannya—bloom, garden stuff
Manobala—vigour of mind
Manobhavana—behaviour
Manobhilasha—ambition, intent, passion
Manobhirama—pleasing to mind
Manochithra—angel of chitram, drawing
Manodhini—one who understands everything

Manogna—clever, ambition, intent, passion, beauty
Manogya—illumination, luminosity, radianceful, pleasing
Manoharita—pretty, lovely, handsome, graceful
Manohari—attraction
Manohari—steals the heart of others
Manoi—pretty, lovely, handsome, graceful, brave, courageous
Manojava—with the speed of thought
Manokiri—pretty, lovely, handsome, graceful name
Manomohine—a enchanted woman with mind
Manonmani—goddess lakshmi
Manopriya—lovely to the soul
Manorama—ambition, intent, passion, desire, aspiration, longing
Manorama—pleasing, favourite, charming, pretty, lovely, handsome, gracefuluch in
Manoranjana—entertainment
Manoranjana—pleasing, entertaining
Manoranjani—one who entertains
Manorata—beauty
Manoratha—desire, aspiration, longing of the mind
Manorathe—heart's happiness ambition, intent, passion
Manorita—beauty
Manoritha—of the mind
Manorma—pretty, lovely, handsome, graceful
Manoshi—pretty, lovely, handsome, graceful name
Manoswee—brilliant, sagacious, gifted, wise, learned
Manovallabha—beloved
Manovati—true dream
Mano—god be with us
Manpala—auspicious
Manpreet—love of heart, happiness of heart
Manraj—ruler of the heart, mind
Mansa—ambition, intent, passion
Mansa—intention, spiritual
Mansha—ambition, intent, passion

Mansha—desire, aspiration, longing
Manshika—mind, clean heart, intellect
Manshi—woman
Manshree—desire, aspiration, longing
Manshul—wormonarch, ruler, prince, earl hard
Manshve—pretty, lovely, handsome, graceful name
Manshwika—holy river ganga
Mansi—pretty, lovely, handsome, graceful birdttainment
Mansi—a goddess
Mansi—plucked bloom, garden stuff, voice of heart
Mansve—brilliant, sagacious, gifted, wise, learned
Mansvi—goddess durga, bottom of the heart
Manswi—brilliant, sagacious, gifted, wise, learned
Mantasa—valuable, valued, rare, lord of specific wood
Mantasha—valuable, valued, rare, lord of specific wood
Manthakini—pleasing, favourite, charming, pretty, lovely, handsome, graceful
Manthana—to extract
Manthika—thoughtful
Manthra—property
Manti—amiable, pleasing, suave, interesting
Mantrana—advice, consultation
Mantra—a holy, pure, sanctified, pious, solemn prayer
Mantra—hymns, holy chants
Mantrine—the highness, empress, queen of chess
Manugna—brilliant, sagacious, gifted, wise, learned
Manuhya—judicial
Manuja—daughter of man
Manuja—woman, great person
Manukarnika—name of a river
Manuprairna—inspiration of original man
Manureet—pretty, lovely, handsome, graceful name

Manushe—human
Manushi—a woman
Manushi—woman, goddess lakshmi, humanity
Manushree—lakshmi deity, lakshmi
Manushritha—goddess lakshmi
Manushri—goddess lakshmi
Manusri—goddess lakshmi and saraswathi
Manu—of the mind, desirable, pretty, lovely, handsome, graceful
Manu—wise, thinmonarch, ruler, prince, earl
Manvati—respectful
Manva—desire, aspiration, longing, mind identifier, mind
Manver—heart winner
Manve—wife of manu
Manvika—as a human being
Manvika—youth, female of maanav
Manvita—most respectable, goddess
Manvitha—happy, goddess durga
Manvit—pretty, lovely, handsome, graceful name
Manvi—humanly, serenity, calm, calmness, stillness, silence of mind, goddess
Manvi—kind hearted, who spread goodness
Manvi—lady
Manyata—belief
Manyata—principles
Manyatha—principles, beliefs
Manya—rebellious agree, great
Manya—the respected one
Manyta—believe and preferences
Maosmi—weather
Maraichelvi—woman
Marakatham—a gemttractive
Marala—swan
Marale—swan
Maralika—small swan
Marava—raga of traditional hnidustani
Mardhini—goddess durga
Mareesha—traveller
Marga—pearl
Margi—traveller

Mariche—a ray of illumination, luminosity, radiance
Marichika—mirage
Marichika—mirage, ray
Marichi—name of a star
Marika—rebellious woman, bitter, star
Marisa—combination of two
Marisha—respectable
Marishthe—dwelling in cleanliness
Markandeya—lord shiva's devotee sage who
Marmi—nice
Marsha—warlike, dedicated to god mars
Marudham—from the lush green fields
Marudhvathi—synonym for durga, goddess durga
Maruff—famous, known, noted, celebrated
Marushika—born with blessings of lord shiva
Maruti—wind, lord hanumanji, lord ganesh
Marvi—beauty redefined, eternal beauty
Maryada—boundry, virtue
Maryada—limit, respect
Marya—mark, limit, beloved
Masara—emerald
Mashika—born during rainy season
Masilmani—holy, sanctified, pious, solemn, chaste, without any blemishes
Mastani—pretty, lovely, handsome, graceful name
Masum—innocent
Matali—a mother's friend, charioteer
Matangee—intellect
Matangi—an intellectual
Matangi—goddess durga
Matangi—goddess parvati
Mateah—honoured, ambition, intent, passion, liked
Mateshwari—mother of humankind
Mathana—name of sri krishna with his
Mathani—god
Mathanki—goddess saraswati
Mathan—god of love

Matharasi—pretty, lovely, handsome, graceful name
Mathara—pretty, lovely, handsome, graceful name
Mathavi—durga
Mathiarasi—very bright life
Mathivani—pretty, lovely, handsome, graceful name
Mathivathani—moon faced
Mathubala—more tamonarch, ruler, prince, earl
Mathulai—fruit
Mathula—fruit name pomegranate
Mathulekha—pretty, lovely, handsome, graceful
Mathullika—a bird
Mathumathi—cute girl
Mathumitha—sweet
Mathuram—sweetness
Mathura—birth place of lord krishna
Mathurekha—pretty, lovely, handsome, graceful name
Mathuri—silent
Mathusha—honey
Mathusri—honey
Matila—earth
Matisha—mother, name of goddess
Matram—changes
Matra—mother, name of goddess
Matrika—mother, name of goddess
Matripuja—worship
Matseyagandha—lady with smells like a fish
Matsyagandha—as sweet as fish
Matsya—fish
Matvi—one who belongs to mother
Maulashree—pretty, lovely, handsome, graceful name
Maulika—original
Maulika—soft, the original
Maulisha—very talented
Mauli—god name
Mauna—silence
Maunita—pretty, lovely, handsome, graceful name
Mauphool—pretty, lovely, handsome, graceful bloom, garden stuff
Mausami—seasonal, weather

Mausam—season
Maushmi—monsoon wind, weather
Maushmi—seasonal
Mausmi—monsoon wind
Mausumi—beauty, monsoon wind
Mausum—season
Mayana—goddess durga
Mayanka—god, season
Mayank—moon, lord krishna
Mayanshi—related to goddess lakshmi
Mayarani—seasonal
Mayari—birds, lunar goddess
Mayasa—walks proudly
Mayavani—creating illusion
Mayavati—pradyumma's wife
Mayavine—one who creates illusions
Mayawati—full of illusion
Maya—illusion
Maya—illusion, goddess durga
Maya—illusion, magical
Maya—name of a woman
Mayilamai—illusion, durga
Mayil—full of grace, like a peacock
Maynta—acceptance, myth
Mayra—moon, beloved plant name
Maysaa—to walk with a swinging gait
Maysha—pretty, lovely, handsome, graceful name
Maytri—friendship
Mayuka—peahen
Mayukha—lustre, sun rays
Mayukhi—peahen
Mayurakhsi—eye, glimmers of the peacock
Mayura—peacock, illusion
Mayuree—peahen, female peacock
Mayure—peahen
Mayurika—baby peahen, peacock feathers
Mayurika—peahen
Mayuri—a female peacock
Mayuri—peacock, pigeon with sweet voice
Mayusha—pretty, lovely, handsome, graceful name
Mayushka—peacock
Meceka—gem, cloud
Medhakara—peacock

Medhana—kedarnath daughter
Medhane—of intelligence
Medhani—of intelligence
Medhant—clever
Medhasvi—goddess saraswati
Medhavine—brilliant, sagacious, gifted, wise, learned woman
Medhavi—brilliant
Medhavi—genius, cleaver, brilliant, sagacious, gifted, wise, learned
Medhavi—peahen, jasmin, wife of madhav
Medha—brilliant, sagacious, gifted, wise, learned, intellect, wisdom
Medha—goddess saraswati
Medhine—earth
Medhya—mighty, clean, fresh
Medh—goddess saraswati
Medine—baby peahen
Medini—the earth
Medini—the earth, goddess lakshmi
Medin—peahen
Medni—the earth
Medura—brilliant, sagacious, gifted, wise, learned girl
Meehika—fog
Meemansha—analyses
Meenaa—cup of wine, fish, descent from
Meenabai—a fish, eye, glimmers
Meenabigai—goddess
Meenakshi—a water fish, eye, glimmers, one with fish eye, glimmers
Meenakshi—woman with pretty, lovely, handsome, graceful eye, glimmers, cloud
Meenakumari—earth
Meenali—goddess
Meenalotchini—valuable, valued, rare stone, fish
Meenal—valuable, valued, rare gem
Meenambal—goddess parvathi
Meena—valuable, valued, rare stone, fish, starling
Meendeity—highness, empress, queen of fishes
Meenu—girl with fish eye, glimmers
Meerabai—the name of famous poet

Meeraja—combination of meenakshi and
Meerakumari—young devotee of lord krishna
Meerant—krishna devotee, meera's moment of
Meera—a saintly woman, one who is circumscribed
Meera—illumination, luminosity, radiance, saintly woman devotee of
Meesha—unlimited, smile
Meeshree—sweet
Meeshvi—god of ambition, intent, passion, pretty, lovely, handsome, graceful, goddess
Meetal—love
Meeta—a friend
Meeta—friend, good behaviour
Meethi—sweet, truthful
Meethu—sweet, amiable, pleasing, suave, interesting
Meetra—sun, illumination, luminosity, radiance
Meetusi—pretty, lovely, handsome, graceful name
Meetu—sweet
Meet—love, friend
Meeza—quarter moon
Megala—symbol
Meganayagi—a devotee of krishna
Megana—clouds
Megan—pearl, strong and capable, strong
Megavalli—line of clouds
Megavana—cloud
Mega—raining, clouds, rain
Megha-sri—cloud
Meghabindu—pretty, lovely, handsome, graceful name
Meghal—rain, cloud
Meghamala—array of clouds
Meghamsha—part of clouds or rain
Meghana—pretty, lovely, handsome, graceful cloud, rain, shower
Meghani—highness, empress, queen of clouds
Meghan—pearl, strong and capable

Meghapushpa—cloud bloom, garden stuff, the rain water
Meghari—cloud
Meghasvana—pretty, lovely, handsome, graceful name
Meghaswi—goddess saraswati
Meghavini—intelligence
Meghavi—cloud
Meghayoni—garland of clouds
Megha—a star
Megha—cloud, rain
Megha—clouds
Meghnathi—born from rain
Meghna—sky, river gangas, rain drops
Meghna—soft hearted
Meghranjane—cloud's glory
Megnaa—cloud
Mehak—sweet smellura, fragrance
Mehal—cloud
Mehanavat—goodness
Mehanaz—moon's glory
Mehandi—a bloom, garden stuffing plan, generally used
Mehar—good desire, aspiration, longinges, courtesy of god
Mehatnu—pretty, lovely, handsome, graceful name
Meha—brilliant, sagacious, gifted, wise, learned, rain, sharp, cloud
Meha—cloud
Meha—rain
Mehbooba—beloved
Mehdi—hena
Mehek—aura, good smell, pretty, lovely, handsome, graceful scent
Mehera—powerful
Meher—benevolence, moon, sweet smell
Mehgna—sky
Mehlaka—chand ki rah
Mehndi—henna hand art, pretty, lovely, handsome, graceful colour
Mehrunissa—benevolent
Mehr—blessing, the seventh solar month
Mehula—rain
Mehuli—a small rain cloud
Mehul—cloud, rain

Mehul—rain, cloud
Meiyammai—truth
Meiyarivu—beloved
Meiyazhagi—beauty, beauty of truth
Mekala—beloved, knower of the self
Mekala—knower of self
Meka—benevolence
Mekhala—slope of a mountain, belt, girdle
Mekhalin—pretty, lovely, handsome, graceful name
Mekhali—sweet
Mekha—rain
Mekhla—girdle
Melapaka—pretty, lovely, handsome, graceful name
Mela—dark, black, religious gathering
Meli—bitter
Menadeity—pretty, lovely, handsome, graceful name
Menagai—dancer
Menaha—celestial damsel
Menaja—goddess parvati
Menakadeity—female parrot
Menaka—a celestial dancern apsara
Menakshi—fish eye, glimmers
Menali—name of a princess
Mena—wife of himalayas woman
Mena—wife of the himalayas, female
Menila—goodness, serenity, calm, calmness, stillness, silence full
Menitha—wise, numerology number
Menka—a celestial woman, an apsara
Menka—an apsara, shakuntala's mother
Menmoli—speaks kindly
Menmozi—speaks kindly
Merait—the earth
Mera—aristocratic lady
Mersiha—the most pretty, lovely, handsome, graceful
Merunisha—pretty, lovely, handsome, graceful name
Merunya—talent, brilliant
Merushree—the most pretty, lovely, handsome, graceful like meru mountain
Meru—meru

Mesha—long life, born under the sign of

Meshva—goddess of ambition, intent, passion, goddess parvati

Meshwa—pretty, lovely, handsome, graceful name of river

Metali—friendship, lovely

Methi—celestial damsel

Methli—language of bihar

Methra—dew drops

Meth—goddesss parvati

Metri—friendship

Mianvi—an angel like a god

Mia—beauty, mine, belovedlways

Michael—who resembles god, one who is like

Midhura—sweet, pleasant

Midunika—good music

Miduni—good music

Miharika—smooth and gentle

Miheka—smile, mist, fog, dew drop, name

Mihika—mist

Mihika—mist, fog, dew drop, goddess name

Mihira—intelligence, feminine form of

Mihishka—part of lord shiva

Mihita—pretty, lovely, handsome, graceful name

Mika—like god, gift from god, pretty, lovely, handsome, graceful

Milana—union, joining together, beloved

Milan—meeting, get together, eager

Milan—union, contract

Milika—desiring union

Milisha—pretty, lovely, handsome, graceful name

Mili—a meeting find, found

Millan—showing matching of relationship

Milly—gentle vigour, industrious

Milone—melodious

Miloni—achiever

Milpa—earth

Mily—found meeting, pretty, lovely, handsome, graceful

Mimansa—a book of philosophy

Mimansa—thinmonarch, ruler, prince, earl

Minakshi—fish eye, glimmers daughter of kubera

Minaksi—fish eye, glimmers

Minalaya—a meeting find

Minal—a valuable, valued, rare stone

Minal—a valuable, valued, rare stone, like a diamond

Minanatha—desire, aspiration, longing

Minarva—intellect

Minati—prayer

Minaxi—one with fish figure, appearance, structured eye, glimmers, goddess

Minaxshi—fish eye, glimmers, goddess parvati

Mina—love, will, ambition, intent, passion, helmet

Minda—fish

Minesh—lord shiva, part of fish

Minimol—small daughter

Minisha—lord krishna's devotee

Mini—small, tiny

Minku—pretty, lovely, handsome, graceful name

Minnalkodi—a valuable, valued, rare stones

Minnal—fish eye, glimmers, illumination, luminosity, radiance

Minnati—prayer

Minnat—grace, kindness, favour, gift

Minnoliyal—pretty, lovely, handsome, graceful name

Minnoli—brilliant like illumination, luminosity, radiance

Minnu—illumination, luminosity, radiance, sky, shining

Minol—pretty, lovely, handsome, graceful, brilliant, sagacious, gifted, wise, learned

Minoti—stuborn

Mintoo—cute

Mintu—illumination, luminosity, radiance of god

Minu—eden gem, valuable, valued, rare stone

Mipasha—lovely

Mirachka—attraction
Mirajkar—surname of a marathi family
Miral—reigning highness, empress, queenngel of heaven
Miranka—pretty, lovely, handsome, graceful name
Miran—princely, noble
Miraya—prosperous, lord krishna's devotee
Mira—devotee of lord krishna
Mirin—happiness
Mirium—desire, aspiration, longed-for child
Mirudhuksha—soft
Mirunalini—lakshmi
Misbah—lamp
Mishali—lord krishna's devotee
Mishal—sparkling, shining, illumination, luminosity, radiance
Mishan—bringer of joy
Mishaye—gift of love
Misha—feminine of michael, like the
Misheta—goddess lakshmi
Mishika—gift of love, goddess durga
Mishil—happy
Mishita—sweet person
Mishka—gift of love
Mishrakeshi—an angel
Mishree—sweet
Mishri—sweet
Mishtee—sweet
Mishthe—sweet
Mishthi—sweet
Mishti—sweet, sweet person
Mishtu—lovely
Mishty—sweet
Mishu—love
Mishva—pretty, lovely, handsome, graceful, beauty
Mishwa—name of river
Misri—loving, sweet
Missi—sweet honey
Missty—sweet
Misthi—sweet
Misti—dim, cloudy, vague, foggy, misty

Mistu—sweet, lovely, pretty, lovely, handsome, graceful
Misty—foggy, misty, sweetness, dim
Mitakshi—goddess durga
Mitale—a bond between friendship and love
Mitali—friendship
Mitali—friendship, lovely, pretty, lovely, handsome, graceful
Mital—friendship
Mitansha—meaningful
Mitanshi—pretty, lovely, handsome, graceful name
Mitansi—friendship, part of friend
Mita—a friend
Mita—a friend, dearest, generous
Miteelai—sweet
Mitesha—support, indoctrination, assuredness
Mithali—friendship
Mithila—a name of the city
Mithila—goddess sita's birthplace
Mithilesh—the monarch, ruler, prince, earl of mithila, janak, father
Mithira—pretty, lovely, handsome, graceful name
Mithi—truthful, sweet, daughter of
Mithlesh—goddess sita
Mithradeity—friend
Mithrai—friendly
Mithra—friendly, friend sun, cute
Mithuna—star name, zodiac
Mithu—friend, sweet, parrot, pretty, lovely, handsome, graceful
Mitiksha—a wonder
Miti—method way to perform a task
Mitrakeshi—sweet person
Mitravinda—possessor of friends
Mitra—friend
Mitra—friend dayillumination, luminosity, radiance
Mitshu—bloom, garden stuffs, the god somnath
Mitsu—honey, illumination, luminosity, radiance
Mittali—friendship
Mittal—friendly
Mitti—soil

Mittu—parrot
Mitul—measured, moderate
Mitusi—pretty, lovely, handsome, graceful name
Mitve—love
Mitwa—love
Mivara—capital of videha
Miya—sacred house, temple, increasingly
Mnnat—desire, aspiration, longing
Moana—from the ocean, brave, cute
Mocaniya—a friend
Mochana—freedom
Mocsha—to relieve, free from births
Modakara—being happy
Modanatha—pretty, lovely, handsome, graceful name
Moda—an apsara's name
Modine—cherful
Modin—illumination, luminosity, radianceful
Moganambal—dancer
Moghana—daughter of emperor mughal
Mohanagee—a woman with pleasing, favourite, charming figure
Mohanakshe—charming eye, glimmers
Mohanam—pretty, lovely, handsome, graceful, good monarch, ruler, prince, earl
Mohanangee—pleasing, favourite, charming body
Mohana—charming
Mohana—pleasing, favourite, charming, charming
Mohanie—angle
Mohani—pleasing, favourite, charming, fascinating, charming
Mohar—coin in ancient times
Mohati—as pretty, lovely, handsome, graceful as pearl
Moha—infatutation
Moha—love
Moha—pleasing, favourite, charming
Mohenie—bewitching, enchantress
Mohica—attractionttractive
Mohika—attraction

Mohima—fame, greatness, glorious
Mohine—pleasing, favourite, charming
Mohinideity—fascinating, the jasmine blossom
Mohini—most pretty, lovely, handsome, graceful, bewitching
Mohini—pleasing, favourite, charming
Mohisha—intellect, sweet
Mohita—attracted, impressing
Mohita—pleasing, favourite, charming, charming
Mohitha—angel of god, infatuated
Mohithira—very pretty, lovely, handsome, graceful, sweet
Mohit—attracted
Mohi—pleasing, lovely
Mohnashini—she who destroys delusion
Mohna—pleasing, favourite, charming
Mohor—gold coin, valuable, valued, rare
Moikuzhali—pretty, lovely, handsome, graceful name
Moitreye, glimmers—an princessn enchantress
Mokshana—salvation
Mokshapaya—pretty, lovely, handsome, graceful name
Mokshasri—free from births
Moksha—freedom, salvation, final destiny
Moksha—salvation
Mokshdha—pretty, lovely, handsome, graceful name
Mokshika—to find good soul, name of goddess
Mokshin—free
Mokshita—salvation, final destiny of god
Mokshitha—freettaining moksham, goddess
Mokshi—liberated, salvation, freedom
Moksika—talent
Moksin—free
Moksitha—humanitarian, determined, goddess
Molina—tree that grow from root

Molisha—princess
Moli—diadem, crown
Molshree—orange coloured very fragrant
Moly—an herb hermes gives to odysseus
Monalika—one of the thousand names of the
Monalisa—noble, the beauty
Monalisa—pretty, lovely, handsome, graceful woman
Monali—name of goddess durga, hill, name
Monal—a bird
Monal—birdmazing
Monaska—desire, aspiration, longing of heart
Monasri—pretty, lovely, handsome, graceful name
Monavi—symbol for silence
Mona—a bird
Mona—solitarydviser, nun, desire, aspiration, longing
Mondira—brilliant, sagacious, gifted, wise, learned, helpful, caring
Monesha—brilliant, sagacious, gifted, wise, learned
Monesha—lord krishna
Monica—adviser, solitarylone, unique
Monieka—solitary, lord of mind wise
Monika—a wise counsellor, goddess durga
Monir—shining
Monisa—intelligence, beaatifull
Monisha—lord of mind
Monisha—tallent, sweet, lord of mind
Monishka—pretty, lovely, handsome, graceful, intelligence
Monita—angel
Monitha—respected, noble, silenced
Moni—brilliant, sagacious, gifted, wise, learned, pretty, lovely, handsome, graceful, nicely
Monjulika—highness, empress, queen
Monpriti—heart lover
Monushree—soft, pretty, consort of vishnu
Monu—soft, pretty

Monvitha—blessed child
Mon—mind, silent
Mookathal—silent rhythm
Mookshika—lord ganesha's vehicle
Moomal—highness, empress, queen, beloved, pretty, lovely, handsome, graceful
Moon—slave, myth name, letters
Moorali—flute
Moorat—the idol
Moovitha—moon
Moraka—known
Morika—pea hen
Morika—peahen
Morli—flute of lord krishna
Moshika—princess
Mosika—god gift in earth
Motana—nice
Motibai—pearl
Moti—pearl
Mottayita—intellectual
Moubani—a bloom, garden stuff
Mouksha—to relieve, free from births
Moukshi—salvation, reliever, liberated
Moukthika—pearl, goddess lakshmi
Moulana—silent, calm
Moulika—love, chief
Mouli—sacred thread, mother, head
Moulyasri—bright, goddess lakshmi
Moulya—together, valuable, valued, rare
Moumita—honey bee, love, sweet friend
Mounavi—silent person
Mouna—silent, quiet
Mounica—silent, silence
Mounika—silence, silent girl
Mounisha—goddess parvati, moon illumination, luminosity, radiance
Mounita—quite, silent
Mouni—silent
Mousami—seasonal, similar to mausami
Mousam—seasons
Moushmee—sesonal
Moushmi—seasonal
Moushumee—mausam
Mousumi—weather, seasons

151 Indian Names For Girls

Mouthika—like a pearl
Mowlisha—pretty, lovely, handsome, graceful name
Mownika—silent
Mradual—very sweet speaker
Mradula—very sweet speaker
Mridane—goddess parvati
Mridanta—passing through a constellation
Mrida—name from lord shiva purana
Mridhula—softness
Mridine—soil
Mridini—goddess parvati
Mridula—gentle, soft, tendernessn ideal, model
Mridula—softness, tenderness
Mridul—soft, tender
Mriduna—gentle, soft, moderate
Mridusmita—with a sweet smile
Mridu—gentle
Mridu—soft, sweet
Mrigakshi—pretty, lovely, handsome, graceful eye, glimmers like deer
Mrigakshi—one with deer like eyes, lovely, handsome, graceful eye, glimmers
Mriganayani—one with deer like pretty eyes, lovely, handsome, graceful eye, glimmers
Mriganayani—with pretty, lovely, handsome, graceful eye, glimmers
Mriganka—the moon
Mrigankhi—deer eye, glimmers
Mrigekshana—deer eye, glimmers
Mrigeshana—doe eye, glimmers
Mrigisha—one who is like a deer
Mriglochana—pretty, lovely, handsome, graceful eye, glimmers as deer
Mriglochni—pretty, lovely, handsome, graceful eye, glimmers like deer
Mrignaini—with pretty, lovely, handsome, graceful eye, glimmers
Mrignayane—a woman with pretty eyes, lovely, handsome, graceful eye, glimmers as deer
Mrignayani—glimmers as deer, lovely, handsome, graceful
Mrignayani—with pretty, lovely, handsome, graceful eye, glimmers like deer
Mrignayni—mrig means deer and nayni means eyes
Mrigtrishna—mirage
Mrigya—deer
Mrikshine—tearing up
Mrinale—lotus stalk
Mrinalika—an apsara
Mrinalika—lotus bloom, garden stuff
Mrinalika—stem of lotus, goddess lakshmi
Mrinaline—lotus
Mrinalini—lotus
Mrinalini—stem of lotus, goddess lakshmi
Mrinali—like a lotus
Mrinali—lotus stem, goddess lakshmi
Mrinallika—stalk of lotus
Mrinal—delicate
Mrinal—lotus, goddess lakshmi
Mrinmaye—deer's eye, glimmers, made of clay
Mrinmayi—name of seeta, covered with mud
Mrinmoye—anything that is made out of mud
Mrishana—reflection
Mrisha—falsehood
Mritanshi—immortal, long life
Mrithubashini—soft spoken girl
Mrithula—softness, goddess lakshmi, cute
Mrithulika—soft
Mritika—one who acceptscceptance
Mriti—acceptance
Mritsana—fertile and fragrant earth
Mritsa—good earth
Mritsha—good earth
Mritsha—sweet smell of earth when water
Mrittika—earth
Mrittika—mother earth, goddess earth
Mritwika—made by soil
Mrityunjay—lord shiva
Mrnalini—a collection of lotuses
Mrridve—soft, delicate, moderate

Mrudali—soft, sweet voice
Mrudane—goddess parvati
Mrudani—another name of goddess parvati
Mruda—goddess parvatiffectionate
Mrudhula—soft, pretty, lovely, handsome, graceful
Mrudini—pretty, lovely, handsome, graceful name
Mrudula—soft natured, tender and pretty, lovely, handsome, graceful
Mrudu—soft
Mrugaja—son of moon
Mrugakshe—deer eye, glimmers
Mrugakshi—doe eye, glimmers
Mrugal—deer
Mrugaya—soft
Mruga—a bird
Mruga—doe
Mrugesha—like a deer
Mrugisha—like a deer
Mrugya—pretty, lovely, handsome, graceful deer
Mrulochana—pretty, lovely, handsome, graceful eye, glimmers like doe
Mrunalavattee—like a lotus
Mrunalini—the goddess of durga, brilliant, sagacious, gifted, wise, learned
Mrunali—lotus stalk
Mrunali—lotus stalk, princess, dancer
Mrunal—lotus stack, brilliant, sagacious, gifted, wise, learned, princess
Mrunmai—soft natured
Mrunmaye—earth, goddess sita
Mrunmayi—made of earth, goddess earth
Mruthula—soft natured
Mubashshara—giver of good news
Mubinah—manifest, clear, one who
Mudhita—sensitive
Mudika—bloom, garden stuff, fragrance
Mudita—cherful, happy
Mudita—glad

Mudra—healing hand movement, expression
Mudra—pose
Mudrika—a ring
Mudrika—ring
Mugdhakshe—fair eye, glimmers
Mugdha—spellbound
Mugdha—spellbound, innocent, innocent
Muhfuza—pretty, lovely, handsome, graceful name
Mukambika—the silent mother
Mukesh—one with loving eye, glimmers heart of gold
Mukitha—sweet
Mukshitha—liberated
Muktaa—pearl
Muktabha—shining like a pearl
Muktagauri—fair women with pearl, liberated
Muktakesha—open tresses, goddess parvati
Muktalata—necklace of pearls
Muktali—a neckless of pearls
Muktavli—a pleased woman
Mukta—face, pearl
Mukta—get rid of everything, liberated
Muktika—a pearl
Mukti—freedom from life and death
Mukti—freedom, salvation
Mukula—a bud
Mukula—bud
Mukulika—small blossom
Mukulita—bud buds
Mukul—bud
Mukunda—a gem
Mukunda—giver of freedom, lord krishna
Mukuta—crown
Mulapurusha—liberation
Mulashanti—garland of pearls
Mula—name of a nakhatra out of
Mulika—bud
Mullai—bloom, garden stuff with lovely fragrance
Multani—pretty, lovely, handsome, graceful name

Mumal—princess of jaisalmer
Mumtaz—the distinguished, the best, the
Mumuksha—ambition, intent, passion of power
Mundari—a ring
Munesa—pretty, lovely, handsome, graceful name
Muneswari—goddess parvathi
Munia—a little girl
Munira—happiness, radiant, luminous
Munisha—lovely
Munita—pretty, lovely, handsome, graceful name
Muniyammal—goddess
Muniya—name of a bird
Muni—a sage, saint
Munjula—goddess parvati
Munmun—love, very pleasant
Munni—small
Murlika—small flute
Murt—the idol
Musakan—smile
Mushika—night
Mushki—fregrance
Muskaan—smiling, smile, symbol of
Muskan—smile, laughter, sweet smile
Musqaan—pretty, lovely, handsome, graceful name
Muthamizharasi—highness, empress, queen of three form of the tamil
Muthamizh—music
Muthammal—holy, sanctified, pious, solemn, chaste, like a pearl
Mutharasi—pretty, lovely, handsome, graceful highness, empress, queen like a pearl
Mutholi—shines like a pearl
Muthumalai—a garland made up of one of the
Muthunagai—smiles like a pearl
Muthuselvi—happy prosperous daughter, she is
Muvetha—cute
Myah—goddess, ornament, jewellery, ornamentation, adornment
Myla—female soldier, merciful, female
Mynadeity—pretty, lovely, handsome, graceful name
Mynavathi—a bird
Myna—a black bird which sings pretty, lovely, handsome, gracefully
Myra—swift and illumination, luminosity, radiance
Mysha—a happy mood, happy for entire
Mythili—goddess sita, princess of mithila
Mythilli—pretty, lovely, handsome, graceful, heart full, wife of
Mythily—goddess sita
Mythradeity—goddess of truth
Mythreyi—daughter of a vedic muni
Mythri—friendship
Myuri—bird
Myvizhiyal—pretty, lovely, handsome, graceful eye, glimmers

****

Indian Names For Girls—N

Nabah—noble, high, sky
Nabanipa—a new bloom, garden stuff
Nabanita—star, new life
Nabeela—noble, high-born
Nabhanipa—a new bloom, garden stuff
Nabhanya—celestial
Nabhanya—heavenly, springing forth from heaven
Nabhan—big sky
Nabhaswatee—one who creates sound in sky
Nabhaswati—creator of noise in sky
Nabha—noble high, sky
Nabhita—fearless
Nabhitha—fearless
Nabhi—central, centre of body
Nabhomani—the sun
Nabhya—central, centre of body
Nabya—new
Nachiketa—fire
Nachiyar—good dancer
Nachi—fire
Nachni—dancer, suggestive look
Nadantika—a name of the river, reed destroyer
Nadavala—a quantity of reed
Nadeen—loveir
Nadhine—river
Nadhiya—simple, soft
Nadia—filled with support, indoctrination, assuredness, caller, moist
Nadina—large
Nadira—pinnacle, rare, valuable, valued, rare
Nadiya—river, support, indoctrination, assuredness, generous, successful
Nadja—support, indoctrination, assuredness
Nadni—gift of sun
Nadya—support, indoctrination, assuredness, generous
Naesha—special, sharp minded
Naffisha—incurable price

Nafrin—negotiable
Nagaja—born of the mountain
Nagajothi—illumination, luminosity, radiance, snake
Nagakanti—tree name
Nagalakshmi—central
Nagalata—snake goddess
Nagamagal—pretty, lovely, handsome, graceful name
Nagamani—monarch, ruler, prince, earl of diamond, gem of serpents
Nagamatree—mother of serpent
Nagammai—mother of snake
Nagamuthu—the beginning, first
Naganalatha—snake goddess
Naganandini—mountain born
Naganika—serpent maiden
Naganjara—elephant
Nagasaishree—god name
Nagasakthi—power of snakes
Nagashree—name of princess
Nagashree—snake goddess
Nagasri—the wealth of serpents
Nagaveni—hair like snake
Nageswari—goddess of the mountain
Nagija—daughter of serpent
Nagila—best among serpent
Nagila—best among serpents
Nagina—ornament, jewellery, ornamentation, adornment, figuration
Nagina—ornament, jewellery, ornamentation, adornment, figuration, gem, pearl
Nagini—snake
Nagma—diamond, melodious song
Nagu—sacred god snake
Nahar—tributary, day
Nahem—praise lord
Naia—boat, flowing
Naidhrua—parvatilmost perfect
Naihita—glorious
Naija—daughter of wisdom
Naila—acquirer, obtainer
Naima—belonging to one

Naima—calm, belonging to one, graceful
Naimee—blinmonarch, ruler, prince, earl of eye, glimmers
Naimiti—earth's daughter
Naimitra—lord shiva
Naimi—joy, sweetness, pleasantness
Naimlochane—with twinkling eye, glimmers
Nainadeity—goddess's eye, glimmers
Nainashree—good monarch, ruler, prince, earl eye, glimmers
Naina—eye, glimmers, goddess
Naina—eye, glimmers, goddess in nainital
Nainika—pupil of the eye, glimmers
Nainisha—pretty, lovely, handsome, graceful eye, glimmers
Naini—a girl with pretty, lovely, handsome, graceful eye, glimmers
Nainshi—pretty, lovely, handsome, graceful like eye, glimmers
Nainsi—grace, graceful
Nain—eye, glimmers, beauty, pleasantness
Naira—woman with big eye, glimmers
Naireeti—pretty, lovely, handsome, graceful name
Nairita—coming from the southwest
Nairiti—fairypsara, princessngel
Naisargi—natural
Naisa—affection
Naiser—founder of clans
Naishada—poetry
Naishadha—poetry
Naisha—special, sharp minded
Naishi—ornament, jewellery, ornamentation, adornment, figuration, rose
Naitee—destiny
Naitika—incessant, regular
Naiti—incessant
Naitree—eye, glimmers
Naitri—eye, glimmers, goddess lakshmi
Naitro—sweet
Naitvika—pretty, lovely, handsome, graceful eye, glimmers

Naivedhi—prasad offered to god
Naivedhya—offering to god
Naivedya—offering to god
Naivya—new, fresh, recent
Naivy—blue related
Naiyah—new
Naiya—boat, water nymph
Najma—star, valuable, valued, rare, sorry, moon
Nakeeta—residency, earth
Nakiska—star
Nakita—victory of the people
Nakkan—brightness of face, new
Nakshanjali—new
Nakshathra—star
Nakshatramala—sequence of stars
Nakshatra—star, pearl, twinkle star
Naksha—map, star
Nakshika—one who love stars
Nakshita—one with pretty, lovely, handsome, graceful features
Nakshthra—star
Nakshtramala—chain of star
Nakshtra—star, map
Nakti—night
Nakula—goddess parvati
Nakuli—lord shiva's wife
Nalada—the nectar
Nalaka—at nanital a goddess in a temple
Nalayini—special
Nala—successful, beloved, highness, empress, queen
Nalika—lotus, lotus stalk
Nalima—pretty, lovely, handsome, graceful name
Nalinakshi—lotus eye, glimmers
Nalinakshi—one with eye, glimmers llike dear
Nalina—lotus, water-lily
Nalindi—river
Naline—god
Nalini—bunch of lotus bloom, garden stuff
Nalini—lotus bloom, garden stuff, noushad
Nalin—lotus bloom, garden stuff
Nalita—lotus

Nalitz—good mind
Nalkubera—pretty, lovely, handsome, graceful
Nallamma—good woman, good mother
Nallarasi—onre with lotus like eye, glimmers
Nallini—excellent and sweet
Nalmee—fragrant, nectar
Nalukine—multitude of lotuses
Namagal—magnificent poetess, orator
Namahaswi—devoted towards respect
Namaha—respect, pray
Namana—bending, salute
Namani—respects
Namankita—good, famous
Namanshi—hello, namaste
Namansika—pretty, lovely, handsome, graceful name
Naman—bow to god
Namashvi—respect, pray
Namashwi—i bow, respect, pray
Namashya—worshipping, worthy of salutation
Namasri—devoted towards respect
Namasvi—goddess parvati, popularity
Namaswi—swan, respectful
Namasya—worthy of salutation, worshipping
Nama—greeting, gift, present, grace
Namisha—twinkling of an eye, glimmers
Namita—humble
Namita—humble, valuable, valued, rare one, kind-hearted
Namitha—simple, humble
Nami—wave, lord vishnu
Namrah—brave, tigress
Namrata—modesty
Namrata—polite nature, politeness
Namratha—obedient, politeness
Namruta—humble
Namrutha—obedient
Namuchi—politeness, permanent
Namu—bow, respect
Namya—the night, to be bowed to
Namya—to be bowed to, quiet
Nanadana—daughter, goddess durga

Nanaki—sister of guru nanak
Nanaki—sister of guru nanaka
Nanak—the first guru
Nancee—grace
Nancy—filled with grace flavour
Nancy—grace
Nandanaa—happiness, daughter, bloom, garden stuff
Nandana—daughter
Nandana—daughter, bloom, garden stuff, happiness
Nandani—goddess durga, holy cow
Nandayantee—bestowing joy
Nanda—born to achieve
Nanda—frolic, dancing
Nanda—joyful, happy
Nandeene—bestower of joy, goddess durga
Nandeeni—illumination, luminosity, radianceful holy cow
Nandeesha—lord shiva guard
Nandha—name of a goddess, parvathi
Nandhika—goddess lakshmi
Nandhine—daughter
Nandhini—a holy cow
Nandika—goddess lakshmi
Nandika—one who gives pleasure
Nandine—goddess ganga, happiness, daughter
Nandini—illumination, luminosity, radianceful, pleasing
Nandini—goddess durga, ganges, a dauther, pretty, lovely, handsome, graceful cow
Nandisa—morning glory
Nandisha—abode of lord shiva
Nanditaa—smile, happy, spread love
Nandita—happy, spread love, overly happy
Nandita—one who pleases
Nanditha—happiness, happy
Nandi—one who pleases others, bull of
Nandni—enjoyment
Nandra—lot of love
Nandu—special, cute than anything
Nangaishree—cultured lady
Nangai—cultured lady
Nanganallal—goddess durga

Nanma—goodness
Nansi—god has favoured me
Nanthini—love, kind, brave
Nanu—small, pretty, lovely, handsome, graceful
Naomika—goddess durga, lakshmi
Naomi—congeniality, enjoyment, pleasure
Narasamma—pretty, lovely, handsome, graceful name
Narayane—goddess parvati
Narayani—goddess lakshmi
Narayani—narayan's consort, goddess lakshmi
Narayini—mother goddess saraswati, lakshmi
Narbda—serenity, calm, calmness, stillness, silence, one who arouses tender
Nareshvari—name of goddess
Nargis—bloom, garden stuff, narcissus
Narine—related to a bloom, garden stuff
Narisha—goddess
Naristha—dear to a woman
Narita—given vigour
Narjee—bloom, garden stuff
Narmadadeity—goddess of narmada
Narmadaichelvi—goddess lakshmi
Narmadai—river
Narmada—a river
Narmada—serenity, calm, calmness, stillness, silence
Narmadha—one who arouses tender feelings
Narmadyutee—bright with joy
Narmatha—awesome highness, empress, queen that rules all lands
Narmeen—a bloom, garden stuff, delicate
Naroga—healthy
Narogi—healthy
Narois—bloom, garden stuff
Narpendyah—highness, empress, queen
Narshika—god gift
Nartan—dance
Narvi—active, leadership, inattentive

Naseeb—devotion luck, future
Naseema—gentle breeze, zephyr, fresh air
Naseem—breeze
Naseen—cool breeze
Nashely—the one that is loved or loved one
Nashika—forgiver, one who forgives
Nashita—energetic and full of life
Nashi—ours
Nashmika—pretty, lovely, handsome, graceful rose
Nasika—nose
Naswitha—another name of goddess parvati
Natali—princess
Natanamani—a dancer
Natanasundari—dance
Natana—makes others dance
Natasha—pretty, lovely, handsome, graceful
Natasha—gentle, simple
Natashree—pretty, lovely, handsome, graceful
Natee—female dancer who perform from place to place
Natesa—lord of dance
Nathika—new one
Nathiya—sweet, eternal, constant
Natika—consisting of actors and dancers
Natika—consisting of dancer and actors
Natisha—star, child of christmas
Natkuna—with good character
Natrisha—pretty, lovely, handsome, graceful name
Natun—new
Natya—dance, love
Nauka—boat
Naumika—one worthy to get praise
Nausat—child of christmas
Navadeep—new creation illumination, luminosity, radiance
Navadha—new comer
Navadha—nine types of worship in jainism
Navadurga—all nine forms of durga

Navajyoti—new illumination,
luminosity, radiance
Navajyoti—new illumination,
luminosity, radiance, new flame
Navakalika—newly married woman
Navalkishoree—very young
Naval—astonishing
Navamallika—new highness, empress,
queen
Navamani—new gem, gems
Navami—new, ninth tithi in astrology
Navaneta—butter
Navanetha—newly illumination,
luminosity, radiance lamp
Navangee—new body
Navangi—pretty, lovely, handsome,
graceful woman
Navanisha—new night
Navanitha—new
Navani—new, youthful woman, young
Navanthikaa—goddess lakshmi
Navanya—pretty, lovely, handsome,
graceful
Navan—champion
Navarasi—fresh jasmine bloom,
garden stuff
Navarasi—magnificent poetess, orator
Navashree—new
Navatara—butter
Navaya—simplest
Navbhagya—new luck
Navdeep—new shine, illumination,
luminosity, radiance
Navdha—new
Navdip—the sweet smell
Navdisha—new direction
Navedita—pretty, lovely, handsome,
graceful name
Navena—new
Navenya—newest
Naven—fresh, new, excellent, pleasant
Naveshni—pretty, lovely, handsome,
graceful name
Naveta—new
Navetha—new
Naveya—new, young
Navgun—nine good qualities
Navika—fresh, young

Navika—new
Navilu—ornamentation, adornment,
figuration
Navinata—newness
Navina—fresh, new
Navina—youthful, younger, new
Navinya—new
Navisha—confident, new, holy,
sanctified, pious, solemn, chaste, lord
shiva
Navishna—lord shiva
Navishthe—song of praise
Navistha—youngest
Navita—new
Navitha—new
Naviya—new one
Navi—new, holy, sanctified, pious,
solemn, chaste
Navjot—new illumination, luminosity,
radiance
Navjyoti—new flame, illumination,
luminosity, radiance
Navlika—name of goddess
Navmalni—a bloom, garden stuff
Navmi—ninth, goddess
Navneta—butter like
Navneta—butter, fresh
Navnet—one who is ever new
Navnidhi—nine treasures
Navnita—everyday new
Navodita—freshly risen
Navodita—newly created
Navpreet—new love
Navroop—new form
Navyamitha—new
Navyasri—new beginning
Navyata—new, fresh
Navya—new
Navya—new, novel, beauty of
highness, empress, queen
Navya—novel, new, worth praising,
young
Navya—worth praising
Nayaja—daughter of wisdom
Nayaki—female leader
Nayanatara—eye, glimmers like a star
Nayana—most pretty, lovely,
handsome, graceful eye, glimmers

Nayana—of the pretty, lovely, handsome, graceful eye, glimmers

Nayanika—one having pretty, lovely, handsome, graceful eye, glimmers

Nayani—sweet eye, glimmers

Nayansi—pretty, lovely, handsome, graceful eye, glimmers

Nayantaara—star of the eye, glimmers

Nayantara—iris, star of the eye, glimmers

Nayantara—star of our eye, glimmers

Nayantika—pretty, lovely, handsome, graceful

Nayan—eye, glimmers

Nayara—very illumination, luminosity, radiance, leadership, leader

Naya—to admire god

Nayera—gift of god, fashionable, lucky

Nayika—actress

Nayna—icywesome, cool, cute

Naynika—eye, glimmers

Nayni—with pretty, lovely, handsome, graceful eye, glimmers

Nayonika—bright eye, glimmers,

Nayra—pretty, lovely, handsome, graceful

Nayrika—pretty, lovely, handsome, graceful name

Naysa—miracale of god

Naysha—life

Nazeena—gift of god, love

Nazima—song, poetess, matron

Naz—pride

Neats—nice

Neebha—resembling, similar

Needhi—principle, treasure, wealth, money

Neeharika—snow, dew drop

Neehar—holy, sanctified, pious, solemn, chaste

Neeha—dew drop, affection, diamond

Neeja—lily bloom, garden stuff

Neekisha—fresh air

Neekita—pretty, lovely, handsome, graceful, residency, earth

Neelabja—blue lotus

Neeladree—blue peak

Neelaja—river starting from blue mountain

Neelakamatchi—iris, eye, glimmers as bright as stars

Neelakanimozhi—dew drops

Neelaksha—blue eye, glimmers

Neelakshi—blue eye, glimmers

Neelakshi—blue-eye, glimmers

Neelambaree—one who is dressed in blue clothes

Neelambaree—one who wears blue clothes, a ragni

Neelambari—blue sky

Neelambika—pretty, lovely, handsome, graceful name

Neelam—blue diamond, sapphire, blue gem

Neelam—blue sapphire

Neelangini—wife of lord shiva

Neelanjana—black surma

Neelanjana—blue eye, glimmers

Neelanjasha—blue hued illumination, luminosity, radiance

Neelashini—pretty, lovely, handsome, graceful name

Neelashni—pretty, lovely, handsome, graceful name

Neelavalli—pretty, lovely, handsome, graceful name

Neelavani—a sapphire

Neelavathi—blue sea

Neelaveni—one with long hair

Neela—blue colour

Neela—blue, green colour

Neelesha—the happy sapphire, bloom, garden stuff

Neelesh—lord krishna, the moon

Neelgandhika—the blue ruby

Neelimaa—blue complexioned

Neelima—blue

Neelima—sky colour, blue sky

Neelimpika—little cow

Neeline—the indigo plant

Neeli—the sky's colour, illumination, luminosity, radiance blue

Neelja—a river

Neelja—blue

Neelkamala—blue lotus

Neelkamal—blue lotus
Neelmani—blue diamond, sapphire
Neelu—a green plant
Neelu—diamond, blue, green
Neema—saint kabir's mother
Neema—very brave
Neemisha—who believe in god
Neenada—melodious sound
Neena—new, emotion, better
Neenika—water, earthir
Neepa—kadamb tree
Neepa—name of a bloom, garden stuff
Neerada—rain clouds
Neerajakshi—one with lotus eye, glimmers
Neerajana—act of adoration
Neeraja—holy, sanctified, pious, solemn, chaste, clean, water born
Neeraja—lotus, goddess lakshmi
Neerajita—illuminated
Neeraj—most popular, lotus
Neerali—unique, different from all
Neeranjana—holy, sanctified, pious, solemn, chaste, spotless
Neera—consisting of water
Neera—holy, sanctified, pious, solemn, chaste water, soft, young one
Neerda—blue
Neerja—avatar, goddess lakshmi
Neerja—lotus
Neeru—water, illumination, luminosity, radiance
Neerva—holy, sanctified, pious, solemn, chaste water
Neeshal—pretty, lovely, handsome, graceful name
Neesha—night
Neeshika—night
Neeshitha—pleasant, kind, generous
Neeshu—night, darkness
Neetaa—with in rules, moral, night
Neetal—holy, sanctified, pious, solemn, chaste
Neeta—upright, bear, night
Neeta—wells behaved, upright
Neethika—angel of valuable, valued, rare stone
Neethi—policy, justice

Neethu—clear, wonderful, pretty, lovely, handsome, graceful
Neetika—angel of valuable, valued, rare stone
Neetima—goddess lakshmi
Neetisha—one who is well-versed in law
Neetiya—name of goddess lakshmi
Neeti—conduct, guidance
Neeti—policy, good behaviour
Neetu—earth
Neeva—blue, radiance
Neevisha—pretty, lovely, handsome, graceful name
Neeyashini—moon nature
Neeyati—nature, behaviour
Nehali—innocent
Nehal—rainy, brilliant, sagacious, gifted, wise
Neharika—blessed, protected by god
Nehar—dew drop, mist, fog
Nehasri—ultimate, absolute, highest, best
Neha—pretty, lovely, handsome, graceful eye, glimmers
Neha—affection, love
Nehha—eye, glimmersight, pretty, lovely, handsome, graceful eye, glimmers
Nehita—glory
Nehula—new
Neilesha—blue colour
Neimisha—twinkling of an eye, glimmers
Neina—eye, glimmers
Neisha—night
Neismitha—smile
Neity—eternal, everlasting, fortune
Nekeisha—women
Nekita—victory, victorious
Nekitha—angel, residency, earth
Nelanjanaa—within rules
Nelika—blue eye, glimmers
Nelima—blue, bloom, garden stuff
Nelu—blue, clever, rich
Nemali—bird, peacock
Nemasha—passionate, pretty, lovely, handsome, graceful, curious

Nema—rules
Nemet—a gift of god
Nemisha—momentary, twinkling of eye, glimmers
Nemishta—sweet, satisfies
Nena—eye, glimmers, favour, grace
Nency—grace, happy
Nenshi—eye, glimmers with pride
Nensi—full of joy, happy
Nerisha—illumination, luminosity, radiance of the home
Nerona—pretty, lovely, handsome, graceful
Nesamani—love, rain
Nesara—sun
Nesa—moral
Nesham—happiness
Nesheka—holy, sanctified, pious, solemn, chaste, night
Neshitha—loveffection
Neshwari—goddess gayatri
Nesika—pretty, lovely, handsome, graceful name
Nethra—eye, glimmers, eye, glimmers
Netrali—pretty, lovely, handsome, graceful eye, glimmers
Netravati—pretty, lovely, handsome, graceful-eye, glimmers
Netravi—pretty, lovely, handsome, graceful eye, glimmers
Netra—eye, glimmers
Netrika—eye, glimmers, part of eye, glimmers
Nevanshi—part of new
Nevedha—lord buddha
Nevika—beauty
Neyamani—new
Neyha—rain, love
Neysa—holy, sanctified, pious, solemn, chaste, brilliant, sagacious, gifted, wise, learned
Niara—of high purpose
Nia—intention, female champion
Nibha—like, similar
Nibha—resembling, similar, like
Nichika—consisting of parts
Nichita—covered, flowing down
Nichya—promising of self

Nicika—a great pleasure, perfect
Nickita—covered, flowing down
Nidali—pretty, lovely, handsome, graceful name
Nidarshna—pretty, lovely, handsome, graceful name
Nida—to call, voice
Niddha—having a treasure
Niddhi—money, cash, goddess lakshmi
Nideesha—pretty, lovely, handsome, graceful name
Nidha—pretty, lovely, handsome, graceful
Nidhepa—giving nature, devotional, knowledge
Nidhersha—discipline
Nidhe—treasure
Nidhiksha—silence beauty, treasure, wealth
Nidhipa—treasure
Nidhisha—treasure, wealth, money, life
Nidhi—treasure, wealth, money, life
Nidhi—wealth
Nidhyana—intuition
Nidhyathi—meditation
Nidi—shine upon, treasure
Nidra—slep
Nidyatee—meditation
Niesha—full of life, holy, sanctified, pious, solemn, chaste
Nigah—eye, glimmers, view, look
Nigama—phrase of music
Nihali—generosity, passing clouds
Nihal—romantic, joyful
Nihanshi—never ending, joyful
Nihara—mist
Nihara—snow drop, waterfall
Nihareeka—bunches of star
Niharikaa—one having pretty, lovely, handsome, graceful eye, glimmers
Niharika—akash ganga
Niharika—first rain drop, goddess lakshmi
Nihari—star
Niharshana—true

Niha—pretty, lovely, handsome, graceful, holy, sanctified
Nihira—treasure, newly found treasure
Nihitha—everlasting, ever living, sweet
Nihu—lovely
Nija—one who is your own
Nija—truth, successful, white rose
Nijitha—devotee of lord viswajith
Nijta—combination of love, union of love
Niju—pan-sophist
Nij—thankful
Nikandarya—goddess saraswati
Nikara—collection
Nikeeta—not scared
Niketak—home
Niketa—goddess lakshmi, home
Nikhara—luster, beautify shine
Nikhila—entire
Nikhila—whole, complete, smart
Nikhisha—brilliant
Nikhita—sharp, the earth
Nikhita—the earth
Nikhitha—earth, victorious people
Nikisha—pretty, lovely, handsome, graceful
Nikitaa—temple
Nikita—residency, earth, victorious
Nikitha—the earth, goddess lakshmi
Nikki—people's triumph
Nikoo—pretty, lovely, handsome, graceful bloom
Nikrritee—dishonesty
Niksha—victorious
Nikshiptha—victory, treasure
Nikula—family art
Nikulinika—inherited the art
Nikunj—bower, birds nest, garden
Niku—people of victory, cute
Nilakshi—blue-eye, glimmers
Nilambari—clothed in blue
Nilam—blue sapphire, blue gem
Nilani—enchanting moon
Nilanjali—blue water, pretty, lovely, handsome, graceful eye, glimmers
Nilanjana—one with blue eye, glimmers

Nilanshi—part of lord shiva, blue ansh
Nilan—blue ornament, jewellery, ornamentation, adornment, figuration
Nilaruna—first illumination, luminosity, radiance of dawn
Nilasha—blueness, starting newly
Nilashri—blue beauty
Nilavarasi—pretty, lovely, handsome, graceful highness
Nilavoli—ray of illumination, luminosity, radiance from the moon
Nilav—bluish, sing of love
Nilaxshi—coordinated
Nilaya—home
Nila—blue
Nila—moon, blue coloured
Nila—moon, enchanting moon
Nilema—a beauty by its blue reflection
Nilen—surrendered
Nilima—blueness
Nilima—new bloom, garden stuff, blue
Nilimpa—name of holy cow
Nilini—perpetrator of the kuru race
Nilmani—a ornament, jewellery, ornamentation, adornment, figuration of heaven
Niloufer—a celestial
Nilsa—life, good
Nilshikha—blue mountain's top
Nilutha—providing water
Nilu—pretty, lovely, handsome, graceful, rich, blue in colour
Nimai—blueness
Nimayak—lord of gem
Nima—renowned adjust measure
Nimeela—pretense
Nimeesha—momentary, split second, princess
Nimiksha—serenity, calm, calmness, stillness, silence, twinkling of an eye, glimmers
Nimila—closing the eye, glimmers
Nimilika—closing the eye, glimmers
Nimisha—serenity, calm, calmness, stillness, silence, twinkling of an eye
Nimisha—the twinkling of an eye, glimmers
Nimita—fixed

Nimittaka—kissing
Nimi—a moment
Nimi—friend of fire
Nimlocha—the setting of the sun
Nimmi—pretty, lovely, handsome, graceful eye, glimmers, home
Nimmi—twinkling
Nimmy—sparkling of eye, glimmers
Nimra—cute girl, soft lion
Nimrit—humble, decided by god
Nimrukree—sun set
Ninarika—misty
Nina—love support, indoctrination, assuredness, lovely-eye, glimmers
Nina—splendour, ornament, jewellery, ornamentation, adornment, figuration
Niomi—pretty, lovely, handsome, graceful love
Nipa—kadamb tree
Nipa—one who watches over
Nipeksha—calm
Nipti—knowledgeable, treasure
Nipuna—expert
Nipuna—perfect
Nipunika—expert woman
Nipurna—perfection
Niradhara—calm
Nirahankara—she who is without egoism
Niraimadhi—full moon
Niraimathi—full moon
Niraj—born of water, lotus bloom, garden stuff
Nirakaari—formless
Nirakari—one without any figure, appearance, structure or form
Nirakula—she who is without agitation
Nirala—exceptional
Nirale—exceptional
Nirale—unique, different
Niralika—unique, different
Nirali—different, unique
Niralya—different, unique
Niral—calm
Niramala—holy, sanctified, pious, solemn, chaste
Niramaya—simplicity, purity, without

Niramaye—holy, sanctified, pious, solemn, chaste, clean, spotless
Niramaye—momentary
Niranjana—joyful, river
Niranjana—name of river, goddess durga, unstained
Niranjini—without blemish
Nirantara—uninterrupted, without interior
Niranya—figure, appearance, structureless
Niravi—bliss
Nira—consisting of water, juice
Nira—liquid
Nirbhaya—fearless
Nirbhaye—fearless, brave
Nirbhayi—fearless
Nirbha—shining appearance
Nirbhetha—fearless
Nirbisha—medicine plant
Nireeksha—support, indoctrination, assuredness, expectation
Nireeksha—to search
Nireesha—happiness, silent nature
Nirel—calm
Nireshika—power of god, love of father
Nirgunayai—name of goddess durga
Nirguna—attribute-less
Nirgundee—the root of lotus
Nirikshana—watching, guarding
Niriksha—unseen, expectation, support, indoctrination, assuredness
Niriksha—unseen, support, indoctrination, assuredness
Nirisha—happiness, silent nature
Niriskhana—no end
Nirjala—love, serenity, calm, calmness, stillness, silence of water
Nirjara—young, not becoming old
Nirjaree—not become old
Nirja—goddess lakshmi, lotus
Nirjhara—immortal
Nirjharine—fountain, victory of death
Nirjhari—watery
Nirmada—who is without pride
Nirmalakumari—holy, sanctified, pious, solemn, chaste, unbiased

Nirmalarani—goddess durga
Nirmala—holy, sanctified, pious, solemn, chaste, clean
Nirmala—the cleanest one, virtuous, holy, sanctified, pious, solemn, chaste
Nirmalya—holy, sanctified, pious, solemn, chaste, devotion, blue eye, glimmers
Nirmal—holy, sanctified, pious, solemn, chaste, without any impurity
Nirmarshtee—washing
Nirmatri—maker, producer
Nirmaya—holy, sanctified, pious, solemn, chaste, clean, kindness
Nirmaye—without blemish, purity
Nirmayi—without blemish
Nirmay—holy, sanctified, pious, solemn, chaste
Nirma—neat, clean
Nirmita—created
Nirmitha—created
Nirmiti—produce, new construction
Niroopan—god like
Niroopa—figure, appearance, structureless
Niroopa—without figure, appearance, structure
Nirosha—pious, goddess lakshmi
Nirritee—calamity
Niruaimi—beloved pretty, lovely, handsome, graceful illumination
Nirupadhih—she who has no limitations
Nirupama—incomparable
Nirupama—unmatched, unique, incomparable
Nirupamma—one who is incomparable
Nirupana—form, sight
Nirupa—bright decree, command
Nirupma—gayatri
Nirupma—incomparable
Nirushi—pretty, lovely, handsome, graceful name
Niruta—pretty, lovely, handsome, graceful name
Niruthiya—pretty, lovely, handsome, graceful name

Niru—beauty of heavenly goddess, water
Nirvana—one who blows out, deep silence
Nirvane—goddess of bliss
Nirvani—goddess of bliss
Nirva—holy, sanctified, pious, solemn, chaste water
Nirveli—water child
Nirvighna—no disturbances, without obstacles
Nirvigna—success in all deeds
Nirvikara—she who is unchanging
Nirvisha—land of bliss
Nirvita—god gift
Nirvi—bliss
Nirwa—holy, sanctified, pious, solemn, chaste water
Niryanshi—pretty, lovely, handsome, graceful name
Niryuha—prominence, chaplet, crest
Nirzara—young, not becoming old
Nisagra—nature
Nisanthi—serenity, calm, calmness, stillness, silence
Nisarga—nature
Nisar—warm cloth
Nisa—night, beauty, lady, women
Nischala—immovable, fixed, quiet
Nischal—a decree, command
Nischera—coming forth
Nischintitia—free from anxiety
Nischitha—sure
Nishadee—night
Nishadi—twiillumination, luminosity, radiance
Nishajala—water of the night
Nishala—constant not moving
Nishali—different style
Nishama—infinite, matchless
Nishandhi—unique, incomparable
Nishanthi—the whole world
Nisharga—pretty, lovely, handsome, graceful name
Nisharvi—night, quite, the whole world
Nishay—a decree, command
Nisha—night

Nisha—night, perfect, quite
Nishchala—constant, unwavering
Nishchala—steady
Nishchith—sure
Nishdha—pretty, lovely, handsome, graceful, honest
Nisheta—deep search
Nishidha—pretty, lovely, handsome, graceful name
Nishidh—gift oblation
Nishigandha—sweet intoxication
Nishikanta—lord of the night
Nishikanta—the moon
Nishika—holy, sanctified, pious, solemn, chaste, honest, night
Nishila—highness, empress, queen of nights
Nishita—alert, sharp night, sharp
Nishita—night
Nishithini—night
Nishittha—devotion, determined
Nishi—alert, getting stronger
Nishi—night
Nishkalanka—who is faultless
Nishkala—linga form of lord shiva
Nishka—holy, sanctified, pious, solemn, chaste, honest, kind, giving
Nishka—undeceitful
Nishkutika—a pleasure grove near the house
Nishma—eye, glimmers or moon, illumination, luminosity, radiance, bright
Nishna—clever
Nishra—in her shadow, night, quite
Nishree—river, goddess lakshmi
Nishta—ambition, intent, passion
Nishtha—devotion
Nishtha—devotion, devotion
Nishtha—loyalty, intention
Nishthha—diligence
Nishu—darkness, night most
Nishva—pretty, lovely, handsome, graceful name
Nisita—night
Nistaranga—lakshmi
Nistha—devotion, firm
Nisu—night, darkness

Niswa—pretty, lovely, handsome, graceful name
Nitajtana—earth, ganges
Nital—joy, win
Nitambine—with pretty, lovely, handsome, graceful lips
Nitanshi—eternal, everlasting, morning sun rays
Nitara—a star, deep rooted
Nitasha—form of natasha, kind, strong
Nita—serious, gracious, with in rules
Nitey—policy, rules
Nithali—never ending
Nitha—carried, red
Nithika—pretty, lovely, handsome, graceful
Nithilamani—honest
Nithilam—holy, sanctified, pious, solemn, chaste like the pearl
Nithila—pretty, lovely, handsome, graceful like pearl
Nithina—pretty, lovely, handsome, graceful
Nithini—principle
Nithisha—goddess of justice, lusters forever
Nithishka—lusters forever, glittering pearl
Nithiyakalyani—devotion
Nithiyakumari—moral
Nithiya—forever
Nithi—destiny
Nithra—slep
Nithura—brilliant, sagacious, gifted, wise, learned
Nithu—adorable, similar to nita
Nithyahasini—always smiling
Nithyakumari—pretty, lovely, handsome, graceful name
Nithyasri—goddess lakshmi
Nithya—always, constant, eternal
Nitigya—knowledge of policy
Nitika—moral person
Nitika—morality, niti means policy
Nitiksha—goddess lakshmi
Nitima—girl of principles
Nitisha—good planning, best creation

Nitish—pretty, lovely, handsome, graceful name
Nitiya—pretty, lovely, handsome, graceful name
Niti—rules, morality, policy
Nitu—adorable, moral
Nityabuddha—who is ever wise
Nityanshi—everyday, constant
Nityapriya—ever pleasing
Nityashree—with eternal beauty
Nityashree—with eternal beauty, soul
Nityashri—with eternal beauty
Nityasree—with eternal beauty
Nityasri—with eternal beauty
Nityasuddha—who is eternally holy, sanctified, pious, solemn, chaste
Nityavinodini—always pleasing, evergreen joy
Nitya—constant, goddess durga
Nitya—everyday, constant, continuously
Nivah—holy, sanctified, pious, solemn, chaste
Nivali—tribute
Nivansha—religious, holy, sanctified, pious, solemn, chaste, holy
Nivanshita—holy, holy, sanctified, pious, solemn, chaste, religious
Nivanshi—cute little baby
Nivashini—place to live, home, lord vishnu
Niva—sun, hug, renew, expression
Niva—to become fat
Niveda—offering to god
Nivedha—offering made to god
Nivedhita—devoted, offered to god
Nivedhitha—offered to god
Nivedhi—offered to god, requestful
Nivedhya—offering to god
Nivedita—offered to god, requestful
Nivedita—surrendered to god
Niveditha—offered to god
Nivedi—requestful, offered to god
Niverta—bliss
Nivesha—goddess lakshmi
Nivessha—prosperity, investment
Nivetaa—creative

Nivetha—holy, sanctified, pious, solemn, chaste, tree branch, sweet
Nivetha—offering made to god
Nivethitha—happiness
Nivika—new
Nivisha—lord shiva
Nivita—creative
Nivitha—creative
Nivitri—goddess durga, princess
Nivi—new born, water
Nivriti—bliss, satisfaction
Nivritti—non-attachment, bliss, retirement
Nivruta—the one who can win
Nivya—highness, empress, queen, freshness, foundation
Niyana—obedient
Niyankita—one having pretty, lovely, handsome, graceful eye, glimmers
Niyanshi—happy
Niyanta—creator, name for brahma
Niyasa—serenity, calm, calmness, stillness, beauty of heart
Niyatha—fate, destiny
Niyathi—fate, fortune, ultimate, absolute, highest, best powers
Niyati—destiny, luck, fate, fortune
Niya—friend, new achievement, graceful
Niyuktha—commanded, sign
Niyutsha—warrior
Nizel—champion pretty, lovely, handsome, graceful bird
Nmi—soft, softness
Noboya—name of goddess durga
Nolly—full of joy
Nona—the ninth one
Nonu—cute
Nooparottama—with the best anklet
Noopur—anklet
Noopur—anklet of lord krishna
Noorani—god's illumination, luminosity, radiance
Noorien—illumination, luminosity, radiance
Noori—shining
Noorjehan—illumination, luminosity, radiance of the world

Noorpreet—illumination, luminosity, radiance and love
Noor—sympathy, compassion
Noshitha—great
Noshi—sweet
Novika—new
Nrideva—pretty, lovely, handsome, graceful name
Nripamala—nice look
Nripa—monarch, ruler, prince, earl, love
Nrithya—an indian dance form
Nrithyika—emerged from dance, lord shiva
Nriti—dance
Nritya—dance
Nrity—dance
Nrupal—pretty, lovely, handsome, graceful name
Nrupa—feet of a monarch, ruler, prince, earl
Nruthya—dance
Nudhar—gold, unattached
Nuha—the sage, intelligence, mind
Numi—pretty, lovely, handsome, graceful name
Nupoor—anklet
Nupura—anklet
Nupur—payal, honest, anklet
Nushi—sweet, sanskrit
Nushka—valuable, valued, rare possession

Nusrat—help, victory, honest
Nutan—new
Nutan—new, modern
Nuthana—new
Nuthan—new, sweet
Nuti—praise
Nuti—worship, praise, reverence
Nutten—new
Nuzha—pleasure trip, excursion spot
Nyamani—good-natured
Nyara—be humble, pretty, lovely, handsome, graceful
Nyarika—justice
Nyasa—purity, divinity within the body
Nyasha—merciful, kind-hearted
Nyayika—logician
Nyja—real, fact
Nymisha—holly place, forest, wood, jungle, dark
Nyneishia—princess
Nynika—pupil of the eye, glimmers
Nyota—warrior, star
Nyra—rose, beauty of goddess saraswati
Nyrudhya—change of wind
Nyrudya—change of wind
Nysha—special, new beginning
Nyshita—illumination, luminosity, radiance climate, goddess lakshmi
Nytra—eye, glimmers

****

Indian Names For Girls—O

Oashni—god's valuable, valued, rare gift
Occhar—lucky
Ochitya—conclusion
Odaka—apple flavour
Odaniya—anklet
Odathi—refreshing, owner
Odika—wild rice, anklet
Oditi—dawn
Oeshi—god's valuable, valued, rare gift
Ohana—friend, family
Oindrila—another name for the wife of indra
Oishi—gift of god, holy, pure, sanctified, pious, solemn
Ojabala—having power
Ojada—vigourening
Ojala—illumination, luminosity, radiance
Ojal—splendour, vision, shelter
Ojasa—splendour, shine, vigour
Ojasbala—goddess of bodhi tree
Ojasini—energetic, vigourous
Ojastara—vigourous, powerful, energetic
Ojasvati—full of brightness
Ojasve—brave
Ojasve—brave, bright
Ojasvini—almighty, fearless
Ojasvini—full of brightness, splendid
Ojasvita—full of brightness, energetic
Ojasvita—personality
Ojasvi—bright
Ojasvi—fearless
Ojaswati—full of brightness
Ojaswine—brave, energetic, powerful
Ojaswini—full of brightness
Ojaswitaa—dawn
Ojaswita—energetic, brightness
Ojasya—mighty
Ojayati—having vital energy, vitality
Oja—vitality
Ojeeta—born in the month of falgun

Ojmana—speedy, vigourous
Ojobala—having power
Ola—wealth, ancestor, valuable, valued, rare, worth
Olevia—leaf
Olichudar—brilliant
Olikodi—brilliant
Olimani—brilliant
Olirmathi—powerful
Olisudar—helping
Oliyarasi—brilliant
Oli—angel, honeybees
Omaira—awesome, star, red
Omaja—result of spiritual unity
Omakshi—auspicious eye, glimmers
Omala—earth
Omala—the sacred word for the earth
Omana—protector, friend, helper
Omana—woman
Oma—leader, giver of life, commanding
Oma—the sound of universe
Omeesha—goddess of birth
Omela—pretty, lovely, handsome, graceful, graceful
Omeswari—devoted towards devotion
Omica—god's blessing, gift
Omika—kind
Omila—protector, friend
Omisha—goddess of birth, death
Omita—lord shiva
Omi—the sound of universe, warrior
Omja—born of cosmic unity
Omkali—pretty, lovely, handsome, graceful name
Omkara—an auspicious beginning
Omkareshwari—goddess parvati, gauri
Omkari—prosperous, auspicious beginning
Omla—earth
Omnavi—love
Omparee—angel of god
Omprabha—power of om
Omprabha—radiance

Omprakash—illumination, luminosity, radiance of god
Omshri—combination of god
Omsi—generous
Omsree—prosperous sacred syllable
Omvati—holy lady
Omvati—sacred, having the power of om
Omyawati—helping, favourable
Omya—help, kindness, favour
Omya—life giver, pretty, lovely, handsome, graceful, prettiest
Omysha—smile
Onalika—the daugher of natraj
Onella—illumination, luminosity, radiancerch
Oni—ambition, intent, passion, wanted, born on a holy
Onkari—goddess parvati
Onkita—intelligence
Ooghavati—a woman
Ooha—a dream, imagination
Oomiya—pretty, lovely, handsome, graceful
Oongaranayagi—shelter
Oongararubini—ganga river's name
Oorjane—belonging to energy
Oorjasvatee—full of energy
Oorjaswati—daughter of monarch, powerful
Oorja—energy
Oorja—the energy
Oormaya—wavy, night
Oormika—wave, humming of a bee
Oormika—wave, ring
Oormila—daughter of king janaka
Oormila—of the waves of passion
Oormi—current
Oormi—goddess of birth and death
Oormy—powerful ray
Oornavati—rich in shep
Oorna—woollen
Oorubilva—broad leaved
Ooruja—born from the thigh

Oorvashi—an angel
Oorvi—earth
Ooshma—heat spring
Ooviyanangai—wave
Ooviyapavai—humming sound of bee
Opalina—ornament, jewellery, ornamentation, adornment, figuration
Opaline—ornament, jewellery, ornamentation
Opal—ornament, jewellery, ornamentation, adornment, figuration
Oparna—parvati
Opel—a ornament, jewellery, ornamentation, adornment, rare stone
Oppilamani—best
Oppilarasi—princess whom cannot be compared
Oppiliya—fearless
Ormi—a wave
Orni—pretty, lovely, handsome, graceful, pretty
Orpita—offering
Orvi—the earth
Oshadhi—medicine, herb
Osha—shining, burning
Oshdhi—medicine
Oshe—born from rivers
Oshika—limitless, successful, happy
Oshima—persevering and strong-willed
Oshin—ocean, sea, successful
Oshma—summer season
Oshmi—personality, shine of ice
Otave—responsible
Ourvi—earth
Oushadhi—plants with healing power
Ova—from a little egg, happy, bright
Ovia—drawing, painting
Oviya—artist, pretty, lovely, handsome, graceful drawing
Ovi—pretty, holy message of saint
Oyshe—holy, pure, sanctified, pious, solemn
Ozal—vision

****

Indian Names For Girls—P

Pabitra—purity, holy
Pachaiamma—green girl
Pacholi—an aromatic oil
Padama—lotus, goddess lakshmi
Padamja—goddess lakshmi
Padamshree—a reward
Padhma—lotus
Padimni—like a bloom, garden stuff
Padmaa—draupadi
Padmabati—goddess lakshmi
Padmadeity—durga deity
Padmagriha—who resides in a lotus
Padmahasta—goddess lakshmi
Padmajai—born from lotus, goddess lakshmi
Padmaja—goddess lakshmi
Padmaja—goddess lakshmi, born from lotus
Padmakala—lotus
Padmakali—lotus bud
Padmakshi—one with lotus-like eye, glimmers
Padmalatha—pretty, lovely, handsome, graceful name
Padmalaya—lake of lotuses
Padmala—born from lotus, lakshmi
Padmala—lotus
Padmalcohan—eye, glimmers like lotus
Padmalochana—eye, glimmers like lotus
Padmalochana—lotus eye, glimmers
Padmalochani—a woman with eye, glimmers like lotus
Padmalya—goddess lakshmi
Padmal—lotus
Padmamalini—goddess lakshmi
Padmamukhi—lotus faced
Padmanayani—lotus eye, glimmers
Padmana—lotus faced
Padmani—excellent woman
Padmanjali—full of lotus in the hand
Padmapatra—goddess lakshmi
Padmapriya—lover of lotus
Padmarane—highness, empress, queen of the lotus
Padmarekha—lotus-like lines on palm
Padmaroopa—like a lotus
Padmasambhava—one who is born out of lotus
Padmasana—goddess lakshmi seated on the lotus
Padmashree—holy, pure, sanctified, pious, solemn lotus
Padmashri—holy, pure, sanctified, pious, solemn lotus
Padmasree—holy, pure, sanctified, pious, solemn lotus
Padmasri—holy, pure, sanctified, pious, solemn lotus
Padmavarana—a woman with colour like lotus
Padmavasa—one who resided in lotus
Padmavathi—goddess lakshmi
Padmavathy—goddess lakshmi
Padmavati—goddess lakshmi
Padmavati—goddess lakshmi, bearer of lotus
Padma—pretty, lovely, handsome, graceful lotus bloom, garden stuff
Padma—goddess lakshmi
Padmine—one who is fond of lotus
Padmini—a collection of lotus
Padmini—lotus pond
Padmin—a female elephant
Padmma—goddess lakshmi
Padmodbhava—sprung from a lotus
Padnuni—lotus
Padvika—designated honour
Pagam—petal of lotus
Pahal—the start
Pahar—hour, time of day
Pahel—good starting
Pahi—petal of a bloom, garden stuff
Pajasvati—firm, strong, brilliant
Pajas—goddess lakshmi
Pajika—lotus pond
Pakala—lotus

Pakasansa—pretty, lovely, handsome, graceful name
Paka—dye, paint, simple, ignorant
Pakhe—a bird
Pakhi—bird, gorgeous bloom, garden stuff
Pakija—holy, pure, sanctified, pious, solemn
Pakima—sweetest
Pakshalika—full of feathers
Pakshalika—on the right path, bird
Pakshi—bird
Paku—nature
Palakshe—white
Palakshi—white
Palaksi—white, one with eye, glimmers like leaf
Palak—eye, glimmer, eye, glimmers lid, eye, glimmers
Palala—a straw
Palaniamma—goddess, respect love
Palashika—petal of palash bloom, garden stuff
Palashine—covered with foliage
Palashkusum—bird
Palas—understanding, rock
Palavi—new leaves, soft, bud, leaf
Palbha—soft, tender
Palchhin—pretty, lovely, handsome, graceful name
Palini—protector
Palin—protecting
Palita—daughter
Palita—guarded, protected
Palka—a remote place
Palkin—sweet eye, glimmers
Palki—blink of the eye, glimmers
Pallabi—tree, leaf
Pallari—an uncommon name
Pallave—bird
Pallave—creeper
Pallavika—new leaf, little blossom
Pallavika—resembling a blossom
Pallavine—new leaves
Pallavine—young shoot
Pallavini—new leaves, bud
Pallavita—eye, glimmers lid, blossoming

Pallavi—first stanza of poem
Pallavi—new leaf, soft
Pallavi—new leaves, sprout
Pallika—a small city
Palli—lamp
Pallvi—new leaves, new charm
Pall—bitter
Palmozi—child language
Palomi—dove, soft
Paluk—eye slashes, glimmer
Palvira—pretty, lovely, handsome, graceful name
Palvi—new leaves, leaf
Pameela—honey
Pamee—tender leaves
Pamela—a popular name
Pamela—honey, glimmers, sweetness, new leaves
Pammie—all-honey, sprouted, growing
Pammi—truly amiable, pleasing, suave, interesting, amiable, pleasing, suave
Pammy—all-honey, with new leaves
Pampa—name of the river
Pampa—river
Panache—fame, sparkle
Panaisha—best
Panchadakine—the fifth deities of energy
Panchale—another name of draupadi
Panchalika—a doll
Panchali—another name of draupadi
Panchali—draupadi
Panchami—illumination, luminosity, radiance of moon, festival
Panchavarnam—parrot, fifth girl of family
Panchhi—a bird
Panchichallika—doll
Panchika—independent free bird
Panchi—a free bird, independent, bird
Pandaribai—pretty, lovely, handsome, graceful name
Pandava—river
Pandavika—pandav's wife
Pandiamma—a doll
Pandita—learned, the wise man, good

Pandi—princess, droupadi
Panduloha—pretty, lovely, handsome, graceful name
Paneri—pretty, lovely, handsome, graceful
Panini—skillful, one of the inhabited
Panishka—water inherent, cool evening
Panishthe—admiration
Panita—admired
Pani—water, holy, sanctified, pious, solemn, chaste
Panjali—highness, empress, queen
Panju—very soft, soft minded
Pankajadharini—lotus holder
Pankajakshe—eye, glimmers like lotus
Pankajalochana—lotus eye, glimmers
Pankajam—lotus, born from mud
Pankajane—lotus plant
Pankajavalli—skilful
Pankaja—a lotus-bloom, garden stuff
Pankaja—mud born, lotus bloom, garden stuff
Pankajine—lotus plant
Pankajnayane—lotus eye, glimmers
Pankaj—lotus
Pankhadi—petal
Pankhdi—bloom, garden stuff petal
Pankhi—feathers
Pankhudi—wing of bird, petal
Pankhuri—petal
Pankhuri—wings of birds, petal of a bloom, garden stuff
Pankita—clayish, sludgy
Pankit—line
Pankti—a line of poem, sentence, pharse
Pankuni—month
Panna—emerald
Panna—emerald, grace, favoured by god
Panshu—it is one type of fruit
Pansve—amiable, pleasing, suave, interesting
Panthini—guider, one who leads the way
Panthi—traveller
Panth—the creed

Panu—admiration
Panvitha—bloom, garden stuff
Panyasree—beauty and goodness of the moon
Panya—admired, glorious, excellent
Paola—tiny, petite, small, petal
Papiha—a bird
Papiha—a sweet singing bird
Pappal—leader, ruler
Pappamma—sentence
Pappa—father, daddy
Parabhrita—cuckoo
Paragati—gyatri
Parag—emerald
Parajal—eye, glimmers-liner of warrior arjuna
Parajika—a ragini in indian music
Parajika—a ragni
Parajita—a lady name
Parala—a bode of cities
Parali—dry grass
Paral—eye, glimmers-liner of lord krishna's eye, glimmers
Paral—name of a bloom, garden stuff
Paramagna—an ancient woman
Paramahansa—ultimate, absolute, highest, best ascetic
Paramatmika—whose nature is the ultimate, absolute, highest, best
Parama—the best, most excellent
Parameshvari—ultimate goddess, goddess parvati
Parameshwari—ultimate, absolute, highest, best sovereign goddess
Paramesvary—the ultimate, absolute, highest, best
Parameswari—goddess durga
Paramita—wisdom
Paramita—wisdom, perfection, virtuous
Paramitha—wisdom
Paramjeet—ultimate, absolute, highest, bestly victorious
Paramjit—ultimate, absolute, highest, bestly victorious
Parana—father of water, the best
Paranjyoti—goddess durga
Parantika—everlasting

Parapushta—female cuckoo
Parashakti—ultimate, absolute, highest, best power
Parashree—ganga river
Parashvi—touchstone, gold maker
Parasmani—a touch stone which change iron metal into gold
Parasmani—touchstone
Paras—touchstone
Paravi—bird
Para—of the heaven
Para—the ultimate, absolute, highest, best
Parbarti—surrender
Parbatie—goddess parvati
Pareeka—pretty, lovely, handsome, graceful name
Pareekshita—ruler
Pareesa—pretty, lovely, handsome, graceful, like a fairy
Paree—fairy, pretty, lovely, handsome, graceful
Paresha—ultimate, absolute, highest, best lord
Pareshka—to challenge
Pareshthi—the highest worship
Parhi—highness, empress, stillness, silence, pretty, lovely, handsome, graceful
Paribhasha—definition
Parichaya—acquaintance
Parichiya—introduction
Paridhana—garment
Paridhi—circumference of the orbit, limit
Paridhi—realm
Parighya—knowledge
Parigyana— knowledged person
Pariha—land of the fairies
Parijatham—bloom, garden stuff
Parijat—a celestial bloom, garden stuff, born in heaven
Parija—fairytale, pleasant smell
Pariksha—exams, test challenge
Paril—love
Parimaladeity—goddess
Parimalam—fragrance, beauty, fairy
Parimalavalli—limit

Parimala—a substance with fragrance
Parimala—fragment, pretty, lovely, handsome, graceful smell
Parimal—fragrant substance
Parimitaa—a bloom, garden stuff
Parimita—moderate
Parinaya—bond of love
Parina—fairy
Parineta—married woman
Parineta—perfectionist, expert
Parinetha—married woman, goddess kali
Parineti—beauty, fairy
Parinet—princess
Parinidhi—pretty, lovely, handsome, graceful name
Parinika—goddess parvati
Parinine—winged
Parinita—expert, married woman, complete
Parinitha—maturity, expert, married woman
Pariniti—matured
Parini—fairy's daughter
Parin—lord ganesha, fairy-like
Parisa—angelic, like a fairy
Parisha—angle, gift of god
Parishil—like an angel
Parishi—like a fairy
Parishmita—fairy's smile
Parishna—lovely, love to life
Parishvi—highness, empress, queen of angle
Parisi—like an angel
Paris—crafty previous stone, lover
Parita—angel, in each detection
Parita—in every direction
Paritosh—satisfaction
Parivita—extremely free
Parivita—not straight, revolving, round
Pariyat—bloom, garden stuff, rose
Pariya—love
Parizad—of holy, pure, sanctified, pious, solemn origin
Pari—angel, fairy, charitable princess
Pari—fairy
Parjanya—rain

Parkeeya—another's wife
Parmangana—excellent woman
Parma—pretty, lovely, handsome, graceful name
Parmeshwari—goddess durga
Parmeshwary—goddess durga
Parmila—new, expert, wisdom
Parmita—wisdom, buddha's teaching
Parmod—growth, happiness, lord ganesha
Parnaa—a prize
Parnal—leafy
Parnanjali—hand-full of leaves
Parnashree—leafy beauty
Parnashri—leafy beauty
Parnavi—a bird
Parnavi—bird, new leaf
Parna—feather, wings, leaf
Parna—leaves
Parnikaa—small leaf, small plant
Parnika—little leaf
Parnika—small leaf, goddess parvati
Parnik—leaf, goddess parvati
Parnita—auspicious apsara
Parnita—married woman
Parnitha—auspicious apsara
Parni—leafy
Parokshe—beyond perception
Paromita—person having selectivity
Paroo—goddess parvati
Paro—master, furnished, knowledge
Parridhe—circumference of the orbit
Parshvi—touchstone
Parthal—highness, empress, queen
Parthavi—goddess sita
Parthav—warrior arjuna
Parthibha—intellect, brightness, talent
Parthive—sita
Parthivi—born from earth
Parthivi—daughter of the earth
Parthi—earth-daughter
Parthi—highness, empress, queen
Parthushti—a person who is totally satisfied
Partibha—talented
Partima—statue
Parul—name of a bloom, garden stuff, graceful

Parul—name of bloom, garden stuff
Parul—pleasing, favourite, charming
Parushi—pretty, lovely, handsome, graceful, brilliant, sagacious, gifted, wise, learned
Paru—master, furnished, knowledge
Parvane—full moon
Parvani—full moon
Parvasee—traveller
Parvatee—wife of lord shiva
Parvatham—goddess sita
Parvathiammal—graceful
Parvathi—name of goddess
Parvathy—wif of lord shiva, goddess parvati
Parvati—a river
Parvati—wife of lord shiva
Parveni—star
Parven—star, collective shining stars
Parvini—festival
Parvita—surrounded, covered
Parviti—a song
Parvi—beginning
Parwan—acceptable
Parwatee—wife of lord shiva, goddess durga
Parwin—new
Parya—angel
Pashasine—controller of thirst
Pasha—bond
Pashupriya—fond of all beings
Pasungodi—pretty, lovely, handsome, graceful name
Pasunkili—durgadeity
Patala—goddess durga
Patalika—a bond
Patalin—pretty, lovely, handsome, graceful name
Patali—a name of bloom, garden stuff
Patangika—small bird
Patanjali—commentator of sanskrit grammar
Patasi—so sweet
Patava—awesome
Patavya—goddess durga, lakshmi
Pata—spectrogram
Pathana—reading
Pathina—virginal

Pathini—belongs to the way, path
Pathvika—toward your goal, path
Pathy—nice
Patika—symbol
Patmanjari—a raga
Patmanjiri—a raga
Patrakshi—eye, glimmers like leaf
Patralekha—a name from ancient epics
Patralika—series of leaves, beauty of a leaf
Patra—a leaf
Patru—goddess
Pattamma—mother of silk
Pattatharasi—a raga, crowned highness, empress, queen
Pattu—silk, wool, song
Paulmi—ray of sun
Paulomi—goddess saraswati
Paulomi—wife of lord indra
Paumi—leaves, plants
Pauralika—a classical rag, pleasant to citizen
Paurave—a girl name
Pauravi—horizon on east and west
Paurnamee—day of full-moon
Paurvi—eastern
Pausthi—strong, satisfied
Pavai—pretty, lovely, handsome, graceful
Pavaki—goddess saraswati, born from fire
Pavaki—name of goddess durga
Pavak—fire
Pavak—fire, holy, sanctified, pious, solemn, chaste
Pavana—holy, sacred
Pavana—holy, sanctified, pious, solemn, chaste, holly
Pavane—holy, sanctified, pious, solemn, chaste, sacred
Pavanika—belongs to the lord of air, wind
Pavanitha—holy, sanctified, pious, solemn, chaste
Pavani—holy, sanctified, pious, solemn, chaste, purifying
Pavani—purifier, ganga, air, wind
Pavani—purity soul, kind hearted

Pavanvenkatsai—god
Pavan—wind, holy, sanctified, pious, solemn, chaste
Pavazhakodi—sage bhirgu's wife
Pavazhavalli—goddess saraswati
Pavena—freshness, purity
Pavetra—holy, sanctified, pious, solemn, chaste
Pavika—goddess saraswati, goddess of
Paviksha—holy, pure, sanctified, pious, solemn, goddess of beauty
Pavinaya—sound, voice of air
Pavina—voice of air
Pavini—purity
Pavishana—holy, pure, sanctified, pious, solemn beauty
Pavishika—pretty, lovely, handsome, graceful name
Pavishka—holy, pure, sanctified, pious, solemn beauty
Pavishna—holy, pure, sanctified, pious, solemn, beauty of goddess
Pavitha—holy, sanctified, pious, solemn, chaste and dignified
Pavithra—holy, sanctified, pious, solemn, chaste, sacred, lovely, softness
Pavitra—holy, sanctified, pious, solemn, chaste
Pavitra—holy, sanctified, pious, solemn, chaste, daughter of god
Pavitra—purity, clean
Pavitree—holy
Pavitrin—purification
Pavi—illumination, luminosity, radiance, sanctified, pious, solemn, chaste
Pavlen—near to god's feet
Pavni—to make holy, sanctified, pious, solemn, chaste something, knowledge
Pavni—true, holy, sanctified, pious, solemn, chaste, holy
Pavu—innocent, purity
Pawana—pretty, lovely, handsome, graceful name
Pawan—wind, holy, sanctified, pious, solemn, chaste, who removes bad energy

Pawne—purity, holy
Pawni—clear, holy, sanctified, pious, solemn, chaste, lord hanuman
Pawni—sacred
Payala—anklet
Payaliya—wisdom, foot ornament, jewellery, ornamentation, adornment, figuration
Payal—anklet
Payal—anklet, type of ornament, jewellery, ornamentation, adornment
Payal—foot ornament, jewellery, ornamentation, adornment, figurationnklet
Payaswini—cow who gives milk
Payaswini—holy, sanctified, pious, solemn, chaste
Payel—anklet, foot ornament, jewellery, ornamentation, adornment, figuration
Payingili—green parrot, foot ornament, jewellery, ornamentation
Payinkodi—a river's name, cow
Payoda—giver of water, milk giver
Payoda—milk
Payoja—lotus
Payoshmi—name of the river
Payoshnika—the ganga river
Payoshni—milky, holy river
Payoshni—name of the river
Pearly—form of pearl
Pearl—the valuable, valued, rare stone
Pea—beloved, lover
Pechika—pretty, lovely, handsome, graceful name
Pechiyammi—goddess parvathi deity
Peehuna—very sweet
Peehu—a bird
Peetashma—topaz
Peeush—nectar
Pehar—dawn, morning
Pehel—starting, first
Peher—dawn, early morning
Pehr—phase, time of day
Pehul—monarch, ruler, prince, earl of heaven
Pekham—peacock's feather

Pennarasi—lotus, highness, empress, queen
Pennazhagu—pretty, lovely, handsome, graceful, pretty woman
Perani—dancing
Perazhagi—pretty, lovely, handsome, graceful women
Perazhagu—very pretty, lovely, handsome, graceful
Peridhi—radius, limits
Pernita—answered prayer
Perumagal—own daughter
Perun—rare, not normal
Peru—guava
Petva—fire
Peya—favourite
Peyusha—nectar
Phalak—sky shield
Phalguni—born in falgun hindu month
Phalline—fruitful
Phanisree—beauty
Phindi—pretty, lovely, handsome, graceful name
Phiroja—turquois
Phiroza—turquoise
Phoolan—bloom, garden stuffing
Phoolan—bloom, garden stuffy
Phoolla—in full bloom
Phoolwati—delicate as a bloom, garden stuff
Phool—bloom, garden stuff
Phulmani—a gem
Phutika—bloom, garden stuff
Pial—anklet
Piasha—thirst
Piavri—your love
Pia—lover, beloved, pious
Pieu—beloved
Pihal—benevolent
Pihika—sweet as always
Pihoo—sweet sound
Pihul—price
Pihuna—very sweet, sweet bird voice
Pihu—sound, chirp voice of peacock
Piki—the cuckoo bird
Piku—sweet, innocent, pretty, lovely
Pinaakee—pretty, lovely, handsome, graceful name

Pinakine—bowfigure, appearance, structured
Pinakini—bow-figure, appearance, structured
Pinal—god of children
Pina—god raises
Pingala—goddess lakshmi, reddish brown
Pingala—money, goddess lakshmi
Pinga—goddess durga
Pingla—goddess durga
Pinita—holy, sanctified, pious, solemn, chaste, chaste
Pinjala—a river
Pinkal—lotus bloom, garden stuff
Pinki—a bloom, garden stuff
Pinki—like a rose
Pinkur—pink hearted
Pinku—pink coloured, most pretty, lovely, handsome, graceful
Pinky—most pretty, lovely, handsome, graceful, the little finger
Pipyana—musical instrument
Pirnoor—shine of god
Pitakavera—pretty, lovely, handsome, graceful name
Pitanila—goddess durga
Pitapushpa—wife of udhava
Pitchaiamma—goddess durga
Pitika—saffron
Pitika—saffron, yellow jasmine
Pitmani—yellow ornament, jewellery, ornamentation, adornment
Piusha—way, nectar
Piu—beloved, love
Pival—a feeling tree
Pivari—wife of sukha
Pivi—type of sweet fruit
Piyalic—a tree
Piyali—a tree
Piyali—name of a river
Piyal—loving
Piyashi—thirst
Piya—beloved
Piya—love or the one who is loved
Piyiush—nectar
Piyuksha—adorable
Piyusha—full of nectar

Piyusha—the food of the gods, necter
Piyushi—holy watermrit, sweet water
Piyu—beloved
Plabani—gentle breeze that touches heart
Plaksha—knowledge, goddess saraswati
Plava—a kind of tree
Poetika—saffron
Pollyam—pretty, lovely, handsome, graceful name
Pomi—expert, smart
Pommi—best girl, responsible
Ponnamal—golden
Ponnamma—golds like golden god
Ponnarasi—golden highness, empress, queen
Ponnazhagi—golden beauty
Ponnazhagu—golden beauty
Ponni—nectar, nature of love
Ponnmani—pretty, lovely, handsome, graceful name
Ponnulakshmi—goddess saraswathi, lakshmi
Ponnu—gold
Ponnvadivu—golden
Ponthara—a big star
Poobavan—love
Poodeity—bloom, garden stuff
Poojal—water used for worship
Poojanya—worship, prayer
Poojan—worship
Poojasri—worship
Pooja—prayer, worship, devoted to god
Pooja—worship
Poojila—honoured
Poojila—venerable, respectable
Poojita—respectable, worshipped, honoured
Poojitha—devoted, the one who is worshipped
Poomagal—daughter of a bloom, garden stuff
Pooma—calm
Poombavai—prayer
Poomitha—strong, golden eye, glimmers

Poonam—full moon night, poornima, merit
Poonam—full moonday
Pooncholai—bloom, garden stuff garden
Poongodi—bloom, garden stuff on a creeper, slender stalk
Poonkodai—full moon
Poonnamma—worshipped
Poorani—fulfilling, satisfying
Poorani—lot of goodness
Poorbi—ancient, eastern
Poorbi—eastern
Poorika—complete
Poornakala—love
Poornakamala—a blooming lotus
Poornamala—gold
Poornashree—full of beauty
Poorna—complete
Poorna—perfect, complete
Poornendhu—full moon, god
Poornika—one who is complete
Poornimaa—complete
Poornimadeity—goddess lakshmi
Poornima—illumination, luminosity, radiance, full moon, beauty
Poorni—love, love and happiness
Poorti—completion
Poorvaganga—river narmada
Poorvaja—elder sister
Poorva—earlier one, elder, east
Poorva—eastern
Poorvika—ancient, from the east
Poorvi—a classical melody
Poorvi—to east
Poosha—dress
Pooshitha—defended, loved
Pootul—full moon
Poovalli—full moon
Poovarasi—pretty, lovely, handsome, graceful, highness, empress, queen
Poovazhagi—beauty of bloom, garden stuff
Poo—worship, bloom, garden stuff, pray bloom, garden stuff
Popi—bloom, garden stuff
Popo—lovely, quiet, sweetheart
Pore—angel, wisdom

Porkodinayaki—a classical melody
Porkodi—gold, leaves
Porti—goddess durga
Poshayitri—pretty, lovely, handsome, graceful name
Poshika—a name
Poshita—one who feeds
Poshitha—incense stick
Poshya—gospel love, good
Postya—dwelling
Pothumani—common time, bell
Potriratha—hog-vehicled female divinity
Potriya—like pot
Poulima—serenity, calm, calmness, stillness, shy
Poulomi—a apsara
Pounami—full moon day
Pouravi—rising sun, from the east
Pourchelvi—golden lady
Pourkodi—name of a tourist place
Pournami—full moon
Pournima—full moon
Poushah—the month of paush
Poushali—of the month poush
Poushila—sculpture
Poverti—the mother of ganesh
Poya—lucky charm
Poyesi—poetry
Prabalika—very strong
Prabalta—vigour
Prabavathi—wife of sun
Prabhada—lady
Prabhadeity—a deity in the court of brahma
Prabhadra—one who is shy
Prabhati—of the morning
Prabhavali—shining, graceful raga
Prabhavanti—effect, goddess of wealth
Prabhavathi—lakshmi and parvathi
Prabhavathy—wife of sun
Prabhavati—a ragini, wife of sun
Prabhava—origin
Prabha—brightness, illumination, luminosity, radiance, luster, shine
Prabha—shine, lustre
Prabhi—angelic, pretty, lovely, handsome, graceful

Prabhner—pretty, lovely, handsome, graceful name
Prabhuti—name of lord shiva, vigour
Prabhuti—well
Prabhu—god
Prabodhine—awakening
Prabuthi—well being, welfare, success
Pracheta—origin, starting point
Pracheta—pretty, lovely, handsome, graceful name
Pracheta—the soul
Prachika—driving
Prachirna—to come forth appear
Prachita—holy, sanctified, pious, solemn, chaste, brilliant
Prachiti—knowledge, information
Prachi—first ray of sun, morning, east
Prachi—the eastern horizon
Pradakshina—origin, starting point
Pradanya—wisdom
Pradatta—gift of god
Pradayani—goddess saraswati
Prada—illumination, luminosity, radiance, luster, shine
Pradeepa—pretty
Pradeepika—one that illuminates small lamp
Pradeepta—lustering
Pradeepta—lustering, illumination, luminosity, radiance, illuminated
Pradeepthi—brightness of illumination, luminosity, radiance
Pradeepti—illumination, luminosity, radiance, radiance
Pradeepti—radiance, illumination, luminosity, radiance, lustering
Pradeesha—worship
Pradhakshina—starting point
Pradhan—leader
Pradha—extremely distinguished
Pradhi—great intelligence
Pradipta—winner of the life, lustering
Pradipti—illumination, luminosity, radiance, lustre, radiance
Pradnaya—knowledge
Pradnya—wisdom, buddhi, intelligence

Pradusa—pretty, lovely, handsome, graceful name
Pradvi—goddess durga
Pradya—pretty, lovely, handsome, graceful name
Pradyna—illuminated, luminous
Pradyumna—bestwoer
Praeksha—vision
Prafula—bloom, blooming, playful
Prafulla—cherful
Prafulla—pleasant, cherful, in bloom
Praful—giver
Pragalbha—goddess durga
Praganya—love
Pragaspathie—circumambulation
Pragathi—progress, success
Pragati—development
Pragati—progress, development, improvement
Praghya—conscious, wisdom
Pragita—sweet person
Pragna—knowledge, consciousness
Pragnika—illumination, luminosity, radiance
Pragnna—thinmonarch, ruler, prince, earl present, consciousness
Pragnya—scholar, goddess gayatri, famous
Pragnye—brilliant, sagacious, gifted, wise, learned
Pragritya—celebrity, excellence
Pragti—development, improvement, progress
Pragun—straight, honest
Pragyaparamita—blossom, wise love
Pragyata—wisdom
Pragyawati—a wise woman
Pragya—another name of goddess saraswati
Pragya—wisdom
Pragya—wisdom, intelligence
Pragya—wisdom, intelligence, calm
Praharsha—always cherful
Praharsha—happy person
Praharshini—good manner, happiness
Praharshita—ever happy girl
Praharshni—pretty, lovely, handsome, graceful name

Prahar—early morning, time
Prahasini—continues smiling girl, smiling
Prahassya—pretty, lovely, handsome, graceful
Prahelika—pretty, lovely, handsome, graceful, progress
Prahi—wellness
Prahlad—lord vishnu's devotee
Prajakta—fragrant, white colour bloom, garden stuff
Prajal—illuminated, luster, shining, illumination, luminosity, radiance
Prajana—wisdom, education
Prajanyaruchi—the worship of knowledge
Praja—public, ordinary people
Prajeetha—valuable, valued, rare gift
Prajina—shine of gloriness
Prajini—kind, shining of glory
Prajisha—morning
Prajna—knowledge, goddess saraswati
Prajul—bright
Prajusha—morning
Prajwala—bright, eternal flame, shining
Prajwal—lamp, illumination, luminosity, radiance
Prajya—wisdom, intelligence, sensible
Prajyoti—illumination, luminosity, radiance
Prakalpa—project
Prakalp—project
Prakarana—more brilliant, sagacious, gifted, wise, learned
Prakarti—nature
Prakashatee—bright, shining
Prakashini—luminous, shining forth, bright
Prakashita—illuminated, irradiated
Prakathambal—wise
Prakathi—a wise lady
Prakhya—appearance, fame
Prakiti—nature
Prakritee—natural
Prakrithi—nature
Prakriti—earth, nature, pretty, lovely, handsome, graceful

Prakriti—nature, famous
Prakri—a song
Prakrthi—nature, goddess lakshmi
Prakruthi—nature, weather
Prakruti—nature, primal substance
Prakshali—purity, holy, sanctified, pious, solemn, chaste
Prakshita—pretty, lovely, handsome, graceful name
Prakshi—prakash ki raksah karne wali
Prakurti—nature
Pramada—young, pretty, lovely, handsome, graceful woman
Pramade—dizzling
Pramanika—wisdom, certificate
Prama—knowledge of truth
Prameela—goddess parvati, honey
Pramila—arjun's wife
Pramila—well behaved, kind, pretty, lovely, handsome, graceful
Pramita—best friend, wisdom, limited
Pramitha—best friend, wisdom
Pramiti—knowledge of truth
Pramitla—wisdom, best friend
Pramoda—joy, pleasure
Pramodini—happy lady
Pramodini—the won who gives joy
Pramodita—giver of joy
Pramud—ecstasy, great happiness
Pranaali—method, system
Pranaarthi—soul
Pranada—creating life, giving life
Pranakshi—pretty, lovely, handsome, graceful eye, glimmers wisdom
Pranali—method, organisation, system
Pranamya—respectful be worshipped, life
Prananjali—joining two hands together to greet
Prananya—leader, intelligence
Pranaswi—soul, spirit, protecting life
Pranathi—greeting, vigour of mind
Pranati—prayer
Pranati—prayer, joy, salutation, bow
Pranauthi—lamp
Pranavati—full of life, living
Pranava—young
Pranave—goddess parvati

Pranavi—goddess parvati
Pranayani—beloved, devotee
Pranaya—life, leader, love
Pranayita—animated, kept alive
Praneka—goddess parvati
Praneshvari—beloved
Praneta—led forward
Praneta—led forward, conducted, advanced
Pranetee—conduct
Pranetha—holy, sanctified, pious, solemn, chaste water
Praneth—sacred fire, knowledgeable
Pranetra—creator, leader, promulgator
Pranhita—name of river
Pranidhi—valuable, valued, rare, spy
Pranika—goddess parvati
Pranikya—goddess saraswati, loved by all
Pranisha—love to life
Pranita—promoted, expert
Pranitha—expert, character, promoted
Pranithi—breath, life
Pranith—with care, love
Praniti—conduct, leading, guidance
Pranjala—leader
Pranjale—respectful
Pranjali—name of a lady
Pranjali—wise
Pranjal—holy water silent, honest, soft
Pranja—very very cute
Pranjeeta—winner of life
Pranmani—ornament, jewellery, ornamentation, adornment, figuration among the leader
Pranoti—welcome
Pranshi—goddess lakshmi
Pransi—goddess lakshmi
Prantika—end
Pranusha—brightness of the rising sun
Pranve—dear one, special
Pranvitha—pretty, lovely, handsome, graceful name
Pranvi—luck, bloom, garden stuff, dear one, special
Pranvuta—praised
Prapatika—one who manifest
Prapti—achievement

Prapti—to get something
Prapulla—a pleasant smiling face
Prarabdha—a collection of past karmas
Prarthana—prayer
Prarthan—prayer
Prarthi—prayer er
Prasamitta—composed
Prasana—cherful, rising
Prasanchita—happy, cherful heart
Prasandhi—serenity, calm, calmness, stillness, silence maker
Prasanna—always very happy, pleasing
Praseeda—name of goddess lakshmi
Praseetha—pleasant, monkey
Prashaha—powerful
Prashami—calm, tranquil
Prashamsa—praise
Prashana—love
Prashani—tender, gentle
Prashansa—admire, prasie
Prashansha—praise
Prashanthi—highest serenity, calm, calmness, stillness, silence
Prashantini—calm and composed
Prashanti—serenity, calm, calmness, stillness, silence
Prashanti—silence, serenity, calm, calmness, stillness, silence
Prashant—serenity, calm, calmness, stillness, silence
Prashasta—praised
Prashasti—fame, praise, poetry
Prashati—mother of draupadi
Prasha—love mark of love
Prasha—love mark of love, ambition, intent, passion
Prasheila—ancient time
Prashetha—origin, starting point
Prashidhi—famousccomplishment, fame
Prashi—goddess lakshmi, good
Prashri—devotion, proud
Prashu—speedy, quick action
Prashvita—parvati, lord shiva's wife
Prasiddhi—fame
Prasidhhi—famous
Prasiga—brightness

Prasnsa—appreciation
Prasobh—one with illumination, luminosity, radiance
Prasoona—budding bloom, garden stuff
Prasoon—advantage
Prasunna—cherful, pleased, happy
Pratapa—glory
Pratapi—brilliant, glorious
Prateechi—prayer
Prateechi—west
Prateeka—the good example
Prateeksha—praise
Prateeksha—waiting, wait
Prateeti—talent
Prathama—the first, goddess shakti
Prathami—the earth
Prathana—prayer
Prathav—always first
Pratha—trend, custom, style, tradition
Pratheba—illumination, luminosity, radiance
Pratheka—symbol, pretty, lovely, handsome, graceful
Prathepa—calm, serenity, calm, calmness, stillness, silence
Prathibha—brilliant, sagacious, gifted, wise, learned
Prathicksha—waiting
Prathicsha—wait, support, indoctrination, assuredness, waiting for something
Prathigna—challenge
Prathika—symbol, proud, symbolic
Prathiksha—wait, timewaiting
Prathiksh—promise
Prathima—pretty, lovely, handsome, graceful pleasant, statue or doll
Prathisha—serenity, calm, calmness, stillness, silence
Prathistha—popularity
Prathithi—famous
Prathi—waiting, every
Prathna—prayer
Prathvi—earth, goddess sita, princess
Prathysha—early morning
Prathyumna—victory

Prathyusha—rising sun, dawn, early morning
Pratibhasha—answer
Pratibha—genius
Pratibha—intellect, splendour, brightness
Pratibtha—ability
Pratichaya—from the west
Pratichi—west
Pratichi—western direction
Pratigna—trust, pledge, vow
Pratigya—pledge, vow
Pratijya—promise, vow, swearssent
Pratika—symbol, shadow, lord indra
Pratiksa—waiting
Pratiksha—wait in support, indoctrination, assuredness
Pratiksha—wait, time waiting
Pratima—image
Pratima—mirror image, reflection, icon
Pratisha—pre eminence
Pratishta—distinguished
Pratishtha—honour
Pratishtha—preeminence, prestige
Pratistha—establish, pre-eminence
Pratitha—well known
Pratiti—devotion, conviction
Pratiti—knowledge
Pratitra—bank of a river
Pratixa—awaiting
Pratosh—a name
Prattysha—morning
Pratulya—incomparable, unique
Pratulya—uncomparable
Pratusha—morningt dawn
Pratushti—gratification
Pratushya—morning
Pratyaksha—appear, respectable
Pratyakshi—always in your front as an inward
Pratyangiree—goddess durga in tantrik form
Pratyangir—form of durga
Pratyanja—inspiration
Pratyasha—support, indoctrination, assuredness, expectation

Pratyeksha—all of them, everyone, whole
Pratyusha—early morning, glad
Praudha—old
Pravalika—question, goodness, special
Pravalikha—a flowing river
Pravalitha—unlimited power
Pravallika—puzzle, bloom, garden stuff, question, god
Pravanya—pretty, lovely, handsome, graceful
Pravara—principal
Pravardhini—development
Pravarsha—rain, highness, empress, queen
Pravashine—one who traval a lot
Pravasree—development
Pravasthika—goddess
Pravasthi—birth, name of lord vishnu
Pravathika—pretty, lovely, handsome, graceful name
Pravati—prayer
Prava—blowing forth
Pravena—clever, expert
Pravena—skilled, goddess saraswati
Praveni—a plate of hair
Praven—expert, experienced, truth, god
Pravesha—entrance
Pravesha—to enter
Praveshika—entrance
Pravesh—entry
Pravidha—pretty, lovely, handsome, graceful name
Pravika—pretty, lovely, handsome, graceful name
Praviksha—goddess lakshmi, long awaited
Pravina—skilled, skillful expert
Pravinu—brilliant, sagacious, gifted, wise, learned, pretty
Pravinya—best at something
Pravisha—illumination, luminosity, radiance
Pravi—incredible, pretty, lovely, handsome, graceful
Pravrita—revolved

Pravya—brilliant, sagacious, gifted, wise, learned
Prayaga—confluence of three sacred river
Prayanshi—thoughtful, expressive
Prayashi—to try
Prayas—practise
Prayati—advance
Prayatna—an attemptn effort
Prayerna—bhakti, worship
Prayukta—motive, consequence
Prayuktha—brilliant, sagacious, gifted, wise, learned
Prayuta—mingled with
Prbhavati—a ragini, wife of sun
Prdyota—bright
Prearna—inspiration, pretty, lovely, handsome, graceful
Preedhika—bloom, garden stuff
Preeha—pretty, lovely, handsome, graceful name
Preena—goddess of bloom, garden stuff, content
Preenithi—loved
Preesa—beloved
Preesha—god gifted, talent given by god
Preeshika—love love
Preetal—fame
Preetami—beloved, loved one
Preeta—loveffection, ambition, intent, passion
Preethal—most loved one
Preethami—pretty, lovely, handsome, graceful name
Preethanjali—pretty, lovely, handsome, graceful name
Preetha—happy, love
Preethika—amiable, pleasing, suave, interesting
Preethisha—god of love
Preethi—love, clean, bonding
Preetijusha—beloved
Preetika—loving actions
Preetilata—legend created by love
Preeti—love
Preeti—loveffection
Preety—love

Preet—love
Preevasee—beloved
Preeyati—beloved
Preity—affection, love
Prekshana—tolerance, durability, toleration
Preksha—goddess laxami, beholding
Preksha—perceive carefully
Preksha—wise
Premalatha—love
Premala—loving
Premal—lovingffectionate
Premanayaki—dear one
Premanidhi—the treasure of love
Preman—lovely, cute
Premavathi—beloved
Premawattee—full of love, beloved
Prema—loving, loveffection
Prembai—full of love
Premell—creeper of love
Preme—loved-one
Premila—highness, empress
Premi—lover
Premja—a brave lady
Premlata—garland of love, type of plant
Premlela—icon, idol, statue
Premsudha—preeminence
Prem—love
Prena—inspiration
Prenetra—creator, leader, promulgator
Prenika—girl with inspiration
Prenita—pretty, lovely, handsome, graceful name
Prenitha—inspiration
Preni—inspiration
Prerana—inspiring, inspiration
Prerena—direction, command
Prerita—to inspire
Prerna—encouragement, inspiration
Prerna—giving inspiration
Preru—love
Presha—beloved, loving gift
Preshtha—most bloved
Preshti—ray of illumination, luminosity, radiance
Prestha—dearest, beloved
Prexa—beholding, viewing

Preyakshana—pretty, lovely, handsome, graceful name
Preyanshi—amiable, pleasing, suave, interesting part
Preyashi—loveable
Preyasi—beloved
Preya—beloved
Pre—beauty
Prgnaya—goddess saraswati
Prianka—princess, favourite
Priavi—joy
Prikshita—pretty, lovely, handsome, graceful name
Prinaka—girl who brings heaven to earth
Prinal—pleased, satisfied
Prina—content, goddess of bloom, garden stuff
Princee—daughter of monarch
Princess—daughter of monarch
Princia—pretty, lovely, handsome, graceful name
Princika—pretty, lovely, handsome, graceful name
Princle—unicorn
Princy—a princess
Prini—goddess of bloom, garden stuffs
Prinjal—highness, empress, queen of angels
Prinkal—who is like love bird, illumination, luminosity, radiance
Prinka—love, beloved, loving gift
Prinsha—pretty, lovely, handsome, graceful name
Prisa—god gift, beloved, praise
Prisca—saintncient
Prisha—beloved, loving
Prishita—gentle, creative and ambitious
Prishi—to be loved and to be praised
Prital—loved one
Pritami—pretty, lovely, handsome, graceful name
Pritanshi—piece of love
Pritan—pretty, lovely, handsome, graceful name
Prita—dear one
Prita—dear one, beloved

Pritee—pretty, lovely, handsome, graceful name
Pritha—extended, kunti
Pritha—unique, name of kunti, mother
Prithe—love
Prithika—bloom, garden stuff, fair
Prithpal—love, moment of life
Prithuloma—fish, pisces, zodiac sign
Prithushri—with great fortune
Prithvika—little earth, cardamom
Prithvi—earth
Prithvi—the earth
Prith—love
Pritibala—full of love
Pritikana—an atom of love
Pritika—beloved
Pritika—love, dear one, loved one, beloved
Pritilata—blossom creeper of love
Pritisha—goddess of love, durga
Pritivi—world, earth
Priti—love, bonding, pretty, lovely, handsome, graceful, illumination
Pritu—bonding, love
Prity—love, pretty, lovely, handsome, graceful
Prit—love
Privika—purity, deityne
Privi—earth
Privya—piece of heart
Priya-dharshini—nice view
Priyabrata—bloom, garden stuff
Priyadarshana—one who is good monarch, ruler, prince, earl
Priyadarshani—nice, pretty, lovely, handsome, graceful view
Priyadarshani—pleasing, favourite, charming
Priyadarshe—love
Priyadarshika—pretty, lovely, handsome, graceful name
Priyadarshini—illumination, luminosity, radianceful to look, loved one
Priyada—beloved
Priyadharshni—honesty
Priyadutta—earth

Priyagya—pretty, lovely, handsome, graceful name
Priyajanani—mother with love
Priyaka—pretty, lovely, handsome, graceful name
Priyalata—loved one, darling
Priyala—bestowing pleasure
Priyala—one who gives love, honourable
Priyali—love, unique, magical
Priyal—beloved
Priyal—emotional, beloved, gold
Priyamanjari—bloom, garden stuffs
Priyammaya—full of love
Priyamvada—silence, sweet spoken
Priyamvada—sweet spoken
Priyamvadhana—pretty, lovely, handsome, graceful
Priyam—beloved
Priyam—love, beloved
Priyana—roses, ideal, model
Priyanga—love
Priyangi—goddess lakshmi
Priyangshi—one with pretty body, lovely, handsome, graceful, amiable
Priyangu—name of the creeper, garden stuff
Priyanivita—loves
Priyani—dearest
Priyanjali—worshipper of one's ideal, model person
Priyankaa—loved one, pretty, lovely, handsome, graceful person
Priyankaree—beloved
Priyanka—pretty, lovely, handsome, graceful, loveable
Priyanka—beloved
Priyankee—one with charming mark
Priyanki—pretty, lovely, handsome, graceful name
Priyank—amiable, pleasing, suave, interesting, lord shiva, ganesha
Priyansha—pretty, lovely, handsome, graceful name
Priyanshe—love
Priyanshi—amiable, pleasing, suave, interesting, intellectual girl

Priyanshu—first ray of sun, illumination, luminosity, radiance
Priyansika—pretty, lovely, handsome, graceful name
Priyansi—pretty, lovely, handsome, graceful name
Priyanvada—one who speaks nicely
Priyaranjeny—loving
Priyashan—loved all
Priyasha—beloved, dear one
Priyasha—dearest
Priyasmita—best friend
Priyatama—lovely
Priyata—beloved
Priyavadami—a bird
Priyavadhana—amiable, pleasing, suave, interesting face
Priyavarchchas—who loves vigour
Priya—dear one
Priya—kind, beloved one, loved one
Priye—beloved
Priym—beloved
Priyu—beloved one, loved one
Priy—love god's gift
Prjal—luster, illuminated, illumination, luminosity, radiance, shining
Profulla—lotus
Progya—prowess
Proma—truth
Promila—a wife of arjuna
Promila—love others
Promita—idol
Pronomita—beloved
Protima—statue
Proxima—a star nearest to sun
Prrishane—tender, the earth
Prrishti—a ray of illumination, luminosity, radiance, touch
Prritha—stout, fat
Prrithika—jasmine
Prrithukeertee—one whose fame is reached far
Prshni—mother of plants
Prthiksha—pretty, lovely, handsome, graceful name
Prthve—the earth
Prtiksa—waiting

Prtyusha—early, bright morning
Prushti—pink
Prusti—pretty, lovely, handsome, graceful name
Prutha—the earth, daughter of earth
Pruthe—creeper of love
Prutholoma—one who has long hair
Pruthushree—one who is very rich
Pruthuvaktra—wide mouthed
Pruthvi—earth
Pubi—the wind which passes through east
Puchi—sweet
Puhu—name
Pujasatya—pretty, lovely, handsome, graceful name
Puja—worship, prayer, idol worship
Pujita—worshipped
Pujitha—prayer, worshipping god
Puji—gentle
Pujya—respectable
Pulak—eye, glimmers, gem
Pulika—obedience
Pulina—little
Pulindee—mountainer
Pulkita—always smiling, prasann mukh
Pulkit—worship
Puloma—to be thrilled
Puloma—wife of the sage bhrigu
Pulomi—worshipped, daughter
Pummy—innocent, pretty, lovely, handsome, graceful
Punam—full moon
Punarnava—a star
Punarnavi—always new
Punarvika—repeat again
Punarvi—new, reborn
Punati—a bloom, garden stuff
Puna—again
Pundarikaksha—lotus eye, glimmers
Pundarika—one who is like a lotus
Pundarishraja—a garland of lotuses
Pundari—lotus
Puneta—full moon
Punet—holy, sanctified, pious, solemn, chaste
Pungodhai—like a bloom, garden stuff

Punika—a star
Punima—full moon
Punita—holy, sanctified, pious, solemn, chaste, holy, love
Punita—pious
Punitham—holy, sanctified, pious, solemn, chaste religious
Punitha—holy, holy, sanctified, pious, solemn, chaste, noble, good character
Punjal—pretty, lovely, handsome, graceful name
Punj—group of power, holy, sanctified, pious, solemn, chaste
Punkodhai—like a bloom, garden stuff
Punkodi—petal of a bloom, garden stuff
Punkuzali—pretty, lovely, handsome, graceful
Punom—full moon
Puntayati—holy, sanctified, pious, solemn, chaste, holy
Punthali—a doll
Punyabrata—heart touch
Punyageha—pretty, lovely, handsome, graceful name
Punyajani—meritorious
Punyaka—dear one
Punyanaman—a doll
Punyapriya—a loving person
Punyasloka—virtuous
Punyata—blessings gained for good work
Punyatha—blessing gained for good work
Punyatrina—goddess
Punyavale—virtuous
Punyavati—virtuous
Punyayi—name of goddess durga
Punya—auspicious, virtuous, good work
Punya—virtue, holy basil
Purabi—from the east
Purab—east
Puradhana—ancient
Purajana—pretty, lovely, handsome, graceful name
Purala—goddess durga
Puramaline—garland with castle

Purambhi—pretty, lovely, handsome, graceful name
Purandara—destroyer of the city
Purandhe—woman
Purandhri—mother of vedas, goddess
Purani—fulfilling, completing
Puranjane—understanding
Puran—complete, perfect
Puraphala—pretty, lovely, handsome, graceful name
Puravi—a rage
Purayana—oldest
Purbali—who worships god sun facing east
Purbasha—support, indoctrination, assuredness of east
Purbi—direction
Puribai—full of devotional
Purisha—bonding
Purishya—pretty, lovely, handsome, graceful name
Purnamita—pretty, lovely, handsome, graceful name
Purnasha—all desire, aspiration, longing is fulfilled
Purnashri—with fortune
Purna—complete, perfect
Purna—completebundant
Purnika—abundant, complete
Purnima—full moon
Purnima—full moon, synonyms
Purnita—complete, fulfilled
Purni—complete
Purobi—pretty, lovely, handsome, graceful raga
Purtika—to satisfy, complete
Purti—goddess direction
Purti—purification satisfy, complete
Purunitha—pretty, lovely, handsome, graceful name
Purushakriti—tamonarch, ruler, prince, earl the form of a man
Purvaja—elder sister
Purvani—full moon
Purvansa—ancient
Purvansha—ancient
Purvanshi—purv disha, sun
Purvansh—east direction

Purva—east
Purva—east, elder, nakshatra
Purve—fulfiller, one that satiates
Purvika—orient, formerly
Purvita—from the east
Purvi—eastern
Purvi—first, pretty, lovely, handsome, graceful, from the east
Purwa—east, elder, breeze
Pushan—status of respect
Pusha—nourishing
Pushika—gentle star
Pushit—nourshing
Pushkala—abundant, full
Pushkala—wealthy
Pushkarine—elder sister
Pushkarni—pretty, lovely, handsome, graceful name
Pushpaanjali—nourishing
Pushpagandha—juhi bloom, garden stuff
Pushpaja—born from a bloom, garden stuff
Pushpaja—born of bloom, garden stuff
Pushpakala—bloom, garden stuff
Pushpakali—from the east
Pushpakanta—bloom, garden stuff bud
Pushpaki—mythical vehicle of lord vishnu
Pushpalata—bloom, garden stuff creeper
Pushpalatha—bloom, garden stuff offering
Pushpamala—garland of bloom, garden stuffs
Pushpamanjaree—a bud of bloom, garden stuff
Pushpamanjari—garland of bloom, garden stuffs
Pushpam—bloom, garden stuff
Pushpangana—one who is as delicate as bloom, garden stuff
Pushpangi—bloom, garden stuff bodied
Pushpangi—bloom, garden stuffy body
Pushpangna—delicate like bloom, garden stuff

Pushpanjali—a handful of bloom, garden stuffs
Pushpanjali—devote bloom, garden stuff to god
Pushpanjli—offering with the bloom, garden stuffs
Pushparani—highness, empress, queen of bloom, garden stuffs
Pushparenu—pollen of the bloom, garden stuff
Pushpashree—one who is pretty, lovely, handsome, graceful as bloom, garden stuff
Pushpasri—bunch of bloom, garden stuffs
Pushpavale—a line of bloom, garden stuff
Pushpavali—bloom, garden stuff vine
Pushpavathi—possessing bloom, garden stuffs
Pushpavati—blossoming bloom, garden stuff
Pushpa—a bloom, garden stuff
Pushpa—blossom, pretty, lovely, handsome, graceful, bloom, garden stuffs
Pushpeeka—a name
Pushpika—decorated with bloom, garden stuffs, bloom, garden stuff
Pushpita—decorated with bloom, garden stuff
Pushpita—decorated with bloom, garden stuffs
Pushpitha—bloom, garden stuff, decorated with bloom, garden stuffs
Pushpi—bloom, garden stuff like, soft, tender
Pushprekha—line of bloom, garden stuffs
Pushpya—bloom, garden stuff
Pushta—bloom, garden stuff petal
Pushtika—well nourished girl
Pushti—possessor of all wealth
Pushyaja—born from bloom, garden stuff
Pushyati—soft
Pushya—bloom, garden stuff, blossom, uppermost

Puspanjali—bloom, garden stuff
Puspita—bloom, garden stuffed, decorated with bloom, garden stuffs
Puspomita—prear
Pusti—a form of the deity
Putakini—full of energy
Putali—puppet

Putana—blowing hard
Puvanika—pretty, lovely, handsome, graceful name
Puvika—good behaviour
Puvisha—extraordinary person
Pwan—holy water, windir
Pyas—thirsty

****

Indian Names For Girls—Q

Qayanat—universe
Qira—generous
Qiyara—very pretty
Quaneisha—a name
Quarrtulain—god's mercy
Quasar—meteor
Queeni—mermaid

Quentin—from the highness, empress, the fifth
Quetzali—hyper
Quincy—like a highness, empress, queen
Quity—pretty, lovely, handsome, graceful girl
Qushi—happy

****

Rabani—holy, pure, sanctified, pious, solemn
Rabhya—worshipped
Rabia—famous, godly, spring
Rabsimar—messenger of god, kind
Rachanaa—built, construction, creative art
Rachana—creation, creater, writer
Rachana—creations
Rachel—innocence of a lamb, shep, ewe
Rachika—creator
Rachita—created
Rachita—creator
Rachitha—smile, created, brilliant, sagacious, gifted, wise, learned
Rachit—creator
Rachi—to form, morning
Rachna—constructionrrangement
Rada—filled with care, glad, happy
Raddha—lord krishna's lover
Radhamani—beloved of lord krishna
Radhana—speech
Radhane—worship
Radhani—worship
Radharani—created, devotee of lord krishna
Radhashree—goddess lakshmi
Radha—beloved of lord krishna
Radha—radha, krishna's beloved
Radha—success, prosperity
Radheswari—beloved of lord krishna
Radhe—belonging to lord krishna
Radhika—goddess radha, lover of krishna
Radhika—lord krishna devotee
Radhika—love of krishna
Radhika—successful, prosper, beloved to lord krishna
Radhish—pretty, lovely, handsome, graceful name
Radhiya—lover of krishna, satisfied
Radhi—forgiveness, pardon, willing

Radhya—name of radha be worshipped
Radnya—daughter of monarch, ruler, prince, earl
Raeleah—rays of sunshine
Raeya—singer
Ragachandrika—lord krishna's lover
Ragajanani—goddess durga
Ragamalika—god vishnu play the raga
Ragasudha—melody with healing touch
Ragasutra—radha, lover of krishna
Ragavarshini—one who showers ragas
Ragavarshini—rain
Ragavarthini—elevation
Ragavi—sings with raga
Raga—belongs to music terms
Raga—harmonious, melody, tune, feeling
Raga—musical notes
Rageshwari—goddess of melody
Rageswari—goddess of melody
Raghavi—goddess lakshmi, music
Raghini—a musical note
Raghvi—sweet
Ragine—love, melody
Ragine—name of a classical melody
Ragini—melodios, love
Ragini—passionate about music
Ragini—singer melody
Ragi—loving
Ragi—music, tune, voice
Ragni—lovely goddess
Ragvi—part of tune, music
Raha—serenity, calm, calmness, stillness, happiness, free, bliss
Rahela—caravan, helpful
Rahini—goddess saraswati
Rahita—friend of traveller
Rahithya—goddess lakshmi
Rahitya—inviting goddess lakshmi
Rahi—good companion, spring, traveller
Rahi—traveller, spring weather, way

Rahni—goddess saraswati
Raida—leader doll
Raieha—fragrance, khushboo
Raieshwari—pretty, lovely, handsome, graceful name
Raihana—aromatic, sweet basil
Raihanna—sweet princess, sweet basil
Raika—good, pretty, lovely, handsome, graceful
Raikha—star, line, beauty, limit
Raima—pleasing
Raina—highness, empress, queendvice, decision
Raina—night
Raini—cherful, pretty, lovely, handsome, graceful and happy
Rainy—rain of love, jolly
Rain—night
Raisa—easy-going, leader, bloom, garden stuff, highness, empress, queen
Raisha—leader, goddess
Raivathi—star in space
Raiva—swift star sweet heart
Raizel—rose
Rajadanya—loving
Rajag—universal awareness
Rajahansa—swan
Rajakokilam—melody
Rajakumari—princess
Rajalakshmi—goddess lakshmi
Rajalaksmi—goddess lakshmi
Rajal—highness, empress, queen of water, brilliant
Rajammal—pretty, lovely, handsome, graceful name
Rajam—goddess lakshmi
Rajanaya—highness, empress, queen
Rajana—colouring, painting, brightening
Rajane—night
Rajanigandha—scented bloom, garden stuff
Rajani—night, serenity, calm, calmness, stillness, darkness
Rajanna—lord shiva
Rajannya—highness, empress, queen
Rajanya—monarch, ruler, prince, earlly

Rajashree—glory of monarch, royality
Rajashree—royalty, loving, goddess
Rajashri—royalty
Rajasi—worthy of a monarch, ruler, prince, earl
Rajasri—grandeur, goddess lakshmi
Rajasulokshana—night
Rajasuya—the monarch, ruler, prince, earl's inauguration sacrifice
Rajas—one of the three expression
Rajata—like silver
Rajata—silver
Rajatha—silver
Rajathi—highness, empress, queen
Rajaveni—ruby ornament, jewellery, ornamentation, adornment, figuration
Rajave—royal bird
Rajbala—princess
Rajdeep—illumination, luminosity, radiance of state, ruler
Rajdip—pretty, lovely, handsome, graceful name
Rajdulari—dear princess
Rajeela—illuminated
Rajeevane—lotus plant
Rajeevani—small lotus
Rajeevlochana—lotus eye, glimmers
Rajeevni—a lotus
Rajeshni—highness, empress, queen, name of goddess parvati
Rajeshree—highness, empress, queen
Rajeshri—highness, empress, queen
Rajeshvaree—good fortune
Rajeshvari—princess
Rajeshvari—princess, goddess durga
Rajeshwari—goddess parvati, great goddess
Rajesh—godness
Rajeswari—highness, empress, queen
Rajeswri—highness, empress, queen
Rajhansa—swan
Rajhans—celestial swan
Rajiffer—princess
Rajika—lamp, line, streak
Rajina—sun, illumination, luminosity, radiance
Rajinder—monarch, ruler, prince, earl indra, the emperor

Rajini—moon, illumination, luminosity, radiance, dark night
Rajisha—moon
Rajita—bright, brilliant, illuminated
Rajita—charming
Rajitha—beauty, winner, illuminated
Rajivini—collection of blue lotuses
Raji—shining, illumination, luminosity, radiance group, smile
Rajju—angel of softness
Rajkala—monarch, ruler, prince, earl
Rajkala—moon's ray
Rajkamal—monarch, ruler, prince, earl of lotus
Rajkumari—princess
Rajlakshmi—goddess lakshmi
Rajlakshmi—wealthy monarch, ruler, prince, earldom, goddess lakshmi
Rajl—god
Rajmattie—shining
Rajnandani—monarch, ruler, prince, earls daughter, goddess lakshmi
Rajnandhini—daughter of a monarch, ruler, prince, earl, princess
Rajnandini—highness, empress, queen of beauty, princess
Rajnandni—pretty, lovely, handsome, graceful name
Rajnesh—night winner
Rajne—highness, empress, queen
Rajnigandha—name of a bloom, garden stuff
Rajnita—daughter of monarch, ruler, prince, earl
Rajni—night
Rajni—night, half name of bloom, garden stuff, highness, empress, queen
Rajonya—member of royal family
Rajoshree—royal shine
Rajpreet—monarch, ruler, prince, earl, love
Rajputana—from royal family, richness
Rajrita—prince of living
Rajshe—the one who belongs to monarch, ruler, prince, earldom
Rajshree—sage likes queen
Rajshri—rajya lakshmi

Rajsi—proudly, monarch, ruler, prince, earl
Rajsri—like a monarch, ruler, prince, earl
Rajula—deity
Rajul—innocent, brilliant, shining
Raju—the monarch, ruler, prince, earl
Rajvanthi—pretty, lovely, handsome, graceful name
Rajvanti—princess
Rajver—brave monarch, ruler, prince, earl
Rajvika—goddess saraswati
Rajvi—pretty, lovely, handsome, graceful, highness, princess, brave
Rajvi—belongs to royal family
Rajwantee—princess
Rajwant—the one of its kind
Rajyashree—goddess of state
Rajyashree—wealth of monarch, ruler, princess, earldom
Rajyashri—state honour
Rajyotika—illumination, luminosity, radiance
Rakanisha—the full moon night
Rakavi—highness, empress, queen of music and songs
Raka—direction, full moon
Raka—full moon
Raka—the full moon night
Rakchi—pretty, lovely, handsome, graceful
Rakeeh—night
Rakhe—a bond of love
Rakhe—symbol of protection
Rakhi—full moon in aswin month
Rakhi—symbol of protection
Rakhi—trustshes
Rakin—respectful
Rakishi—wide load
Rakma—consort of lord vishnu
Rakshadashri—the protector
Rakshana—protect
Rakshana—protection
Rakshanda—protected
Rakshanda—protecting
Rakshanshi—protection
Rakshati—one who protects

Raksha—protection
Rakshika—one who protects
Rakshika—protector
Rakshita—protection, protector
Rakshita—secure
Rakshitha—protected guard
Rakshitree—guardian
Rakshma—rich girl
Rakshovikshobhini—goddess
Rakshta—protector, guardian
Raksita—protected
Raksitha—a guard
Raktahansa—red swan
Raktakanchana—red gold
Rakta—painted
Rakta—painted, beloved, red, dear
Raktima—goddess saraswati, goddess durga
Rakti—pleasing
Ramaa—goddess lakshmi, wife, lord ram
Ramadasa—sevak of god ram
Ramadeity—goddess of beauty, lovely woman
Ramagauri—goddess lakshmi, fair women
Ramakrrit—causing rest
Ramamani—ornament, jewellery, ornamentation, adornment, figuration adorned by lord rama
Ramana—pretty, lovely, handsome, graceful
Ramana—enchanting, pretty, lovely, handsome, graceful
Ramane—lakshmi
Ramanika—charming, pleasing
Ramanika—illumination, luminosity, radianceful, lovely woman, pleasing
Ramani—pretty, lovely, handsome, graceful girl
Ramani—a lady
Ramanjeet—loveable of all
Ramaprabha—brightness of goddess lakshmi
Ramapriya—beloved of lord rama
Ramarani—highness, empress, queen of rama

Ramavina—pretty, lovely, handsome, graceful
Ramayane—one who is well-versed in ramayana
Ramaye—devotee of lord rama
Ramayi—beauty of lord ram
Rama—goddess lakshmi
Rama—lord rama, pleaser of the lord
Rambha—an apsara
Rambha—name of an apsara (angel)
Rambhine—the staff of a spear
Rameela—lover
Rameetha—goddess sita
Rameshvari—goddess parvati
Rameshwari—goddess parvati
Ramesh—rest, cherfulness, lord rama
Ramgauri—goddess lakshmi, pretty, lovely, handsome, graceful women
Ramila—god of love
Ramila—lover, bestowed of pleasure
Ramini—pretty, lovely, handsome, graceful girl
Ramisa—white rose
Ramita—happiness, pleasing, pleasant
Ramita—pleasing
Ramitha—pleasing, pretty, lovely, handsome, graceful
Ramkumarie—pretty, lovely, handsome, graceful name
Ramkur—pleaser of the lord rama
Ramla—prophet, predictor of the future
Ramneka—pretty, lovely, handsome, graceful
Ramnek—pretty, lovely, handsome, graceful
Ramni—pretty, lovely, handsome, graceful, loveable
Ramola—charming
Ramola—who takes interest in everything
Ramona—advice, decision
Ramona—protector
Ramrati—beloved, devotee of lord rama
Ramra—splendour
Ramuniqe—pretty, lovely, handsome, graceful girl

Ramyadeity—name of an apsara
Ramyakumari—parvati
Ramya—pretty, lovely, handsome, graceful
Ramya—pretty, lovely, handsome, graceful, natural
Ranadurga—goddess druga
Ranagana—full of pleasure
Ranajana—full of pleasure
Ranajeeta—victorious in battle
Ranamita—a friend in ned, war friend
Rananjoy—winner of war
Rana—blessing, elegant
Ranchi—pretty, lovely, handsome, graceful name
Rane—highness, empress, queen
Rane—highness, empress, queen, holy, sanctified, pious, solemn, chaste
Rangammal—splendour
Rangana—a bloom, garden stuff, happy
Rangati—classical song
Rangat—colourful
Rangavali—a highness, empress, queen
Rangavalli—rangoli
Rangeeta—illumination, luminosity, radiance, painted
Ranginwala—person of colours
Rangitha—charmed
Ranhita—quick, swift
Ranhita—swift, quick
Ranhitha—swift
Rania—contented, highness, empress, queen
Ranisha—rae plus aisha
Ranita—graceful, tinkling, lovely tune
Ranitha—tinkling, cute and pretty
Raniya—gazing, illumination, luminosity, radiance
Rani—highness, empress, queen
Rani—highness, empress, queen, princess
Ranjana—entertainment, illumination, luminosity, radiance
Ranjana—pleasure
Ranjanbala—enjoyment joy
Ranjani—full of joy, pleasingttraction

Ranjan—enjoyment, entertainment
Ranjeeka—one of the shruti
Ranjeetha—adorned
Ranjeet—the illumination, luminosity, radiance one, victorious
Ranjika—exciting, one who pleases
Ranjika—one who pleases
Ranjima—pretty, lovely, handsome, graceful name
Ranjina—pleasant and charming
Ranjini—pleasing
Ranjinni—pleasing
Ranjita—adorned, successmusing
Ranjita—decorated
Ranjitham—love
Ranjitha—pretty, lovely, handsome, graceful, colourful and charming
Ranjitha—charming, colourful face
Ranjith—pleasing
Ranjudeep—pleasant
Ranjula—charming, pleasing
Ranju—sweet, pretty
Ranni—night
Ranshu—cherful, illumination, luminosity, radiance
Rantika—pretty, lovely, handsome, graceful name
Ranuska—enjoyment
Ranu—heaven
Ranva—pleasant, illumination, luminosity
Ranvita—joyous
Ranvitha—joyous
Ranvi—smartness
Ranya—pleasant, war like, gazer
Ranya—war, pleasant
Ran—pleasing, goddess of storms
Raqueliza—pretty, lovely, handsome, graceful name
Rarosa—rose
Rasajna—knowledgeable about different art
Rasamani—gem of a monarch, ruler, prince, earl
Rasamanjari—an auspiou sign
Rasanjna—river ganga
Rasa—nectar
Rasa—play, full of sentiments

Rasbihari—lord krishna
Raseeka—full of passion, connoisseur
Rasham—traditions
Rashana—a ray of illumination,
luminosity, radiance
Rashanika—full of feeling
Rasha—the first drops of rain
Rasheda—wise, mature, conscious,
pious
Rashenthri—innocence
Rashe—wealth, pretty, lovely,
handsome, graceful
Rashika—descended from royalty,
noble
Rashika—sentimental
Rashila—tasty
Rashima—radha
Rashim—illumination, luminosity,
radiance
Rashita—gilded
Rashi—collection
Rashi—cute, wealth, money, pretty,
lovely, handsome, graceful
Rashi—sign of the zodiac
Rashmika—ray of illumination,
luminosity, radiance
Rashmika—tiny ray of illumination,
luminosity, radiance
Rashmisreya—sunrays, silk, soft in
sanskrit
Rashmita—sun, illumination,
luminosity, radiance, beam of moon
Rashmi—a first ray of sun ray of
Rashmi—ray of early morning sun
Rashpal—all loving, purity, love
Rashtree—ruler
Rasiga—fan
Rasika—connoisseur passion
Rasila—interesting person, very sweet
Rasma—ray of illumination,
luminosity, radiance, smooth, silk
Rasmeen—well-established, well-
founded
Rasmeet—pretty, lovely, handsome,
graceful princess
Rasmita—beam of moon, illumination,
luminosity, radiance

Rasmi—beam of moon, sun,
illumination, luminosity, radiance
Rasna—the tongue
Rasna—the tongue, taste
Rasnika—full of feelings
Raspriya—a gopi
Rasvali—full of nectar, illumination,
luminosity, radiance
Rasvitha—sunshine
Rasya—emotional
Rasya—rose, bloom, garden stuff
name
Rasya—secret
Ratana—crystal, gem, ornament,
jewellery, ornamentation, adornment,
figuration
Ratanjali—red sandal wood
Ratan—ornament, jewellery,
ornamentation, adornment, figuration,
ornament
Rathideity—holly goddess of kama
Rathika—satisfied
Rathimeena—pretty, lovely,
handsome, graceful eye, glimmers
Rathinadeity—connoisseur
Rathinaprabha—ray
Rathiya—royal, sweet, pretty, lovely,
handsome, graceful
Rathi—a ray of illumination,
luminosity, radiance
Rathnabai—praise, gem, gold, pearl
Rathna—diamond, pearl
Rathya—cross road
Rathyni—satisfied
Rathy—pretty, lovely, handsome,
graceful
Ratida—giving pleasure
Ratideity—love goddess, wife of
kaamadeva
Ratikara—one which cause pleasure
Ratika—lovettachment, pleasure
Ratimada—a celestial woman
Ratima—fame
Rati—consort of cupid
Rati—most pretty, lovely, handsome,
graceful lady
Ratnabala—girl of ornament,

jewellery, ornamentation, adornment, figuration

Ratnabala—ornament, jewellery, ornamentation, adornment, figurationled

Ratnabali—string of pearls, beornament, jewellery, ornamentation, adornment

Ratnajyoti—lustrous ornament, jewellery, ornamentation, adornment, figuration

Ratnajyoti—lustrous ornament, jewellery, ornamentation, adornment, figuration

Ratnajyouti—a very pretty, lovely, handsome, graceful woman

Ratnalekha—splendour of ornament, jewellery, ornamentation, adornment, figurations

Ratnali—a ornament, jewellery, ornamentation, adornment, figurationled neckless

Ratnali—jewellery, ornamentation, adornment, figurationled ornament

Ratnamaala—strring of pearls

Ratnamala—string of ornament, jewellery, ornamentation, adornment, figuration

Ratnamala—string of pearls, necklace of gems

Ratnambaree—dressed in ornament, jewellery, ornamentation, adornment, figuration

Ratnangee—with ornament, jewellery, ornamentation, adornment, figurationed limb

Ratnangi—pretty, lovely, handsome, graceful girl

Ratnangi—ornament, jewellery, ornamentation, adornment, figuration-bodied

Ratnanjali—red sandal

Ratnaprabha—earth, illumination, luminosity, radiance from a ornament, jewellery

Ratnapriya—lover of ornament, jewellery, ornamentation, adornment, figurations

Ratnarchisha—shining like ornament, jewellery, ornamentation

Ratnashoo—neclace of ornament, jewellery, ornamentation, adornment, figuration

Ratnashu—the earth

Ratnavali—bunch of gems, earth

Ratnavati—the earth

Ratnawali—wife of the famous poet

Ratna—ornament, jewellery, ornamentation, adornment, figuration

Ratna—ornament, jewellery, ornamentation, adornment, figurationlery

Ratnika—princess of jems

Ratnolka—a tantrik deity

Ratnottama—best ornament, jewellery, ornamentation, adornment, figuration

Ratooja—daughter of truth

Ratoo—truthful

Ratreehasa—laughing night

Ratree—night

Ratri—night

Ratri—night, bow

Ratti—wife of kamdeva

Ratuja—season, daughter of truth

Raudramukhi—fierce face like destroyer rudra

Raudri—a garland of gems

Raupya—made of silver

Ravali—a way of sound, cute, eshwara

Ravena—bright, sunny, beauty of the sun

Raven—pretty, blackbird

Rave—awesome, first sun ray on earth

Ravichandrika—a garland of gems, glory of sun

Ravija—daughter of the sun, yamuna

Ravija—sun, daughter of the sun

Ravikiran—rays of sun illumination, luminosity, radiance

Ravinasri—beauty of sun, bright illumination, luminosity, radiance

Ravina—sunny, beauty of the sun

Ravinder—sun god

Raviprabha—illumination, luminosity, radiance of the sun

Ravishta—loved by sun

Ravishta—loved by the sun
Ravita—daughter of sun god
Raviyanki—daughter of the sun god, sunshine
Ravi—the sun, river, first ray of sun
Ravva—beauty
Ravyanki—sunshine
Ravya—worshipped
Rawdha—garden bunch of gems, meadow
Rawina—beauty of sun, sunny
Raxa—protection
Raxitha—guardian, protector
Rayana—gates of paradise heaven
Rayantika—pretty, lovely, handsome, graceful name
Raya—flow, sated with drink
Rayesha—knowledgeable
Rayna—highness, empress, queen, holy
Rddhi—a classical melody
Rea—poppy, earth
Rebha—singer of praise
Rechal—responsible
Recika—amiable, pleasing, suave, interesting
Redansha—part of heart
Redhanya—highness, empress, queen of jungle
Redha—lover of krishna
Reecha—chants, hymn
Reeday—heart
Reedhima—goddess lakshmi, pearl
Reedisha—satisfy
Reehanshiks—sweet
Reeha—air, smell
Reeja—lord
Reejh—dedication, desire, aspiration, longing
Reema—goddess of durga, white antelope
Reemsha—bunch of bloom, garden stuffs
Reem—gazelle, white antelope
Reem—name of goddess
Reenadeity—flow, sated with drink
Reenal—pleased, satisfied

Reenarani—pretty, lovely, handsome, graceful name
Reenasri—pretty, lovely, handsome, graceful name
Reena—artistic, gem, dissolve, reborn
Reenika—song
Reeni—serenity, calm, calmness, stillness, silenceful
Reenu—amiable and cooperative
Reepal—love
Reesha—feather, sanity
Reeshika—saintly
Reetadeity—pearl
Reeta—pearl
Reethana—sweet saffron
Reethuchandra—pretty, lovely, handsome, graceful name
Reeth—traditions, goddess durga
Reetika—of a stream
Reetika—one who follows traditions
Reetisha—goodness of truth
Reeti—culture, traditional, course
Reeti—motion
Reetul—according to season
Reet—pearl, tradition, rule
Reevaa—pretty, lovely, handsome, graceful name
Reeva—tied, joined, beauty
Reeya—gem, graceful, singer
Regani—ruling the world
Regina—highness, empress, queen, purple bloom, garden stuff
Reguna—soul freedom
Rehana—fragranceir
Rehanshi—sweet basil
Rehansi—good luck
Reha—star
Reheila—who shows the way
Rehma—silk
Rehnugha—pretty, lovely, handsome, graceful name
Rehwa—ancient name of river narmada
Reia—highness, empress, queen
Reina—night, highness, empress, queen
Rejaksha—fiery eye, glimmers
Rejani—night

Reji—rejoice
Rekha—line, gentle
Rekha—star, linertwork, beauty
Remanika—pretty, lovely, handsome, graceful name
Reman—song
Remika—holy, sanctified, pious, solemn, chaste beauty
Remitha—pleasing, loved
Remmi—love, serenity, calm, calmness, stillness, silence
Remya—charming, pretty, lovely, handsome, graceful
Rena—of the sea, born again, reborn
Rency—to be reborn, greek
Reneka—song
Renesh—lord of love
Renisha—reborn
Renita—love, reborn
Renjini—pretty, lovely, handsome, graceful name
Renjith—goddess lakshmi
Renji—joyful make happy
Renjoo—lord krishna
Renn—night, sun, illumination, luminosity, radiance
Renoo—earth, universetom
Rensi—brilliant
Renuga—mother
Renukadeity—moon, illumination, luminosity, radiance
Renuka—moon, illumination, luminosity, radiance
Renuka—parsuram's mother
Renukhadeity—with pretty, lovely, handsome, graceful figure
Renukha—another name of yellama deity
Renusri—pretty, lovely, handsome, graceful name
Renu—beauty, gracetom, universe
Renu—earth, atom, dust
Renzy—the heart of god
Resham—silk
Reshavi—serenity, calm, calmness, stillness, silence, beauty of goddess
Resha—line

Reshika—illumination, luminosity, radiance
Reshitha—rising of end, beginning
Reshmaa—silk
Reshman—of silk, soothing
Reshma—silkyurvedic medicine, silken
Reshmithashree—silk
Reshmi—silken, silky
Reshudha—holy, sanctified, pious, solemn, chaste
Reshu—holy, sanctified, pious, solemn, chaste soul
Resigna—daughter of goddess lakshmi
Resmi—smooth, silk
Retham—music, tune
Rethanya—one with great, loving heart
Rethi—sand
Rethushana—goddess lakshmi
Reth—sand
Retica—pretty, movement
Retika—pretty, lovely, handsome, graceful name
Reti—sand
Rett—sand
Revani—repeat speech, words, voice
Revanthi—pretty, lovely, handsome, graceful
Revatee—silk
Revathi—wealth, cute, star
Revathy—star, wife of moon
Revati—wife of balarama star
Reva—active, agile
Reva—sweat heart star
Revi—a star
Revti—name of a river
Rewanshi—part of lord vishnu
Rewati—nakshatra
Rewa—swift
Reyana—jasmine bloom, garden stuff
Reyanshi—ray of illumination, luminosity, radiance
Reyaz—practise
Reya—highness, empress, queenngel, graceful, singer
Reyi—night
Reyna—highness, empress, queen

Reyona—gift of god
Reza—summer, reaper
Rezhitha—brilliant
Rheana—graceful
Rhea—to flow, stream, flowing, river
Rhesha—holy, pure, sanctified, pious, solemn beauty
Rheya—singer
Rhia—good heart
Rhidayanshi—part of heart, from the heart
Rhiday—heart
Rhidima—prosperity love
Rhim—white antelope
Rhishika—saint, saintly
Rhithika—generous
Rhitika—generous
Rhitu—season
Rhoma—goddess lakshmi, sensitive
Rhonna—mighty, wise ruler
Rhudaina—part of heart
Rhudai—heart
Rhudhi—pretty, lovely, handsome, graceful name
Rhudri—worship offering to lord shiva
Rhutu—season
Rhutvika—pretty, lovely, handsome, graceful name
Rhu—soul
Rhyah—highness, empress, queen of the sun
Rhydm—instrumental
Rhythma—a music, a node of music
Rhythm—music flow, taal, sur
Riana—love, happiness and luck, highness, empress, queen
Rianchi—cherful
Riansha—ray of sun, happiness
Rianshi—cherful, happiness
Riaz—practise
Ria—singer, love flow, earth
Ribha—lion face
Ribhya—worshipped
Richal—creative, resourceful, decisive
Richa—chants, hymn
Richa—worship
Richika—one who praises
Richika—rich, celebrating

Richitha—hymn, the writing of the vedas
Richu—ric means to praise
Ridansha—given to me
Ridaya—heart
Riddhika—prosperity, wealth
Riddhima—full of love
Riddhima—full of wealth
Riddhisha—goddess lakshmi
Riddhishi—goddess lakshmi
Riddhishree—knowledge, wealth, prosperity
Riddhita—wealthy, prosperity
Riddhiyanshi—wealth giver
Riddhi—growth, wealth, prosperity
Riddhi—wealth, goddess lakshmi
Riddima—great guru's wife name
Riddi—consort of lord ganesh, fortune
Rideepta—pretty, lovely, handsome, graceful name
Rideiya—from the heart
Ridey—heart
Ridham—music
Ridhanya—spring season, girl with music
Ridha—tone
Ridhika—to increase make gain
Ridhiksha—to increase make gain
Ridhima—full of love, pearl
Ridhisha—satisfy
Ridhita—pretty, lovely, handsome, graceful name
Ridhi—prosperity be successful
Ridhma—prosperity love
Ridhushni—season
Ridhvika—good prosperity
Ridhwi—prosperity
Ridika—to make gain increase
Ridima—prosperity, pearl love
Ridita—prosperity
Riditta—pretty, lovely, handsome, graceful name
Ridnya—going on
Ridoo—charming
Ridvika—prosperity
Ridvi—close to heart, belongs to heart
Riena—best
Rigdha—one of the veds

Righna—world, love, profit
Rigvedha—one of the name of seven veda
Rigvedita—knowledge
Rigvedya—who blessed with rig veda
Rihana—sweet basil
Rihani—entrance of heaven, spiritual
Rihanna—sweet scent, great, highness, empress, queen
Rihanshi—cherful, name of goddess
Rihansi—part of sun, part of lord vishnu
Riha—bloom, garden stuff, fragrance
Rihu—pretty, lovely, handsome, graceful name
Riitu—ideal, model of serenity, calm, calmness, stillness, silence
Rijak—earning, tradition, way
Rijul—innocent
Rijuta—innocence
Rijuta—straightness
Riju—helpful, innocent, pleasing
Riju—innocent
Riketa—season
Rikhasa—the highness, empress, queen of session
Rikisha—rose
Rikita—pleasing, season, innocent
Rikshana—passionate, extremely sensitive
Rikshitha—pretty, lovely, handsome, graceful name
Rikta—empty
Riktisa—happy
Riku—innocent
Rile—valiant, courageous
Rima—goddess lakshmi
Rima—white antelope, siddhi
Rimisha—pretty, lovely, handsome, graceful name
Rimi—sweet, loving and caring, pretty
Rimjhim—other name of rain in hindi
Rimnish—pretty, lovely, handsome, graceful name
Rimpal—stream
Rimpa—full of joy, happiness
Rimple—soft, gentle spirit
Rimpy—good, pretty

Rimsha—sweet, bunch of bloom, garden stuff
Rimzim—rain
Rinal—satisfied, pleased
Rinayra—princess
Rina—gentle, honest
Rina—serenity, calm, calmness, stillness, solemn, chaste
Rinesha—perfectionist, bright
Rinesh—pretty, lovely, handsome, graceful name
Rinika—love for other
Rinisha—perfectionist, bright
Rinishka—pretty, lovely, handsome, graceful
Rinita—pretty, lovely, handsome, graceful name
Rini—cute, smiling, little bunny
Rinkal—nice, eye, glimmers
Rinka—dissolved
Rinkey—pretty, lovely, handsome, graceful name
Rinkita—love
Rinki—regal one, calm personality
Rinku—sweet nature, well
Rinky—a name
Rinnie—pretty, lovely, handsome, graceful name
Rinsha—pretty, lovely, handsome, graceful name
Rinshi—cute
Rinti—clever
Rintu—pretty, lovely, handsome, graceful name
Rinu—freelance of bloom, garden stuffs, smart
Rin—dignified, cold
Riona—a highness, empress, queen, royal
Ripal—sweet, cute
Ripanshi—god's child
Ripdika—river
Risa—smile, laughter
Rischita—writing of vedas, saintly, best
Rishaka—feather, saintly, purity
Risham—pretty, lovely, handsome, graceful name

Rishani—happy
Rishank—devotee of lord shiva
Risha—feather, line, saintly, highness, empress, queen
Rishbha—innocent
Risheka—saint, saintly
Rishika—saint, saintly
Rishikha—saintly
Rishiki—ray of illumination, luminosity, radiance, kindness
Rishikulya—innocense
Rishikulya—virtuous
Rishima—moonbeam
Rishita—saintly, message for happiness
Rishitha—message for happiness
Rishi—saint
Rishka—pretty, lovely, handsome, graceful name
Rishma—smart, pretty, funny, saintly
Rishmita—saintly
Rishmitha—saintly
Rishona—first
Rishta—sword
Rishtha—relationship
Rishu—cute
Rishva—lawful, loyal, lawmaker
Rishvika—saintly
Rishvitha—pretty, lovely, handsome, graceful name
Rishvi—female saint
Risika—saintly
Risna—wise, pretty, lovely, handsome, graceful
Risu—believern explorer, cute
Risva—great one
Ritah—valuable, valued, rare pearl
Ritambara—progressive
Ritambhara—a saint lady
Ritambhara—ultimate, absolute, highest, best state of mind
Ritambhra—universal knowledge
Ritanshi—not being afraid of anyone, brave
Ritanya—name of goddess saraswathi
Rita—gentle
Rita—pearl, child of illumination, luminosity, radiance

Riteeka—motion
Ritesh—lord of truth
Rithanyasri—goddess saraswati
Rithanya—goddess sarasvathi
Ritheka—flow of river, command river
Ritheka—name of goddess lakshmi, movement
Ritherka—pretty, lovely, handsome, graceful name
Rithika—flowing water, brass, of a stream
Rithula—season
Rithuvarna—colour season
Rithu—season
Rithvika—priest, rays, pretty, lovely, handsome, graceful, moon
Rithvi—goodness, scholar
Rithya—charming, lucky, beauty of nature
Ritica—pretty, highness, empress, queen of weather, movement
Ritija—innocent, brave, brilliant, sagacious, gifted, wise, learned
Ritika—flowing
Ritika—movement, pretty, cute, of brass
Ritiksha—highness, empress, queen of season
Ritil—creeper of love
Ritisha—the goddess of truth
Ritishka—daughter of the god
Riti—ritual, culture, memory, well
Riti—tradition, moving, path
Ritka—a holy, sanctified, pious, solemn, chaste white river
Ritkriti—creation of god sun
Ritoma—pretty, lovely, handsome, graceful
Ritoshree—pretty, lovely, handsome, graceful nature
Ritshika—pretty, lovely, handsome, graceful name
Ritsika—traditional
Ritujaa—moonbeam
Ritul—talentedctive, butterfly
Ritumbari—pretty, lovely, handsome, graceful name

Ritumbhara—of holy, pure, sanctified, pious, solemn truth, the earth
Rituparan—way of life
Rituparna—leafy season, spring, productive
Ritusha—pretty, lovely, handsome, graceful, caring
Ritushri—splendour and highness, empress, queen of the seasons
Ritu—season
Ritu—season, mausam
Ritvika—pretty, lovely, handsome, graceful, goddess of truth
Ritvi—female priest, scholar
Ritwika—princess, moon, priest
Rit—tradition
Rivaa—form of rebecca river, tied
Riva—form of rebecca, tied, joined
Rivya—pretty, lovely, handsome, graceful name
Riwa—joined, beauty, tied
Riyanci—part of sun, first ray of sun
Riyanika—holy, sanctified, pious, solemn, chaste, pretty, lovely, handsome, graceful
Riyanshi—cherful
Riyansika—truthful, goddess
Riyansi—part of sun, large settlement
Riya—graceful, singer, one who sings
Riya—graceful, singer, pretty, lovely, handsome, graceful
Riya—singer
Riza—pleasure
Rizma—winner, bloom, garden stuff, pretty, lovely, handsome, graceful
Rizmi—heart
Rizul—illumination, luminosity, radiance
Rizvika—pretty, lovely, handsome, graceful name
Rochak—pleasant
Rochamana—consisting of illumination, luminosity, radiance
Rochana—pretty, lovely, handsome, graceful woman
Rochana—red lotus
Rochane—pretty, lovely, handsome, graceful

Rochani—illumination, luminosity, radiancegreeable
Roche—illumination, luminosity, radiance
Rochira—illumination, luminosity, radiance
Rochishan—brightness
Rochisha—illumination, luminosity, radiance
Rochita—creator, season
Rochit—embellished
Rochi—illumination, luminosity, radiance, illumination, luminosity, radiance
Rochuka—one who gives pleasure
Rodasi—the earth and sky
Rodhasvatee—a holy river in india
Roepwatie—pretty, lovely, handsome, graceful
Rohana—sandalwood
Rohane—pretty, lovely, handsome, graceful
Rohane—most beloved, sacred, spiritual
Rohanika—pretty, lovely, handsome, graceful name
Rohani—most beloved, powerful
Rohanna—illumination, luminosity, radiance
Rohanshi—ascending, healing, medicine
Rohantee—vine
Rohanti—climbing, vine
Rohan—ascending, healing, medicine
Rohash—momory of movement
Rohena—splendid
Rohe—rising up
Rohila—pretty, lovely, handsome, graceful name
Rohine—increasing, mother of all cows, goddess
Rohine—the earth and skies star, fire
Rohini—fire, heat
Rohini—increasing, a star
Rohin—rising, lord vishnu
Rohita—brahma's daughter, red coloured
Rohita—red

Rohitha—another name of lord vishnu
Rohi—soul, a river
Rohma—kind hearted
Rojamani—pearl rose
Rojaramani—pretty, lovely, handsome, graceful rose, lakshmi
Rojarani—rose highness, empress, queen
Roja—pretty, rose, sensitive
Rojitha—rose
Roji—pretty, lovely, handsome, graceful, love, satisfaction
Rokshada—possessing illumination, luminosity, radiance
Role—sindoor
Roli—name of river in afghanistan
Roli—red powder
Roly—princess
Romanshi—pretty, lovely, handsome, graceful name
Roman—of rome, talented
Romasha—full of hair
Roma—goddess lakshmi
Roma—superior, elevated, lofty, goddess lakshmi
Romica—princess of heart
Romika—sky girl
Romila—pretty, lovely, handsome, graceful, deeply
Romil—full of love, cherful
Romini—pretty
Romi—wealth, money
Rommi—pretty, lovely, handsome, graceful name
Romola—charming
Romola—roman woman, hairy, charming
Romona—protective advice, protector
Ronak—illumination, luminosity, radiance, bright
Roneka—embellishment
Ronika—victory bringer
Ronita—brilliant, bright, shining, joy
Roobal—pretty
Roobhavani—spirit
Roobha—attraction
Roochie—interest
Roodhi—birth, fame

Roohanika—belongs to soul
Roohica—soul
Roohika—soul, goddess lakshmi, ambition, intent, passion
Roohi—soul
Rookmin—love, happiness, illumination, luminosity, radiance
Rooma—brahma's daughter
Roona—red colour, lakshmi
Roonhi—god's obligation, gift
Rooni—star
Roopakala—with a form like a work of art
Roopala—beauty
Roopalekha—streak of beauty
Roopali—pretty, lovely, handsome, graceful, pretty
Roopal—silver, pretty, lovely, handsome, graceful
Roopamala—blessed with beauty
Roopambara—pretty, lovely, handsome, gracefully dressed
Roopambaree—pretty, lovely, handsome, gracefully dressed
Roopam—pretty, lovely, handsome, graceful
Rooparani—pretty, lovely, handsome, graceful like goddess lakshmi
Rooparashmi—rays of beauty
Rooparekha—name of a highness, empress, queen
Roopashri—pretty, lovely, handsome, graceful
Roopasi—pretty, lovely, handsome, graceful
Roopasree—pretty, lovely, handsome, graceful
Roopavani—pretty, lovely, handsome, graceful
Roopa—beauty
Roopa—blessed with beauty, pretty, lovely, handsome, graceful
Roopeni—lord of beauty
Roopeshwari—most pretty, lovely, handsome, graceful, goddess
Roopini—pretty, lovely, handsome, graceful
Roopi—name of a gem

Roopkala—pretty, lovely, handsome, graceful arts
Rooplakshmi—sugreeva's wife name
Roopmati—heartfelt, pretty, lovely, handsome, graceful natured
Roopshika—serenity, calm, calmness, stillness, silence and love
Roopsi—pretty, lovely, handsome, graceful
Roop—look, beautyppearance
Rootra—durga deity
Rooyi—cotton
Ropana—healing
Rosa—rose, little rose, bloom, garden stuff name
Rosey—rose
Rose—rose bloom, garden stuff, bush, bloom, garden stuff name
Roshana—bright, passionateuchstone
Roshani—illumination, luminosity, radiance, goddess of success
Roshan—bright, illumination, luminosity, radiance
Roshen—rose, little rose
Roshika—never forgotten by people, shining
Roshini—illumination, luminosity, radiance, brightness, charming
Roshita—illuminated
Roshitha—bright illumination, luminosity, radiance
Roshna—bright, shining, illumination, luminosity, radiance
Roshni—shining, radiant, rays of the sun
Rosy—deep pink, pretty, lovely, handsome, graceful, rose
Rouble—money
Royina—growing
Royina—rising, growing
Roza—rose blossom, bloom, garden stuff name
Rrijuvani—the earth
Rrikshambika—mother of the stars
Rriksha—the best
Rrishva—elevated
Rritushala—abode of illumination, luminosity, radiance

Rritu—season
Ruana—string musical instrument
Ruani—from the soul
Rubaina—bright, pretty, lovely, handsome, graceful, gift of god
Rubai—bloom, garden stuff
Rubanya—bright, the sun
Ruban—hill, plural of rubwa, bright
Rubby—red gemstone
Rubeena—face reader
Rubie—red gemstone, ruby ornament, jewellery, ornamentation
Rubina—the red gemstone, red, ruby
Rubini—cute
Rubisha—part of gemstone
Rubi—red gemstone
Ruby—reddish
Rucha—lustre, illumination, luminosity, radiance
Rucha—splander, bright, brilliant
Ruche—hobby
Ruchika—interest, shining, pretty, lovely, handsome, graceful
Ruchika—pleasing, favourite, charming
Ruchila—pretty, lovely, handsome, graceful
Ruchila—bright, names of goddess lakshmi
Ruchiraj—pretty, lovely, handsome, graceful
Ruchira—pretty, lovely, handsome, graceful, like to all, tasty
Ruchira—shining, charming
Ruchir—pretty, lovely, handsome, graceful
Ruchismita—pretty, lovely, handsome, graceful smile
Ruchita—curiosity, splendorous
Ruchita—shining
Ruchitha—bright, illumination, luminosity, radiance, interested
Ruchi—beauty, taste
Ruchi—interest, lustre, beauty, love
Ruchu—sweet, cute, clever
Rudatha—taste
Ruddhima—full of prosperity
Ruddhira—one who endows properity

Ruddhi—growth
Rudhira—one who is prosperous
Rudhi—risescent, birth, fame
Rudhrama—courageous
Rudhve—pleasant
Rudrabhiravi—goddess durga
Rudragita—tasty
Rudrakali—goddess durga
Rudrakshi—eye, glimmers of lord shiva, goddess parvati
Rudrambika—the angry mother
Rudramma—angry
Rudrana—goddess parvati
Rudrane—a wife of lord shiva
Rudrane—wife of rudra
Rudrani—goddess rudrama deity
Rudranshi—part of lord shiva
Rudrapriya—goddess durga
Rudrashe—rudra like
Rudrasi—red
Rudra—belonging, devotee of lord shiva
Rudra—consort of lord shiva
Rudra—goddess durga
Rudresha—belongs to lord shiva
Rudri—the pooja of the lord shankar
Rugma—pretty, lovely, handsome, graceful name
Rugmini—wife of lord krishna
Rugu—soft
Rugveda—part of one of vedas
Rugvedha—name of one of the vedas
Rugvedi—type of a veda
Rugvija—powerful goddess
Ruhane—soul, spiritual, holy, pure, sanctified, pious, solemn
Ruhanika—pretty, lovely, handsome, graceful
Ruhani—spiritual, sacred, holy, pure, sanctified, pious, solemn, shine
Ruhani—spirituality, soul, most beloved
Ruhanshi—spiritual
Ruha—grown, risen
Ruhe—soul bloom, garden stuff, who touches the
Ruhika—ambition, intent, passion

Ruhika—goddess lakshmi, ambition, intent, passion
Ruhina—with a soul
Ruhine—cute, sweet
Ruhin—spiritual
Ruhi—soul, of spirit, serenity, calm, calmness, stillness, silenceful
Ruh—soul
Rujala—honest
Rujana—goddess durga
Rujula—honest
Rujula—soft, one who endows wealth
Rujul—soft spoken
Rujumriti—a person having a sober memory
Rujusmiriti—soul
Rujusmita—a person having a sober smile
Rujusmita—pretty, lovely, handsome, graceful name
Rujuta—honesty, sincerity, integrity
Ruju—soft
Rujvi—honest woman
Rukaiya—best of the best
Ruka—gold
Rukhmanideity—who endows wealth, lakshmi, soft
Rukhmanikumari—soft, innocent
Rukhmani—wife of lord krishna
Rukhmini—goddess lakshmi
Rukhsana—pretty, lovely, handsome, graceful
Rukmabha—shining like god
Rukmani—ornament, jewellery, ornamentation, adornment, figuration of gold
Rukmapura—pretty, lovely, handsome, graceful name
Rukmavati—beloved of lord krishna
Rukma—golden
Rukmine—a wife of lord krishna
Rukmini—wife of krishna
Rukmini—wife of lord krishna
Ruksana—brilliant
Ruksane—brilliant
Rukshana—pretty, lovely, handsome, graceful
Rukshara—flow of water

Rukshara—goddess lakshmi, goddess lakshmi

Rukshi—pretty, lovely, handsome, graceful name

Rukumani—god name

Rumali—pretty, lovely, handsome, graceful name

Rumana—heavenly fruit

Rumaya—innocent

Ruma—a goddess

Ruma—wife of sugriva, vedic hymn

Rumi—pretty, lovely, handsome, graceful name

Rumnita—pretty, lovely, handsome, graceful

Rumpa—innocent

Runali—red coloured, lakshmi

Runal—kind

Runaskara—pretty, lovely, handsome, graceful name

Runa—secret tradition, secret love

Runi—a traditional name

Runi—i, you owe me

Runjhun—voice of anklet

Runzhun—sweet sound

Runzun—sweet music

Rupaale—silver

Rupak—pretty, lovely, handsome, graceful name

Rupalata—flow of water

Rupala—brilliant

Rupalekha—vedic hymn

Rupale—pretty, lovely, handsome, graceful girl

Rupali—pleasing, favourite, charming

Rupali—silver, pretty, pretty, lovely, handsome, graceful

Rupaly—beauiful, silver

Rupal—made of silver, beauty, cool

Rupamanjari—made of silver

Rupam—pretty, lovely, handsome, graceful, lovely beauty

Rupangee—with pretty, lovely, handsome, graceful body

Rupangi—pretty, lovely, handsome, graceful figure

Rupangi—with pretty, lovely, handsome, graceful body

Rupanjan—beauty, pretty, lovely, handsome, graceful

Rupansha—part of beauty

Rupanshi—pretty, lovely, handsome, graceful

Rupasee—pretty, lovely, handsome, graceful

Rupashi—pretty, lovely, handsome, graceful

Rupashree—pretty, lovely, handsome, graceful

Rupashree—pretty, lovely, handsome, graceful lakshmi

Rupashri—pretty, lovely, handsome, graceful

Rupasi—pretty, lovely, handsome, graceful lady

Rupasi—good-monarch, ruler, prince, earl

Rupasri—holy, pure, sanctified, pious, solemnly pretty, lovely, handsome, graceful

Rupa—beauty, silver

Rupeksha—the structure of god

Rupeshvaree—goddess of beauty

Rupeshwari—goddess of beauty

Rupika—pretty, lovely, handsome, graceful figure

Rupika—pretty, lovely, handsome, graceful woman, gold coin, form

Rupinder—pretty, lovely, handsome, graceful

Rupinika—one who possess good form and figure

Rupitha—pretty, lovely, handsome, graceful

Rupi—pretty, lovely, handsome, graceful, beauty

Rupi—pretty, lovely, handsome, graceful, pleasing, favourite, charming

Rupmati—most pretty, lovely, handsome, graceful

Rupmati—possessing beauty

Rupsa—pretty, lovely, handsome, graceful

Rupshika—zenith of beauty

Rupshree—most charming

Rupvati—pretty, lovely, handsome, graceful
Ruqaya—name of the prophet's daughter
Rusa—the world, bride
Ruscha—bright
Rushada—good news
Rushali—pretty, lovely, handsome, graceful, bright girl
Rusham—serenity, calm, calmness, stillness, silenceful
Rushana—adorning, ornamentation, adornment, figuration
Rushatee—fair complextion
Rushati—white, fair complexion
Rushda—guided one, guidance, good news
Rushika—a god, graceful
Rushikulya—sprout of beauty
Rushina—adorning, charming
Rushita—goddess
Rushitha—bright girl
Rushiti—saintly, sage
Rushi—saintess, taste
Rushminta—pretty, lovely, handsome, graceful name
Rushmitha—sun, illumination, luminosity, radiance, beam of moon
Rushvi—female saint
Rutaja—pretty, lovely, handsome, graceful
Ruta—pretty, lovely, handsome, graceful, friend, companion
Ruthrabala—a river's name
Ruthranayagi—daughter of truth
Ruthrapriya—season
Ruthrasri—pretty, lovely, handsome, graceful name

Ruthu—season
Ruthvija—priestess
Ruthvika—speech, goddess saraswati
Ruth—mate, companion, friend
Rutika—garden of bloom, garden stuffs
Rutti—season
Rutuja—highness, empress, queen of seasons
Rutumbhara—pretty, lovely, handsome, graceful, pretty
Rutu—the season
Rutvaa—season, speech
Rutva—season, speech
Rutveka—goodness of life, holy life
Rutvika—goodness of life, holy life
Rutvi—cherful, blossom, desire, aspiration, longing
Rutwa—season
Ruvanshi—part of lord shiva
Ruvanthika—satisfaction
Ruvika—splendid
Ruvina—pretty, lovely, handsome, graceful name
Ruvi—look, season, weather
Ruxmani—the consort of god krishna
Ruzal—delicate
Ryena—highness, empress, queen, holy, sanctified, pious, solemn, chaste
Ryka—born out of a prayer
Ryna—night
Rysa—laughter
Rytasha—highness, empress, queen of night
Rythem—bunch of bloom, garden stuffs, musical

****

Indian Names For Girls—S

Sabeena—pretty, lovely, handsome, graceful
Sabhnam—water drops on leaves
Sabhya—mannered
Sabita—pretty, lovely, handsome, graceful sunshine
Sabitha—sunshine, loveable, clever
Sabi—young, teen, intelligence, grace
Sabrang—rainbow
Sabri—lord rama's devotees, patient
Sachana—gentle
Sacha—truthful, defender, helper of
Sachika—lord krishna's flute, kind
Sachita—consciousness
Sachi—blessed child, wife of lord indra
Sachi—lord indra's wife
Sachi—truth, goddess indrani
Sachu—true
Sachvi—truthful
Saci—humanity, right
Sadabhilasha—wife of lord indra
Sadabhuja—goddess durga
Sadaf—pretty, lovely, handsome, graceful stone, pearl, sea shell
Sadagati—liberation
Sadamundi—consciousness
Sadan—house, home
Sadashaya—member
Sadayilatchmi—goddess durga
Sada—good luck, holy, sanctified, pious, solemn, chaste onelways
Sadesh—pearl
Sadgata—who moves in the right direction
Sadgati—correct path, liberation
Sadguna—good virtues, virtuous
Sadhaka—effective, efficient
Sadhanaa—practise quest
Sadhana—long practise, study, fulfilment
Sadhana—performance, concentration
Sadhana—practise
Sadhan—fulfilment

Sadhavi—simplicity, virtuous
Sadhika—accomplished
Sadhika—achiever, simple
Sadhika—simplechiever
Sadhita—completed
Sadhna—long practise, study, worship
Sadhna—worship, long practise, study
Sadhree—conqueror
Sadhri—conqueror
Sadhumati—virtuous minded
Sadhve—honest, chaste
Sadhvika—more polite
Sadhvi—a woman with high character
Sadhvi—chaste woman
Sadhvi—sanguine, goddess parvati
Sadhvi—virtuous woman, simplicity
Sadhya—accomplishment
Sadhya—good habits, highness, empress, queen, perfection
Sadhya—simplicity, meditated
Sadiqua—kindly
Sadique—good virtues
Sadri—pretty, lovely, handsome, graceful
Sadvatee—rightous
Sadvati—righteous, truthful, pious
Sadvikha—truth
Sadvita—combination
Sadvi—simplicity, more polite
Sadwika—cool
Saeeda—priestly
Saeeda—priestly, prosperous, lucky
Saeenaz—alone
Saee—bloom, garden stuff, female friend, memory
Saesha—goddess durga
Saeyami—one who has self conrol
Safala—achieved, success, fruitful
Safia—chaste, lion's share, holy, sanctified, pious, solemn, chaste
Sagarambara—ocean clad
Sagara—ocean
Sagaree—of the ocean
Sagarika—ocean, related to sea, wave

Sagarika—of the oecan
Sagarika—of the sea
Sagari—pertaining to the sea
Sagari—river, of the ocean
Saga—seeing one long journey
Sagnika—with fire, lord shiva's third eye, glimmers
Sagnira—pretty and honesty
Sagrika—water, ocean, waves
Saguna—calm, possessed of good qualities
Sagun—auspicious
Sagun—name of a girl
Sahadeity—protected by the goddesses
Sahae—help, the friend
Sahajadeity—wave
Sahajanya—born together
Sahaja—natural, original, innate, normal
Sahaj—female friend
Sahala—simple, smooth
Sahanaa—tolerance, durability, toleration
Sahanaz—pretty, lovely, handsome, graceful
Sahana—a raga, tolerance, durability, toleration, vigour
Sahana—long life
Sahanya—pretty, lovely, handsome, graceful name
Saharika—helper
Saharsha—sun, dawn, morning, bewitch
Sahasara—pretty, lovely, handsome, graceful name
Sahashra—a new beginning
Sahashree—born from desert, strong
Sahasranjali—thousand namaskar
Sahasra—a new beginning, thousand times
Sahasta—pretty, lovely, handsome, graceful name
Sahastra—thousand
Sahasvitha—goddess lakshmi
Sahaswini—courageous
Sahasya—confidence
Saha—breath
Saha—enduring, mighty

Sahej—serenity, calm, calmness, stillness, easy, tolerance, durability, toleration
Saheli—friend
Saheli—friend, beloved
Sahera—mountain, wakeful, natural
Saher—morning, dawn, awakening
Saheythika—devotee of lord shiva
Sahiba—the lady, highness, empress, queen
Sahika—correct
Sahila—guide
Sahil—pretty, lovely, handsome, graceful name
Sahima—snowed
Sahinia—pretty, lovely, handsome, graceful name
Sahira—mountain, natural
Sahista—pretty, lovely, handsome, graceful name
Sahita—being near river
Sahitee—literature, literature of music
Sahitha—being near, tolerance, durability, toleration
Sahithi—goddess, literature
Sahithya—literature
Sahiti—literature of music, literature
Sahitra—full of tolerance, durability, toleration
Sahitya—knowledge, literature
Sahi—cute, pretty, lovely, handsome, graceful, devotion, innocent
Sahoj—easy
Sahrudee—kind hearted
Sahura—strong, the earth
Sahya—a mountain in india
Sai-ishita—wealth superior
Sai-jesal—holy water
Sai-krisha—holy, pure, sanctified, pious, solemn
Sai-vaishnavi—god sai, vigour of lord vishnu
Sai-vani—sweet voice of saibaba
Saiaashvi—pretty, lovely, handsome, graceful name
Saiananya—matchless, incomparable
Saibha—rani, jaan

Saidhanya—pretty, lovely, handsome, graceful name
Saijal—pretty, lovely, handsome, graceful name
Saijasi—goddess
Saija—princess
Saijil—strong, proud
Saikara—cherry blossoms of the world
Saikirana—a beam of illumination, luminosity, radiance from deity saibaba
Sailaja—lord parvati, daughter of parvati
Saila—dwelling in the mountains
Sailendri—goddess parvati
Saile—name of bloom, garden stuff, shadow of lord sai
Saili—carved in rock, style, custom
Sailu—soft devotee stone
Saima—mother of bloom, garden stuffs, illumination, luminosity, radiance
Saineha—lord sairam
Sainika—strong, soldier
Saioni—eager, clever
Saipriya—beloved of saibaba
Sairah—on the way to saibaba
Sairandhri—maidservant
Saisagun—blessings of sai
Saisha—pretty, lovely, handsome, graceful name
Saisha—truth of life, ornament, jewellery, ornamentation, adornment, figuration
Saishree—everywhere, saibaba
Saishri—respected towards sai baba
Saishta—pretty, lovely, handsome, graceful name
Saismriti—pretty, lovely, handsome, graceful
Saisree—grace of sirdi sai
Saisri—lord sai baba
Saiti—friend
Saivandana—prayer of sai baba
Saivarsha—pretty, lovely, handsome, graceful name
Saive—auspiciousness, holy
Saivi—auspicious

Saiyami—one with self control
Saiyan—lord
Saiya—shadow
Saiyette—princess
Saiyogeeta—one who can concentrate
Saiyogita—one who can concentrate
Saiyoni—pretty, lovely, handsome, graceful name
Sai—a bloom, garden stuff
Sajala—sea, clouds
Sajal—full of water
Sajana—beauty, lover, beloved
Sajani—loving, well loved, night
Sajda—pray, prayer of god, worship
Sajeeni—pretty, lovely, handsome, graceful name
Sajee—bucket that carry bloom, garden stuff
Sajel—river water, little charm, sun
Sajidha—pretty, lovely, handsome, graceful name
Sajili—decorated
Sajina—valuable, valued, rare, pretty, lovely, handsome, graceful, princess
Sajini—beloved, friend
Sajiri—pretty, lovely, handsome, graceful
Sajitha—morality
Sajjana—a good person
Sajjata—confidence
Sajjita—decorated
Sajna—beloved
Sajni—beloved
Saj—music
Saketha—shri krishna
Sakhi—friend
Sakhi—true friend, storey, life partner
Sakina—friend, tranquillity calm, devout
Saki—blossom, bloom, blossom of support, indoctrination, assuredness
Sakree—consort of indra
Sakriya—thank you
Sakshami—capable
Saksham—competent
Sakshe—proof
Sakshe—witness

Sakshika—holy, sanctified, pious, solemn, chaste, love, moon
Sakshita—witness
Sakshi—witness
Sakshi—witness, justice, proof
Sakshmita—pretty, lovely, handsome, graceful name
Saksi—witness, evidence
Sakthi—power, goddess
Sakti—energy, goodness, power
Sakula—loving, well loved
Sakuntala—bird, goddess
Sakunthaladeity—witness
Sakunthala—kind, friend
Salauni—most pretty, lovely, handsome, graceful, preety, fair
Sala—prayer
Salena—the moon
Saleshni—correctgreeable
Salika—flute
Salila—water
Salima—happy, safe, healthy, sound
Salini—with a fixed abode, settled
Salma—safe be safe, pretty, lovely, handsome, graceful woman
Salonia—serenity, calm, calmness, stillness, silence
Salonika—victory
Saloni—pretty, lovely, handsome, graceful
Saloni—pretty, lovely, handsome, graceful, smart, innovative
Saloshini—pretty, lovely, handsome, graceful name
Samaa—sky, environment
Samadu—daughter
Samaera—goddess of beauty, girl of shine
Samah—pretty, lovely, handsome, graceful sky, generosity
Samaira—goddess of beauty, enchanting
Samaiya—heavenly
Samaja—equal
Samajya—fame, reputation
Samajya—reputation
Samakhya—fame, celebrity
Samakshi—present, i am here

Samala—requested of god
Samale—a collection of bloom, garden stuff
Samalika—chain of bloom, garden stuffs
Samali—bouquet
Samangine—complete in all parts
Samanmitha—equal to all, pleasing
Samantha—lord has heard, listener, bloom, garden stuff
Samanvita—goddess durga
Samanvitha—victorious
Samanvi—equal
Samaptika—concluding
Samapti—the end
Samaridhi—fortune, wealth, prosperity
Samarpan—close, devotion
Samarpita—offered, gift of god, dedicate
Samastee—totality
Samasti—all that is reaching, the universe
Samata—equality
Samaya—sunrise princess, opportunity
Sama—weather, of a serenity, calm, calmness, stillness, silenceful nature
Sambathkumari—pretty, lovely, handsome, graceful
Samba—serenity, calm, calmness, stillness, silence
Sambhabi—chanting, mantra of lord shiva
Sambhavana—probability
Sambhave—goddess durga
Sambhavi—everything possible to her
Sambha—to shine, bright
Sambhootee—origin
Sambhooti—pretty, lovely, handsome, graceful name
Sambodhi—full of knowledge
Samboornadeity—bouquet
Samboornavalli—dedicating
Sambuddhi—perfect knowledge
Samdarshi—lord krishna
Samedee—one who moves
Sameeche—praise
Sameeha—ambition, intent, passion

Sameeksha—abstract, forecast, understanding
Sameeksha—critical analysis
Sameena—happy, fatty, plump, clean
Sameera—early morning fragrance
Sameesha—dart
Sameesha—nearby, pretty, lovely, handsome, graceful
Sameetee—committee
Sameira—goddess of beauty destiny
Sameksh—abstract, present
Samhita—a vedic composition
Samidha—an offering for a sacred fire
Samiha—desire, aspiration, longing, magnanimous, ambition, intent, passion
Samika—serenity, calm, calmness, stillness, high, superior, elevated, raised
Samiksha—analysis, overview research
Samiksha—overview
Samikshya—to find, examinenalysis
Samira—a chameli bloom, garden stuff, pleasant
Samisa—love
Samisha—pretty, lovely, handsome, graceful
Samishtee—group of all
Samishti—group of all
Samiska—nearby
Samita—collection of knowledge, collected
Samithra—good friend
Samiti—committee
Samit—collected
Samiya—incomparable celestial dancer
Sammada—joy, happiness
Sammani—equally in everything, honourable
Sammathi—agreement
Sammati—good wisdom
Sammati—permission
Sammohini—hypnotise
Sampada—wealth, money, wealthy
Sampada—wealth, property
Sampad—perfection

Sampangi—one who has balanced body
Sampati—collected
Sampattee—wealth
Sampatti—wealth
Sampavi—one who has everything
Sampoorna—complete
Sampreeta—incomparable
Sampreethi—joy, satisfaction, illumination, luminosity, radiance
Sampreeti—complete joy
Sampreeti—real love and attachment
Sampreti—serenity, calm, calmness, stillness, silence
Samprita—goddess durga
Sampritha—satisfied, contented
Samprithi—real love
Sampriti—attachment
Sampuja—reverence, esteem
Sampurna—complete
Sampushti—perfect, prosperity
Samragee—an empress, the companionship
Samragi—an empress, the companionship
Samragyi—empress
Samreen—beauty of sun, moon, bloom, garden stuff
Samriddhi—prosperity, wealth, rich
Samridha—prosperity
Samridhi—wealth, prosperity, richness
Samrita—provided with nectar
Samrithi—prosperity, goddess lakshmi, meeting
Samriti—memory
Samriti—memory, meeting together
Samrit—collection of tradition
Samrpit—praise of god
Samrriddhe—wealth
Samrriddhin—full of wealth
Samrritee—meeting
Samrta—provided with nectar
Samruddhi—prosperity, prosper
Samrudhe—great, success
Samrudhi—prosperity, goddess lakshmi
Samrutha—amrutham
Samruthi—pleasant, kind

Samshini—destroyer of evil
Samskara—ethics
Samsritha—goddess lakshmi, saraswati
Samstuti—an offering for a sacred fire
Samta—equality
Samudita—wealthscended
Samudrasri—beauty of the ocean
Samudrika—from the ocean, spiritual
Samundeeswari—completetal
Samvarna—of the gold
Samvedhya—pretty, lovely, handsome, graceful name
Samveta—adorned, covered over
Samvidha—direct, lead
Samvrita—invisible due to illusion, maya
Samvriti—the golden
Samvrutha—completeness
Samyama—tolerance, durability, toleration, quiet, serenity, calm, calmness, stillness, silenceful
Samyatha—endowed with complete
Samya—fasting, equality
Samyukhta—united
Samyukhthai—dedicated
Samyukta—goddess durga, united
Samyuktha—united, goddess deity
Samyuktheswari—an indian princess
Samyutha—goddess saraswathi
Sanaaya—love
Sanaa—piece of art, work of art
Sanabhi—wealthy, befitting
Sanam—beloved
Sananda—full of joy
Sananda—look, happy
Sanashisha—good blessing
Sanasi—bringing wealth
Sanatani—goddess durga
Sanavi—memory, goddess lakshmi
Sanaya—ancient, perpetual, long lasting
Sana—prayer, resplendence, brilliance
Sanbanki—bloom, garden stuff
Sanchaita—saving, collection
Sanchala—sanskrit synonym for water
Sanchali—movement
Sanchal—trembling

Sanchana—pretty, lovely, handsome, graceful name
Sancharane—delivering a message
Sanchari—traveller
Sanchaya—collection
Sanchayeta—pretty, lovely, handsome, graceful name
Sanchayita—a poem
Sanchay—collection
Sanchika—great beauty
Sanchita—collection
Sanchita—collection, savings
Sanchita—collection, savings, pretty, lovely, handsome, graceful
Sanchitha—collection of verses
Sanchi—goddess lakshmi
Sanchi—name of goddess lakshmi
Sandana—moon, fragrance, redolence
Sandeeptha—pretty, lovely, handsome, graceful name
Sandeep—goddess lakshmi, ray of illumination, luminosity, radiance
Sandesha—messenge
Sandhana—worship, hard practise
Sandhaya—collection
Sandhia—evening
Sandhiya—cute, valuable, valued, rare
Sandhi—compact, promise
Sandhra—soft, intense, strong
Sandhu—the blessed ones
Sandhyaprabha—preety
Sandhyaraga—the colour of twiillumination, luminosity, radiance
Sandhya—evening, valuable, valued, rare mind, twiillumination, luminosity, radiance
Sandhya—religious act performed during evening time
Sandika—vibrant, pretty, lovely, handsome, graceful
Sandipta—true friend
Sandip—union, serenity, calm, calmness, stillness, silenceful
Sandita—bound
Sandra—form of alexander
Sandya—sunset time, god
Sandy—protector of mankind
Saneha—affection, love

Saneh—love
Sanemi—perfect
Sangamithirai—melody of evening
Sangamithra—pretty, lovely, handsome, graceful name
Sangamitra—friendly with social
Sangami—together, union
Sangani—friend
Sangari—cute
Sangati—union
Sangavi—goddess paarvati
Sangeena—polite
Sangeetaa—rugmangad's wife name
Sangeeta—concert, music
Sangeeta—musical, music
Sangeetha—sweet music, music, musical
Sangeeti—concert
Sangeet—music
Sanghamitra—devotee of lord buddha
Sanghavi—goddess lakshmi
Sanghita—music
Sanghvi—goddess lakshmi
Sangine—companion
Sangini—companion, life partner
Sangir—promise
Sangita—musical, music
Sangiti—music concert
Sangvi—where river ends at beach
Sangya—consciousness, intellect
Sangya—number, definition
Sanheta—vedic text
Sanhita—collection of vedic hymns
Sania—brilliant, moment, happy
Saniddhi—nearness
Sanidhi—temple
Sanidhya—under the guidance of guru
Saniha—near
Sanika—flute, true
Sanimit—a good woman
Sanipriya—emerald, sapphire
Sanitha—lucky
Sanithi—obtainment
Saniti—obtainment
Sanitra—gift, oblation
Sanitree—gift
Sanivka—pretty, lovely, handsome, graceful name

Saniya—moment in time, radiant
Sani—gift, prayer, radiance, brightness
Sanjala—companion
Sanjali—fold hand in prayer
Sanjali—inner beauty
Sanjanaa—creator
Sanjana—gentle, serenity, calm, calmness, stillness, silenceful nature
Sanjana—goddess parvati
Sanjana—perfect knowledge
Sanjanthi—pretty, lovely, handsome, graceful name
Sanjaya—triumphant, happy, victorious
Sanjeeta—evening
Sanjeetha—the beauty of music
Sanjeet—illumination, luminosity, radiance
Sanjeevani—life giver, immortality
Sanjeevan—pretty, lovely, handsome, graceful name
Sanjeevini—medicine to stay alive
Sanjeevitha—beauty
Sanjeevni—immortality
Sanjeev—very good, long life, medicine
Sanjhi—name of gods place, evening
Sanjhune—pretty, lovely, handsome, graceful
Sanjh—evening
Sanjh—eveningttachment
Sanjibani—mantra of immortality, rebirth
Sanjini—pretty, lovely, handsome, graceful name
Sanjita—triumphant, successful, victorious
Sanjitee—full victory
Sanjitha—triumphant, flute
Sanjiti—complete victory
Sanjivani—immortality
Sanjivika—long live
Sanjivini—immortality
Sanjivne—immortality
Sanjivni—immortality
Sanjiya—love, beauty, speak less
Sanjna—well known, wife of sun, scholar

Sanjogita—attached
Sanjogita—attached, related, conjoined
Sanjoli—period of twiillumination, luminosity, radiance
Sanjukta—one who joint
Sanjukta—wife of monarch, ruler, prince, earl prithviraj, union
Sanjuktha—pretty, lovely, handsome, graceful name
Sanjula—pretty, lovely, handsome, graceful
Sanjushree—pretty, lovely, handsome, graceful
Sanju—hanuman, similar to sanjay
Sanjyani—producing harmony
Sanjya—consciousness, command
Sanjyoti—illumination, luminosity, radiance of sun
Sankalpa—pretty, lovely, handsome, graceful, resolve
Sankalpa—resolution
Sankaravadivu—union
Sankareswari—lord shiva and parvati
Sankari—goddess parvati
Sankata—goddess who removes danger
Sankata—goddess who removes dangers
Sankavai—organise
Sankeerna—preety, pretty, lovely, handsome, graceful
Sankeertana—type of music
Sankeerthana—music, god songs
Sankeisha—holy, pure, sanctified, pious, solemn
Sankhya—comforts, happiness
Sankhya—welfare, comfort, health
Sankita—brave, vigour, happiest
Sankriti—pretty, lovely, handsome, graceful name
Sanksha—praise, blessings
Sankul—full of
Sanmani—genuine ornament, jewellery, ornamentaiion, adornment, figuration
Sanmathi—noble minded
Sanmati—noble mind
Sanmati—noble minded

Sanmayi—who is holy, sanctified, pious, solemn, chaste live, exist, rise, being, entity
Sanmay—pretty, lovely, handsome, graceful name
Sanmika—lord shiva
Sanmita—complex
Sanmitha—complex
Sannatee—humility
Sannati—bending down, humility
Sannaya—fortunate, splendid, radiant
Sannidhi—gold, nearness, holy place
Sannidi—temple
Sannihatee—one who destroys easily
Sannihitha—pretty, lovely, handsome, graceful name
Sanno—pretty, lovely, handsome, graceful name
Sannu—lily bloom, garden stuff name
Sannvi—beauty, goddess lakshmi
Sanobar—palm tree, fir
Sanoja—eternal
Sanole—introspective
Sanoli—possessed with self penance, earth
Sanrakta—red colour blood
Sanshatee—doubt
Sanshika—sun shine
Sanshita—ambition, intent, passion
Sanshi—super
Sanshkriti—culture
Sansiddhi—perfection
Sansita—praise
Sanskritee—culture, preparation concentration
Sanskrithi—tradition
Sanskriti—culture
Sanskrit—good ethics and moral values
Sanskruti—culture, traditional
Santanikee—made from the bloom, garden stuff of kalpa tree
Santani—continuing
Santani—harmony
Santati—granter of issues, goddess durga
Santavana—condolence
Santawana—consolation

Santayani—of the evening
Santa—serenity, calm, calmness, stillness, silence, calm, giver of gifts
Santhamani—eternal
Santhanalakshmi—praise
Santha—calm
Santhibai—pretty, lovely, handsome, graceful name
Santhini—be loved, serenity, calm, calmness, stillness, silence
Santhi—serenity, calm, calmness, stillness, silence, enjoy, silence
Santhosha—satisfaction
Santhoshitha—happiness
Santhoshi—happiness, happy girl
Santini—love
Santok—tolerance, durability, toleration
Santosa—content, satisfied
Santosha—content, satisfaction
Santoshi—satisfactionlways smiling
Santoshi—satisfied
Santosh—satisfaction, happiness
Santosi—satisfied
Santpreet—pretty, lovely, handsome, graceful name
Santra—orange, sweet like an orange
Santushti—complete satisfaction
Santu—kind and pretty, lovely, handsome, graceful girl
Santya—bestowing gifts, kind
Sanuja—joyful
Sanumati—mountain
Sanusha—innocent
Sanu—young
Sanvali—dusky
Sanve—goddess lakshmi, durga, beauty
Sanvika—goddess lakshmi
Sanvika—goddess lakshmi, goddess durga
Sanvitha—goddess durga, lakshmi, saraswati
Sanvitha—lakshmi, goddess lakshmi
Sanviti—intelligence
Sanvitti—knowledge, intellect
Sanviya—butterfly, goddess lakshmi
Sanvi—beauty, goddess lakshmi

Sanvi—rainbow, goddess lakshmi, parvati
Sanvritty—fulfilment, live, exist, riseing
Sanvy—expert advice
Sanwariya—satisfaction
Sanwari—dusky
Sanwika—goddess lakshmi
Sanyakta—joined, united
Sanyam—to have control
Sanya—beneficent, fortunate, splendid
Sanyha—incomparable
Sanyogita—complete satisfaction
Sanyukta—conjoined
Sanyukta—union, goddess durga
Sanyyah—pretty, lovely, handsome, graceful, moment
Sapanaa—dusky
Sapana—pretty, lovely, handsome, graceful girl
Sapana—dream
Saparna—leafy
Saparya—adoration, homage
Saphala—successful
Sapna—dream, mighty, will, vigour
Sapni—dreamim
Sapriti—with love
Saptajita—winning the seven elements
Saptashree—pretty, lovely, handsome, graceful name
Sarabai—dream
Sarabjeet—the mother of all mothers
Saradambal—successful
Saradayamine—a night in autumn
Sarada—goddess saraswati
Saradha—goddess of education, trust
Sarahna—praiseppreciation
Sarah—princess, lady
Sarakshi—good sight
Saraladeity—goddess saraswati
Sarala—straight, honest, simple
Saral—honest, sincere, simple
Sarama—the flet footed one
Sarama—wife of bibhisan
Saranga—a bird
Sarangee—a name of the musical instrument, spotted deer
Sarangi—a musical instrument

Saranika—one who gives shelter
Saraniya—calm
Sarani—protecting
Sarani—way, path
Saranna—compound of sarah, princess
Sarannya—pretty, lovely, handsome, graceful name
Saranyadeity—truth, simple
Saranyakumari—simple, honest
Saranya—defender, surrendered
Saranyoo—flet footed
Saran—protection, joy
Sarasabharathi—surrendered
Sarasakshe—lotus eye, glimmers
Sarasangi—surrendered
Sarasavane—sweet voiced
Sarasa—swan
Sarasika—surrendered
Sarasi—lake, jolly, happy
Sarasu—swan, brilliant, sagacious, gifted, wise, learned
Sarasvati—a goddess of learning
Saraswatee—goddess
Saraswathideity—a parroy
Saraswathi—goddess of knowledge
Saraswati—goddess of learning
Saras—juicy
Saratha—goddess saraswati
Saravati—name of a river
Saravika—happy
Sarawathi—name of goddess
Sarayoo—moving fast, a name of the puranic river
Sarayu—a holy river in ayodhya
Sarayu—a river
Sara—holy, sanctified, pious, solemn, chaste, lady, excellent
Sara—solid, valuable
Sarbani—goddess durga
Sarda—the name of goddess saraswati
Sardha—devotion, grace
Sarengi—musical instruments
Sargam—seven notes of music
Sargam—tune, basic notes of music
Sargha—indian beech tree
Sargine—composed of parts
Sargini—composed of parts, love
Sargun—all the quality

Sargun—all the quality, speamonarch, ruler, prince, earl truth
Saridha—goddess of learning, birdrrow
Sariga—really smart
Sarikaa—a bird, nightingale, cuckoo
Sarika—cute name parrot
Sarika—lake, pond
Sarika—the brave princess parrot
Sarika—woman, bird
Sarikha—pretty, lovely, handsome, graceful name
Sarila—water fall
Sarina—princess, lady, form of sarah
Sarisha—gods bride, pretty, lovely, handsome, graceful, blessed
Sarita—a river
Sarita—river, princess, lady, stream
Saritha—river, princess, river
Sarit—river, princess
Sarit—river, steam
Sariyah—clouds at night, column
Sariyu—river
Sarjana—creation
Sarjena—creative
Sarjita—the one who creates
Sarla—honest
Sarla—straight forward
Sarmila—shy, happy, modest
Sarmishtha—goddess durga
Sarmista—sweet talmonarch, ruler, prince, earl
Sarmistha—a daughter of vrsaparvan
Sarmitra—pretty, lovely, handsome, graceful
Sarmi—healer, serenity, calm, calmness, stillness, silence and harmony
Saroja—lotus
Saroja—lotus, born in a lake
Sarojine—straight forward
Sarojinideity—lotus
Sarojini—lotus
Sarojini—the lotus
Sarojmala—river
Sarojni—lotus, goddess parvati
Sarojrani—pretty, lovely, handsome, graceful name

Saroj—unique, lotus bloom, garden stuff
Sarovari—form the lake
Sarpani—snake (female)
Sarpasya—face like snake
Sarpee—snake
Sarras—nice
Sarsija—lotus
Sarswati—goddess of learning
Sarthaka—success, well done
Sarthaki—achievement, success
Sartha—having
Sarthika—achievement, success
Sarthi—helpful
Sarti—a river
Saruchi—wonderful
Sarulatha—cluster of lotuses
Sarupani—in the lotus
Sarupa—pretty, lovely, handsome, graceful
Saruprani—pretty, lovely, handsome, graceful woman
Saruta—pretty, lovely, handsome, graceful name
Saru—garland of lotuses
Sarvada—always
Sarvagjna—goddess durga, Annapurna deity
Sarvagjna—one who knows everything
Sarvagna—one who knows everything
Sarvagnya—all knowing
Sarvagya—one who knows everything
Sarvajina—who knows everything
Sarvamangala—universally auspicious
Sarvane—perfect
Sarvani—the all, goddess durga, universal
Sarvapa—one who drinks everything
Sarvari—commander, night, year name
Sarvastra—with all weapons
Sarva—complete, perfect
Sarva—perfect, complete
Sarvesha—god of all things
Sarvesha—goddess of all
Sarveshe—desire, aspiration, longed by all
Sarvika—universal
Sarvika—whole, complete

Sarviniswari—beauty, lovely
Sarv—cypress
Sarya—a pious woman
Saryu—a river
Saryu—river sharayu river in ramayana
Sar—explanation
Sasaile—lord sai shadow bloom, garden stuff
Sashini—moon
Sashini—moon nature god
Sashi—beauty, moon
Sashi—moon, shining, talented, the world
Sashmati—soft character
Sashmita—ever smiling
Sashmi—full moon
Sashreeka—one who is pretty, lovely, handsome, graceful
Sashrika—goddess durga, prosperous
Sashti—goddess durga, lord murugan
Sashvena—goddess saraswathy
Sashvina—goddess saraswati
Sasideity—moon
Sasireka—pretty, lovely, handsome, graceful name
Sasirekha—good fortune
Sasi—river sharayun apsara, moon
Sasmita—smiling
Sasmita—with a smile
Sasnitha—smile
Sassy—breath
Sasthita—pretty, lovely, handsome, graceful name
Sasthi—goddess durga
Sastika—lord murugan
Saswati—eternal
Sasya—rain, grain
Satajyoti—the moon
Satakhi—eye, glimmers
Satakirti—fame
Satakshe—goddess durga
Satakshi—eye, glimmers, goddess durga
Sataroopa—kind hearted
Satej—soft, smooth
Sathakshi—hundered eye, glimmers
Sathana—very sweet

Satha—devotion, dishonest
Sathiyachithra—always laughing
Sathiya—friend
Sathvika—serenity, calm, calmness, stillness, silenceful
Sathwika—pretty, lovely, handsome, graceful, pretty
Sathyapriya—truth loving
Sathyavathi—truthful
Sathya—truth, true
Sati—chaste, virtuous woman
Sati—gift, goddes parvati
Satmika—goddess of rain
Satoguni—who has knowledge of all
Satprabha—radiant, brilliant
Satpreetika—one who loves truth
Sattvikee—energetic, true essence
Sattviki—of true essence, holy, sanctified, pious, solemn, chaste, honest
Satvanti—full of truth, devotionful
Satvanti—truthful
Satvari—night
Satvati—loyal, truthful
Satvati—pleasant, illumination, luminosity, radiance
Satveka—goddess durga
Satve—true, live, exist, rise
Satvika—goddess durga, true, virtuous
Satvika—simplicity, pious, calm, virtuous
Satviki—goddess durga
Satvik—virtuous, simplicity, honesty
Satvi—live, exist, rise, being, entity
Satwanti—speamonarch, ruler, prince, earl truth
Satwika—calm
Satwika—god of mother, hills, silence
Satyabhama—beaming with truth
Satyadeity—goddess of truth
Satyajyoti—having real splendour and beauty
Satyaki—one who is truthful
Satyakshi—true, fire
Satyam—honesty, truth
Satyangita—truth and knowledge
Satyaprema—wife of lord shiva

Satyapriya—lover of truth, goddess durga
Satyarata—devoted to truth
Satyarata—one who is devoted to truth
Satyarpita—dedicated to truth
Satyarupa—truth, personified
Satyashesha—one who prayer or ambition, intent, passion is realised
Satyasri—truth and wealth women
Satyavatee—truth
Satyavathi—who speaks truth
Satyavati—mother of vyasa, truthful
Satyavati—truthful
Satyavela—time of truth
Satyaveni—lord of beauty, goddess parvati
Satya—truth
Satyvadini—speamonarch, ruler, prince, earl the truth
Saubale—daughter of mighty
Saubhagya—good fortune
Saubhgya—welfare, good fortune
Saudamani—illumination, luminosity, radiance
Saudamine—illumination, luminosity, radiance
Saudamine—lover of truth
Saudamini—full of illumination, luminosity, radiance
Saudamini—illumination, luminosity, radiance, thunder
Saugandhika—good fragrant
Saujanya—friend, generosity
Saujanya—kind
Saukhya—happy, comfortable
Saumaya—calm, sober, related to moon
Saumila—easily available
Saumyata—pretty, lovely, handsome, graceful, soft
Saumya—gentle
Saumya—goddess durga
Saumya—polite, soft, mild, gentle
Saumye—moonshine
Saumyi—moon illumination, luminosity, radiance shining
Saunanda—one who is joyous nature
Saunanda—sweet natured

Saundarya—beauty
Saurabhi—sweet-smell
Sauraja—pretty, lovely, handsome, graceful name
Sauratee—one who is always pleasing
Saurati—always pleasing
Saurave—bravery, courage
Sauravi—sun
Saura—the sun worshipper, celestial
Saurika—heavenly
Sauri—the sun
Saurvi—bravery, courage
Sauvarna—made of gold
Sauvarna—one whose complexion is like gold
Sauvasa—a fragrant species of tulsi
Sauvasa—basil fragrant
Sauveree—daughter of hero
Sauviri—daughter of hero
Savana—treeless plain
Savani—early morning raga sung in rainy
Savani—spring season
Savannah—grassland without trees
Savanthika—monsoon
Savaree—with saffron
Savarna—daughter of ocean
Savarna—of the same colour or appearance
Savasi—the strong one
Savera—morning, illumination, luminosity, radiance
Savera—morning, new start
Saveri—with saffron ragini
Savidharani—sun god
Savine—one who prepare nectar
Savini—one who prepares soma
Saviona—gift of god
Savitashri—lustre of the sun
Savita—moon, sun
Savita—the sun
Savitha—sun, illumination, luminosity, radiance, sun, bright
Savithrideity—sun
Savithri—daughter of the ocean
Savitree—a pious lady
Savitri—a river, goddess saraswati, holy, sanctified, pious, solemn, chaste

Savitri—sun, illumination, luminosity, radiance
Savitri—wife of satyavan
Savitur—word from mantra sloka
Savi—goddess lakshmi, sun
Savi—sun, goddess durga, lakshmi, star
Savni—spring season
Savree—pretty, lovely, handsome, graceful name
Savyani—pretty, lovely, handsome, graceful
Savya—pretty, lovely, handsome, graceful, perfect
Savy—sun, star
Sawali—shadow
Sawani—a river
Sawari—dusky, gentle
Sawasti—wellness
Sawhali—speaks sweet
Sawini—name of river
Sawitri—a river, goddess saraswati, holy, sanctified, pious, solemn, chaste
Sawra—voice
Sayadhwani—melodious
Sayali—pretty, lovely, handsome, graceful bloom, garden stuff
Sayani—clever, evening
Sayantica—evening, burning candle
Sayantika—burning candlerising
Sayantini—evening
Sayanti—symbol of serenity, calm, calmness, stillness, silence, unity
Sayantoni—pretty, lovely, handsome, graceful name
Sayan—valuable, valued, rare friend, companion
Saya—close of day, shadow
Saya—shadow
Sayeda—leader
Sayentika—the arised one, burning candle
Sayesha—god, shadow of god
Sayesha—goddess durga
Saye—friend
Sayichitra—pretty, lovely, handsome, graceful name

Sayjal—river water, holy, sanctified, pious, solemn, chaste water
Sayli—sweat, jasmine
Sayma—goddess durga, fasting, time
Sayna—love, shine
Sayni—shine, love, sign, fasting women
Sayntika—burning candlerising
Sayona—to decorate, decorated
Sayoni—dusk, clever, brilliant, sagacious, gifted, wise, learned
Sayonna—glory of evening, shining
Sayoojya—satisfaction
Sayra—a new star
Sayuri—goddess durga, bloom, garden stuff
Sayzal—flowing calm water, holy, sanctified, pious, solemn, chaste water
Schaely—fairy forte
Scruthi—candle, god, illumination, luminosity, radiance
Seaa—bright, variant form of shiya
Seajol—sea water
Seara—holy, sanctified, pious, solemn, chaste, holy
Searria—pretty, lovely, handsome, graceful name
Seejal—correct
Seeksha—education
Seela—mountain
Seemantini—woman
Seemanti—parting line
Seema—border
Seema—limit, boundary, border, face
Seemha—limit, boundary, border
Seemika—love
Seemran—pretty, lovely, handsome, graceful name
Seena—a river
Seentahna—vigour, courage
Seepika—small pearl
Seepi—small pearl
Seep—pearl
Seerat—beauty of soul, heart
Seerat—inner charm
Seetal—creative, cool
Seeta—wife of lord rama
Seethabai—parting line of hair

Seethaiyammal—inner beauty
Seethalakshmi—wife of lord sri ram
Seetha—holy, sanctified, pious, solemn, chaste, wife of lord rama, limit
Seettal—cool
Seetu—pretty, lovely, handsome, graceful name
Sehaj—tolerance, durability, toleration
Sehej—tolerance, durability, toleration, quite, serenity, calm, calmness, stillness, kind
Sehnaz—pretty, lovely, handsome, graceful name
Seira—a new star
Sejal—river water, holy, sanctified, pious, solemn, chaste water
Sejol—holy, sanctified, pious, solemn, chaste water, flowing calm water
Sejuti—sweet, cute
Selina—star in the sky, moon
Selma—fair, protected by god
Selvakumari—the priness of money
Selvam—proprerty
Selvanayaki—holy, sanctified, pious, solemn, chaste, depth in character
Selvarani—fair, charming, good monarch, ruler, prince, earl
Selvi—happy prosperous daughter
Selvy—happy prosperous daughter
Semantee—indian white rose
Semantika—indian white rose
Semanti—a white rose
Sema—to speak, omen
Senajita—vanquishing armies
Sena—army
Sena—goddess of the moon, blessed
Senbagam—lustering bloom, garden stuff
Senisa—brilliant, sagacious, gifted, wise, learnedrtist
Senni—highness, empress, queen
Senorita—sweet
Serena—joy, quiet, calm, serenity, calm, calmness, stillness, silenceful
Seshaveni—lord krishna dancing on the snake
Sesha—serpent who symbolises time
Setaara—star

Setara—a star
Setasree—pretty, lovely, handsome,
graceful name
Sethuammal—pretty, lovely,
handsome, graceful name
Sethuramani—quiet, calm
Sethurani—highness, empress, queen
of bridge
Setu—bridge, sacred symbol
Sevali—smart
Sevanthi—pretty, lovely, handsome,
graceful bloom, garden stuff
Sevantika—pretty, lovely, handsome,
graceful bloom, garden stuff
Sevanti—bloom, garden stuff
Sevatee—indian white rose
Sevati—a rose
Sevati—white rose
Seva—worship
Sevita—cherished, worshipped
Seya—shadow, evening
Sezal—river, holy, sanctified, pious,
solemn, chaste water, real
Shabab—beauty
Shabalini—a mossy
Shabana—decorated, belonging to
night
Shabari—a tribal devotee of lord rama
Shabhayata—culture
Shabnam—mist, snow, dew, morning
dew
Shabnum—sew
Shabri—a devotee of lord rama
Shabu—calm, dewdrop, snowdrop,
serenity, calm, calmness, stillness,
silence
Shache—a holy's cow name
Shachi—wife of lord indra
Shadhana—worship, long practise,
study
Shadhani—aim of goal
Shadhwi—simplicity, virtuous woman
Shaela—from the fairy palace
Shae—admirable, from the fairy fort
Shafali—pretty, lovely, handsome,
graceful bloom, garden stuff
Shafa—cure

Shafu—pretty, lovely, handsome,
graceful, brilliant, sagacious, gifted,
wise, learned
Shagana—one of raga
Shagufta—happy, bud of bloom,
garden stuff, blooming
Shaguftha—fragrance
Shagun—auspicious moment
Shahana—princess, one with tolerance,
durability, toleration, highness,
empress, queen
Shaharika—pretty, lovely, handsome,
graceful name
Shaharsa—pretty, lovely, handsome,
graceful name
Shahavilasa—dew
Shahbala—cherished
Shahd—honey, perfect
Shahena—tender, falconess, soft,
gentle
Shahen—royal, falcon, tender, bird
Shahika—being near
Shahila—being near river
Shahina—princess, falconess
Shahin—royal
Shahista—never changed, the
highness, empress, queen
Shahita—being near river
Shahitha—being near river
Shahnas—a tune
Shahnzay—princess of royal
Shahzeela—pretty, lovely, handsome,
graceful
Shaifali—sweet smell
Shailabala—speech
Shailaja—name of a river, goddess
parvati
Shailalokhini—tender
Shailarani—stone, mountain
Shailasha—abode in mountain
Shailasha—parvati
Shailashree—goddess of mountain
Shaila—goddess parvati
Shaila—stone, mountain, goddess
Shailbala—goddess parvati
Shaileja—daughter of mountains
Shailender—monarch, ruler, prince,
earl of mountains

Shaileshi—monarch, ruler, prince, earl of mountain, lord shiva
Shaileshri—near
Shaile—style
Shaili—life-style
Shaili—style, traditional, behaviour
Shailja—daughter of mountain
Shailja—strong, goddess parvati
Shaille—style
Shailli—creating arts
Shailu—goddess parvati
Shailvi—goddess parvati
Shaily—style, way
Shail—mountain, rock
Shaina—pretty, lovely, handsome, graceful, happiness, lucky
Shaine—always shining, brightest
Shaine—fasting woman
Shaini—shine, fasting women
Shaira—poetess, princess
Shairve—pretty, lovely, handsome, graceful name
Shaisha—lord shiva
Shaista—pretty, lovely, handsome, graceful, gentle, courteous
Shaitha—god
Shaive—prosperity
Shaivi—a goddess
Shaivi—prosperity
Shaivya—auspicious
Shaivya—pretty, lovely, handsome, graceful name
Shajee—bold, clever, courageous
Shajitha—friendly
Shajiyaparven—pretty, lovely, handsome, graceful star
Shaji—pretty, lovely, handsome, graceful name
Shaj—pretty, lovely, handsome, graceful name
Shakambari—goddess durga
Shakambari—goddess parvati
Shakambharee—worship
Shakaya—voices in the wind life
Shaka—pretty, lovely, handsome, graceful, the sun
Shakeela—pretty, lovely, handsome, graceful, well figure, appearance
Shakeel—handsome
Shakha—branch of a tree
Shakila—pretty, lovely, handsome, graceful, kind, figure, appearance, structurely
Shakini—goddess parvati
Shaksha—witnesses
Shakshitha—goddess deity
Shakshi—evidence, witness, goddess durga
Shakshya—pretty, lovely, handsome, graceful name
Shaksika—witness, goddess durga, evidence
Shakthi—power, goddess durga, fire
Shakti—energy, power, goddess durga
Shakunika—a name of the bird
Shakunika—goddess parvati
Shakuni—a bird
Shakuni—prosperity
Shakuntala—a highness, empress, queen
Shakuntala—brought up by birds
Shakuntee—bird
Shakunthala—brought up by birds
Shakuntika—a small bird
Shakunti—daughter of shakuni bird
Shakuntla—flying bird
Shakun—good omen
Shakya—capable
Shalabha—butterfly
Shalada—one who procure spear
Shalaka—goddess parvati
Shalakha—goddess parvati
Shalalu—perfume
Shalbha—grass hopper
Shalbhe—grass hopper
Shaleni—settled, with a fixed abode
Shalen—praiseworthy
Shalika—a bird
Shalika—flute
Shaline—a bloom, garden stuff
Shaline—well settled, fixed, dwelling
Shalini—brilliant, sagacious, gifted, wise, learned, sensible, talented
Shalini—gentle, modest
Shalin—a tree
Shalin—silk cotton tree

Shallu—calm pretty, lovely, handsome, graceful, old ancient cloth
Shalmala—goddess parvati
Shalmali—name of a tree, silk cotton tree
Shalni—settled, with a fixed abode
Shaloni—charming
Shalu—old ancient cloth, calm, pretty, lovely, handsome, graceful
Shalu—pleasing, favourite, charming
Shalvi—serenity, calm, calmness, stillness, silence of god
Shalya—wonderful
Shal—mountain
Shamali—colours of krishna
Shamal—lord krishna
Shamani—serenity, calm, calmness, stillness, silence
Shamani—serenity, calm, calmness, stillness, silence, night
Shamanta—love, passion, equality
Shamata—modesty
Shama—a flame
Shama—illumination, luminosity, radiance flame, silk-cotton tree
Shambari—a boddh power
Shambari—illusion
Shambhava—possible
Shambhave—sacred grass
Shambhavi—consort of shambhu
Shambhavi—goddess parvati, durga
Shambhukanta—wife of shambhu, parvati
Shambhvi—goddess durga
Shambuti—born, manifested
Shameeka—serenity, calm, calmness, stillness, silenceful
Shameena—super, pretty, lovely, handsome, graceful
Shameera—a chameli bloom, garden stuff
Shamee—tree which like lord ganesha
Shamiana—tent
Shamika—dark beauty
Shamiksha—nearby
Shamila—a fragrant breeze
Shamili—pretty, lovely, handsome, graceful angel stone slab

Shamim—fragrance, fire, sweet scent
Shamina—serenity, calm, calmness, stillness, silence, tolerance, durability, toleration
Shamini—heaven star, cute
Shamir—rock that can penetrate metal
Shamiska—lovely, lord shiva
Shamita—calmed, serenity, calm, calmness, stillness, silence maker
Shamitha—who is calm and disciplined
Shami—leaves offered to lord ganesha
Shamla—air, breeze, gorgeous
Shamla—dark evening
Shamla—dark, evening, candle
Shamle—dawn
Shamli—love of lord krishna, radha
Shammy—god ganesha's fev plant
Shampa—thunder, illumination, luminosity, radiance
Shamruti—love
Shamsini—fulfilled
Shamugapriya—fragrance
Shamya—pretty, lovely, handsome, graceful
Shanasa—praise, desire, aspiration, longing
Shanata—serenity, calm, calmness, stillness, silenceful
Shanavi—goddess lakshmi
Shanaya—god gift, first ray of the sun
Shanda—god is gracious, stone, goddess
Shandera—pretty, lovely, handsome, graceful name
Shandile—collection, goddess of curd
Shaneta—pretty, lovely, handsome, graceful name
Shanishka—pretty, lovely, handsome, graceful name
Shanish—amazing, generous
Shanive—pride
Shanivi—pride
Shaniya—holy, sanctified, pious, solemn, chaste beauty, form of shana
Shani—pretty, lovely, handsome, graceful face, inspiring

Shanjanaa—gentle in harmony, serenity, calm, calmness, stillness
Shanjhana—gentle
Shanjhavi—evening
Shanjhune—devoted to lord hanuman
Shankara—lord shiva
Shankari—goddess parvati
Shankhalika—as perfect as conch shell
Shankhamala—illumination, luminosity, radiance fairy tale princess
Shankharine—ultimate, absolute, highest, best among all other branches
Shankhine—mother of pearl
Shankhini—mother of pearls
Shankhmani—ornament, jewellery, ornamentation, adornment
Shankhvati—a river full of shells
Shanmathy—pretty, lovely, handsome, gracefulrise, noble minded
Shanmika—lord shiva
Shanmitha—goddess lakshmi
Shanmuganayaki—wife of lord shiva
Shanmuka—nice face, six faced
Shanoli—sweet hearted, kind hearted
Shanooja—pretty, lovely, handsome, graceful name
Shanoo—wife of shan
Shansa—invocation
Shansa—praise
Shantaa—white rose
Shantachi—beneficial
Shantagauri—serenity, calm, calmness, stillness, calm
Shantah—serenity, calm, calmness, stillness, silence, god
Shantala—goddess parvati
Shanta—gentle
Shanta—serenity, calm, calmness, stillness, silenceful
Shanthadeity—praise
Shanthakumari—serenity, calm, calmness, stillness, silenceful
Shanthala—calm cool
Shanthamma—mother of serenity, calm, calmness, stillness, silence
Shantha—serenity, calm, calmness, stillness, silenceful

Shanthini—serenity, calm, calmness, stillness, silence, calm, quiet
Shanthi—calm, serenity, calm, calmness, stillness, silence
Shantiva—bearer of serenity, calm, calmness, stillness, silence
Shantiva—friendly, kind, deity
Shanti—calmness, serenity, calm, calmness, stillness, silence
Shanti—clam, quiet
Shanti—serenity, calm, calmness, stillness, silence, silent
Shanusa—innocent
Shanu—innocent, smile, dark, richest
Shanve—beautyttractive, lustering
Shanvika—goddess lakshmi
Shanvitha—goddess lakshmi
Shanvi—sun, lusteringttractive
Shanvi—sunttractive, goddess lakshmi
Shanya—beneficent, radiant
Shanz—evening
Shan—moderate, pride, prestige, famous
Sharadamani—ornament, jewellery, ornamentation, adornment
Sharadashree—beauty of heaven
Sharadashri—beauty of autumn
Sharada—a season, winter
Sharada—goddess of learning, saraswati
Sharadee—as pretty, lovely, handsome, graceful as autumn
Sharadee—autumn, modest
Sharadika—of autumn
Sharadini—autumn
Sharadi—as lovely as an autumn
Sharad—autumn
Sharali—union
Sharangee—guarding
Sharanika—shelter of god, lord
Sharani—the earth, protector, guardian
Sharankumari—a goddess
Sharann—under blessing of lord
Sharanya-sri—serenity, calm, calmness, stillness, silence
Sharanya—protectress
Sharanya—to give home, shelter,

serenity, calm, calmness, stillness, silence

Sharat—a season

Sharavani—flow

Sharav—holy, sanctified, pious, solemn, chaste and innocent

Sharaya—durga, giver of refuge

Sharayu—a holy river, river in ayodhya

Shardambha—goddess saraswati

Sharda—goddess saraswati

Sharda—the goddess of art and literature

Shardha—concentration, veneration, desire, aspiration, longing

Shardhya—bold, strong

Shardoole—tigress

Shariba—lakshmi

Sharidya—pretty, lovely, handsome, graceful name

Sharika—goddess durga

Sharika—goddess durga, partner

Sharini—earth

Sharitha—princess, lady, river, stream

Shari—from fertile fields, forest, wood, jungles

Sharjana—creation

Sharjeel—simple

Sharlen—little and womanly

Sharmada—earth, one who confers happiness

Sharmadha—shy

Sharmika—beauty

Sharmila—a popular name

Sharmila—preety

Sharmila—shy, shyness, modest, happy

Sharmishta—beauty and brilliant, sagacious, gifted, wise, learned

Sharmishtha—goddess durga

Sharmista—wife of yavati

Sharmistha—shelter, wife of yayati

Sharmistha—very fortunate, wife of yayati a puranic monarch

Sharmita—friend

Sharmitha—shinning

Sharmi—goddess saraswati

Sharnali—sunset

Sharnie—dirty stunted grass

Sharnika—shelter of god

Sharnya—pretty, lovely, handsome, graceful name

Sharnya—shelter

Sharon—plain, princess

Sharoon—sweet, fragrance, honey

Sharoo—lord vishnu, full moon

Sharshti—universe

Sharumathi—full moon

Sharvali—pretty, lovely, handsome, graceful name

Sharvani—goddess saraswati, goddess parvati

Sharvaree—evening, twiillumination, luminosity, radiance

Sharvaree—modest, modern

Sharvaree—night

Sharvari—the night, name of goddess

Sharva—auspicious one

Sharva—consort of lord shiva

Sharvika—perfected

Sharvila—universal, beauty, sun

Sharvina—sound of vina, goddess durga

Sharvi—pretty, lovely, handsome, graceful, goddess durga, parvati

Sharvi—holy, pure, sanctified, pious, solemn

Sharvya—bright, loving

Sharwali—pretty, lovely, handsome, graceful name

Sharwani—goddess lakshmi, durga

Sharwari—night

Sharya—sweetie and lovely

Sharyu—name of a river

Shasha—moon

Shashibala—goddess durga

Shashibala—the moon

Shashikaanta—twiillumination, luminosity, radiance

Shashikala—activities of moon

Shashikala—moon illumination, luminosity, radiance, brightness of moon

Shashika—pretty, lovely, handsome, graceful moon

Shashikiran—the moon

Shashimani—the moon stone
Shashine—a digit of moon
Shashini—moon
Shashiprabha—moon illumination, luminosity, radiance
Shashipriya—pearl, the moon
Shashirekha—moon rays
Shashi—the moon
Shashmita—ever smiling
Shashmi—illumination, luminosity, radiance
Shashtee—praise
Shashthe—goddess durga
Shashthika—the sixth day after birth of a child
Shashwatee—moon
Shashwathi—eternal
Shasika—part of moon, female ruler
Shastee—praise
Shasthika—goddess durga
Shasti—praise, hymn
Shaswathi—eternal
Shaswati—eternal
Shatabdi—period of years, century
Shatadrutee—flowing in branch
Shatajyoti—moon, illumination, luminosity, radiance
Shatakshe—hundred eye, glimmers
Shatakshi—goddess durga
Shatarupa—goddess saraswati, lord shiva
Shatavari—eternal
Shatha—aromatic, eternal
Shathurikasri—silent
Shathvika—goddess durga
Shatice—ninth child
Shatodara—one whose waist is slender
Shatodari—with hundred bellies
Shatrunjaya—one who attain victory over enemies
Shatvaree—night
Shaumita—good friends
Shaunakshi—lovely
Shaurya—brave
Shaury—brave
Shavalini—beloved to lord shiva
Shavana—mother
Shavantika—absorbed in monsoon

Shavan—monsoon, rain during monsoon
Shavena—gods gift
Shaveta—saraswati
Shavika—pretty, lovely, handsome, graceful name
Shavita—the sun
Shavi—brightness like sun
Shawan—rain
Shawna—god is merciful
Shawran—pretty, lovely, handsome, graceful name
Shaxi—witness
Shayamali—goddess durga
Shayama—radha
Shayan—companion, kind hearted, valuable, valued, rare
Shayari—poetry
Shaya—salvation of god, gift of god
Shaya—worthy
Shayesha—shadow of god
Shayle—blinded, style
Shayna—pretty, variant of shane
Shay—supplanter gift, fairy palace
Shazia—princess, happiness, fragrance
Shazmin—princess
Shazna—active
Sheaddha—reverence
Shea—fairy palace, from the fairy fort
Shefalika—a bloom, garden stuff, little bloom, garden stuffing plant
Shefali—a bloom, garden stuff
Shefali—pretty, lovely, handsome, graceful and fragrant bloom, garden stuff
Shehla—dark brown, almost black
Sheila—blinded, slang term for woman
Sheile—pretty, lovely, handsome, graceful name
Sheil—cultured
Shejali—a fruit
Shekhar—lord shiva
Shekhsa—education
Sheladeity—indrani, night
Shelarani—decent
Shela—behaviour
Shela—wife of lord brahma
Shelly—from the ledge meadow

Shelza—goddess durga
Shema—limit, border
Shemunshi—the indian white rose
Shemushi—intellect, understanding
Shemyukta—pretty, lovely, handsome, graceful eye, glimmers
Shena—female version of john
Shenbagam—most pretty, lovely, handsome, graceful bloom, garden stuff
Shenetha—graceful
Shenita—pretty, lovely, handsome, graceful name
Shenoa—dove of serenity, calm, calmness, stillness, silence
Shen—brightness, snow white
Shen—spiritual, deep-thinmonarch, ruler, prince, earl
Sheoli—lover
Shephale—sweet fragrant
Shephalika—the fruit of jasmine tree
Sherin—very sweet
Shershika—title, headline, important
Sheryl—form of cheryl, similar to cherry
Shesha—mirror
Sheshma—goddess lakshmi
Sheshna—god
Shetala—a virtuous woman
Shetala—cool, gentle
Shetal—cold, very cool
Shetal—cool
Shetu—bridge
Shetu—support, indoctrination, assuredness
Shevaani—wife of lord shiva, beauty
Shevadhi—wealth, ornament, jewellery, ornamentation, adornment, figuration
Shevaline—a name of the river
Shevalini—name of river
Shevali—a green plant
Shevane—beauty, wife of lord shiva
Shevanti—a bloom, garden stuff
Sheva—goddess parvati
Sheva—happiness
Shevi—odddipoli
Sheyali—a beginning of new work

Shezal—flowing calm water, holy, sanctified, pious, solemn, chaste water
Shezreen—particle of gold
Shibani—goddess durga
Shichi—luster, goddess durga
Shiddhi—to aim, wife of lord ganesha
Shidheswari—goddess of knowledge, wisdom
Shidhi—achievementbility of success
Shielawatti—river
Shiesta—modest, disciplined, cultured
Shifali—member of the orchid family
Shifana—curing girl, gods gracious, soft
Shighra—a river
Shijina—god lord shiva, parvati
Shika—deer, gentlep of hill
Shikhandi—yellow jasmine
Shikhara—a river
Shikharine—excellent
Shikharini—nature
Shikha—flame, peak
Shikha—flamep of a mountain
Shikhi—fire
Shikhi—peacock, flame
Shikin—good
Shikra—clever
Shikra—skillfulrtistic
Shikriti—the brighting stars of sky
Shiksha—education
Shilavatia—name of a river
Shilavati—name of river
Shila—rock, thunder
Shila—variegated
Shilla—rock
Shilna—perfectly created
Shilpashree—peak
Shilpa—pretty, lovely, handsome, graceful girl
Shilpa—artist, statue, well-proportioned
Shilpee—pretty, lovely, handsome, graceful name
Shilpika—skilled in art
Shilpita—most pretty, lovely, handsome, graceful
Shilpita—well proportioned
Shilpi—a sculptor

Shilpi—white shellsrtisan, water lilly
Shilu—rock, stone
Shimaa—mirth, joy, ecstasy, gladness
Shimida—giving work
Shimla—pretty, lovely, handsome, graceful name
Shimran—remembrance, meditation
Shinaa—shining illumination, luminosity, radiance, sun, virtue, good
Shinat—pretty, lovely, handsome, graceful lady
Shinaya—shine
Shina—virtue, good
Shinchana—pretty, lovely, handsome, graceful name
Shine—brightness, sun rays
Shine—full of brightness
Shini—to shine among all
Shinjani—sound of ankle bell
Shinja—jingle, tinkling
Shinjini—ankle-bellsnklet
Shinjini—anklebells
Shinjitha—sweet noise
Shinu—successful
Shiny—glorious, shining, brightness
Shiphalika—coral jasmine tree
Shipi—illumination, luminosity, radiance way
Shipli—statue
Shipra—holy, sanctified, pious, solemn, chaste, river
Shirali—peacock
Shirat—inside, internal beauty, good
Shiravani—goddess saraswati
Shiraz—flame
Shireen—sweet, charming, pleasant, gentle
Shireesha—bloom, garden stuff
Shirina—night, singing sweetly
Shirin—kind, sweet, pleasant, gentle
Shirisha—shining sun, goddess lakshmi
Shiromani—crest ornament, jewellery, ornamentation
Shiromauli—figuration, disciplined, cultured
Shirsa—pretty, lovely, handsome, graceful name

Shirshita—goddess lakshmi, parvati
Shisa—pretty, lovely, handsome, graceful name
Shishira—a delicate bloom, garden stuff, winter
Shishirkana—particles of dew
Shishta—goodness
Shistha—polite, modest, disciplined
Shitala—cold
Shital—very cool, cold
Shitama—pretty, lovely, handsome, graceful name
Shitara—star
Shitari—transformer
Shitashe—cold eater
Shitasi—a river
Shita—cold
Shitel—cold, very cool
Shitija—goodness sita, horizon
Shitij—sky and land meet together
Shitu—support, indoctrination, assuredness
Shiulie—a bloom, garden stuff
Shiuli—a bloom, garden stuff, night bloom, garden stuff jasmine
Shivaangi—goddess parvati
Shivaani—beauty, wife of lord shiva
Shivaanya—part of lord shiva
Shivadeity—goddess of grace
Shivadha—pretty, lovely, handsome, graceful name
Shivadooti—ambassador of lord shiva
Shivaduti—messenger of lord shiva
Shivai—lord shiva
Shivaja—a creeper
Shivakami—beloved of lord shiva
Shivakanta—goddess durga
Shivakari—source of auspicious things
Shivakumar—lord shiva
Shivale—beloved of lord shiva
Shivalini—devotee of lord shiva
Shivali—goddess parvati
Shivali—goddess parvati, durga
Shivalya—related to lord shiva
Shival—wife of lord shiva
Shivami—lord shiva and nectar
Shivamsha—desire, aspiration, longing of lord shiva

Shivananda—belongs to lord shiva
Shivana—goddess parvati
Shivangi—pretty, lovely, handsome, graceful, part of lord shiva
Shivangi—more pretty, lovely, handsome, graceful
Shivanija—goddess parvati
Shivanika—devotee of lord shiva
Shivaniya—part of lord shiva
Shivani—beauty, belonging to lord shiva
Shivani—goddess parvati
Shivanjali—offering with both hands to lord
Shivanki—goddess parvati
Shivanna—lord shiva
Shivanne—goddess parvati
Shivannya—part of lord shiva
Shivansee—a part of lord shiva
Shivanshi—a part of lord shiva
Shivansi—part of lord shiva
Shivantika—lord shiva's princess
Shivanya—lord shiva, part of lord shiva
Shivapriya—beloved of lord shiva, goddess durga
Shivarani—wife of lord shiva
Shivashri—glory of lord shiva
Shivasri—belonging to lord shiva
Shivasundari—goddess durga
Shivasunu—lord shiva
Shivathy—lord shiva
Shivati—shiv and parvati
Shivatmika—the essence of lord shiva
Shiva—name of lord, the ultimate, absolute, highest, best spirit
Shivea—lord shiva
Shivechha—desire, aspiration, longing of lord shiva
Shiveka—palanquin
Shivena—parvati
Shivgamini—follower of lord shiva
Shivgami—follower of lord shiva
Shivika—goddess parvati
Shivika—palanquin river, lord shiva
Shivina—sweet, goddess parvati
Shivi—name of a great monarch, ruler, prince, earl

Shivkanya—daughter of lord shiva
Shivkriti—acceptance
Shivkumari—daughter of lord shiva
Shivle—image of lord shiva, name of bloom, garden stuff
Shivle—of lord shiva
Shivlika—belonging to lord shiva
Shivlila—holy, pure, sanctified, pious, solemn drama of lord shiva
Shivli—bloom, garden stuff
Shivmati—the brain of lord shiva
Shivnaya—part of lord shiva
Shivneya—devotee of lord shiva
Shivni—devoted to lord shiva
Shivnya—wife of lord shiva
Shivohne—god is gracious
Shivoo—devotee of lord shiva
Shivosree—devoted to lord shiva
Shivrina—lord shiva
Shivriti—tradition of lord shiva
Shivsha—absorbed in lord shiva
Shivta—white, clear
Shivu—lord shiva
Shivya—devoted to lord shiva
Shivyya—goddess parvati
Shiv—lord shiva, ultimate, absolute, highest, best spirit
Shiwangi—goddess durga
Shiwani—belonging to lord shiva
Shiwanya—part of lord shiva
Shiyahi—ink
Shiya—goddess lakshmi, bright
Shlaghya—excellent
Shlesha—more than enough
Shloka—a sacred chant, verse
Shmeeta—ever smiling
Shmita—every smiling
Shmrit—remembrance
Shneha—loveffectionate
Shobana—goddess parvati
Shoba—beauty, nice
Shobhadeity—goddess parvati, wife of lord
Shobhana—handsome
Shobhana—the pretty, lovely, handsome, graceful one, splendid
Shobhanbabu—splendid
Shobhavati—decorated woman

Shobha—pleasing, favourite, charming, splendour, beauty
Shobha—splendour
Shobhika—beauty
Shobhini—graceful, splendid
Shobhishtha—most pretty, lovely, handsome, graceful
Shobhita—decorated
Shobhita—splendid be adorned, beauty
Shobhna—pretty, lovely, handsome, graceful
Shobhna—ornament, jewellery, ornamentation, figurational, shining
Shobika—friendly
Shobitha—who is brilliant
Shoche—flame
Shoha—a star, princess, sunrise
Shohini—pretty, lovely, handsome, graceful
Shohna—gold, cute, amiable, pleasing, suave, graceful
Shomdutta—daughter of god lord shiva
Shomili—elegant and pretty, lovely, handsome, graceful
Shomtirtha—the birth of lord shiva, powerful
Shonali—helpful girl
Shonamani—red gem, ruby
Shona—a river
Shona—gold, red tributary of ganga
Shoneta—blooded
Shonima—redness
Shonita—brightness
Shoni—one of complexion of red lotus
Shoni—red coloured woman
Shony—pretty, gold, pretty, lovely, handsome, graceful
Shon—female version of john
Shorashi—young woman
Shotika—beauty of life
Shoumili—where beauties meet
Shoumo—the learned one
Shoumya—heart touching, soft
Shounak—pretty, lovely, handsome, graceful name
Shouraya—courageous
Shourya—courageous

Shrabana—name of a star
Shraddhanve—goddess durga, lakshmi
Shraddha—believe, devotion, confidence
Shraddha—veneration
Shradha—devotion, concentration, trust
Shradha—respect
Shradhdha—devotion, trust, devotion
Shraghvi—tulsi
Shrai—credit give credit to someone
Shramidhi—girl who likes to work hard
Shramika—hard worker
Shram—hard work, devoted towards work
Shrankhla—chain
Shrashti—universe
Shrasti—universe
Shrathi—veda
Shravana—name of a star, sense of hearing
Shravaneya—worthy to listen
Shravane—the day of full moon
Shravaniya—worthy to listen
Shravani—a hindu festival
Shravani—born in the month of shravan
Shravani—worthy to listen
Shravanthika—pretty, lovely, handsome, graceful, flowing
Shravanthi—a name in buddhist literature
Shravanti—a name in buddhist literature
Shravasta—much heard, famous
Shravasti—an ancient indian city
Shravasti—an old city of india
Shravena—pretty, lovely, handsome, graceful name
Shravishtha—most famed
Shravi—basil plant, cool
Shravni—innovative perfectly
Shravya—melodious, good listener
Shrawani—name of hindu month
Shrawantika—lengthy greatness like rainfall
Shraya—shresth

Shrddha—devotion wife of lord shiva, trust
Shrdha—devotion, belief
Shreddhi—achievement, prosperity
Shreea—goddess lakshmi
Shreebani—born in month of shravan
Shreebhu—name of a river
Shreedeity—goddess
Shreedeve—an ancient indian city
Shreedha—give beauty, wealth prosperity
Shreedhi—shree means goddess lakshmi
Shreedula—blessing
Shreehita—well desire, aspiration, longinger
Shreelataa—pretty, lovely, handsome, graceful language
Shreelatha—bloom, garden stuff of prosperous
Shreela—pretty, lovely, handsome, graceful
Shreelekha—prosperous writing, gods gift
Shreemahi—prosperous earth, world
Shreemani—pretty, lovely, handsome, graceful, rich
Shreemanjari—basil plant
Shreematee—wonderful knowledge
Shreemayi—fortunate
Shreema—prosperous
Shreenandan—the god of love
Shreena—spiritual, goddess lakshmi
Shreenidhi—goddess lakshmi
Shreenidhi—goddess lakshmi, gold
Shreeparna—tree adorned with leaves
Shreeprada—goddess radha
Shreeprada—radha
Shreepriya—goddess lakshmi
Shreeradha—goddess lakshmi
Shreeraksha—protection in the name of god
Shreeranjani—prosperous
Shreesha—wealthy
Shreeshti—universe, world
Shreeta—most pretty, lovely, handsome, graceful, goddess lakshmi
Shreetija—prayer

Shreeti—prayer
Shreevani—holy, pure, sanctified, pious, solemn speech
Shreeya—goddess lakshmiuspicious
Shree—prosperous, wife of the god
Shrejal—foremost, best, first
Shreja—better
Shrena—foremost, best, first
Shrenika—organised
Shreni—grading, step by step achiever
Shresha—special bloom, garden stuff
Shreshi—pretty, lovely, handsome, graceful name
Shreshta—the best, fortunate, marvellous
Shreshtha—perfection
Shreshthi—best of all
Shreshthta—a person who greater than anyone
Shrestajna—top knowledge
Shresta—great, purity, foremost, best
Shrestha—full of praise, best, responsible
Shresthi—best of all
Shresth—best of all
Shreyansha—gives credit to others
Shreyanshi—superior, famen important women
Shreyan—nice
Shreyashi—credit gives, credit to someone
Shreyashree—credit
Shreyashri—pretty, lovely, handsome, graceful name
Shreyasi—one who is most pretty, lovely, handsome, graceful, lucky
Shreya—better
Shreya—lucky, excellent, credit
Shreyu—auspicious
Shribala—holy, pure, sanctified, pious, solemn maiden
Shribhadra—a goddess, best among people
Shribha—goddess lakshmi
Shribindu—mark of fortune
Shrida—bestowing fortune
Shrideity—goddess lakshmi
Shridula—blessing

Shridulla—blessing
Shrieya—first, best, shreshth
Shrigauri—goddess parvati
Shrigeeta—the sacred geeta
Shrii—respected, richness
Shrijani—creative
Shrijita—respected winner
Shrikala—goddess lakshmi
Shrikama—radha
Shrikanta—creative, goddess lakshmi
Shrika—fortune, wealth, prosperty
Shrikha—pretty, lovely, handsome, graceful name
Shrikirti—lustrous fame
Shrikumari—lustrous
Shrilakshmi—goddess lakshmi
Shrilalita—graceful, prosperous
Shrilata—lustrous creeper
Shrila—wonderful, pretty, lovely, handsome, graceful
Shrilekha—lustrous essay
Shril—lustrious
Shrimala—pretty, lovely, handsome, graceful name
Shrimani—pretty, lovely, handsome, graceful, ornament
Shrimata—holy, pure, sanctified, pious, solemn mother goddess
Shrimati—goddess lakshmi, fortunate
Shrimayi—fortunate
Shrima—pretty, lovely, handsome, graceful name
Shrimukhi—with a radiant face
Shrimurti—holy, pure, sanctified, pious, solemn image
Shrinandini—daughter of prosperity
Shrina—night,—holy, pure, sanctified, pious, solemn
Shringanka—love, beauty, ornamentation, adornment, figuration
Shringine—cow
Shrinidhi—goddess lakshmi
Shrinika—goddess lakshmi
Shrinita—respected with in rules
Shrinitha—night, goddess lakshmi
Shrinka—goddess lakshmi
Shriparna—tree adorned with leaves
Shriranjani—radha

Shrisha—goddess lakshmi, god power
Shrishthi—earth, serenity, calm, calmness, stillness, silence
Shrishti—earth, universe
Shrishty—universe, world
Shristhi—creation, remembrance
Shristih—creation
Shristika—pretty, lovely, handsome, graceful name
Shristi—world, universe, entire world
Shrita—one of the name of goddess lakshmi
Shriti—memory
Shrity—respected, richness
Shrivali—goddess lakshmi
Shrivalli—goddess lakshmi
Shrivani—holy, pure, sanctified, pious, solemn speech
Shrivarsha—rain
Shriveda—pretty, lovely, handsome, graceful name
Shrive—devotee of lord shiva
Shrividhya—goddess durga
Shrividya—goddess durga
Shrivi—devotee of lord shiva
Shriyadita—lord surya, sun
Shriyani—pretty, lovely, handsome, graceful name
Shriyanka—goddess lakshmi
Shriyanshi—part of god
Shriya—prosperity and happiness
Shriya—prosperity, wife of lord
Shri—respect, lustre
Shrmila—hard wormonarch, ruler, prince, earl
Shromika—pretty, lovely, handsome, graceful name
Shruhani—pretty, lovely, handsome, graceful name
Shrujana—creative and brilliant, sagacious, gifted, wise, learned girl
Shruja—to love
Shrujeshwari—goddess of creativity
Shrunali—born in month of shravan
Shrunga—point of hill, crest
Shrushti—world, earth
Shrusti—world, universe
Shrutadeity—goddess of knowledge

Shrutadeva—with holy, pure, sanctified, pious, solemn knowledge
Shrutakeerti—wife of shatrugna, goddess lakshmi
Shrutakirti—of well known glory, famous
Shrutaly—lyrics, musical notes
Shrutashrava—goddess durga
Shrutavati—famous, well known
Shrutavinda—knower of scriptures river
Shruta—famous
Shruta—heard, knowledge
Shruthika—lord parvati
Shruthi—melody, music, lyrics
Shrutika—a person
Shruti—pretty, lovely, handsome, graceful, different, hearing
Shruti—vedic words
Shrutuja—auspicious
Shruva—blessed
Shrvani—month of shravan
Shrya—best
Shryu—name of a river
Shubakshna—pretty, lovely, handsome, graceful
Shubaksna—pretty, lovely, handsome, graceful name
Shubhabrata—auspicious vow
Shubhada—giver of luck, prosperity
Shubhaga—gracious
Shubhagi—auspicious, shining, fortunate
Shubhalakshmi—holy, pure, sanctified, pious, solemn fortune
Shubhali—best friend
Shubhamayi—full of splendour, pretty, lovely, handsome, graceful
Shubhamvi—auspicious
Shubham—auspicious, lucky
Shubhangini—best
Shubhangi—most-handsome
Shubhangi—one who brings happiness
Shubhani—splendour, beauty, ornament, jewellery, ornamentation
Shubhanjali—auspicious offering
Shubhankari—door of good deeds

Shubhaprada—granter of auspicious things
Shubhara—auspicious, goodness
Shubhasree—goddess lakshmi
Shubhavi—she who does good
Shubha—auspicious, shining
Shubha—glorious
Shubhechha—good ambition, intent, passion
Shubhika—a garland of auspicious bloom, garden stuffs
Shubhi—to be lucky, cherfulness
Shubhrata—pretty, lovely, handsome, graceful name
Shubhrata—white
Shubhravati—fair complexioned river
Shubhra—ganga river
Shubhra—whitening of sacret, holy, sanctified, pious, solemn, chaste
Shubravi—fair, respectable character
Shubra—white
Shuchika—holy
Shuchika—sacred
Shuchimukhi—holy, sanctified, pious, solemn, chaste faced
Shuchismita—one who has a holy, sanctified, pious, solemn, chaste, sweet smile
Shuchita—purity
Shuchi—bright, holy, sanctified, pious, solemn, chaste
Shuchi—holy, sanctified, pious, solemn, chaste
Shuddhawati—holy, sanctified, pious, solemn, chaste
Shuddhi—goddess durga, clearance
Shuddhi—purification
Shudeeksha—goddess lakshmi
Shudha—holy, sanctified, pious, solemn, chaste, food for god
Shudhi—pretty, lovely, handsome, graceful name
Shuhana—holy, sanctified, pious, solemn, chaste, bright ray of sun
Shuhana—sanctified, pious, solemn, chaste, bright ray of sun
Shuhani—bright ray of sun, pleasant, holy, sanctified, pious, chaste

Shuhani—pleasant, holy, sanctified, pious, solemn, chaste
Shuki—bright, quickwitted
Shukla—goddess saraswati
Shukla—saraswati
Shukti—a power
Shukti—pearl-oyster
Shuladhara—goddess durga
Shulini—goddess durga
Shulka—goddess saraswati
Shumati—good minded, wisdom
Shunayna—pretty, lovely, handsome, graceful eye, glimmers
Shun—coral, fan, good-natured
Shurya—brave
Shushana—graceful lily
Shushila—true beauty and kindness
Shushma—fragrant, pretty, lovely, handsome, graceful woman, sun
Shushmita—pretty, lovely, handsome, graceful name
Shushmi—wind
Shutimati—a river, having oyster shells
Shutradeity—goddess saraswati
Shuvangi—another name of goddess durga
Shuvarna—pretty, lovely, handsome, graceful, gold, golden
Shvasa—breath
Shvene—white
Shveni—white
Shvetambara—dressed in white
Shvetashva—goddess name
Shveta—white, holy, sanctified, pious, solemn, chaste heart, brave
Shveti—white, river
Shvetlana—white colour
Shvita—white, brightness, holy, sanctified, pious, solemn, chaste
Shviti—whiteness
Shwarayi—pretty, lovely, handsome, graceful name
Shweeta—bright, white
Shwetambari—goddess saraswati
Shwetambri—goddess saraswati
Shweta—holy, sanctified, pious, solemn, pleasing, suave, interesting

Shweta—white, pretty, lovely, handsome, graceful
Shwetha—white
Shwetika—white
Shweya—good attitude
Shwiti—fairness
Shyaina—pretty, lovely, handsome, graceful name
Shyala—lord krishna
Shyamaa—white
Shyamala—dusky
Shyamalika—dusky
Shyamalima—dusky
Shyamali—dusky
Shyamal—lover, dusky
Shyamangi—dark-complexioned
Shyamangi—darkcomplexioned
Shyamari—dusky
Shyamasri—dusky
Shyama—dark as cloud, goddess kali
Shyama—lord krishna
Shyambhavi—goddess durga
Shyamini—a creeper with dusky leaves
Shyamlata—a creeper with dusky leaves
Shya—tradition, purity, water
Shyeti—white
Shylaja—god of parvathi
Shyla—blind, daughter of the mountain
Shyla—goddess parvati
Shyna—one who feels shy
Shyne—pretty, lovely, handsome, graceful name
Shyni—bright
Shyra—a new star
Siahi—ink
Sian—the lord has been gracious
Siara—holy, sanctified, pious, solemn, chaste, holy
Sia—one who brings joy, moving, help
Sibani—gorgeous, pretty, lovely, handsome, graceful
Siddhama—goddess durga
Siddhangana—an accomplished woman
Siddhani—blessed

Siddhanth—principle
Siddhanti—principle for life
Siddhartha—one who attains wealth
Siddhavati—achieving perfection
Siddha—a form of deity
Siddha—dusky
Siddheshvaree—goddess of accomplishment
Siddheshwari—lord shiva
Siddhika—one who attains, lord ganesh
Siddhiksha—a religious ceremony
Siddhima—achievement
Siddhita—ability of success
Siddhi—achievement
Siddhi—prosperity, wealthychievement
Siddhma—goddess durga
Siddika—belongs to lord ganesha
Siddiksha—goddess lakshmi
Siddi—achievement, wife of lord ganesha
Siddyayika—one who accomplished
Sidhantika—principle
Sidhika—pretty, lovely, handsome, graceful name
Sidhiksha—goddess lakshmi
Sidhima—achievement
Sidhi—success, perfection, in worship
Siena—a town in italy
Sifa—purity, truthful, salvation
Sigappi—a goddess
Sihana—bright ray of the sun, holy, sanctified, pious, solemn, chaste
Sihi—sweet, kind
Sikata—sand
Sikhsha—education
Sikhxa—education
Sikta—pleasing, favourite, charming, wet
Siladitya—sun of stone
Silky—very soft, smooth
Silpa—stone, devoted, honest
Silu—rock, stone
Simantika—illumination, luminosity, radiance
Simar—simplewesome
Sima—border, limit, boundary, symbol

Simbala—a small pod
Simbala—pond
Simi—limit behold, gracious
Simmi—cute, pretty, lovely, handsome, graceful, lovely girl
Simmi—modesty
Simone—god has heard, one who hears
Simone—to listen
Simoni—obedient
Simpal—gentle
Simran—memory
Simran—remembrance, meditation
Simren—meditation
Simrita—loved and honoured by all
Simrit—rememberance
Simrit—remembered
Simron—meditation, remembrance
Simrun—in remembrance of god, meditation
Simu—happy, love
Sinaya—pretty
Sinchana—droplets, sprinkle of water
Sinchan—sprinkling
Sindhiya—evening
Sindhoori—bloom, garden stuffura of sunset
Sindhuja—born of ocean
Sindhuja—goddess lakshmi, pretty
Sindhura—responsibility, charming
Sindhuri—goddess durga, who wears sindhoor
Sindhusuta—goddess lakshmi
Sindhu—ocean
Sindhu—sea, ocean, river, water
Sindooja—goddess lakshmi
Sindoori—red colour, married
Sinduja—holy river, meditation
Sinduri—red coloured
Sinevale—day before the new moon
Singdha—holy, sanctified, pious, solemn, chaste, goddess parvati
Singhgamine—walks like lioness
Sinhamati—lion hearted, brave
Sinhayana—goddess durga
Sinhika—lioness
Sinhini—lioness
Sinjini—sound of anklet

Sinsapa—ashok tree
Sinu—love, pretty, lovely, handsome, graceful
Siphali—pretty, lovely, handsome, graceful name
Sirali—angel, cute
Sireesha—tender bloom, garden stuff
Sirihasini—always smiling, goddess lakshmi
Sirisha—bloom, garden stuff, sacred
Siri—richness, beauty, diamond, gold
Sisa—mirror
Sisira—cool, winterdorable
Sista—last one, disciplined, polite
Sital—cool, cold
Sitara—a star, morning star
Sitar—musical instrument
Sitashi—like goddess sita
Sita—goddess, wife of lord rama
Sita—wife of shree ram
Sitesh—wife of lord ram
Sithara—morning star, lucky star
Sithika—quiet, cool
Siti—lady, noble woman, earth
Sitta—lord ram's wife
Sivaanya—goddess parvati
Sivadharshini—reflection as lord shiva
Sivagami—lord shiva's wife shakti
Sivakooval—lord shiva
Sivamathy—knowledge or moon
Sivanandhini—devotee of lord shiva
Sivancy—a part of lord shiva
Sivaneswary—lord shiva
Sivane—goddess parvathi
Sivangini—part of god
Sivani—goddess parvati
Sivanjali—lord shiva
Sivanshi—part of lord shiva
Sivanthika—pretty, lovely, handsome, graceful name
Sivanya—goddess parvati
Sivapriya—a goddess
Sivasankari—goddess parvati
Sivasathi—companion of lord shiva
Sivashine—devotee of lord shiva
Sivasree—god lord shiva and goddess sakthi
Sivasri—worshipper of lord shiva

Sivathanu—goddess parvati
Siva—the ultimate, absolute, highest, best spirit, lord shiva
Sivgami—follower of lord shiva
Sivitha—pretty, lovely, handsome, graceful name
Sivi—deer
Siwani—belonging to lord shiva, beauty
Siyahi—ink
Siyali—desire, aspiration, longingful
Siyana—protection
Siyani—pretty, lovely, handsome, graceful name
Siyanshi—pretty, lovely, handsome, graceful name
Siya—goddess sita, illumination, luminosity, radiance, blessings
Siya—sita
Siyona—graceful, happy
Skandajit—wife of lord vishnu
Skanda—son of lord shiva
Skandha—wife of lord shiva
Skandini—princess, effusing, spurting
Skendha—branch
Sleja—goddess saraswati
Sloka—hymn, words
Smahi—progress
Smana—a holy, pure, sanctified, pious, solemn, unique soul
Smaradootee—messenger of love
Smaraduti—messenger of love
Smarami—remind of god
Smaram—remembrance
Smarata—memory
Smarti—rememberance
Smaya—love, smile
Smeera—smile
Smeetha—smiles
Smera—pretty, lovely, handsome, graceful, smiley
Smera—smiling
Smile—always happy
Sminal—always smile
Smirit—memory, remembrance
Smirtee—rememberence
Smirti—memory, remembrance, ambition, intent, passion

Smitakshi—the girl who possess calmness
Smital—always smiling
Smita—full of smile
Smita—smiling, smile, ever smiling lady
Smitha—smiling, blossomed, smiling face
Smithu—pretty, lovely, handsome, graceful smile, great, wise
Smiti—a smile, laughter, happiness
Smiti—smile
Smitojjala—pretty, lovely, handsome, graceful name
Smit—with smile
Smrita—remembered
Smrithi—wisdom, memories
Smriti—immortal, recollect, recollection
Smriti—memory
Smrutika—remembrance, memory
Smruti—memory, remembrance
Snaya—princess
Sneahal—love, friendly
Snehabhi—love
Snehakanshi—love
Snehalata—creeper of love
Snehalatha—full of love, compassion
Snehala—affectionate
Snehala—full of affection
Snehali—love affection
Snehal—love, friendly, bring love to
Snehamayi—full of friendship
Snehanshi—pretty, lovely, handsome, graceful name
Sneha—affection, wife of rishi sandeep
Sneha—love, affection
Sneha—loveffectionate, wife of rishi
Snehelata—vine of love
Snehida—amiable, pleasing, suave, interesting
Snehika—loveffection, friendliness
Snehil—symbol of love, loveffection
Snehita—loveffection, friendliness
Snehitha—friendly
Snehi—loving, dashing, friendly
Snehjeet—win the love

Snehlata—amiable, pleasing, suave, interesting, pretty, lovely
Snehlata—lovely
Sneh—love
Sneh—love, attraction
Snigda—affectionate
Snigdha—holy, soft, delicate, smooth
Snigdha—tender, soft
Snigtha—pretty, lovely, handsome, graceful name
Snija—scent, bloom, garden stuff
Snikitha—smiling face
Snita—soft
Snithika—very active
Snitica—independent
Soamlata—pretty, lovely, handsome, graceful name
Sobaika—good, gold
Sobhabati—rich, goddess lakshmi
Sobhana—atractive, splendid
Sobina—atractive
Sobitha—creative
Sobodhine—one who wakes the god
Sochayantee—a name of the celestial woman
Sofiya—shyness, good character
Sohalia—moon-luster
Sohana—graceful
Sohane—pretty, lovely, handsome, graceful
Soha—sunrise star, princess
Sohini—splendiddorned, pretty, lovely, handsome, graceful
Sohita—well-desire, aspiration, longinger for everyone
Sohna—cute, amiable, pleasing, suave, interesting, pretty
Sohni—pretty, lovely, handsome, graceful
Sohvat—appreciation, ornamentation, adornment, figuration
Sohvi—wisdom, woman of wisdom
Soiree—song
Sokkammal—bloom, garden stuffing
Sokkanayaki—moon-luster
Sokki—moon, illumination, luminosity, radiance
Solaikuil—a cuckoo in a garden

Solanlle—pretty, lovely, handsome, graceful name
Somabha—bright like the moon
Somabha—like the moon
Somada—pretty, lovely, handsome, graceful like moon
Somada—like a moon
Somadeity—goddess of nectar
Somalakshmi—lustre of the moon
Somalata—the creeper
Somale—beloved the moon
Somali—beloved of the moon
Somali—moon's beloved
Somansh—half moon
Soman—pretty, lovely, handsome, graceful name
Somashree—pretty, lovely, handsome, graceful type of wine
Somashree—holy, pure, sanctified, pious, solemn nectar
Somasuta—daughter of the moon
Somatra—excelling the moon
Somaya—calm, graceful
Soma—like moon
Soma—moon-rays, somras type of wine
Soma—nectar, juice
Somdutta—daughter of lord shiva
Someshwari—lord of moon
Someswari—the moon, devoted to lord shiva
Somila—like moon
Somila—tranquil
Somita—pretty, lovely, handsome, graceful name
Somiya—soft, smooth
Somi—daughter of lord
Somlata—pretty, lovely, handsome, graceful name
Sompriti—pretty, lovely, handsome, graceful name
Somsutaa—pretty, lovely, handsome, graceful name
Somyata—soft, softness
Somya—mild, soft, devotion, pretty, lovely, handsome, graceful
Sonaira—good time, era of sun
Sonakshe—golden eye, glimmers

Sonakshi—pretty, lovely, handsome, graceful
Sonakshi—golden-eye, glimmers, fairy face
Sonala—golden
Sonale—golden
Sonalika—gold, golden
Sonalika—golden
Sonalisa—most charming
Sonali—golden, special, goldness
Sonali—self-examination
Sonaltasha—lord of lord shiva
Sonal—golden
Sonal—golden, soft hearted
Sonamani—ornament, jewellery, ornamentation, adornment, figuration of gold
Sonam—pretty, lovely, handsome, graceful, gold, made of gold
Sonam—like gold
Sonanshi—piece of gold
Sonan—gold, golden
Sona—gold
Sona—gold, prayer
Sonera—clean water
Sonia—pretty, lovely, handsome, graceful
Sonia—pretty, lovely, handsome, graceful, pretty, wise, wisdom
Sonibai—gold
Sonica—pretty, lovely, handsome, graceful
Sonika—gold, golden, true beauty
Sonika—with golden beauty
Sonima—pretty, lovely, handsome, graceful name
Sonita—young sun, pretty, lovely, handsome, graceful
Soniya—gold, clever
Soni—gold, pretty
Soni—golden
Sonny—son of god
Sonom—gifted, fortune, made of gold
Sonurita—young girl
Sonu—gold
Sonu—gold, loving
Sonvi—learning

Sonwani—voice as holy, sanctified, pious, solemn, chaste as gold
Sony—beauty
Soodnya—wise
Soohaney—ray of sun
Soohini—pretty, lovely, handsome, graceful
Sooktee—wise saying
Sooline—armed with spear
Soonera—holy, sanctified, pious, solemn, chaste holy water
Soorat—beauty, face
Sooriyabai—golden
Soorya—sun
Sopana—dream
Sophia—woman of wisdom
Sophiya—knowledge, wisdom, will
Sorupa—illumination, luminosity, radiance
Sorya—brave, warrior, courage, eloquent
Sosamma—nice
Soubarna—girl with a golden complexion
Soubhagya—lucky
Soudhrita—pretty, lovely, handsome, graceful name
Sougandika—sacred river, good smell
Soujanya—calm, sensitive, honesty
Soukhya—well being, harmonious
Soumili—good, intteligent, confidence
Soumita—nice rose, pretty, lovely, handsome, graceful heart
Soumitra—son of sumitra
Soumiya—pretty, lovely, handsome, graceful
Soumyasri—illumination, luminosity, radiance
Soumya—gentle
Soumya—gentle, pretty, lovely, handsome, graceful, soft nature
Soundaradeityl—illumination, luminosity, radiance, illumination, luminosity, radiance
Soundarya—pretty, lovely, handsome, graceful, beauty, cute, pretty
Soundhika—fragrance, clouds
Soundhi—nice, good

Souparnika—name of a river
Souprity—pretty, lovely, handsome, graceful name
Sourabhi—fragrance, the celestial cow
Souravi—sun ray
Sourikta—pretty, lovely, handsome, graceful name
Souromi—pretty, lovely, handsome, graceful name
Souvira—one of the indian rag or taal
Sova—one's own
Sovi—charity
Sowbaghyam—wealth
Sowjanya—polite nature, tender
Sowmea—moon
Sowmikashree—pretty, lovely, handsome, graceful name
Sowmiya—gentle, soft, fragrance
Sowmya—beauty, calm, maa durga's name
Sowndariya—angel, pretty, lovely, handsome, graceful
Sowndarya—angel
Sowpi—princess
Sowrabha—fragrance
Sowravi—pretty, lovely, handsome, graceful name
Sowri—star
Sowshya—goddess lakshmi
Spandana—motivation, competition, react
Spandana—throbbing
Spardha—compitition
Sparshananda—joy of touch
Sparsha—touch
Sparshika—pleasant touch
Sparshita—touch, feel, sensation
Sparshitha—touch, feel, sensation
Sparshla—soft touch of mind
Sparsh—touch
Sphatika—crystal
Sphurti—full of energy
Spoorthi—inspiration
Spoorthy—inspirations
Spoorti—enthusiasm
Spriha—being attached to the world
Spruha—ambition, goal, desire,

aspiration, longing, ambition, intent, passion
Spurthi—encourage, inspiration
Sraddha—devotion wife of lord shiva
Sradha—trust, concentration
Sragvi—tulasi, sacred basil plant
Sraiya—credit give credit to someone
Sramana—in tune with natureustere
Srashti—beauty of nature, universe
Srasti—universe, world
Sras—goddess saraswati study
Sravana—sense of hearing, star
Sravani—aspirant, pretty, lovely, handsome, graceful
Sravanthi—continuous flow, goddess lakshmi
Sravanti—flowing river, unstoppable
Sravine—a goddess
Sravni—worthy to listen
Sravya—melodious, melody
Sra—whole
Sredha—part of goddess lakshmi
Sreea—pretty, lovely, handsome, graceful, goddess lakshmi
Sreedeityka—lakshmi
Sreedeity—goddess lakshmi
Sreeganga—name of a holy river
Sreeharshitha—goddess lakshmi
Sreejamya—goddess lakshmi
Sreejata—best, pretty, lovely, handsome, graceful, excellent
Sreeja—daughter of goddess lakshmi
Sreejita—best, winner
Sreejith—one who conquered prosperity
Sreekala—symbol of goodness
Sreeka—love
Sreelakshmi—goddess, goddess lakshmi
Sreelekha—good writing
Sreemayi—fortunate
Sreemoye—goddess durga, ambition, intent, passion, gifted, wise, learned
Sreenanda—happiness, like goddess lakshmi
Sreenandha—pretty, lovely, handsome, graceful name
Sreenayana—beauty of eye, glimmers

Sreenidhi—goddess lakshmi
Sreenika—bloom, garden stuff of lord vishnu
Sreenitha—goddess, bloom, garden stuff, soft minded
Sreepadma—lotus
Sreeshanvika—goddess lakshmi
Sreesha—goddess lakshmi, lord venkateswara
Sreeshma—pretty, lovely, handsome, graceful name
Sreeta—goddess lakshmi, most pretty, lovely, handsome, graceful
Sreeti—memory
Sreeveda—one with knowledge of vedas
Sreeyanshi—part of god
Sreeya—goddess lakshmi, prosperity
Sree—happy, radiance, prosperity
Sreshtha—perfection
Srestha—the best in number and quality
Sreta—beauty, gold, gifted by god
Sreyanshi—give credit to others
Sreya—auspicious, goddess lakshmi
Sreya—excellent, credit
Sri-varsha—goddess lakshmi
Sri-varshini—sun rays, bright illumination, luminosity, radiance
Sri-vidhya—goddess saraswati
Sriaditha—goeddess durga, son
Srianusha—god, pretty, lovely, handsome, graceful morning, richness
Sria—happy, joy
Sribindu—lakshmi
Srichaitra—month in indian calendar
Sridatri—goddess lakshmi
Sriddhika—another name of goddess lakshmi
Srideity—goddess lakshmi
Sridhari—prosperity
Sridharshna—pretty, lovely, handsome, graceful, god, religious
Sridha—part of goddess lakshmi
Sridhika—full of knowledge
Sridhi—knowledge
Sridima—good
Sriharini—padmanabhan's wife

Srihita—goddess lakshmi
Srihitha—goddess lakshmi, knowledge
Srijani—creativity
Srija—who creates
Srijita—creative woman
Srijla—pretty, lovely, handsome, graceful
Srijothi—bright illumination, luminosity, radiance
Srikanya—daughter of goddess lakshmi
Srikari—goddess saraswati
Srikhandini—sister of draupadi
Srikshitha—name of saraswati, lakshmi
Srilakshmi—holy, pure, sanctified, pious, solemn lakshmi
Srilakshmi—pretty, lovely, handsome, graceful name
Srilatha—wealth creeper
Srilaya—rhythm
Srilekha—good writing
Srimaa—desire, aspiration, longing of god
Srimathi—moon, good knowledge
Srimedha—knowledge of god
Srimukhi—with a radiant face
Sringarika—to beautify
Sringa—beautify
Srinidhi—wealth and treasure, goddess
Srinika—goddess lakshmi
Srinita—goddess lakshmi
Srinithi—goddess lakshmi
Srinivasa—lord venkateswara
Srini—love
Srinu—pleasing, favourite, charming, creative
Srinwanti—voice of god
Sripada—feet of god
Sriparna—pretty, lovely, handsome, graceful
Sriprada—goddess lakshmi
Sripriya—favourite person of goddess
Sripu—bloom, garden stuffs devoted to god
Sriranjani—pretty, lovely, handsome, graceful name
Srirenukha—name of a hindu goddess

Srirudra—goddess durga
Srirupa—lakshmi's beauty
Srisaahnika—name of goddess lakshmi
Srishani—who is at the top
Srisha—bloom, garden stuff, goddess lakshmi
Srishtika—one who created the world
Srishti—universe, world, earth
Srishty—creation
Sristi—creation
Sristu—create
Sristy—universe
Srita—goddess lakshmi
Srithasree—goddess lakshmi
Sritha—goddess lakshmi, referring to god
Srithika—simple
Sritija—charming
Sriti—path, producing, roadiming
Sritoma—pretty, lovely, handsome, graceful, goddess lakshmi
Srivaishnavi—goedess maha kali
Srivalli—goddess lakshmi
Srivani—holy, pure, sanctified, pious, solemn speech
Srivanya—calm
Srivarshini—pretty, lovely, handsome, graceful
Srivathi—goddess saraswathi
Srivatsa—son of lakshmi, goddess of wealth
Sriveda—auspicious knowledge, helpful
Srivedha—auspicious knowledge
Sriveni—holy, pure, sanctified, pious, solemn weaving, stream
Srividhya—lakshmi and sarasvati
Srividya—the goddess of wealth
Sriyanshi—part of goddess lakshmi
Sriya—goddess lakshmi, prosperity
Sriza—pretty, lovely, handsome, graceful name
Sri—radiance, diffusing illumination, luminosity, radiance
Sroni—pretty, lovely, handsome, graceful goddess parvati
Srozza—mind
Srrinjaye—one who given victory

Srujana—beautyrt
Srujanika—unique and creative girl
Sruja—created
Srujeeta—pretty, lovely, handsome, graceful name
Srumol—everything
Srushti—world, universe, earth
Srusti—creation
Srutakeerthi—one who is of sharp intellect
Srutakirti—wife of shatrughna in ramayana
Sruthika—lord of music
Sruthisha—sweet, amiable, pleasing, suave, interesting
Sruthi—knowledge of vedas
Sruti—rhythm, hearing, ear
Srutkirti—wife of satrughna
Ssriambal—pretty, lovely, handsome, graceful name
Stambhakee—goddess, pillar
Stambhiki—post, pillar goddess
Stava—one who praise
Stava—that which praises
Stavita—praised
Sthavara—immovable
Sthavara—stable, immovable
Sthira—without movement, strong minded
Sthita—stable
Sthiti—circumstances
Sthuthi—praise to god
Streetama—complete woman
Striratna—goddess lakshmi
Stritama—a complete woman
Stutee—praise, goddess durga
Stuti—goddess durga, praises, prayer
Stuti—praise
Stuvi—praiser, worshipper
Suachi—good
Subakshna—pretty, lovely, handsome, graceful
Subali—very strong, powerful
Subarnarekha—goddess lakshmi line of gold
Subarna—colour of gold
Subarta—pretty, lovely, handsome, graceful name

Subashini—generous, soft or well spoken
Subasini—soft spoken
Subasree—lakshmi
Subasri—monarch, ruler, prince, earl of study
Subathirai—lord arjuna's wife
Subathra—mother of abimanyurjun's wife
Suba—morning, pretty, lovely, handsome, graceful, sweet
Subbareddy—god
Subela—subh ghari
Subhadra—lord krishna's sister
Subhadra—source of great welfare
Subhagai—pretty, lovely, handsome, graceful name
Subhaga—a fortunate person
Subhaga—fortunate
Subhaga—good fortune
Subhagee—pretty, lovely, handsome, graceful name
Subhagya—lucky
Subhakshna—pretty, lovely, handsome, graceful name
Subhandhava—good friend
Subhangini—pretty, lovely, handsome, graceful name
Subhangi—good luck
Subhani—splendour, beauty
Subhara—clean, goddess lakshmi
Subhasane—speaks softly
Subhasa—pretty, lovely, handsome, graceful, shining, soft, well
Subhasha—soft, well spoken, pretty, lovely, handsome, graceful
Subhashini—wellspoken
Subhashree—name of goddess lakshmi
Subhasini—softspoken, wellspoken
Subhasita—pretty, lovely, handsome, graceful
Subhasita—well-spoken
Subhasmita—holy smile
Subhasree—goodness, good monarch, ruler, prince, earl
Subhasri—god lakshmi
Subha—nectar

Subha—splendour, beauty, ornament, jewellery, ornamentation
Subhema—terrible
Subheshitha—pretty, lovely, handsome, graceful name
Subheta—ease
Subhga—pretty, lovely, handsome, graceful
Subhichha—greetings
Subhiksha—full-fill, prosperous
Subhi—splendour, dawnurora
Subhlakshmi—goddess
Subhodhini—clever
Subhooti—one enjoying prosperity
Subhothini—learned woman
Subhraya—prosperous and graceful lady
Subhra—radiant
Subhuja—auspicious apsara
Subhulakshmi—auspicious, goddess lakshmi
Subhuti—well behaved
Subhuudi—of good intellect
Subhu—auspicious, good
Subiksha—prosperous
Subisha—greetings, dawn
Subitha—pretty, lovely, handsome, graceful, nice girl
Subi—one with simplicity
Subodhini—a learned lady
Subrata—devoted to what is right
Subreena—pretty, lovely, handsome, graceful
Subuddhe—good mind
Suchandra—pretty, lovely, handsome, graceful
Suchara—very skillful good performer
Sucharita—of good character, good reputation
Sucharita—well behaved
Sucharitha—one having a very clean character
Sucharu—good skill
Sucharu—to do something systematically
Suchetana—good intelligence
Sucheta—fragrance, with pretty, lovely, handsome, graceful mind

Sucheta—one with a very sharp mind
Suchhaya—shining
Suchika—indicating
Suchinta—deep nice thoughts
Suchira—eternity
Suchira—tasteful
Suchismita—with a pious smile
Suchita—indication, pretty, lovely, handsome, gracefuluspicious
Suchithra—pretty, lovely, handsome, graceful picture, image
Suchitra—pretty, lovely, handsome, graceful picture
Suchitta—good heart, mind
Suchi—holy, sanctified, pious, solemn, chaste
Sudakshima—wife of monarch, ruler, prince, earl dilip
Sudakshina—sincere, upright
Sudamani—as bright as illumination, luminosity, radianceining, wealthy
Sudamine—as bright as illumination, luminosity, radiance
Sudarshana—handsome, pretty, lovely, handsome, graceful
Sudarshane—one who is pleasing to eye, glimmers
Sudarshani—pleasing to the eye, glimmers, lotus pond
Sudarshini—pretty, lovely, handsome, graceful lady, sundari
Sudar—nice, pretty, lovely, handsome, graceful
Sudatta—well given wife of krishna
Sudaya—good, kindness
Suddha—clean, holy, sanctified, pious, solemn, chaste, holy
Suddhi—purification, holiness, truth
Suddhrita—holy, sanctified, pious, solemn, chaste, kind, softness
Sudeeksha—goddess lakshmi
Sudeeksha—goddess lakshmi, parvati
Sudeena—good, kindness, mercy
Sudeepa—bright, excellent lamp
Sudeepta—bright
Sudeepthi—dazzling bright
Sudeepti—illumination, luminosity, radiance

Sudeity—wife of krishna
Sudeksha—goddess lakshmi
Sudena—a real goddess, goddess lakshmi
Sudesha—a son of krishna
Sudeshna—highness, empress, queen, wife of monarch
Sudeshna—wellborn
Sudesh—my pretty, lovely, handsome, graceful country
Sudeve—lamp
Sudhamani—bright, wealthy
Sudhamayi—full of nectar
Sudhama—bountiful river
Sudhanjan—holy, sanctified, pious, solemn, chaste enjoyment
Sudhanya—pretty, lovely, handsome, graceful name
Sudharma—of right path, follower of law
Sudha—food for god, nectar
Sudha—nectar
Sudheksha—goddess lakshmi
Sudhendra—lord of nectar
Sudhesha—good initiation, goddess lakshmi
Sudhika—purified
Sudhiksha—good concentration
Sudhik—concentration, waiting for someone
Sudhinaa—good day
Sudhina—pretty, lovely, handsome, graceful as sun, good day
Sudhira—calm
Sudhita—kind, benevolent ambrosia
Sudhithi—bright flame
Sudhi—sensible
Sudhrita—holy, sanctified, pious, solemn, chaste, kind, softness
Sudhriti—very patientlerant
Sudika—purified
Sudiksha—goddess lakshmi
Sudikshya—goddess lakshmi
Sudimna—the holy, pure, sanctified, pious, solemn power
Sudipta—sweet, bright, illumination, luminosity, radiance
Sudipti—brightness

Sudipti—shining
Sudita—wise
Suditi—bright
Suditi—brightest flame, bright, shining
Sudnya—wise
Sudrishi—pretty, with pretty, lovely, handsome, graceful eye, glimmers
Sudrrishe—pleasing to eye, glimmers
Sudrshi—a pleasant sight
Sugamya—most pretty, lovely, handsome, graceful
Sugam—easy
Sugana—noble attendant
Sugana—pretty, lovely, handsome, graceful name
Suganda—good smell, fragrance
Sugandha—fragrant
Sugandha—sweetsmelling
Sugandhe—sweet smell
Sugandhika—sweet smell
Sugandhita—a woman with good smell
Sugandhi—fragrance
Sugand—fragrance
Suganthi—good fragrance, brightness
Suganya—sugam, goddess parvati
Sugashini—pretty, lovely, handsome, graceful name
Sugasini—fragrant
Sugatee—happiness
Sugathri—sweet voice, pretty, lovely, handsome, graceful eye, glimmers
Sugati—wellbeing
Sugatree—pretty, lovely, handsome, graceful
Sugauri—goddess parvati
Sugeshna—one who sings pretty, lovely, handsome, gracefully
Sugita—pretty, lovely, handsome, gracefully sung
Sugitta—holy book, pretty, lovely, handsome, gracefully sung
Sugna—pretty, lovely, handsome, graceful name
Sugouri—goddess parvati
Sugreeva—one with pretty, lovely, handsome, graceful neck
Sugumari—a delicate

Sugunambal—sung pretty, lovely, handsome, gracefully
Suguni—with good qualities
Suhag—love, life
Suhaila—moon-luster, ease, star, moonshine
Suhali—pretty, lovely, handsome, graceful
Suhana—pleasant, holy, sanctified, pious, solemn, chaste, bright ray of the
Suhani—cherful, pleasant, pretty
Suhanya—holy
Suhanya—holy girl
Suhan—pretty, lovely, handsome, graceful, pleasant
Suhara—pretty, pretty, lovely, handsome, graceful
Suharika—lucky, goddess parvati
Suharsana—pretty, lovely, handsome, graceful smile, joyful
Suharshana—joyful, one with pretty, lovely, handsome, graceful smile
Suhashini—ever smiling
Suhasine—one who smiles pretty, lovely, handsome, gracefully
Suhasini—eversmiling
Suhasi—simple monarch, ruler, prince, earl, good smile
Suhas—one with good smile, laughter
Suhavi—like your heart
Suhela—easily accessible
Suhika—pretty, lovely, handsome, graceful
Suhili—pretty, lovely, handsome, graceful companion
Suhina—pretty, lovely, handsome, graceful
Suhitha—suitable
Suhrita—good heart, well-disposed
Sujaataa—pleasing
Sujah—civilization
Sujaishini—pretty, lovely, handsome, graceful
Sujala—affectionate
Sujala—cloud
Sujal—holy, sanctified, pious, solemn, chaste water, sacred water
Sujana—a great success

Sujanya—honest, wise, superior, elevated knowledge
Sujan—wise, learned
Sujapriya—love
Sujata—of noble birth, beauty, sun, illumination, luminosity, radiance
Sujatha—god, pretty, lovely, handsome, graceful
Sujaya—victory, winner
Sujay—victory
Sujeet—auspicious victory
Sujhata—sun, illumination, luminosity, radiance, beauty
Sujita—great conqueror
Sujitha—smooth, great conqueror
Sujithra—pretty, lovely, handsome, graceful
Sukanta—pretty, lovely, handsome, graceful, radiant
Sukanthe—sweet voiced
Sukanya—pretty, lovely, handsome, graceful girl
Sukanya—a good girl, comely, pretty, lovely, handsome, graceful
Sukavya—good holy poetry
Sukeertee—well-praised
Sukeerthana—prayer
Sukeerthi—good fame
Sukeerti—good fame, of good caste
Sukee—lily
Sukesha—well-bred
Sukeshe—victory
Sukeshi—with good hair
Sukeshi—with pretty, lovely, handsome, graceful hair
Sukeshni—having pretty, lovely, handsome, graceful hair
Sukhada—joy-giver
Sukhada—one who gives happiness
Sukham—joy, happiness
Sukhavati—happy
Sukhayani—one who gladdens
Sukha—happiness, ease, comfort
Sukhda—a woman who gives happiness
Sukhda—one who gives solace
Sukhi—at serenity, calm, calmness, stillness, silence, happy, blessed

Sukhmane—pretty, lovely, handsome, graceful name
Sukhmani—contented soul, bringing serenity, calm, calmness, stillness, silence
Sukhmeet—friend of happiness
Sukhyati—fame
Sukirti—fame, well praised
Suki—beloved, happy
Sukmani—bringing serenity, calm, calmness, stillness
Sukomal—gentle-hearted
Sukomal—very tender
Sukratee—a person who does good deeds
Sukrati—pretty, lovely, handsome, graceful design
Sukrida—sportingn angel
Sukriti—pretty, lovely, handsome, graceful creation of god, wise
Sukriti—well-behaved
Sukrit—wise
Sukrutha—pious
Sukruthi—god's artwork, pretty, lovely, handsome, graceful art
Sukruti—a good conduct, kindness, tolerance, durability, toleration
Suksha—pretty, lovely, handsome, graceful eye, glimmers
Suksha—nice eye, glimmers
Sukshma—fine, subtle
Sukshmita—pretty, lovely, handsome, graceful name
Suksma—fine
Sukthi—shining
Sukti—shining, bright
Sukukshe—born from good womb
Sukula—born in a noble family
Sukumari—soft, meritorious
Sukuna—wise
Sukushi—noble
Sukusuma—ornament, jewellery, ornamentation, adornment
Sulabha—easily available
Sulabha—easy, natural
Sulagna—shy, good time, lucky time
Sulaikha—pretty, lovely, handsome, graceful handwriting

Sulakshami—goddess lakshmi
Sulakshana—well brought up
Sulakshana—with good qualities
Sulaksha—lucky
Sulakshmika—goddess lakshmi
Sulakshmi—goddess lakshmi
Sulakshna—lucky, with good character
Sulalita—very pleasing
Sulalit—pretty, lovely, handsome, graceful, charming
Sulasa—calm
Sulbha—easily available
Sulbha—which is available easily
Sulebha—lucky
Sulekha—good handwriting
Sulekha—good writing
Sulka—goddess sarasvati
Sulochana—having pretty eyes, lovely, handsome, graceful eye, glimmers
Sulochana—one with pretty eyes, lovely, handsome, graceful eye
Sulohita—one of the seven tongues of fire
Sulojana—somebody with pretty, lovely, handsome, graceful eye, glimmers
Suloma—gentle-hearted
Suloma—with pretty, lovely, handsome, graceful hair
Sultana—highness, empress, queen, empress, writing
Sumadhya—graceful woman, slender-waisted
Sumaira—brownish, princess, highness, empress, queen
Sumaiyah—first lady
Sumalatha—bloom, garden stuff creeper
Sumanasri—pretty, lovely, handsome, graceful
Sumana—good-natured, bloom, garden stuff
Sumangala—auspicious
Sumangale—auspicious
Sumangali—greatly auspicious
Sumangli—goddess parvati
Sumanna—pretty, lovely, handsome, graceful name

Sumanolata—bloom, garden stuffy
Sumansa—goddess saraswati
Sumanta—pretty, lovely, handsome, graceful name
Sumantini—pretty, lovely, handsome, graceful name
Sumantra—good advice
Sumanya—respectable
Suman—pretty, lovely, handsome, graceful bloom, garden stuffs
Suman—bloom, garden stuff
Sumapriya—another name of goddess lakshmi
Sumatha—bloom, garden stuff
Sumathi—knowledgeable, sharp
Sumati—good advisor, brilliant, sagacious, gifted, wise, learned
Sumati—good minded, wisdom
Sumavali—garland
Sumaya—with excellent plans
Suma—bloom, garden stuff, natural, everywhere, god
Sumedha—pretty, lovely, handsome, graceful, wise, brilliant
Sumedha—clever
Sumeena—pretty, lovely, handsome, graceful fish
Sumeera—the goddess of wealth
Sumeesha—pretty, lovely, handsome, graceful
Sumeeta—good friend, soul mate
Sumeeta—having a balanced form
Sumegha—pretty, lovely, handsome, graceful clouds
Sumegha—rain, good cloud
Sumeha—brilliant, sagacious, gifted, wise, learned
Sumeshne—well linmonarch, ruler, prince, earl
Sumiran—meditation, in remembrance of god
Sumiran—to remember
Sumira—much remembered
Sumita—a good friend, beauty
Sumita—good-monarch, ruler, prince, earl
Sumitha—one who has pretty, lovely, handsome, graceful body

Sumiti—good friend, great wisdom
Sumitra—mother of lord lakshman
Sumitra—wife of dashratha
Sumi—good, friendly, pretty, lovely, handsome, graceful
Summaya—the first lady
Sumnavari—bringing joy
Sumona—calm, with good heart
Sumukhe—pretty, lovely, handsome, graceful face
Sumukhi—a woman with pretty, lovely, handsome, graceful face
Sumukhi—very pretty, lovely, handsome, graceful
Sumundika—with a nice head
Sunadamala—god gift
Sunaina—pretty, lovely, handsome, graceful eye, glimmers
Sunaini—one with pretty, lovely, handsome, graceful eye, glimmers
Sunairah—pretty, lovely, handsome, graceful
Sunaira—pretty, lovely, handsome, graceful
Sunaiyna—one with pretty, lovely, handsome, graceful eye
Sunakshi—self centred
Sunakus—pretty, lovely, handsome, graceful name
Sunami—well named
Sunamya—sweet chartered
Sunanda—pleasing, favourite, charming
Sunanda—sweet charactered, good-natured
Sunandini—happy
Sunandita—happy
Sunandita—joyful
Sunandi—pleasing
Sunannda—sweet charactered, pretty, lovely, handsome, graceful
Sunantha—goodness of cow
Sunashi—lord indra
Sunayana—a woman with lovely eye, glimmers
Sunayana—having pretty, lovely, handsome, graceful eye, glimmers

Sunayani—a woman with lovely eye, glimmers
Sunaya—very just, good conduct
Sunaya—well-conducted
Sunayna—pretty, lovely, handsome, graceful eye, glimmers
Sundarakshi—one with pretty, lovely, handsome, graceful eye, glimmers
Sundarani—pretty, lovely, handsome, graceful
Sundaravadivu—happy
Sundara—pretty, lovely, handsome, graceful
Sundari—pretty, lovely, handsome, graceful, daughter of rishabhdev
Sundari—most pretty, lovely, handsome, graceful
Sundeep—guider of the illumination, luminosity, radiance
Sundha—a character in ramayana
Sundhuja—born of the ocean, goddess lakshmi
Suneha—pretty, lovely, handsome, graceful, beloved
Sunehri—golden
Sunekhasri—beauty, smart, honest
Sunekha—honest, writing, wonder
Sunela—dark blue
Sunela—deep, dark blue colour
Sunena—a girl with pretty eyes, lovely, handsome, graceful eye, glimmers
Sunera—good time, good truth, era of sun
Suneri—golden
Sunesha—pretty, lovely, handsome, graceful night
Sunetaa—well behaved
Suneta—one with good principles
Sunetha—well mannered, conducted
Sunethra—one with lovely eye, glimmers
Suneti—good advice
Suneti—mother of dhruva
Sunetra—pretty, lovely, handsome, graceful eye, glimmers
Sunetra—one with pretty, lovely, handsome, graceful eye, glimmers

Sunhera—golden
Sunidhi—auspicious, excellent treasure
Sunila—blue
Sunina—pretty, lovely, handsome, graceful eye, glimmers, tree of heaven
Sunisha—pretty, lovely, handsome, graceful night
Sunishka—pretty, lovely, handsome, graceful ornament
Sunishka—graceful ornament, jewellery, ornamentation, adornment
Sunishtha—full belief, full confidence
Suniska—with pretty, lovely, handsome, graceful smile
Sunistha—good devotion, clean
Sunita—well-behaved, polite
Sunita—with pretty, lovely, handsome, graceful body
Sunitee—good conduct
Sunitha—well disposed, righteous
Sunith—just-lover
Suniti—good conduct, good principles
Sunity—woman with good virtues
Sunjana—lord shiva
Sunlima—bright, blue, dark
Sunmaya—silence and discipline
Sunny—joyful, bright, brilliant
Sunrita—gladness, joy
Sunu—sweet little lady
Supal—whiten, serenity, calm, calmness, stillness, valued, rare time
Supanna—valuable, valued, rare diamond
Suparna—pretty, lovely, handsome, graceful, charming
Suparna—leafyttractive, good behave
Suparni—with pretty, lovely, handsome, graceful wings
Suphulla—with pretty, lovely, handsome, graceful blossoms
Suprabhata—a morning prayer
Suprabha—radiant
Suprabha—resplendent, grand
Supraja—good person, su means good
Supranya—beauty
Suprasada—auspicious, gracious, favourable

Suprasanna—very serene
Suprateekine—pretty, lovely, handsome, graceful form
Supratishtha—famous
Supratishthita—celebrated
Supreeta—adored one, beloved
Supreetha—beloved endearing to all, beloved
Supreeti—love
Supreet—loving, amiable, pleasing, suave, interesting love
Supreeya—pretty, lovely, handsome, graceful name
Suprema—loving
Suprita—well pleased
Supriti—pretty, lovely, handsome, graceful friendship, true love
Suprit—loving
Supriya—beloved, wonderfuldorable
Supriya—much-loved
Supta—goddess
Suptha—hidden
Supti—sun, slep
Supunya—very virtuous or holy
Supushpa—pretty, lovely, handsome, graceful bloom, garden stuff
Surabhe—fragrance, wild basil, sandal wood
Surabhi—pretty, lovely, handsome, graceful, desire, aspiration, longing-yielding cow
Surabhi—good smell, sandal wood
Surabhu—born of the gods
Suraganga—celestial woman
Suragi—song
Suraja—born of gods
Surajni—pretty, lovely, handsome, graceful night
Suraksha—protection
Surala—one who brings the gods
Surama—very pleasing
Suramya—very pretty, lovely, handsome, graceful
Surananda—joy of the gods river
Surana—joyous, pleasing sounds
Surangana—heavenly woman
Suranga—holy, pure, sanctified, pious, solemn

Surangi—colourful
Surangna—wife of god
Surani—river in heaven
Suranjana—pleasing, charming
Suranya—goddess saraswati
Surasa—goddess durga
Surasa—good essence
Surasoo—mother of god
Surasree—song highness, empress, queen
Surasti—perfect
Surastree—celestial woman
Surastri—celestial woman
Surasu—mother of gods
Surata—another name of ganges
Suratna—possessing rich ornament, jewellery, ornamentation, adornment
Suravahini—river of the gods
Suravani—earth as the mother of the gods
Suravinda—pretty, lovely, handsome, graceful yaksa
Suravi—fragrance, sun
Surayanshi—part of sun
Surbala—good singing girl
Surbhi—fragrance
Surbhi—sweet fragrance, illumination, luminosity, radiance
Surbie—fragrance, illumination, luminosity, radiance
Surdhirgika—mandakini
Surdhuni—mandakini
Sureena—pretty, lovely, handsome, graceful name
Suree—wife of god
Surejya—worshipped by the gods
Sureka—pretty, lovely, handsome, gracefully
Surekha—pretty, lovely, handsome, gracefully drawn
Surekha—drawn with pretty, lovely, handsome, gracefully
Surenoo—very small particle
Surenu—very smalln atom
Sureshe—ultimate, absolute, highest, best goddess
Sureshi—goddess durga

Sureshwari—sovereign goddess of gods
Surina—a Goddess, wise
Surinder—the monarch, ruler, prince, earl of gods, lord indra
Surishvari—pious, holy, sanctified, pious, solemn, chaste, the river ganga
Surit—good knowledge
Suriyakala—sun
Suriya—brightness of sun
Suri—little princess, red rose, consort
Surjanika—pretty, lovely, handsome, graceful name
Surmidhi—fluency as in singing for music
Surmya—channelled
Surochana—much liked
Surochana—very pretty, lovely, handsome, graceful
Surohine—pretty, lovely, handsome, graceful red
Surohini—pretty, lovely, handsome, gracefully red
Surojita—mighty
Surona—pleasing
Surotama—auspicious apsara
Surottama—best among the goddess
Surottama—best among the goddesses
Surshri—the best voice, melody
Surubi—music
Surucha—bright illumination, luminosity, radiance, with fine taste
Suruchi—good natured
Suruchi—one with good taste, good taste
Surukhe—with pretty, lovely, handsome, graceful face
Surukhi—having pretty, lovely, handsome, graceful face
Surupa—pretty, lovely, handsome, graceful
Surupika—well formed, pretty, lovely, handsome, graceful
Suruthi—auspicious apsara
Suryabha—as bright as the sun
Suryadita—sun
Suryaja—born of the sun

Suryakala—sun of art portion of the sun
Suryakamala—the sunbloom, garden stuff
Suryakantam—brightness of the sun
Suryakanta—lustering, good, ornament, jewellery
Suryakanti—sun's rays
Suryakanti—sun's rays
Suryamukhi—sun faced
Suryane—the wife of the sun
Suryani—sun's wife
Suryani—wife of the sun
Suryanka—who describe sun
Suryaprabha—as bright as the sun
Suryashobha—sunshine
Suryasree—holy, pure, sanctified, pious, solemn sun
Suryatanya—river yamuna
Surya—sun
Surya—the sun, glittering sun, sun god
Sur—fluency as in singing, songs
Susama—exquisite beauty, splendour
Susangata—good companion
Susantika—patient, calm
Susatya—always truthful
Suseela—good charactered woman
Sushama—beauty
Sushanta—very calm, placid
Sushanti—serenity, calm, calmness, stillness, silenceful
Sushela—easy to get
Sushela—good conduct, chaste
Sushela—lord krishna's wife name
Sushela—of good disposition
Sushema—well parted hair
Sushila—good conduct
Sushilika—of good character bird
Sushita—so sweet
Sushita—suitable
Sushi—lord parvati
Sushma—pretty, lovely, handsome, graceful woman
Sushma—very handsome
Sushmeeta—with pleasing smile
Sushmita—pretty, lovely, handsome, graceful smile, good smile

Sushmitha—pretty, lovely, handsome, graceful smile
Sushobhana—very pretty, lovely, handsome, graceful
Sushobhita—very pretty, lovely, handsome, graceful
Sushrava—much heard of, famous
Sushrava—very famous
Sushreeka—good monarch, ruler, prince, earl, wealthy, prosperity
Sushree—very rich
Sushreya—pretty, lovely, handsome, graceful
Sushrita—pretty, lovely, handsome, graceful name
Sushri—very splendid, rich
Sushroni—a goddess
Sushsam—smiling face
Sushubha—very pretty, lovely, handsome, graceful and auspicious
Sushumna—holy, pure, sanctified, pious, solemn power
Sushyama—most pretty, lovely, handsome, graceful, well adorned
Susila—wife of krishna, clever
Susita—white
Susma—pretty, lovely, handsome, graceful woman, part of god
Susmita—smiling, sweet smile
Susmiti—pretty, lovely, handsome, graceful smile
Susmi—pretty, lovely, handsome, graceful, amiable
Susneha—who gives love, friendly
Susumna—a dark complexioned
Susvara—sweet voiced
Susvara—with pretty, lovely, handsome, graceful voice
Sutanuka—pretty, lovely, handsome, graceful
Sutanu—pretty, lovely, handsome, graceful
Sutanu—a woman with pretty, lovely, handsome, graceful body
Sutapa—seeker of god
Sutaraka—with pretty, lovely, handsome, graceful stars
Sutara—holy star

Sutarka—with pretty, lovely, handsome, graceful stars
Suta—begotten
Sutharshni—lotus
Suthipha—bright
Sutirtha—lord shiva, the almighty god
Sutithi—good time, moment of good luck
Sutoya—with pretty, lovely, handsome, graceful water
Sutoya—with pretty, lovely, handsome, graceful water river
Sutrama—protecting well
Sutree—bloom, garden stuff
Sutroishi—lady highness, empress, queen
Suvachani—always speamonarch, ruler, prince, earl well
Suvachan—speamonarch, ruler, prince, earl well
Suvacha—speamonarch, ruler, prince, earl well
Suvale—graceful
Suvali—full of grace
Suvama—pretty, lovely, handsome, graceful woman
Suvama—a river
Suvana—melodious, sweet voice
Suvangi—good
Suvanthini—brilliant, sagacious, gifted, wise, learned
Suvan—the sun
Suvarnaprabha—lustre of gold
Suvarnarekha—line of gold, ray of gold
Suvarna—pretty, lovely, handsome, graceful complexion
Suvarna—pretty, lovely, handsome, graceful golden colour, golden
Suvarnmala—golden necklace
Suvarta—good news
Suvasini—pretty, lovely, handsome, graceful fragrance
Suvasu—fragrantn angle
Suvasu—good smell
Suvathini—pretty, lovely, handsome, graceful name

Suveda—very brilliant, sagacious, gifted, wise, learned
Suveira—pretty, lovely, handsome, graceful name
Suvena—nice plait of hair
Suvena—with pretty, lovely, handsome, graceful plait of hair
Suvesha—pretty, lovely, handsome, graceful clothes
Suvetha—welfare, prosperity
Suvida—cultured
Suvidha—ease
Suviksha—wealthy and powerful
Suvisha—beloved one, pretty, lovely, handsome, graceful star
Suvitha—welfare, prosperity,
Suvittee—good knowledge
Suvitti—good knowledge
Suvramoni—purified gem
Suvrana—pretty, lovely, handsome, graceful name
Suvrata—daughter of daksa
Suvrate—very religious
Suvratta—a virtuous lady
Suvra—wife of rukmi
Suvreena—pretty, lovely, handsome, graceful name
Suvreen—pretty, lovely, handsome, graceful, bold
Suvrita—well conducted, virtuous
Suvyooha—a name of heavenly woman
Suvyuha—angel
Suweeta—attitude-less, silent, sweet
Suyashas—very famous
Suyasha—good achievent
Suyati—lord vishnu
Suyesha—innocent
Suyogi—good concentration, timing
Suyosha—perfect woman
Suzainpreet—pretty, lovely, handsome, graceful name
Svabhila—very formidable
Svadha—self power
Svadha—self-power
Svadhe—thoughtful
Svadhi—pretty, lovely, handsome, graceful, thoughtful

Svaha—oblation
Svaha—wife of fire god
Svakritee—good monarch, ruler, prince, earl
Svakritee—permission granted
Svakriti—good monarch, ruler, prince, earl
Svalada—one who gives a little
Svamini—lady of the house
Svana—sound
Svany—pretty, lovely, handsome, graceful like a swan
Svapana—dream
Svapna—dream
Svarashri—respected voice
Svara—goddess of sound
Svarenu—good note
Svarganga—the celestial ganga
Svarnanjali—hands full of gold, prosperity
Svarna—golden
Svarvethe—abode of music
Svastee—fortune
Svati—the wife of the sun
Svayi—pretty, lovely, handsome, graceful name
Svechha—freedom
Svene—pretty, lovely, handsome, graceful name
Svikritee—silver
Svinny—pretty, lovely, handsome, graceful
Svitee—whiteness
Svitra—white
Svra—sweet voice musical tone, tune
Swaachha—purity
Swaarah—interesting, musical notes
Swadha—name of goddess durga
Swadhini—self dependent
Swadhinta—independence
Swadhi—well minded, thoughtful
Swadhurni—ganga
Swagata—welcome
Swagatika—love, welcome
Swagati—welcome
Swaha—wife of agni, the lord of the fire

Swai—pretty, lovely, handsome, graceful name
Swajitha—self victory
Swaksha—pretty, lovely, handsome, graceful eye, glimmers
Swakshi—pretty, lovely, graceful eye, glimmers, lord vishnu
Swamini—devoted toward master
Swamini—female preacher
Swananda—pretty, lovely, handsome, graceful name
Swanandi—from name of lord ganesha
Swani—pretty, lovely, handsome, graceful like a swan
Swapana—dream
Swapanthi—goddess lakshmi
Swapnalatha—sweet
Swapnali—dreamlike
Swapnam—dream
Swapnasundari—dream girl, woman of dreams
Swapna—dream girl
Swapna—dream, dream-like
Swapnika—dream
Swapnita—dream
Swapnshree—prosperous dream
Swapriya—self loving
Swaradhna—pretty, lovely, handsome, graceful name
Swaragi—one who having good voice
Swarajita—freedom
Swarali—sweet voice, happy, radiance
Swarali—sweet voice, sound, goddess
Swaramgi—a musical tone
Swaranbala—of the gold
Swaranchi—the one who is with golden heart
Swarangi—a musical tone
Swaranika—a spice
Swaranjali—musical, gold
Swaranya—like a fairy
Swaraswi—one with sweet voice
Swara—a musical tone, musical notes
Swara—wife of brahma
Swarda—nice vocal quality
Swardhuni—river, holy river ganga
Swargi—heavenly
Swarn-kanta—gold

Swarnakshi—one with golden eye, glimmers
Swarnalakshmi—goddess parvati
Swarnalata—lustrous
Swarnamala—garland of gold
Swarnamisha—pretty, lovely, handsome, graceful voice, eye, glimmers
Swarnamugi—gold
Swarnaprabha—golden illumination, luminosity, radiance
Swarna—gold
Swarne—golden, fair complexioned
Swarnika—fair complexioned, gold
Swarnima—golden
Swarnim—gold
Swarnisha—devotion, pretty, lovely, handsome, graceful, goddess
Swarnprabha—glorious
Swaroop—own image
Swarupa—truth, beauty
Swashti—source of all auspiciousness
Swastee—source of all auspiciousness
Swasthika—goodness
Swasthitha—auspicious
Swasthi—healthy
Swasthya—healthy
Swastikaa—holy sign
Swastika—cherful, lucky, sun, power
Swastik—welfare sign
Swasti—a star, star
Swasty—source of auspiciousness
Swatee—brightest star
Swathini—holy, sanctified, pious, solemn, chaste as a pearl, clean, bright
Swathi—holy, sanctified, pious, solemn, chaste as a pearl star, clean
Swathy—star
Swatika—auspicious beginning
Swati—a star
Swati—valuable, valued, rare drop
Swati—wife of sun
Swayamprabha—own illumination, luminosity, radiance, gods gift
Swayamprabha—own-luster
Swayamvara—woman who has selected her husband own
Swayam—self

Sweat—white, fair, beauty
Swecchha—freedom
Sweena—only mine
Sweeta—lovely, sweet
Sweetie—lovely
Sweeti—lovely
Sweeti—sweet
Sweetu—lovely
Sweety—lovely, happiness
Sweni—river
Sweren—wife of sun
Swesha—holy, sanctified, pious, solemn, chaste
Swetalin—whites holy, sanctified, pious, solemn, chaste as milk

Sweta—as holy, sanctified, pious, solemn, chaste as milk, fair complexioned
Swetha—white, serenity, calm, calmness, stillness, silence, lovely
Swetparna—white leaf
Swikriti—agree
Swini—pretty, lovely, handsome, graceful name
Swity—sweet, happiness
Swra—sweet voice
Swroopa—figure
Sxama—forgiveness
Syetee—white
Syra—princess
Syun—a ray
Syvetashva—with white horse

****

Indian Names For Girls—T

Tabassum—pretty, lovely, handsome, graceful, bloom, garden stuff
Tabasumm—sweet smile, happiness, laughter
Tabbu—height
Tabitha—like a gazelle, roe, beauty
Tabreesha—free as a bird
Tabu—army, excellentrmy body
Tadakayana—fair complexioned
Tadyata—self awareness
Tahani—branch, congratulations, greetings
Tahila—dark, darkness
Tahnyat—congratulate
Taija—crown
Taisha—full of aliveness life
Tajagna—brilliant
Tajana—princess
Tajasri—illumination, luminosity, radiance
Takira—lord, master, goddess durga
Taksha—eye, glimmers like a pigeon
Taksha—pretty, lovely, handsome, graceful name
Takshila—beauty
Takshvi—goddess lakshmi
Talakya—pretty, lovely, handsome, graceful name
Talavali—head pain
Tala—bottom, gold, stalmonarch, ruler, prince, earl wolf
Talika—a bird
Talika—nightingale
Talikha—nightingale, goddess durga
Tallaja—excellent, happiness
Tallen—engrossed
Talli—young, pretty, lovely, handsome, graceful
Taluna—young, wind
Talune—maiden, virgin
Tamalika—belonging to a place full of tamal
Tamali—a tree with very dark bark

Tamana—ambition, intent, passion, desire, aspiration, longing
Tamani—possibility
Tamanna—desire, aspiration, longing bird, ambition, intent
Tamann—ambition, intent, passion
Tamanvi—desirable win
Taman—philosophers stone,
Tamarai—pretty, lovely, handsome, graceful, lotus bloom, garden stuff, great
Tamara—spice, date tree, palm tree
Tamasa—a river, darkness
Tamashree—doughter
Tamasi—night
Tamasvini—night
Tamasvi—darkness
Tamas—fast, creative, young, darkness
Tamaya—in the middle
Tambura—a musical instrument
Tamira—a spice or palm tree, date palm
Tamisha—god form of tamesha
Tamisra—darkness
Tammana—ambition, intent, passion
Tamoghna—lord vishnu, lord shiva
Tamojita—conquer of darkness
Tamrapushpa—name of a river
Tamra—copper, palm tree
Tamrika—coppery
Tamsa—copper-coloured
Tamsi—moon illumination, luminosity, radiance
Tanam—slender, increment
Tanashvi—blessing for richness
Tanasi—pretty, lovely, handsome, graceful princess
Tanasvi—a blessing for richness
Tanatswa—purified
Tanava—a musical instrument
Tanavi—delicate
Tanavya—daughter, cute
Tanaya—daughter
Tana—body

Tandava—violent dance of lord shiva
Tanda—sign
Tandi—beloved
Tandra—a daughter, team
Tandra—fatigue
Tandya—fight
Tanesha—ambition, fairy highness, empress, queen
Taniamitra—friend of fairy highness, empress, queen
Tania—fairy princess
Tanika—rope
Taniksha—golden stone, goddess of gold
Tanima—pretty, lovely, handsome, graceful, god, slenderness
Tanima—slimness
Tanirika—a bloom, garden stuff
Tanisa—nightmbition, born on monday
Tanisha—ambition, ambition, intent, passion, fairy highness, empress, queen
Tanishiqa—graceful, goddess durga
Tanishi—goddess durga, holy, sanctified, pious, solemn, chaste
Tanishka—graceful
Tanishqa—goddess of gold
Tanishree—pretty, lovely, handsome, graceful
Tanish—bloom, garden stuff, happy
Tanisi—cute, goddess durga
Taniska—goddess of gold or angel
Taniya—giant, fairy highness, empress, queen
Tani—encouragement, devotion
Tanmai—sweet, very calm
Tanmanyi—ecstasy
Tanmaya—absorbed, gold
Tanmaya—fully absorbed
Tanmaye—ecstasy, deep
Tanmayi—concentrate
Tanmita—pretty, lovely, handsome, graceful name
Tannishtha—devotion, dedicated
Tannistha—devoted
Tannushri—beauty
Tannu—body, vigour, power
Tannya—fairy, of the family

Tanoobhava—daughter
Tanoo—delicate
Tanseem—salute of paradise
Tanshika—goddess lakshmi
Tansi—pretty, lovely, handsome, graceful princess
Tansnem—a river in paradise
Tantra—treatises on ritual, meditation
Tantrika—ecstasy, engrossed
Tanubhava—daughter
Tanuja—daughter
Tanuja—goddess, daughter, sky
Tanuka—slender, pretty, lovely, handsome, graceful body
Tanuka—slim
Tanukesha—delicate hair
Tanulata—slim, creeper like body
Tanul—river that flows delicately
Tanupa—hunger
Tanupriya—pretty, lovely, handsome, graceful, body lover
Tanurikia—a bloom, garden stuff
Tanusha—a blessing, delicate, special
Tanushiya—soul of god, pride of all
Tanushi—pretty, lovely, handsome, graceful
Tanushka—goddess of gold, goddess
Tanushree—beauty, pretty, lovely, handsome, graceful, sharp pleasant
Tanushree—holy, pure, sanctified, pious, solemn body, pretty, lovely
Tanushri—pretty, lovely, handsome, graceful, pretty
Tanushee—little moon, pretty, lovely, handsome, graceful body
Tanushvi—acceptable
Tanusiya—a great devotee
Tanusree—with a holy, pure, sanctified, pious, solemn body, beauty
Tanusri—with a holy, pure, sanctified, pious, solemn body, beauty
Tanusya—cool wind
Tanuvangi—slim body girl
Tanuvi—a slender woman
Tanu—body
Tanu—body, delicate, sweet, power
Tanvaya—pretty, lovely, handsome, graceful name

Tanver—delicate woman
Tanveta—caring, goddess durga
Tanve—slender, pretty, lovely, handsome, graceful, delicate
Tanvida—pretty, lovely, handsome, graceful name
Tanvija—daughter of the goddess saraswathi
Tanvika—pretty, lovely, handsome, graceful person, goddess durga
Tanvika—gold, goddess durga
Tanvisha—pretty, lovely, handsome, graceful as nature, soft
Tanvita—caring, goddess durga
Tanvitha—goddess lakshmi, goddess saraswati
Tanvi—delicate, goddess of beauty
Tanvi—prosperity, delicate one, love
Tanvi—slim
Tanya—daughter
Tanya—fairy princess, worthy of praise
Tanya—of the family, fairy princess
Tanysha—ambition
Tanzil—princess of god
Tapamita—never do bad
Tapanatanaya—daughter of the sun
Tapanatee—a name of the river
Tapana—illuminating, burning
Tapaniya—a delicate girl
Tapani—heat, a name of the river
Tapani—the river godavari
Tapanti—warming river
Tapara—of the family
Tapasavi—an ascetic
Tapasee—a nakshatra
Tapashvi—a sage
Tapashwini—one who does meditation
Tapasi—a female ascetic
Tapasree—meditation
Tapasvine—a woman who performs penance
Tapasvi—devotee of god
Tapaswine—godavari river
Tapaswi—one who spiritual and meditate of
Tapasya—devotee of god, prayer
Tapasya—worship

Tapatee—warm, heat
Tapati—the sun's daughter
Tapa—penance
Tapi—name of a river in india
Tapi—name of the river
Tapi—sun-daugther
Tapni—a river in india, godavari river
Tapshaya—very long meditation
Tapsi—one doing penance
Tapti—a river
Tapti—name of a river, daughter of sun
Tapti—sun's daughter, a river
Tapushe—a burning weapon
Tapvi—shining
Tarai—rocky hill hill
Taraka—falling star
Taraka—star
Tarakeshwari—name of a river, goddess parvati
Tarakine—night
Tarakini—starry night
Taraksha—star
Tarala—honeybee
Tarala—splendid
Taralikaa—a star
Taralika—star
Taralitaa—goddess parvati
Taralita—shamonarch, ruler, prince, earl
Tarali—group of stars shining in the sky
Taral—to flow
Taramani—starry night
Taramati—wife of monarch, queen
Taramati—with a glorious mind
Taramba—mother star
Tarana—a musical composition
Tarane—a ray of illumination, luminosity, radiance
Taranga—wave
Tarangine—god
Tarangine—river
Tarangini—a river
Tarangini—river
Tarang—a wave
Taranija—river yamuna
Tarani—a boat

Tarani—a ray of illumination, luminosity, radiance, boat, sun
Tarannum—a bloom, garden stuff, pretty, lovely, handsome, graceful, melody
Tarantha—good luck
Taranum—melody
Taranya—among all others
Taran—earth, melody, rocky hill
Tarapushpa—a river, star blossom, jasmine
Tarasha—created
Taras—pretty, lovely, handsome, graceful, thirst
Taravali—a lot of stars
Taravali—a name of river multitude of
Taravanti—from stars
Taravati—having stars
Tara—hillwer, crag, star, rocky
Tara—self luminous
Tara—star
Tarbini—a river
Tareshvari—goddess parvati
Taria—melody
Tarikaa—sage shandilya's daughter
Tarika—a small actress
Tarika—a small star
Tarika—actress, a star
Tarika—starlet
Tarina—pretty, lovely, handsome, graceful bloom, garden stuff, hill
Tarine—enables to cross over, a raft
Tarini-tanaya—daughter of the sun
Tarinira—having the quality of liberation
Tarini—goddess parvati
Tarishi—a raft, boat, the ocean
Tarishi—daughter of indra
Tarita—goddess durga
Tarita—the leader
Tari—hill, fresh, ripe
Tarjani—ring finger, the first finger
Tarjani—the first finger
Tarjni—index finger
Tarka—a star
Tarkeshwari—goddess parvati
Tarla—a bee
Tarla—star, nectar

Tarlika—goddess durga
Tarlika—shamonarch, ruler, prince, earl
Tarli—star
Tarna—lord vishnu
Tarnija—daughter of sun
Tarpana—satiating, refreshing
Tarpani—a tree, river ganga
Tarpini—satisfying
Tarpini—satisfying, offering oblations
Tarra—hill creek, rocky hill
Tarshini—donate
Tarshini—pretty, lovely, handsome, graceful name
Tarulata—a creeper
Tarulata—melted creeper
Tarul—underground fruit
Taruna—young
Taruna—young girl
Tarune—a young woman
Tarune—woman
Tarunikaa—a creeper
Tarunika—young girl
Tarunika—youth
Tarunima—youth
Taruni—a maiden
Taruni—young girl
Tarunlata—young leaf
Tarunya—young girl, youthfulness
Tarusha—pretty, lovely, handsome, graceful name
Tarushe—victory
Tarushi—courages, victory
Tarushree—goddess
Taru—a tree
Taru—tree, myth, legend, destiny
Taryn—combination of tara and erin
Tarz—music, rhythm
Tasha—born on christmas day, young girl
Tashi—prosperity bird of fillumination, luminosity, radiance
Tashmaya—up to her
Tashmayi—up to her
Tashu—pretty, lovely, handsome, graceful
Tashu—kind, cute, talented in many ways

Tashvini—composed, charming, prosperity
Tashvi—composed
Tashvi—composed, charming, prosperity
Tashwini—pretty, lovely, handsome, graceful, brilliant
Tashya—bonding, resurrection
Tasmaya—devotional feeling
Tasmeya—up to her
Taspandra—young girl
Tasu—sacrifice
Tathya—truth
Tatine—bank of the river
Tatini—river
Tatrripi—one who is satisfied
Tatsavi—pretty, lovely, handsome, graceful name
Tatshae—part of shloka, word from shloka
Tatshai—word from mantras
Tatshaye—word taken from sloka
Tatshayi—part of shloka, word from shloka
Tatva—knowledge
Tauhed—victorious
Tavare—lotus
Taveshi—the name of goddess durga
Taviksha—gourageous
Tavisa—victorious
Tavisha—heaven
Tavishi—courage
Tavishi—earth, durga, indra's damsel
Tavishka—courageous
Tayana—a form of taya
Taya—form of tea, valley field
Tayin—name of a river
Tayja—god gift
Tdesire, aspiration, longinga—lustre
Tdesire, aspiration, longingi—lustrous
Teaana—pretty, lovely, handsome, graceful
Teanna—free spirit, pretty, lovely, handsome, graceful mind
Teartha—holy place
Teeksha—sharp
Teekshika—on the name of rashi libra
Teekshna—sharp, lotus

Teena—claynointed
Teenu—illumination, luminosity, radiance star
Teertha—holy place
Teertha—place of pilgrimage holy place
Teesha—thirst, strong-willed, frighten
Teesta—a river
Teesta—a river bridge
Teethi—auspicious date
Tehak—fragrance
Tehihya—pretty, lovely, handsome, graceful name
Tehni—tree branch
Tehya—valuable, valued, rare
Tehzeeb—elegance
Tej-vani—brightness of goddess saraswati
Tejali—bright girl
Tejal—brightness
Tejal—lustrous, water, brightness
Tejamayi—lalithamba's other name
Tejanshi—bright girl
Tejasee—brightness
Tejasee—lustre
Tejashree—brightness, radiant
Tejashree—lustrous beauty
Tejashri—a lady with brightness and luster
Tejashvini—full of brightness
Tejashvita—full of brightness
Tejashvitha—full of brightness
Tejashwini—one who has brightness
Tejashwi—brightness, strong rays of sun
Tejasi—sharpness, brightness, brilliance
Tejaskara—radiant
Tejaskaya—pretty, lovely, handsome, graceful name
Tejaska—radiant
Tejasmita—beauty, brightness
Tejasree—sharpness
Tejasri—illumination, luminosity, radiance
Tejasvati—vigour, grand
Tejasvini—goddess, brilliant
Tejasvita—full of brightness

Tejasvita—one who possesses illumination, luminosity, radiance and splendour
Tejasvi—energetic, gifted, brilliant
Tejaswani—one who spreads illumination
Tejaswari—lalithamba's other name
Tejaswari—lustrous
Tejaswa—pretty, lovely, handsome, graceful
Tejaswine—beauty of lust
Tejaswini—bright, brave, radiant, lustrous
Tejaswini—lustrous
Tejaswita—brightness
Tejaswi—full of illumination, luminosity, radiance
Tejaswi—shining, lustrous
Tejas—brightness, brilliance, sun raise
Tejas—brilliance
Tejata—strong illumination, luminosity, radiance
Tejati—energetic, gifted, brilliant
Tejavati—lustrous
Tejavi—win
Teja—a strong ray of sun, brightness
Teja—luster
Teja—radiant, illumination, luminosity, radiance of moon, love
Tejesh—brilliance, brightness, lustre
Tejeswani—bright
Tejeswari—glorious
Tejeswari—lalithamba's other name
Tejini—a reed, energetic
Tejini—sharp, bright, energetic
Tejita—radiant
Tejiyas—good girl
Teji—bright, very fast, radiant
Tejni—a reed
Tejomayi—bright with shine
Tejomayi—consisting of illumination, luminosity, radiance and splendour
Tejovali—sharp, bright, splendid
Tejsavi—win
Tejshree—with holy, pure, sanctified, pious, solemn power, graceful
Tejshri—of holy, pure, sanctified, pious, solemn powers

Tejshvani—illumination, luminosity, radiance of the words, voice
Tejshwini—full of brightness
Tejsvini—brilliant, goddess
Tejswani—brightness like sun
Tejunya—brightness
Tejusri—brightness, sharpness, brilliance
Tejuswani—brilliant, sagacious, gifted, wise, learned
Teju—luster, bright illumination, luminosity, radiance
Tejvi—full of brightness
Tejwati—splendour
Temin—pretty, lovely, handsome, graceful, one who is honest
Tena—follower of christnointed
Tentuka—pretty, lovely, handsome, graceful name
Tenzing—protector of dharma
Tenzin—protector of dharma
Tesha—survivor
Teshine—pretty, lovely, handsome, graceful name
Tesu—a bloom, garden stuff name
Teta—innocent beauty
Tevana—sister of ravana
Thahiya—gold
Thailammal—name of a goddess
Thaiyal—a lady
Thaiyamma—just like mother
Thaiya—melody
Thaksajini—a god
Thamarai—lotus bloom, garden stuff, holy, sanctified, pious, solemn, chaste and lovely
Thamilselvi—pride of the tamilians
Thamizmari—rain
Thamizvani—pretty, lovely, handsome, graceful name
Thanavi—delicate
Thaneksha—ambition, intent, passion
Thanesha—ambition
Thangamalar—golden bloom, garden stuff
Thangamari—rain of gold, golden rain
Thangammal—golden girl, valuable, valued, rare

Thangathai—gold
Thanga—gold, power
Thanha—alone
Thanigaivalli—wife of god murugan
Thanika—turmeric
Thanima—pretty, lovely, handsome, graceful
Thanirika—goddess of goldngel
Thanisha—ambition
Thanishka—goddess of gold and angel
Thankam—gold in sikh or punjabi
Thanmaya—reincarnated
Thanmaye—awesome
Thanmayi—concentration, ecstasy
Thanmayu—richbsorbed, careful
Thanoushe—a kind, brilliant, sagacious, gifted, wise, learned, helpful
Thansi—the princess
Thanuja—daughter, pretty, lovely, handsome, graceful, brightness
Thanumitha—most pretty, lovely, handsome, graceful
Thanusha—the first sun ray
Thanushka—pretty, lovely, handsome, graceful, brave
Thanushree—beauty
Thanushri—name of a goddess
Thanuvarshini—shining, beauty
Thanvia—gold
Thanvika—goddess durga
Thanvita—great
Thanvitha—caring, cool joy
Thanvi—great, grace, beauty
Thanyasri—love, sincereaffection
Thanyasri—of the family
Thapaswini—name of goddess parvati, highness, empress, queen
Thapasya—silent
Thapswi—yogi, sadhuscetic
Tharaka—dancing stars
Tharane—world
Tharangini—beauty, bird, river
Tharanika—god for earth
Tharani—the earth
Tharani—the earth, love of god
Tharanum—pretty, lovely, handsome, graceful name
Tharanya—shine

Thara—health, wealth
Thara—wealth, star, wife of bali
Tharchana—offers
Tharcika—happy
Tharika—group lets of stars
Tharini—earth
Tharisha—desire, aspiration, longing, ambition, intent, passion
Tharshini—offering
Tharunika—goddess lakshmi
Tharunima—star
Tharushe—victory
Tharu—tree form of goddess parvati
Thaswika—goddess parvati
Thavamani—thavam, varam
Thayammai—pretty, lovely, handsome, graceful name
Thayi—mother
Thdesire, aspiration, longinga—radiance, brightness, beauty
Thejasree—a lady with brightness and luster
Thejasri—pretty, lovely, handsome, graceful name
Thejasvini—bright, energetic, gifted
Thejaswini—horse of brightness
Thekshana—god
Thenammai—honey like mother
Thenmalar—honey bloom, garden stuff
Thenmoli—speaks sweet like honey
Thenral—cool breeze, encouraging
Thertha—valuable, valued, rare water given in temples
Theshne—pretty, lovely, handsome, graceful moodek
Thha—pretty, lovely, handsome, graceful name
Thiksha—bright
Thilagam—a mark in fore head
Thilaka—caring, holy, pure, sanctified, pious, solemn, amiable, pleasing, suave, interesting
Thillaiarasi—mother of world
Thimalini—pretty, lovely, handsome, graceful name
Thiriveni—adding the ganga, yamuna

Thirsha—three stars with illumination, luminosity, radiance
Thirthana—achieved salvation
Thirumagal—goddess lakshmi
Thirumangai—live long
Thivya—star, pretty, lovely, handsome, graceful
Thogai—pretty, lovely, handsome, graceful feathers
Tholakshi—wife of lord shiva, parvati
Thoyalakshi—born in water, goddess lakshmi
Thridha—name of goddess durga
Thrinisha—pretty, lovely, handsome, graceful name
Thrisha—ambition, intent, passion, thirst, power of three
Thrishika—trident
Thrivanika—pretty, lovely, handsome, graceful name
Thrivarna—three colours and three goddesses
Thriveni—where three rivers meet
Thulaja—the kundalini energy of the
Thulasibai—holy plant with sweet fragrance
Thulasi—god tree
Thumri—illumination, luminosity, radiance classical melody
Thuraya—great, star, the planets
Thushara—snow
Thusharika—goddess lakshmi
Thushitha—goddess sarasvati
Tiana—princess, star of family
Tiara—crown, highness, empress, queen, royalty
Tiasa—ambition, intent, passion for illumination, luminosity, radiance, night
Tia—happiness, princess, bird, crown
Tibna—long kite
Tika—spicy
Tikeshwari—pretty, shy
Tikkate—pretty, lovely, handsome, graceful name
Tikshanarashmi—the sun
Tikshana—sharp
Tikshna—a classical melody

Tikshna—sharp
Tilabhavani—pretty, lovely, handsome, graceful
Tilakavati—decorated, river
Tilaka—a kind of necklace
Tilashree—goddess durga
Tilika—auspicious symbol
Tilottama—a celestial maiden, celestial
Tilottamma—guardian of the sun, celestial woman
Timayati—pretty, lovely, handsome, graceful name
Timee—fist
Timila—a music instrument
Timila—a musical
Timsy—star
Tina—little one, river, clay, holy
Tinkal—butterfly
Tinka—heavenly
Tinki—innocent
Tinku—pretty, lovely, handsome, graceful name
Tinuja—illumination, luminosity, radiance star, brighting
Tinu—little one
Tiraya—searching for something
Tira—landuspicious symbol
Tirna—clean, holy, sanctified, pious, solemn, chaste
Tirna—sing pretty, lovely, handsome, gracefully
Tirsha—sight of happiness, joy of life
Tirtharaji—pretty, lovely, handsome, graceful name
Tirthaseva—pretty, lovely, handsome, graceful name
Tirtha—holy place
Tirthi—place of god, place of ram
Tirthya—three gods vishnu
Tisata—beautify others
Tisha—thirst, frighten, be nervous
Tishya—a star
Tista—a river
Tista—a tributary of ganga river
Tistha—a river
Tisya—auspicious
Titas—river

Tithavati—holy, pious river
Tithi—date, timeuspicious date
Tithi—day, date, time
Titiksha—fortitude
Titiksha—illumination, luminosity, radiancelrate, tolerance
Titir—a bird
Titli—butterfly
Titly—butterfly
Tivisha—fire
Tivrananda—pretty, lovely, handsome, graceful name
Tivraya—pretty, lovely, handsome, graceful name
Tivra—intense, strong, vigour
Tivri—auspicious
Tivyapurusha—endurance, tolerance, durability, toleration
Tiyasha—good, little
Tiya—a bird, parrot, pretty, lovely, handsome, graceful
Tizal—brilliant, sagacious, gifted, wise, learned, valuable
Tnishka—goddess of gold
Todara—pretty, lovely, handsome, graceful name
Todika—breamonarch, ruler, prince, earl
Todi—satisfying
Tokavati—pretty, lovely, handsome, graceful name
Tokaya—mountain
Tokini—a bird
Tokma—japan's capital
Tolana—serenity, calm, calmness, stillness, silence
Tomadhara—pretty, lovely, handsome, graceful name
Tomali—tree with very dark bark
Tomara—your own
Tonya—praiseworthy
Toolikaa—cradle
Tooline—the cotton tree
Toral—a folk heroine
Toral—soft
Tora—thunder, tiger
Tori—triumphant, winner, conqueror
Torsha—river in assam, name of river

Torul—rhythm
Toshale—one who satisfy
Toshal—association
Toshana—lover of life
Toshane—satisfying
Toshani—goddess durga
Tosha—contentment, satisfaction
Toshika—clever child
Toshitaa—satisfied
Toshita—satisfying
Toshita—serenity, calm, calmness, stillness, silenceful garden, satisfied
Toshitha—a word in bhagwadgita
Toshitu—satisfied
Toshi—dearestlert, doctor
Toushini—goddess durga
Toyalaya—contented
Toyaneve—the earth
Toyanjali—goddess durga
Toya—watery, woman of victory
Toyika—satisfied
Trapti—satisfaction, part of life
Trariti—agile, efficient
Trasarenu—wife of the sun
Trati—clever
Trayambaka—word from sloka, the three-eye, glimmers
Trayambaki—the three eye, glimmers one
Trayathi—holy, pure, sanctified, pious, solemn protection
Trayi—intellect
Treena—holy, sanctified, pious, solemn, chaste
Treesha—ambition, intent, passion
Treeshita—three lines
Treeshna—thirst
Trejoye—who can win heaven, earth
Treya—monarch, ruler, prince, earl in three path
Treya—monarch, ruler, prince, earl in three paths
Triaksha—three eye, glimmers, goddess durga
Triambika—goddess parvati
Tribhuvaneshwari—goddess of the three worlds
Tridaeshvaree—goddess durga

Tridhara—the river ganga
Tridiva—heaven
Trigarta—woman pearl
Triguna—maya or illusion, goddess durga
Triguni—the three dimensions
Trijagati—goddess parvati
Trijal—combination of rivers
Trikala—pieces
Trikaya—three dimentional
Trilaksha—three eye, glimmers durga
Trilochana—goddess parvati, a woman with three eye, glimmers
Trilochana—three eye, glimmers, lord shiva
Trilochan—goddess durga
Trilokee—three world
Triloki—three dimension
Trilokyadeity—goddess of the worlds
Trilokya—goddess of the three world
Trilottama—goddess durga
Trimatha—goddess parvati, lakshmi,
Trinaa—pretty, lovely, handsome, graceful name
Trinayani—goddess durga
Trina—holy, sanctified, pious, solemn, chaste, short form of katrina
Trinetra—goddess durga
Trinetri—having three eye, glimmers, goddess durga
Tripada—god of fever
Triparna—leaf of sacred bael, three-leafed
Tripathaga—flowing through three regions
Tripa—goddess durga
Tripda—god of fever
Tripta—satisfied
Tripthi—satisfaction, goddess name
Tripti—satisfaction, pretty, lovely, handsome, graceful
Tript—contentment
Tripurasundari—damsel of gold, silver and iron
Tripura—goddess durga
Tripuri—goddess parvati
Triputa—goddess durga
Triput—goddess durga

Trisa—noble
Trishalana—a river in heaven
Trishala—mother of lord mahavir
Trishala—name of the mother of lord mahavira
Trisha—noble woman, power of three sea
Trisha—thirst
Trishika—thirst, brave, pretty, lovely, handsome, graceful, goddess
Trishisa—aristocratic, power of three sea
Trishitaa—goddess parvati
Trishita—thirsty
Trishla—ambition, intent, passion, mother of mahavir
Trishla—mother of mahavir swami
Trishna—ambition, intent, passion
Trishna—thirst
Trishona—ambition, intent, passion
Trishulini—goddess durga
Trishulliene—goddess durga
Trishu—independent, self taught
Trishvi—pretty, lovely, handsome, graceful name
Trista—bold, feminine of tristan noisy
Tritha—pretty, lovely, handsome, graceful name
Tritiya—a river
Triti—gods gift moment in time
Trivarna—pretty, lovely, handsome, graceful name
Trivedha—pretty, lovely, handsome, graceful name
Trivene—trident
Trivene—triple braided
Triveni—confluence of three sacred rivers
Triveni—sangam of three rivers
Trivika—baby
Trivisha—one who knows three vedas
Triyama—night
Triyan—lord shiva, who with three eye, glimmers
Triya—young woman
Tri—third, the third child
Trotakee—a ragini
Trpti—satisfaction

Trripta—contentment, satisfaction
Trriptee—satisfaction
Trrishala—desiring
Trrishana—ambition, intent, passion, thirst
Trrisha—thirst
Trriteeya—third
Trsna—thirst
Trupta—satisfaction, satiated
Trupti—satiated-ness, satisfaction
Trusa—thirst, curiosity
Trusha—thirst
Trusha—thirst, curiosity
Trushita—desirous of profit
Trushna—thirst
Trushti—satisfaction, goddess, satisfied
Tshering—graceful
Tualshi—holy basil plant
Tuhina—snow, cold, dew drop
Tuhira—pretty, lovely, handsome, graceful
Tuhisha—bird sound
Tuhi—bird sound
Tuisha—first ray of moon falling on water
Tuja—thunderbolt
Tujita—pretty, lovely, handsome, graceful
Tulaja—goddess of maharashtra
Tulana—compare
Tulasa—a sacred plant, tulsi plant
Tulasi—a sacred plant basil, clever
Tula—balance zodiac sign, beloved
Tulika—artistic paint brush
Tulika—brush
Tulini—thirst
Tuliphala—bird sound
Tulip—bloom, garden stuff
Tuli—painting brush in oriya
Tulshi—basil plant, the sacred basil
Tulsilata—basil plant
Tulsi—a medicine plant, basil plant
Tulsi—a sacred plant, basil
Tulya—equalled
Tumpa—happy
Tunava—a paint brush
Tungabhadra—name of the river

Tungabhadra—very noble, sacred
Tungavena—loving heights
Tunga—strong
Tunga—strong, plant
Tungee—night
Tungi—night
Tuni—goodness, shower of happiness
Turanya—swift
Turee—a brush of the painter
Turi—a painter's brush, bear
Turvayana—amazing, loyal, brilliant, sagacious, gifted, wise, learned
Turvi—superior
Turyamaya—full of spiritual power
Turya—holy, pure, sanctified, pious, solemn power
Turya—spiritual power
Tusara—cold, frost, snow, mist, dew
Tusarika—pretty, lovely, handsome, graceful name
Tushara—dew drops
Tusharika—water drop, frost, mist
Tusharkana—a particle of snow
Tushar—water drops, hero, snow
Tushika—snowfall
Tushina—satisfaction
Tushita—contented, satisfied
Tushita—satisfied, pleased
Tushitha—satisfied
Tushnika—holy, sanctified, pious, solemn, chaste soul
Tushnimsila—snow particles
Tushnim—pretty, lovely, handsome, graceful name
Tushti—satisfaction
Tushti—sufficiency
Tusi—resurrection
Tusti—serenity, calm, calmness, stillness, silence, happiness
Tutaka—pretty, lovely, handsome, graceful name
Tuvikshatra—aditi
Tuvya—god goodness
Tuya—clean, ray of illumination, luminosity, radiance
Tvadeeya—belongs to lord
Tvarika—swift, quick
Tvarita—goddess durga

Tvarita—swift, fast
Tvesa—brilliant, glittering
Tvesha—brilliant, bright
Tvisha—lustre, spendour
Tvisha—sunshine, perfect, bright
Tvishe—lustrous
Tvishi—beauty of nature, ray of illumination, luminosity, radiance

Twarita—fast
Twesha—bright illumination, luminosity, radiance
Twinkal—star, brightness
Twinkle—sparkle, gleam of eye, glimmers, brilliant
Tyna—rivernointedn instrument

****

Indian Names For Girls—U

Ubika—growth
Ucchal—perception
Uchimakali—one of the hindu god
Uchita—right going girl
Uchita—right thing to do
Uchit—correct
Udaiyal—helping hand
Udakanjali—lustrous
Udantika—great, satisfaction
Udantika—satisfaction
Udanya—growth, rising
Udaramati—noble minded, highly brilliant, sagacious, gifted, wise, learned
Udaranga—endowed with pretty, lovely, handsome, graceful body
Udara—bellies
Udayalakshmi—groth of lakshmi, surya
Udayanati—risen, virtuous, excellent
Udayanjali—virtuous
Udayantee—risen
Udayanti—morally upright
Udayarani—rise
Udayati—daughter of the mountain
Udayavani—goddess saraswati
Udaya—born, rise
Udaya—create a lord, dawn, morning
Udayti—pretty, lovely, handsome, gracefully
Uday—to rise, the beginning, victory
Udbala—strong
Udbhuti—coming forth, live, exist, rise, being, entity
Uddeeptee—illumination, luminosity, radiance
Uddhavi—pretty, lovely, handsome, graceful name
Uddipta—shined
Uddipti—illumination, luminosity, radiance
Udeepti—charming
Udeshne—pretty, lovely, handsome, graceful name

Udgeeta—sung
Udgita—a hymn
Udgiti—group-song
Udhayakala—rising
Udhayamala—morning or garland of sun rise
Udhayarani—rising highness, empress, queen
Udhayasri—raisin sun, first illumination, luminosity, radiance
Udhaya—rising sun, first illumination, luminosity, radiance
Udhgitha—group of lotus bloom, garden stuffs
Udhvitha—sunrise
Udichi—one who grows with prosperity
Udipta—fiery
Udipti—on fire
Udiramalara—fresh bloom, garden stuff
Udisha—morning illumination, luminosity, radiance
Udita—one who has risen
Udita—risen
Uditi—rising
Uditi—rising of the sun
Udit—the rising sun
Udu—water, star
Udvaha—continuing
Udvahne—sparkling, glittering
Udvahni—gleaming, sparkling
Udvita—river filled with lotus bloom, garden stuffs
Udweksha—pretty, lovely, handsome, graceful name
Udyati—elevated
Udyati—elevation
Ugracharine—goddess durga
Ugraduhitrri—daughter of powerful man
Ugragandha—strong fragrance
Ugrajita—one who attain victory over passion

Ugrakali—fierce and black
Ugrakali—goddess durga
Ugrakarnika—large ear-ring
Ugrasene—wife of akroora
Ugrata—anger, violence
Ugrata—violence, passionnger
Ugratejasa—possessing great energy
Ugrateja—one who is energitic
Ugra—strong, goddess kali
Ugra—terrible, powerful
Ugree—angry
Uhana—brighted
Ujala—illumination, luminosity, radiance, luminous
Ujala—illumination, luminosity, radiance, on fire
Ujali—moon, illumination, luminosity, radiance
Ujas—bright, first illumination, luminosity, radiance
Ujhala—illumination, luminosity, radiance
Ujila—bright
Ujila—sunrise
Ujjaini—rising
Ujjala—bright
Ujjal—bright
Ujjam—very cute
Ujjanini—an ancient city
Ujjavala—brightness, cleanliness
Ujjavalita—brightening
Ujjayatee—victorious
Ujjayati—one who has won, victorious
Ujjayati—successful
Ujjayini—an ancient city
Ujjeevayatee—animated
Ujjesha—first, victorious
Ujjesha—victorious
Ujjitee—victory
Ujjiti—victory
Ujjivati—brought to life life
Ujjivyati—restored to life
Ujjootita—with upgoing hair
Ujjrrimbhita—stretched
Ujjvala—bright, shining
Ujjvala—grandeur, shining
Ujjwala—bright, lustrous
Ujjwalkeerti—bright

Ujvalata—splendour, radiant, beauty
Ujvala—bright, illumination, luminosity, radiance, lustrous
Ujvalita—illumination, luminosity, radiance, shining
Ujval—bright
Ujwala—illumination, luminosity, radiance, bright, lustrous
Ujwani—he who wins the struggle
Uktharka—hymn of the sun
Ukthashansin—one who recite hymn
Uktika—act of creativity
Ukti—method, speech
Ulagammal—mother of the world
Ulapa—lustre, brightness
Ulasa—happiness
Ulas—joyful
Ulhasine—cherful person
Ulhasini—bright, illumination, luminosity, radiance
Ulka—a meteor
Ulka—meteorite, wealthy
Ulkushi—meteor
Ullalagi—with inner beauty
Ullasine—a happiest
Ullekh—one who is always cherful
Ullupi—pretty face
Ulookee—female owl
Uloopee—one who has pretty, lovely, handsome, graceful face
Ulupika—free falling rocks
Ulupi—arjuna's wife
Ulupi—wife of arjuna, the pandava prince
Ulupya—pretty face
Umadeity—pretty face, goddess parvati
Umaimah—little mother
Umaima—pretty face
Umaiyal—god
Umai—goddess parvathi
Umakanta—goddess parvati
Umakant—lord ganesh
Umalakshmi—goddess parvati
Umali—enchantress
Umamaheswari—goddess parvati
Umangini—full of happiness, joy
Umangi—happy

Umang—happiness, aspiration
Umang—happiness, enthusiasm
Umarani—goddess parvati, highness, empress, queen of highness, empress, queen
Umasankari—goddess parvati
Umasri—goddess parvati
Umati—helpful
Umayal—goddess parvati
Uma—goddess parvati
Uma—goddess parvati, durga, nation
Umber—moon
Umeeka—pretty girl
Umeksha—pretty, lovely, handsome, graceful name
Umesha—support, indoctrination, assuredness
Umika—goddess parvati
Umiksha—pretty, lovely, handsome, graceful name
Umlocha—eyes, eyes are questioning
Umrao—noble
Unaisa—sweetheart
Unisha—pretty, lovely, handsome, graceful name
Unita—oneness, sisterly unites
Unjali—blessing
Unkushe—exercising restraint
Unmada—passionate beauty
Unmadine—intoxicating
Unma—joy
Unmeelan—pretty, lovely, handsome, graceful name
Unmuktee—deliverance
Unmukti—deliverance
Unnamulai—goddess parvati
Unnatee—progress
Unnathi—progressive, progress
Unnati—progress
Unnati—progress, prosperity
Unni—lead, modest
Unnti—progress, development
Unntti—progress
Upaasana—prayer
Upabhuktee—enjoyment
Upada—a gift present, offering
Upada—offering
Upadhriti—a ray

Upadhrritee—ray of illumination, luminosity, radiance
Upaghaya—knowledge
Upagya—joy
Upala—sandy shore, stone, gem
Upama—comparison, simile
Upama—example, comparison, respectful
Upaneti—initiation
Upangana—possessing intimate knowledge
Upanya—rare piece of art
Uparnika—good
Upasana—fasting, devotion, homage
Upasana—worship, prayer
Upasa—homagedoration, worship
Upashanta—a ray
Upashanti—sandy shore
Upashna—fasting
Upashruti—one who listen attentively
Upasna—worship, veneration, sadhana
Upasti—adoration, worship
Upavena—with small tributaries
Upda—gift
Updeshna—give instruction in spiritual matters
Upeksha—a kind of yoga
Upeksha—waiting wait patiently
Upendra—sister of lord indra
Uphar—gift
Upma—example
Upmiti—knowledge
Upsana—prayer
Ura—heart
Ura—the heart, earth, love
Urevijya—victory of the earth
Urishilla—excellent
Urishita—firm
Urjani—belonging to energy
Urjaswati—the best
Urjaswitaa—earth
Urja—energy
Urja—energy, power
Urjita—excited, energetic
Urma—lovely, beloved
Urmesha—pretty, lovely, handsome, graceful name
Urmika—ring, wave

Urmika—small wave
Urmilarani—wife of laxman
Urmila—god's bird, enchantres
Urmila—wife of lakshman
Urmil—wife of lakshmana
Urmimala—pretty, lovely, handsome, graceful, garland of waves
Urmiya—goddess of illumination, luminosity, radiance
Urmi—illumination, luminosity, radiance, rays
Urmi—wave
Urmya—night
Urna—cover
Urshila—outstanding
Urshita—determined confident person
Ursula—strong as a little bear
Urti—earth
Uruchaksha—big eye, glimmers
Uruchaksha—wife of sage marichi
Urukeerti—a far reaching fame
Urukirti—of far reaching fame
Urunjira—one who pleases the heart
Urunjira—pleaser of heart
Uruta—vastness
Uruvi—great
Uru—big
Urvara—fertilized
Urvashe—firm, steady
Urvashi—an apsara
Urvashi—to rise, celestial maiden
Urvasi—most pretty, lovely, handsome, graceful of apsaras
Urva—a sage
Urva—huge, big
Urveja—born of the earth
Urven—sam, sdw
Urvesha—lord of the earth
Urve—fertile land
Urve—the earth
Urvijaa—a celestial dancer name
Urvijaya—the ganges
Urvija—born of the earth
Urvija—goddess lakshmi, earth
Urvisha—rainy cloud, highness, empress, queen, lord of the
Urvi—princess, earth

Urvshi—to rise, most pretty, lovely, handsome, graceful women
Urwashi—most pretty, lovely, handsome, graceful apsaras
Usaravali—bright, gold
Ush-rani—sun rays
Ushadeity—earth
Ushakanta—dawn
Ushakant—the sun
Ushakiran—rays of morning sun
Ushakiran—the first ray of the sun at dawn
Ushalakshi—sun illumination, luminosity, radiance
Ushana—dawn
Usharani—daughter of heaven
Usharvi—raga in the morning
Ushasee—twiillumination, luminosity, radiance
Ushashi—morning
Ushasree—pretty, lovely, handsome, graceful name
Ushas—day break
Usha—evening
Usha—joy, sun rise, dawn, happiness
Usheha—desiring
Usheka—one who worship at dawn
Usheta—a person who dwells
Ushija—lovely, charmingmiable
Ushika—love, dawn worshipper
Ushi—a plant
Ushi—ambition, intent, passion, desire, aspiration, longing
Ushma—energy
Ushma—heat, warmth, fire, summer
Ushmil—warm hearted
Ushmi—energy, heat
Ushnaa—heat
Ushna—warmctive, innocent, pretty, lovely, handsome, graceful
Ushnima—heat, splendour
Ushta—everlasting happiness
Usma—pretty, lovely, handsome, graceful, spring, warmth
Usmita—determine
Usra—first illumination, luminosity, radiance
Usri—name of river

Utalika—wave
Utalita—opened, blossoming, brilliant
Utanika—ambition, intent, passion, longing
Utanka—warmth
Uthami—honest
Uthra—wife of warrior abhimanyu
Uthviksha—pretty, lovely, handsome, graceful name
Utika—rising
Uti—desire, aspiration, longing, ambition, intent, passion
Uti—help
Utkala—exellence
Utkala—one who comes from odisha
Utkalita—opened, loosened
Utkanika—ambition, intent, passion
Utkantha—strong ambition, intent, passion
Utkanti—excessive splendour
Utkanti—splendour
Utkarika—made of a valuable, valued, rare metal
Utkarsha—prosperity, proud progress, proud
Utkarsh—progress, height, happiness
Utkartini—fulfilling one's ambitions
Utkhala—perfume
Utkhala—perfumed
Utkuja—a cooling note

Utpalakshe—best
Utpalakshe—lotus eye, glimmers
Utpalakshi—goddess lakshmi
Utpalavati—made of lotuses
Utpala—lotus
Utpala—lotus, water lily
Utpalini—lotus pond, lake of lotuses
Utpatti—creation
Utprabha—sun, illumination, luminosity, radiance
Utpreksha—indifference
Utsah—goddess lakshmi
Utsava—festival
Utsavi—joyful, festive
Utsa—spring, fountain
Utsha—joyfully
Utsuka—excitement
Uttama—best, excellent, eminent
Uttamika—best worker
Uttaragita—enthusiasm, zeal
Uttara—daughter of monarch, ruler, prince, earl virata star
Uttarika—crossing river, coming out
Uttira—downward
Uttiya—a star
Uvanjana—greenery
Uvigna—pretty, lovely, handsome, graceful name
Uzma—greatest, grand, ultimate, absolute, highest, best

****

Indian Names For Girls—V

Vacasya—readiness of speech
Vachana—oath, speech, utterance
Vachana—spoken words, speech
Vachasri—pretty, lovely, handsome, graceful name
Vacha—speech
Vachi—goddess lakshmi
Vachya—blamed, goddess sita
Vachya—expressed
Vadhana—face
Vadhi—devotion
Vadhu—bride
Vadhu—bride, daughter in law
Vadika—restoring knowledge
Vadivambal—pretty, lovely, handsome, graceful name
Vadivazhagi—promise, word
Vadivukarasi—lord ranganatha
Vadivu—expressed, pretty, lovely, handsome, graceful
Vadya—clouds
Vaethisha—pretty, lovely, handsome, graceful name
Vagada—goddess saraswati
Vagai—name of pretty, lovely, handsome, graceful bloom, garden stuff
Vagavadine—one who takes part in discussion
Vagda—goddess saraswati
Vagdeity—goddess of learning
Vagdeity—goddess of speech
Vagdeity—goddess saraswati
Vageshwari—goddess of speech
Vageshwari—goddess saraswati
Vagheshwaree—goddess durga
Vagini—good speaker
Vagisha—goddess saraswati
Vagishwari—goddess durga
Vagmine—doughter of goddess saraswati
Vagmi—name of god vishnu
Vagula—awesome
Vaguna—a powerful dragon

Vahila—name of air
Vahine—flowing
Vahine—lustering
Vahini—flowing
Vaibavi—landlord, rich person
Vaibhave—richness, goddess lakshmi
Vaibhavi—richness, brilliant, sagacious, gifted, wise, learned
Vaibhvi—knowledge, wealthy
Vaibhvi—tich person
Vaichali—who has everything
Vaidahi—goddess sita
Vaidarbhe—grass
Vaidarbhi—rukhmini, wife of krishna
Vaidavi—knowledge
Vaidehi—a name of sita
Vaidehi—goddess sita, wife of lord rama
Vaidharbhe—rukmani
Vaidhe—goddness sita
Vaidhi—sita mata
Vaidhoorya—a river
Vaidhriti—properly adjusted
Vaidika—knowledge of ved
Vaiga—goddess parvati river in
Vaihayasi—aerial
Vaiishale—the great princess, fortunate
Vaijantimala—prize, garland of lord vishnu
Vaijanti—flag, banner, bloom, garden stuff
Vaijayanthi—prize, garland of lord vishnu
Vaijayantika—a garland of pearl
Vaijayantimala—garland of vaijayanti bloom, garden stuff
Vaijayantimala—garland of victory
Vaijayanti—a garland of lord vishnu, prize
Vaijayanti—flag
Vaikha—goddess parvathi
Vaikuntha—heaven
Vaikunthi—from heaven

Vainavi—gold
Vairagi—detached
Vairocana—pretty, lovely, handsome, graceful name
Vaisakhi—auspicious day in punjab
Vaisali—goddess
Vaishakhi—a hindu festival
Vaishakhi—who support others, festival
Vaishale—a river
Vaishalini—great
Vaishali—fortunate
Vaishali—great
Vaishanavi—worshipper of lord vishnu
Vaishanvi—goddess parvati
Vaishavi—goddess parvati
Vaishika—pretty, lovely, handsome, graceful name
Vaishnava—the devotee or consort of lord vishnu
Vaishnave—shakthi rupam
Vaishnavi—lord vishnu's worshipper
Vaishnavi—worshipper of lord vishnu
Vaishnodeity—goddess durga
Vaishno—goddess parvati
Vaishnvi—goddess
Vaishnwi—worshipper of lord vishnu
Vaishonavi—goddess name
Vaishu—goddess lakshmi
Vaishve—pretty, lovely, handsome, graceful name
Vaishvini—goddess
Vaishvi—goddess parvati
Vaishwanaree—omnipresent
Vaish—worshipper of lord vishnu
Vaisnavi—worshipper of vishnu
Vaisvi—belonging to the world
Vaitarani—to cross over to the other world
Vaitarni—a river in paradise
Vaitehi—pretty, lovely, handsome, graceful name
Vaivasvati—belonging to the sun, river yamuna
Vaivaswatee—belonging to the sun
Vaivi—individual
Vaji—strong

Vajramala—with a diamond necklace
Vajrashri—holy, pure, sanctified, pious, solemn diamond
Vajra—diamond
Vajra—goddess durga
Vajreshwari—buddhist goddess
Vaka—speech
Vakine—one who speaks
Vakini—one who recites
Vaksani—vigourening
Vaksi—nourishment, flame
Vakula—a bloom, garden stuff
Vakula—bloom, garden stuff
Vakuli—a bloom, garden stuff tree
Vakul—mythological bloom, garden stuff
Vak—speech, the spoken word
Valakaa—pretty, lovely, handsome, graceful name
Valambigai—goddess
Valarmathi—growing moon
Valarpirai—moon in ascension, encouraging
Valayi—a girl, mischievous girl
Valguki—very pretty, lovely, handsome, graceful
Valika—diamond
Valine—tailed constellation
Valini—stars
Vallabai—beloved
Vallabha—beloved
Vallabhe—beloved
Vallabhe—loving, beloved, hindu god
Vallabhi—beloved
Vallakee—musical instrument
Vallaki—a lute
Vallaree—strong, healthy
Vallari—goddess parvati, creeper
Vallari—of the bloom, garden stuffs
Valle—wife of subrahmanya
Valliammai—wife of lord murugan
Vallika—creeper
Vallika—earth
Vallimayil—goddess sita
Vallini—a creeper
Valli—a creeper
Valli—bloom, garden stuff, vine,

pretty, lovely, handsome, graceful goddess
Vamaakshe—goddess of learning
Vamaa—come
Vamakshe—with pretty, lovely, handsome, graceful eye, glimmers
Vamakshi—pretty, lovely, handsome, graceful eye, glimmers
Vamakshi—with pretty, lovely, handsome, graceful eye, glimmers
Vamalochna—fair eye, glimmers
Vamanie—power of sky, land and water
Vamani—dwarf
Vama—pretty, lovely, handsome, graceful
Vama—a mythological character
Vama—woman
Vamdeity—goddess durga, savitri
Vamika—goddess durga
Vamil—pretty, lovely, handsome, graceful
Vamita—kiran, river
Vamsee—flute of sri krishna
Vamshika—flute
Vamshitha—flute
Vamsi—flute of lord krishna
Vamya—big of big, great
Vamya—great, big of big
Vanadeve—goddess of forest, wood, jungle
Vanadhi—milky way
Vanadurga—goddess parvati
Vanaika—loving
Vanajadeity—pretty, lovely, handsome, graceful eye, glimmers
Vanajakshi—blue lotus eye, glimmers
Vanajaksi—blue lotus eye, glimmers
Vanaja—daughter of forest, wood, jungle, forest, wood, jungle girl
Vanaja—forest, wood, jungle girl
Vanajyoti—goddess durga
Vanalakshmi—goddess of the woods
Vanalika—sunbloom, garden stuff
Vanamala—garland of forest, wood, jungle
Vanamala—garland of forest, wood, jungles

Vanamallika—highness, empress, queen of the forest, wood, jungle
Vanamalli—wild jasmine
Vanani—forest, wood, jungle
Vanapushpa—bloom, wood, jungle, wild bloom, garden stuff
Vanasarojini—the wild cotton plant
Vanashree—sunbloom, garden stuff
Vanashree—wealth of the wood
Vanasundari—forest, wood, jungle beauty
Vanathe—of the forest, wood, jungle
Vanathi—of the forest, wood, jungle
Vanca—desire, aspiration, longing, ambition, intent, passion
Vancha—ambition, intent, passion
Vandanai—beloved of the woods
Vandana—prayer, worship, obeisance
Vandana—worship, respect
Vandaneya—adorable
Vandaneya—saluted
Vandane—goddess of vegetation
Vandane—worship
Vandani—adoration
Vanda—a plant
Vandineka—honoured
Vandita—respected
Vandita—saluted, worshipped
Vanditha—prayer, beginner
Vandna—salutationdoration, worship
Vandurga—goddess of forest, wood, jungles
Vandya—adorable
Vandya—worthy of salutation
Vanesa—holy, sanctified, pious, solemn, chaste
Vanesha—highness, empress, queen of the universe
Vanet—slender, brilliant, sagacious, gifted, wise, learned
Vaneza—cute
Vangmatee—goddess saraswati
Vangmaye—holy, sanctified, pious, solemn, chaste and sweet voice
Vangmaye—pretty, lovely, handsome, graceful name
Vanhishikha—flame
Vanhi—fire

Vania—butterfly
Vanii—goddess saraswati
Vanika—eloquent in words, sound
Vanika—sita
Vanila—flavour
Vanini—soft spoken
Vanipriya—respectable
Vanisha—highness, empress, queen of the universe
Vanisha—holy, chaste cute, highness, empress, queen of the universe
Vanishka—highness, empress, queen of the universe
Vanishree—goddess saraswathi, pretty, lovely, handsome, graceful
Vanishri—goddess saraswati
Vanishta—saraswati
Vanisree—goodness
Vanisri—goddess saraswati
Vanita—a woman
Vanita—woman, graceful lady
Vanithasri—goddess lakshmi
Vanitha—graceful lady, goddess saraswati
Vani—goddess saraswati
Vani—guru's voice, speech
Vani—speech, voice, muse
Vani—voice
Vanjan—wildbloom, garden stuff garland, graceful lady
Vanja—blue lotus
Vanjikodi—daughter of raja shanmugavel
Vanjimagan—pretty, lovely, handsome, graceful name
Vanjula—a name of the river
Vanjul—beauty of the forest, wood, jungle
Vanksha—pretty, lovely, handsome, graceful name
Vanksu—a tributary of the ganges
Vanlataa—pretty, lovely, handsome, graceful name
Vanlata—a creeper in forest, wood, jungle
Vanmaala—jungle garland
Vanmala—garland of the forest, wood, jungle

Vanmala—wildbloom, garden stuff garland
Vanmalli—wild bloom, garden stuff
Vanmathi—highly knowledgeable
Vanmayi—goddess saraswati
Vannakili—wild bloom, garden stuff
Vanni—goddess saraswati, grace
Vanshalakshmi—the wealth of the family
Vansha—dauther, family, offsping
Vansha—offspring, daughter, descendant
Vanshe—flute
Vanshika-sahasra—flute of lord krishna
Vanshika—flute
Vanshika—flute, forwarding of generation
Vanshikha—forwarding the generation
Vanshita—enchanting
Vanshi—flute
Vansika—forwarding the generation
Vansita—goddess of forest, wood, jungle
Vansni—illumination, luminosity, radiance of a family
Vantika—smart, from the forest, wood, jungle
Vanti—smart
Vanuja—pretty, lovely, handsome, graceful girl of forest, wood, jungle
Vanusha—rain
Vanvitha—pretty, lovely, handsome, graceful name
Vanvi—tree
Vanya—goddess belonging to the forest, wood, jungle
Vanya—idle daughter
Vapra—bed of garden
Vapusa—nature, beauty
Vapusha—a goddess, pretty, lovely, handsome, graceful, nature
Vapushe—beauty personified as a daughter
Vapu—body
Varada—goddess lakshmi
Varada—goddess lakshmi, one who got

Varadhadeity—one having pretty, lovely, handsome, graceful body
Varahi—goddess parvati
Varajakshe—lotus eye, glimmers
Varajakshi—with lotus eye, glimmers
Varalakshmi—goddess lakshmi, rich
Varalakshmi—the consort of lord vishnu
Varalika—goddess durga
Varali—moon
Varanana—pretty, lovely, handsome, graceful face
Varana—a river
Varana—surrounding
Varangana—pretty, lovely, handsome, graceful woman
Varangee—days vise
Varangee—tumeric
Varangi—one who possesses pretty, lovely, handsome, graceful body
Varangi—with an elegant body
Varangna—pretty, lovely, handsome, graceful woman
Varanika—pearl
Varanmaala—pretty, lovely, handsome, graceful name
Varanya—forest, wood, jungle, goddess lakshmi
Vararoha—elegant
Vararoha—goddess lakshmi
Varastri—noble woman
Varasya—ambition, intent, passion
Varati—moon
Varavarnine—fair and beautiful complexion
Varayoshita—pretty, lovely, handsome, graceful woman
Vara—blessing, goddess parvati
Vara—boon
Vara—goddess parvati
Varbi—original, holy, sanctified, pious, solemn, chaste
Varcha—goddess durga
Varcha—power, bloom, garden stuff
Varcheka—pretty, lovely, handsome, graceful name
Vardani—goddess durga
Varda—granting boons

Varda—increasing deity river
Vardhini—blossom, happiness lovely lady
Varenya—goddess parvati, desirable
Varidhi—speech
Varidi—treasure of water
Varijaa—water born ie lotus
Varija—lotus, born in water
Varij—high, lotus
Varine—a woman
Varini—rich in gifts
Varishapriya—lotus
Varisha—love, rain, the rainy season
Varisha—rainy season, rain
Varivasya—service, devotion, honour
Vari—river
Vari—water, sea, crop
Varnali—lotus
Varnamalika—rain
Varnana—description
Varnarpriya—colour
Varna—goddess saraswati, colours
Varnika—fire colour, holy, sanctified, pious, solemn, chaste gold
Varnika—holy, sanctified, pious, solemn, chaste
Varnisha—garnishing, pretty, lovely, handsome, graceful night, rain
Varni—pretty, lovely, handsome, graceful, colours
Varni—colourful
Varnu—coloured
Varouna—pretty, lovely, handsome, graceful name
Varsa—rain, monsoon
Varshana—birth place of radha
Varshani—pretty, lovely, handsome, graceful name
Varshati—rain
Varsha—rain
Varsha—rain, shower, year
Varsheni—one who brings rain, rain
Varshica—rained goddess
Varshika—a goddess name, rain
Varshika—the dress of an actress
Varshikha—the dress of an actress
Varshini—the one who brings rain

Varshiny—holy, pure, sanctified, pious, solemn
Varshitaa—rained
Varshita—rain, raining, pretty, lovely, handsome, graceful
Varshita—rained
Varshitha—rained, pretty, lovely, handsome, graceful, showered
Varshnika—year, rain, shower
Varshya—rained
Varsni—rained
Vartika—a figure, appearance, structure, goddess, lamp, deep
Varudhini—name of god
Varuhi—pretty, lovely, handsome, graceful name
Varunanai—doughter of rain, doughter of sky
Varunane—goddess of water
Varunavi—goddess lakshmi
Varuna—a river
Varuna—wife of the lord of the sea
Varune—the rain
Varunika—goddess of rain
Varunisha—rain
Varuni—goddess durga
Varuni—wife of lrod of the sea
Varuni—wife of the lord of the sea
Varunya—goddess durga
Varusha—year, rain
Varushka—giver of happiness
Varutree—protectress
Varutri—protector
Varya—form, treasure, valuable, valued, rare, foreign
Varya—water born
Vasaki—goddess lakshmi
Vasalika—attraction
Vasana—good smell, pleasant smell
Vasantabrabha—spring blossom
Vasantaprabha—spring blossom
Vasanta—spring
Vasantee—spring
Vasanthadeity—form
Vasantham—spring
Vasantha—spring, goddess of rain
Vasanthi—of spring
Vasantikar—a ragni

Vasantika—goddess of spring
Vasanti—of the spring
Vasanti—spring festival, durga
Vasanti—vaidehi, of spring, happy, spring
Vasanti—youthful
Vasant—season, spring
Vasatee—down
Vasatika—morning illumination, luminosity, radiance
Vasati—dawn
Vasave—treasury
Vasavi—lord indra's wife
Vasavi—respect, wife of lord indra
Vashanta—spring, goddess of rain, spring
Vashanti—one who belongs to spring season
Vasha—agree, control
Vasha—willing, under control
Vashika—the one who can control
Vashini—attaractive
Vashini—to live somewhere
Vashishka—without fear
Vashista—lakshmi
Vashnie—a beloved blessing
Vashti—lovely, pretty, lovely, handsome, graceful
Vashudha—earth
Vashudha—pretty, lovely, handsome, graceful name
Vashundra—earth, daughter of earth
Vashya—under control
Vasishta—maharshin ancient guru , rishi
Vasistha—without fear, saint
Vasmika—to submit
Vastrri—illuminating
Vasuda—earth
Vasuda—the earth
Vasudeva—goddess of wealth
Vasudhara—daughter of earth, goddess lakshmi
Vasudha—collector of wealth, earth
Vasudha—earth
Vasudhitee—one who is prosper
Vasudhi—earth, goddess lakshmi

Vasuki—monarch, ruler, prince, earl of snake, snake of lord shiva
Vasulakshmi—goddess of wealth
Vasumathi—giver of wealth
Vasumati—apsara of unequalled splendour
Vasumati—the earth
Vasumitha—brightest friend
Vasundara—pretty, lovely, handsome, graceful name
Vasundhara—earth
Vasundhara—world, earth
Vasundhareye, glimmers—daughter of the earth
Vasundhra—earth, similar to vasundhara
Vasundra—apsara of unequalled splendour
Vasuprada—bestower of wealth
Vasuta—prosperous
Vasu—lord vishnu, wealth
Vasve—earth
Vasvi—of the god
Vathani—earth
Vathsala—giving love to everyone
Vati—nature
Vatoo—one who speaks the truth
Vatsadeity—goddess
Vatsala—beloved
Vatsala—love form parentsffectionate
Vatsalika—affectionate
Vatsalika—nature
Vatsalya—motherly love
Vatsalya—wife of vyas, loving nature
Vatsa—calf, young one
Vatsa—daughter
Vatsla—daughter, loving
Vatya—storm
Vavdita—a person who is praised by others
Vaya—a branch
Vayshali—name of the city in india
Vayuna—active, moving
Vayuna—movinglive, knowledge, wisdom
Vayu—loving, wind godir
Vea—chief, seen

Veda-varshini—wisdom, who brings rain
Veda-varshitha—monsoon
Vedabha—obtained
Vedabha—obtained from knowledge
Vedachandrika—pretty, lovely, handsome, graceful name
Vedadharma—good justice
Vedaini—knowledge
Vedai—admire of knowledge
Vedakshari—pretty, lovely, handsome, graceful name
Vedakshe—the one who knows knowledge
Vedamantra—memory of the vedas
Vedananda—the brilliant, sagacious, gifted, wise, learned
Vedanayagam—original name of sita, knowledge
Vedana—perception
Vedangi—a part of vedas
Vedangi—part of vedas
Vedankita—serenity, calm, calmness, stillness, silenceful storey
Vedanki—filled with vedas
Vedanshi—the scared knowledge
Vedansita—part of veda's
Vedansi—the scared knowledge
Vedanta—the last knowledge of vedas
Vedantika—knowing vedas
Vedanti—wisdom, follower of the vedas
Vedapunya—best work according to veda
Vedashine—one who carry wealth
Vedashree—pretty, lovely, handsome, graceful, goddess saraswati
Vedashri—beauty of the vedas
Vedashruti—famous in the vedas
Vedashya—the one who knows knowledge
Vedasini—carrying wealth river
Vedasmrita—one who remember scriptures
Vedasmriti—loveffection
Vedasmriti—memory of the veda
Vedasri—beauty of the vedas, goddess

Vedasya—the one who knows knowledge
Vedavalli—language of vedas
Vedavathi—familiar with the vedas
Vedayasana—admire of knowledge
Veda—famous
Veda—understanding
Vedehi—goddess sita
Vedeshva—a name of the river
Vedeshva—a river, born of the vedas
Vedham—a truthful person
Vedhari—goddess saraswati
Vedhashree—goddess saraswati
Vedhasree—goddess saraswati
Vedhasya—worship, piety
Vedhavalli—name of god
Vedha—pious, truth
Vedhika—stage knowledge
Vedigna—full of knowledge
Vedika—a river in india
Vedine—an apsra
Vedine—feeling, knowing
Vedisha—lord of vedas
Veditha—goddess lakshmi, goddess saraswati
Vediti—pretty, lovely, handsome, graceful name
Vedi—altar knowledge
Vedna—knowledge, perception, pain
Vedu—true speaker, understanding
Vedvalli—joy of the vedas
Vedya—knowable, what is to be known
Veedhi—method, law, goddess of destiny
Veeharika—flying
Veeha—serenity, calm, calmness, stillness, silence, heaven
Veeksha—knowledge
Veeksha—vision, knowledge
Veekshitha—developed
Veenadeity—joy of the
Veenadhari—goddess saraswati
Veenagana—consciousness
Veenakumari—vedas
Veenapani—goddess saraswati
Veenarani—song from vena
Veenavani—goddess saraswati

Veena—a musical instrument, instrument
Veenela—moon
Veenila—moon illumination, luminosity, radiance, blue sky, moon
Veenu—musical, respect
Veeraj—biggest in universe
Veeralakshmi—goddess parvati
Veeral—brave
Veerambal—pretty, lovely, handsome, graceful name
Veerangana—brave
Veeranna—desert
Veerasundari—goddess of bravery
Veera—brave, devotion, truth
Veerbala—brave girl
Veerini—pretty, lovely, handsome, graceful name
Veerupakshi—goddess parvati
Veesha—well behaved, polite
Veethikasri—love
Veethika—a sub-way
Veethika—nerve in brain
Veethi—way
Veeti—lustre
Vegadhya—radha name
Vegavati—rapid river
Vega—falling star, meadow, plant
Veghana—rain
Vegine—a river, going fast
Veidika—one who has knowledge of the vedas
Vekshana—daksha's wife name
Vekuri—good accompany
Velanila—pretty, lovely, handsome, graceful name
Velayani—pretty, lovely, handsome, graceful name
Velayi—melodious
Vela—beginning, time, starting
Vela—shore, bank, boundary
Velli—silver
Velunachiyar—time, season
Velvizhi—spear like eye, glimmers
Vemmati—a river
Venah—pining
Vena—excitement
Vency—pony, sun ray

Venela—moon illumination, luminosity, radiance
Vene—river, near
Venikara—pining
Venika—flowing stream
Venika—holy river
Venisha—dedicated
Venishka—amiable, pleasing, suave, queen of the universe
Venita—goddess of love and beauty, ambition, intent, passion
Veni—braid, moon illumination, luminosity, radiance
Veni—lord krishna
Venkatesh—lord venkateshwara
Vennela—illumination, luminosity, radiance
Vennila—moon, enchanting
Vennmathi—holy river
Vennmukil—white cloud
Venpa—poem, classical form
Venshika—brave, glorious
Venugeeta—devotional song
Venukashree—flute
Venukashri—pretty, lovely, handsome, graceful name
Venuka—flute
Venukiya—pretty, lovely, handsome, graceful name
Venusha—pretty, lovely, handsome, graceful name
Venu—goddess saraswati, bansari
Venya—desirable
Venya—god gifted, amiable, pleasing, suave, interesting
Verkanni—pretty, lovely, handsome, graceful name
Vernika—pretty, lovely, handsome, graceful name
Verni—colourful
Veronica—one who brings victory
Versha—rain
Vershitha—pretty, lovely, handsome, graceful name
Vertika—lamp
Veshadana—song of the flute
Veshalini—rinds
Veshana—flute

Veshanta—pretty, lovely, handsome, graceful name
Veshpa—amiable, pleasing, suave, interesting
Veshtita—love, heart, wonderful
Vetali—goddess durga
Vetasini—arth
Vetasi—varsini
Vetha—truth
Vetravatee—pretty, lovely, handsome, graceful name
Vetravati—a river in india, name of river
Vetravati—door keeper
Vetrichelvi—name of celesital dancer
Vetri—victory
Viaana—full of life
Vibale—young
Vibali—young, sweet
Vibhangini—radiance, illumination, luminosity, radiance, sunshine
Vibhanshi—sunshine, radiant, illumination, luminosity, radiance
Vibhasatika—smiling, laughing
Vibhashri—sunshine, radiant
Vibhasvati—brilliant
Vibhavana—daughter of night
Vibhavaree—illuminating, glory, night full of stars
Vibhavari—starry night
Vibhavari—starry night, goddess saraswati
Vibhava—cause of emotion
Vibhavi—goddess
Vibhavri—sunshine
Vibhawari—highness, empress, queen of night
Vibhawati—splendourous
Vibha—bright
Vibha—sunshine, radiance, night
Vibhisha—pretty, lovely, handsome, graceful, talented
Vibhi—fearless
Vibhooshana—ornament, jewellery, ornamentation
Vibhoosha—ornament, jewellery, ornamentation, adornment, figuration
Vibhooshita—adorned

Vibhootee—abundance, ashes, welfare, pleanty
Vibhooti—resplendent, powerful, magnificent
Vibhor—ecstatic
Vibhrashtee—flame
Vibhrasti—radiance, flame, blaze
Vibhushana—decorated, splendour
Vibhusha—illumination, luminosity, radiance, splendour, beauty
Vibhusha—ornament, jewellery, ornamentation, adornment, figuration, grandeur
Vibhushita—adorned, decorated
Vibhuti—goddess lakshmi
Vibhuti—great personality, wealth
Vibhu—lord vishnu, powerful
Vibishika—daughter of balavinayagam
Vibusha—bright
Vichitra—strange, variegated
Victoria—woman of victory, victorious
Vidarbha—without darbha grass
Vidarshana—true perception
Viddhi—method, law, most pretty, lovely, handsome, graceful
Videepta—shining, bright
Videeptia—illuminating
Videsha—devotion, happiness
Vidhanshi—part of rules
Vidharti—fearless
Vidhata—maker, creator, dispenser
Vidhatree—goddess
Vidhatri—goddess saraswati
Vidha—a way of wormonarch, ruler, prince, earl
Vidhighna—method
Vidhisha—special for someone
Vidhita—loveable, goddess of mexico
Vidhi—method, goddess of destiny
Vidhi—nature
Vidhubala—goddess lakshmi
Vidhulata—a streak of illumination, luminosity, radiance
Vidhuna—brilliant, sagacious, gifted, wise, learned
Vidhuni—amiable, pleasing, suave, interesting
Vidhunya—pretty, lovely, handsome, graceful name
Vidhushi—brilliance, wise
Vidhutri—pretty, lovely, handsome, graceful name
Vidhut—electricity
Vidhu—bright, moon
Vidhu—the moon
Vidhyadeity—moon
Vidhyagauri—goddess of knowledge
Vidhyasri—electricity
Vidhyavathi—a scholar
Vidhya—education, knowledge, learning
Vidhyotama—a wise girl
Vidhy—tradition
Vidipta—bright
Vidisha—an intermediate region
Vidisha—happiness, smile, devotion, night
Vidita—known, informed goddess
Vidita—understood, known
Vidmahi—name of lord ganesha
Vidmaya—name of lord ganesha
Vidoushi—knowledge, wise girl
Vidujvala—illuminating
Vidula—brilliant, sagacious, gifted, wise, learned
Vidula—moon, planet earth, god muruga
Vidushe—brilliant, sagacious, gifted, wise, learned
Vidushi—a scholar
Vidushi—brilliant, sagacious, gifted, wise, learned, learned
Viduveshe—resentment
Vidvathi—scholar
Vidvi—pretty, lovely, handsome, graceful name
Vidwath—highly qualified, most brilliant
Vidyadeity—goddess of knowledge, saraswati
Vidyadhari—supporter of knowledge
Vidyadhar—wisdom holder
Vidyagauri—goddess of wisdom
Vidyalakshmi—knowledge and lakshmi

Vidyane—knowledge
Vidyani—knowledge
Vidyashree—holy, pure, sanctified, pious, solemn knowledge
Vidyasree—knowledge
Vidyavati—well known, learnedpsara
Vidya—knowledge
Vidya—knowledge, goddess saraswati
Vidyota—consisting of illumination, luminosity, radiance, shining
Vidyota—glory, shining, illumination, luminosity, radiance
Vidyullata—illumination, luminosity, radiance plant
Vidyul—illumination, luminosity, radiance
Vidyuta—illumination, luminosity, radiance
Vidyuta—illumination, luminosity, radiance flashing, thunderbolt
Vidyutprabha—illumination, luminosity, radiance flash
Vidyut—electricity
Vidyut—illumination, luminosity, radiance
Vielashini—loving truth
Viendri—goddess of the brave
Vighneshwari—to end evil, bad
Vigna—pretty, lovely, handsome, graceful
Vigneshwari—daughter of lord ganesha
Vignita—pretty, lovely, handsome, graceful name
Vignyapna—request
Vignyatri—goddess parvati
Vigya—knowledge, wise
Vihadhya—pretty, lovely, handsome, graceful name
Vihana—early morning, ray of sun
Vihana—flying high, dawn
Vihane—early morning, ray of sun
Vihanginee—educated woman
Vihangi—free bird, goddess
Vihangne—one who flies like a bird
Vihani—early morning
Viharikaa—beauty, great
Viharika—great, beauty

Vihari—lord krishna
Viha—heaven
Viha—heavennkle, sanskrit
Vijaita—winner
Vijalakshmi—goddess
Vijali—sparkling
Vijana—illumination, luminosity, radianceining
Vijanti—knowledge
Vijara—one who never grow old
Vijayabanu—winner
Vijayachandrika—moon of victory
Vijayakumari—victorious
Vijayalakshmi—goddess lakmi
Vijayalakshmi—goddess of victory
Vijayalaksmi—goddess of victory
Vijayamala—garland of victory
Vijayanthi—winning
Vijayantika—ultimate victory
Vijayanti—victorious bramhi medicine
Vijayashree—glorious vicory
Vijayasree—a winning girl
Vijayata—winner
Vijaya—goddess durga, victory
Vijaya—victory of goddess durga
Vijaya—viktoriya, vijayam
Vijayeta—victorious
Vijaylakshmi—goddess of victory
Vijaynti—success
Vijayshree—victory
Vijayshree—win, victory
Vijayshri—glorious victory
Vija—thunder
Vijeta—victorious
Vijita—always winning
Vijiti—victory
Vijittaree—vanquisher
Vijiya—born to win
Viji—cute win, charming
Vijja—victory
Vijul—a silk-cottom tree
Vijul—a tree
Vijyagauri—fair women born to win
Vijyalakshmi—born to win, goddess lakshmi
Vijya—born to win, victory
Vijyesh—lord shiva
Vikanshi—bright, cherful

Vikashini—devlopment
Vikashni—progress
Vikashvi—pretty, lovely, handsome, graceful name
Vikasine—progressive
Vikasine—victorious
Vikasini—radiant, cherful, shining
Vikasni—goddess lakshmi
Vikathini—boasting
Vika—god's power full of life
Vikchalamba—goddess durga
Vikeshe—without hair
Vikhyatee—fame
Vikil—the epitome of power, vigour
Vikisha—holy, sanctified, pious, solemn, chaste, brightness, brilliant, sagacious, gifted, wise, learned
Vikitha—pretty, lovely, handsome, graceful name
Vikrama—violent, goddess parvati
Vikrantee—powerful
Vikranti—bold, brave
Vikriti—a silk cotton tree
Vikrrita—strange, deformed
Vikruti—goddess lakshmi
Viksah—knowledge
Vikshika—stars
Vilasantee—glittering, shining
Vilasanti—flashing, shining, glittering
Vilashini—one who gives pleasure
Vilash—coolness, playful
Vilasine—graceful movement, playful
Vilasine—happiest
Vilasini—playful, goddess lakshmi
Vilasita—glittering, shining
Vilas—goddess durga, playful
Vilaxa—specific
Vilina—dedicated
Vilochana—the eye, glimmers
Vilohita—deep red
Vimaladeity—playful
Vimalai—pretty, lovely, handsome, graceful name
Vimalakumari—dedicated
Vimalarani—holy, sanctified, pious, solemn, chaste
Vimala—clean

Vimala—holy, sanctified, pious, solemn, chaste
Vimala—holy, sanctified, pious, solemn, chaste, clever, clean
Vimali—goddess parvathi
Vimal—wiseffectionate, holy, sanctified, pious, solemn, chaste, honest
Vimisha—wonder, smart, cute
Vimish—good
Vimla—clean
Vimlesh—the holy, sanctified, pious, solemn, chaste lord
Vimli—sweet
Vimmi—gentle, simple
Vimmu—sky
Vimochane—emancipation
Vimochani—liberation, freedom river
Vimple—loved one
Vimrantee—powerful
Vimudha—goddess lakshmi
Vinaaya—kind hearted
Vinadee—a name of the river
Vinadi—noisy
Vinaha—together
Vinakshi—pretty, lovely, handsome, graceful name
Vinal—vine hall
Vinamrata—politeness, modesty
Vinamrat—polite speaker
Vinamra—modest, humility
Vinanthi—request
Vinantika—humble
Vinanti—prayer, request
Vinanya—humble
Vinanya—sky, request
Vinapani—goddess saraswati
Vinataa—pretty, lovely, handsome, graceful name
Vinata—humble
Vinata—humble, mother of garuda
Vinatee—humility, prayer
Vinathi—request
Vinati—request, prayer
Vinavati—goddess saraswati
Vinayaka—another name of lord ganesha
Vinayaki—lord ganesha

Vinaya—humble, mother of garuda
Vinaya—silent, modesty
Vinayika—the consort of lord ganesha
Vinayra—pretty, lovely, handsome, graceful name
Vinay—modesty
Vina—a musical instrument
Vina—amiable, pleasing, suave, interesting, beloved, favourite
Vincy—victory, winner
Vincy—winner
Vindhuja—knowledge
Vindhu—point, brilliant, sagacious, gifted, wise, learned
Vindhyanilaya—a form of durga, wind of vindhyas
Vindhyasri—pretty, lovely, handsome, graceful name
Vindhyavaasini—goddess durga, prayer
Vindhyavasini—goddess parvati
Vindhya—a river
Vindhya—knowledge, name of goddess
Vinela—moon, illumination, luminosity, radiance, lord vishnu
Vinela—pretty, lovely, handsome, graceful name
Vinesha—efficient
Vineta—unassuming, humble, knowledgeable
Vinetha—humble, sacrifice, respectful
Vineti—good behaviour
Vinet—kind, decent, domesticated
Vinija—rukmini
Vinila—deep blue
Vinil—morning
Vinima—knowledge
Vinisha—leader, goddess of love
Vinishka—leader
Vinita—dare, polite, sweet
Vinita—garuda's mother
Vinitee—good behaviour
Vinitha—humble, sacrifice
Vinithra—knowledge
Viniti—modesty, good behaviour
Vini—rukmani, dream, goddess of beauty

Vinmaya—pretty, lovely, handsome, graceful name
Vinoda—pleasing
Vinodhini—loved one, humble, playful, happy
Vinodini—pleasing
Vinodini—pleasing, brilliant, sagacious, gifted, wise, learned
Vinodita—amused, illumination, luminosity, radiance
Vinodita—happy
Vinodne—joyous
Vinod—smiling, pleasant, cherful
Vinola—pretty, lovely, handsome, graceful name
Vinoliya—sky spark
Vinoothna—new
Vinshika—flute, brave
Vinthi—request
Vinupama—pretty, lovely, handsome, graceful name
Vinuta—requester, unique, modest, humble
Vinutha—exceptionally new, special
Vinu—popular name
Vinu—vinanth, devotionful ask
Viny—pretty, lovely, handsome, graceful name
Vipanche—one who removes troubles
Vipanchi—lute
Vipasa—name of river
Vipasha—old name of the river vyas
Vipa—speech
Vipodha—giving inspiration
Vipodha—one who gives inspiration
Viprachittee—sagacious
Vipransee—pretty, lovely, handsome, graceful name
Vipra—priest
Vipsa—repetition
Vipula—a river
Vipula—plenty
Vipula—the earth, abundant
Virabala—brave maiden
Virachanaa—moon
Virachana—arrangement
Virahi—genius, loving, passionate
Virajaa—the earth abundant

Viraja—freedom from passion
Viraja—passionless
Virajini—brilliant, splendid
Viraj—name of a celestial dancer, monarch, ruler, prince, earl
Virakshi—powerful women
Virali—priceless, valuable, rare
Viral—priceless, natural
Virane—courageous woman
Virangana—brave lady, rani lakshmibai
Virangi—strong
Viranshu—strong
Virashree—goddess of victory
Virata—bravery
Virati—to denounce sin
Viravine—weeping
Vira—devotion, truth, heroine, heroic
Virendree—goddess of valour
Virendri—goddess of beauty
Viresha—brave
Virika—bravery
Virini—of whom the brave are born
Viri—bloom, garden stuff of pleasant fragrance
Virja—lord shiva
Virochana—illuminating
Virta—bravery, power, spirit
Virtee—pretty, lovely, handsome, graceful name
Virudha—sprouting, grown, formed
Virupa—manifold
Virupa—manifold, variegated
Viruthula—prize
Viryvati—strong, powerful
Visalam—broad minded
Visalatchi—huge
Visala—celestial apsara
Visalini—pretty, lovely, handsome, graceful name
Viseshi—different
Vishaika—part of subject
Vishaka—stars
Vishakha—a star
Vishakha—a star, birth star of lord muruga
Vishakha—sixteenth nakshatra
Vishalakshe—larged eye, glimmers

Vishalakshe—one with big eye, glimmers
Vishalakshi—broad eye, glimmers, one with big eye, glimmers
Vishalakshi—with large eye, glimmers
Vishala—daughter of daksha
Vishala—large
Vishala—wide, spacious
Vishalini—god murugan, goddess saraswati
Vishali—a creeper
Vishali—one with big heart
Vishalya—free from pain
Vishalya—painless
Vishaya—subject
Vishayka—part of subject
Visha—intellect, wisdom, tree
Visheka—additional, spietal
Vishesha—special
Visheta—self control
Vishetha—quality
Vishhara—removing venom
Vishika—lamp, stars
Vishikha—pin
Vishita—twiillumination, luminosity, radiance
Vishma—goddess parvati
Vishmita—pretty, lovely, handsome, graceful name
Vishnavi—lord venkateswara, goddess
Vishnuka—the true beauty
Vishnumaya—goddess parvati
Vishnupriya—dear to vishnu, goddess lakshmi
Vishoka—exempted from grief
Vishranti—rest, relaxation
Vishrutee—fame
Vishrutee—famous, celebrated, fame
Vishrutha—goddess of durga, expanding
Vishruti—fame, celebrated
Vishuddhe—purity
Vishuddhi—purity, holiness, perfect
Vishu—lord vishnu, poison, earth
Vishvaani—pretty, lovely, handsome, graceful name
Vishvache—universal
Vishvadhaya—all-nourishing

Vishvagabha—world's womb
Vishvambharee—the earth
Vishvambhari—the earth
Vishvamhara—earth, universe
Vishvamshu—producer of everything
Vishvanjali—offering to entire universe
Vishvaruche—illuminator of the universe
Vishvashri—treasure of the universe
Vishvasvam—source of everything
Vishvavati—universal, river ganga
Vishva—the earth, world
Vishva—world, universe
Vishvesha—lady of the universe
Vishvita—the universe, world
Vishwaja—earth, whole world
Vishwambhara—earth
Vishwani—lord of universe
Vishwanjali—pretty, lovely, handsome, graceful name
Vishwa—entirell, earth, world
Vishweswari—subject
Vishweta—holy, sanctified, pious, solemn, chaste, purity, clear by heart
Vish—poison, earth
Visishta—special
Vismaya—surprise, wonder of lifemazing
Visma—goddess parvati
Vismita—wondermentmazement
Vismitta—pretty, lovely, handsome, graceful name
Visrutha—vishvam, known to many
Visruthi—pretty, lovely, handsome, graceful name
Vistarine—extended
Vistarini—a goddess
Visu—pretty, lovely, handsome, graceful name
Visvaani—pretty, lovely, handsome, graceful name
Visva—entirell, world
Viswarupa—pretty, lovely, handsome, graceful name
Viswa—universe, world
Vitabhi—fearless
Vitachinta—goddess lakshmi

Vitakama—pretty, lovely, handsome, graceful name
Vitaka—world
Vitana—extension, heap, plenty, abundance
Vitaraga—a goddess
Vitasta—a river, measure of length
Vitasta—jhelum river
Vita—life, desire, aspiration, longing, filled with life
Vithika—pathway, path between greenery
Vithi—fate
Viti—illumination, luminosity, radiance
Vitola—very calm river
Vitrishna—content, satisfied
Vittada—wealth giver
Vittee—gain
Vitti—consciousness, understanding
Vivadhit—fighter
Vivandisha—ambition, intent, passion to worship
Vivarsha—rain
Vivashvati—shining
Viva—long-live, springlike, fresh
Vivdha—different
Vivedha—different
Vivedhya—ved
Viveka—brain, right
Viveka—wise
Vivekine—tolerance, durability, toleration
Vivekini—discriminating
Vivekka—brilliant, sagacious, gifted, wise, learned and witty
Vivekta—success
Vivek—tolerance, durability, toleration, conscience
Vividha—strange, miscellaneous
Vivika—alive, war fortress, life
Viviksha—brilliant, sagacious, gifted, wise, learned, smiler
Viviktha—logically brilliant, sagacious, gifted, wise, learned
Vivitha—kind
Vivitsa—ambition, intent, passion of knowledge

Viyana—respect, valuable, valued, rare
Viya—breeze, poem, sweet
Viyogine—one who is separated
Viyogine—pathway
Viyogini—one who is separated
Viyogi—pretty, lovely, handsome,
graceful name
Viyom—sky
Vodala—shine, illumination,
luminosity, radiance
Volaka—achiever
Vola—discriminating
Vopalita—pretty, lovely, handsome,
graceful name
Vorukana—pretty, lovely, handsome,
graceful name
Vovika—respectful
Vrachaya—searching
Vradhika—always growing
Vrajabala—girl from mathura
Vrajbhamini—pretty, lovely,
handsome, graceful name
Vranda—radha, basil
Vrasha—cow
Vrashbha—a river
Vrashti—rain
Vrata—fast
Vreeha—creative
Vriddhi—growth, progress
Vridha—growth, progress
Vridhi—increase, growth
Vriha—creative, goddess of education
Vriksh—tree
Vrinda—basil, cluster of bloom,
garden stuff
Vrinda—basil, tulsi, goddess radha
Vrinda—tulsi
Vrindha—a garden
Vrischika—star
Vrishali—karana's wife in the
mahabharata
Vrisha—cow
Vrishika—scorpio
Vrishni—pretty, lovely, handsome,
graceful name
Vrishti—rain
Vristi—rain, shower
Vritee—nature, behaviour

Vriteka—success in life
Vritika—thought
Vritikka—goddess radha
Vriti—popularity
Vrittee—creative
Vritti—nature, temperament
Vritti—temperament
Vriyana—pretty, lovely, handsome,
graceful highness, empress, queen
Vrrishaka—cow
Vrritee—live, exist, rise, being, entity,
moral conduct
Vruddhi—grow, increase, progress
Vrudhi—increase, gain, increment
Vruksha—tree
Vrundali—one who belongs to lord
krishna
Vrundana—belongs from lord
krishna's place
Vrunda—basil, goddess radha, tulsi
Vrushali—prosperity, who give
happiness
Vrushitha—prosperity
Vrushti—forest, wood, jungle, rain
Vrusti—heavy rain
Vrutali—pretty, lovely, handsome,
graceful name
Vruthika—pretty, lovely, handsome,
graceful name
Vrutika—develop
Vrutiksha—goddess lakshmi
Vrutti—live, exist, riseing
Vrutti—nature, tamper
Vyadhi—epidemic, trouble
Vyaghree—tigress
Vyaghrritee—speech
Vyahruthi—name of goddess parvati
Vyaka—river
Vyakhya—explain
Vyana—graceful
Vyanjana—rhetorical suggestion
Vyanjana—word-power
Vyapti—accomplishment
Vyapti—accomplishmentttainment
Vyapti—widespread, rain
Vyashalani—natural beauty
Vyashtee—success
Vyasti—success, individuality

Vyatibha—shining, fame
Vya—the arranger
Vyene—dawn
Vygha—river
Vyjayanthi—garland of lord krishna
Vyjayanti—victorious women
Vyna—vineyard, the universe
Vyomaa—temparament
Vyoma—bird, who lives in sky
Vyoma—the sky
Vyomikaa—stay on sky

Vyomika—reside in the sky
Vyomine—heavenly
Vyomine—name of saraswati deity
Vyomini—holy, pure, sanctified,
pious, solemn
Vyshali—great
Vyshnavi—name of goddess lakshmi
Vyushtee—grace, beauty, first ray of
the dawn
Vyusti—the first gleam of dawn, grace

****

Indian Names For Girls—W

Wafiya—loyal, devotionful

Wageeshwari—goddess saraswati

Waheda—pretty, lovely, handsome, graceful, sole, single, unique

Waida—promise

Wajeeha—eminent, distinguished

Wakeeta—pretty, lovely, handsome, graceful bloom, garden stuff

Wamika—pretty, lovely, handsome, graceful

Wamika—goddess durga

Wamila—pretty, lovely, handsome, graceful

Wamil—pretty, lovely, handsome, graceful

Wani—daring

Wanuka—goddess durga

Warda—a girl, earth

Warda—rose, guardian, pretty, lovely, handsome, graceful, giver

Warisha—illumination, luminosity, radiance

Warrachna—good attitude

Watika—garden

Widisha—wife of monarch, ruler, prince, earl ashoka

Winisha—highness, empress, queen of universe

Winmathi—bright moon

Wira—white skinned

Wishi—fulfil desire, aspiration, longing

Worda—rose

Wridhima—full of love, goddess lakshmi

Writi—popularity, thought

Writtika—pretty, lovely, handsome, graceful season autumn

****

Indian Names For Girls—X

Xagar—ocean, pass through
Xama—forgiveness
Xaria—melody
Xena—brave, pretty, lovely, handsome, graceful

Xiti—pretty, lovely, handsome, graceful
Xoti—small
Xyla—dream

****

Indian Names For Girls—Y

Yachana—pleading, pray for something
Yachana—prayer
Yachana—to pray
Yachika—to praisepplication
Yachna—sing, prathna, establishes
Yadamma—mother of remembrance
Yadave—goddess durga
Yadavi—goddess durga
Yadhana—smile
Yadika—pretty, lovely, handsome, graceful name
Yadita—silence, lord of night
Yadnika—little, nearest, holy, sanctified, pious, solemn, chaste fire
Yadni—kind heart
Yadva—devotee of lord vishnu, mind
Yadvesh—very brilliant
Yadwiga—bringer of luck
Yad—remembrance
Yaganya—sacred fire
Yagasri—pretty
Yagavi—bright
Yagini—quiet, swift
Yagna—sacrificial offerings
Yagnetri—ceremonial rites to god
Yagnitha—worship
Yagnya—goddess durga
Yagnya—new, beauty
Yagya—holy sacred fire, hawan
Yahavi—bright
Yahsmita—powerful
Yahvi—heaven, earth
Yajah—devotee
Yajaira—form of yahaira
Yaja—worshipper
Yajika—goddess parvati
Yajmadaya—risen from sacred fire
Yajnadaya—risen from sacred fire
Yajnaseni—another name of draupadi
Yajna—fire, worship
Yajneshvari—goddess of sacrifice
Yajnika—flame of the forest, wood, jungle

Yajushi—nice
Yaju—power, the yajur veda
Yakshangane—river
Yakshangi—a river
Yakshara—unalterable, indestructible
Yaksha—confidence, waiting
Yaksha—waiting, confidence
Yakshe—female yaksha
Yakshine—female yaksha
Yakshini—attendants of durga
Yakshita—pretty, lovely, handsome, graceful, wonder girl
Yaksini—prayer, worship
Yalaini—rose
Yaline—goddess saraswati
Yalini—melodious
Yalini—melodious, music melodies
Yalisai—melodious
Yallini—melodious
Yamabhagine—yamuna river
Yamahardika—heart piercing
Yamala—a twin
Yamal—a twin deity
Yamangika—destroyer of yama
Yamani—restraining
Yamavatee—night
Yama—restrainer
Yamee—goddess durga
Yamee—pair, twin, couple
Yamee—progress, motion
Yamika—night
Yamika—pretty, night
Yamini—illumination, luminosity, radiance in the dark, night
Yamini—night
Yami—pretty, lovely, handsome, graceful
Yami—elder
Yami—illumination, luminosity, radiance in dark, twinkling star
Yamni—costly stone
Yamni—night
Yamoli—melodious
Yamshith—good person

Yamunai—brilliant, sagacious, gifted, wise, learned
Yamuna—a river
Yamuna—quick action, jamuna river
Yamune—a indian river
Yamuni—river
Yamura—goddess lakshami
Yamya—night
Yana—god gifted, valuable, valued, rare to god
Yanti—goddess parvati, vichar, thoughts
Yanvi—illumination, luminosity, radiance in the dark
Yara—little butterfly
Yarima—appointed by god
Yasahvi—rise
Yasalima—wellbeing
Yasana—ambition, intent, passion
Yasana—prayer
Yasashwi—having fame
Yasasri—like shree
Yasaswi—successful, goddess lakshmi
Yashada—the one who gives success
Yashana—a bloom, garden stuff
Yashasri—goddess of success
Yashasvati—famous
Yashasvine—famous, pretty, lovely, handsome, graceful
Yashasvini—glorious, famous
Yashasvi—successful, famous, giving joy
Yashaswati—famous
Yashaswine—famous mother
Yashaswi—famous, successful
Yashavi—fame, victorious, famous
Yasha—fame
Yasha—goddess parvati
Yashica—successful, brave girl
Yashika—famous, glory, successful
Yashila—famous
Yashila—success, famous
Yashini—sweet, one who be gets fame
Yashita—successful, winner, pretty, lovely, handsome, graceful
Yashitha—glorious, famous
Yashi—glory, victory, fame, righteous

Yashka—glory, gifted, successful, famous
Yashmika—god's bloom, garden stuff
Yashmita—symbol of famelways successful
Yashna—one with fame, prayer
Yashna—to pray
Yashneil—famous, glorious, successful
Yashni—illumination, luminosity, radiance, successor
Yashoda—famous, successful
Yashodha—lord krishna's mother
Yashodha—mother of lord krishna
Yashodhra—buddha's wife
Yashomati—krishna's mother
Yashonidhi—ocean of fame
Yashovati—famous, glorious
Yashraj—monarch, ruler, prince, earl of victory
Yashree—star, goddess lakshmi
Yashri—greatness, goodness lakshmi
Yashshri—fame, cooperative
Yashtika—a string of pearl
Yashti—pearls string
Yashti—twinkling star, slender creeper
Yashu—beauty, holy, sanctified, pious, solemn, chaste soul, target
Yashvati—famous
Yashve—god gifted, goddess lakshmi
Yashvini—pretty, lovely, handsome, graceful name
Yashvita—famous, successful, pretty, lovely, handsome, graceful
Yashvi—fame, victorious, famous
Yashvy—fame
Yashwina—successful
Yashwini—successful lady succeed
Yash—fame, success
Yasika—famous, glory
Yasina—little heart
Yasmeen—highness, empress, queen, jasmine bloom, garden stuff
Yasmina—jasmine bloom, garden stuff
Yasmin—sweet smelling, jasmine bloom, garden stuff
Yasmita—famous, glorious

Yasmitha—pretty, lovely, handsome, graceful name
Yasodha—famous, successful, mother of lord
Yassika—glory, famous
Yastika—a string pf pearls
Yasti—slim
Yasve—joy
Yasvita—good
Yasvitha—pretty, lovely, handsome, graceful name
Yasvi—famous, victorious, fame
Yaswini—joy, praiseworthy
Yaswitha—success
Yas—a bloom, garden stuff, jasmine
Yatee—goddess durga
Yathika—goddess durga
Yathisha—new learning
Yathi—one who strives with pertinacity
Yathra—travel, journey
Yathvika—goddess durga
Yatika—name of goddess durga
Yatisa—cute
Yati—goddess durga
Yatna—agony
Yatna—effort, perseverance
Yatra—journey, travel
Yatri—traveller
Yatudhane—magician
Yatvika—nice
Yauvani—goddess gayatri, mother of vedas
Yauvna—youth
Yavaksha—a name of the river
Yavana—quick, swift, youth, young
Yavanika—curtain of stage
Yavani—quick, swift
Yavi—pretty, lovely, handsome, graceful, cute
Yavna—quick, swift
Yavnika—protected by god, powerful
Yavyavati—a name of the river
Yayati—wanderer, traveller
Yazhika—pretty, lovely, handsome, graceful name
Yazhini—joy with love, musical instrument

Yazmozi—ruler
Yeetika—pretty, lovely, handsome, graceful name
Yeghna—pretty, lovely, handsome, graceful name
Yemaya—goddess of the ocean
Yema—happiness, our joy
Yesa—famous, glorious, right
Yesha—fame, famous, glorious, fate
Yeshika—cute
Yeshna—happiness
Yeshvini—winner of fame
Ykshara—powerful, best
Yochana—thought, thinmonarch, ruler, prince, earl
Yodha—soldier, heroic warrior
Yogamaya—magical power of meditation
Yogammal—blessed
Yogandri—happiness
Yogasri—cute girl
Yogavati—intergrated
Yoga—an art of achieving happiness
Yogdipika—illumination, luminosity, radiance of yoga
Yogeeni—lord krishna
Yogeeta—goddess parwati
Yogeetha—goddess parvati
Yogeshri—god of goddess santoshi
Yogeshwari—goddess durga
Yogindra—slep while meditating
Yogini—one who can control senses
Yogini—pleasing, favourite, charming
Yogin—devotee
Yogita—attraction
Yogita—one who can concentrate
Yogitha—saint, yogability
Yogi—sage, saint
Yogmaya—a name of yoga
Yogmaya—meditation for wealth
Yognavi—one who can concentrate
Yogna—ceremonial rites to god
Yogtara—a star
Yogyasri—goddess lakshmi, money
Yogyata—ability, capacity
Yogya—perfect, fame
Yohitha—another name of river ganga
Yojana—planning

Yojana—planning, plan, scheme
Yojitha—organised help
Yojna—planing
Yokitha—pretty, lovely, handsome, graceful name
Yomana—holy river in india
Yongari—goddess, god
Yonita—dove, lady, women
Yosana—young, lady, women, girl
Yoshana—young woman
Yosha—young woman
Yoshika—cute, successful, brave, honest
Yoshine—brilliant, pretty, lovely, handsome, graceful
Yoshini—think
Yoshita—a girl
Yoshita—women, lady
Yosita—successful
Youjana—thought
Yousha—lord krishna, young girl
Yshaswi—having fame
Yuaani—pleasant
Yuavteeshta—yellow jasmine
Yugandhara—earth
Yugandhra—earth
Yuga—era, years, generation
Yugitha—goddess lakshmi
Yugla—name of a lake
Yugma—pair
Yuhisha—path to heven
Yukasri—lucky
Yukta—absorbed
Yukta—idea, latitudettentive
Yuktha—absorbedttentive

Yukthi—trick, power, strategy
Yuktika—act of creativity
Yukti—inventive, skill
Yukti—strategy, idea, trick, solution
Yumai—senseless
Yunita—loveable
Yunna—some one special, success
Yunuen—god's wife
Yurda—bestower of longevity
Yuridia—invented name
Yushi—popular around
Yushna—pretty, lovely, handsome, graceful name
Yuthika—like a bloom, garden stuff, multitude
Yuthika—multitude
Yutika—bloom, garden stuff, jasmine white bloom, garden stuff
Yutika—jasmine bloom, garden stuff
Yuti—a mythological character
Yuti—success, union
Yuvasri—pretty, lovely, handsome, graceful
Yuvatee—a woman
Yuvati—young lady
Yuvigna—pretty, lovely, handsome, graceful name
Yuvika—young woman, maid
Yuvina—young lady
Yuvisha—young
Yuvi—respect of mother
Yuvna—young, strong, healthy
Yuvragi—princess of hearts
Yuvrani—princess
Yuvti—a woman

****

Indian Names For Girls—Z

Zachni—most pretty, lovely, handsome, graceful dancer
Zaei—name of a bloom, garden stuff in marathi
Zafira—victorious, successful
Zahbia—pretty, lovely, handsome, graceful
Zahera—expression, shining, brilliant
Zahira—shining, luminous, brilliant
Zahra—radiant, pretty, lovely, handsome, graceful, fair, white
Zahril—poisonous
Zahrin—pretty, lovely, handsome, graceful
Zaida—to raise, boostbundance
Zaina—lovely, pretty, strong, cherful
Zain—grace, beauty, good
Zakiya—holy, sanctified, pious, solemn, chaste
Zalak—instant appearance
Zalika—well born, wondrously pretty, lovely, handsome, graceful
Zallary—mermaid
Zamina—elegant, pretty, lovely, handsome, graceful
Zamuni—a holy river of hindu
Zana—flow of water
Zanie—god grace
Zanisha—most pretty, lovely, handsome, graceful
Zankar—melodious voice
Zankhana—deep ambition, intent, passion
Zankhi—pray of god
Zankhna—deep ambition, intent, passion
Zankrut—highness, empress, queenuspicious
Zanshi—highness, empress, queen
Zaqaria—cute
Zaral—easy
Zara—illumination, luminosity, radiance, brave, pretty, lovely, handsome, graceful bloom, garden stuff
Zara—princess, lady, shining, bloom, garden stuff
Zareen—golden expression
Zarinaa—highness, empress, queen
Zarina—the gold one, golden, highness, empress, queen
Zarna—a small stream of sweet water
Zaveri—deityne
Zayka—flavour
Zebidiah—purple panguin cherios
Zeel—waterfall
Zeenat—beauty and happiness of home
Zeena—a hospitable woman, welcoming
Zelam—name of river in punjab
Zena—moon, fame, news
Zenia—hospitable, welcoming, bloom, garden stuff
Zenisha—most pretty, lovely, handsome, graceful
Zenobia—given life by zeus, power of zeus
Zenoushka—little maid, pretty, lovely, handsome, graceful highness, empress, queen
Zenshi—sweet, complete
Zerelda—brave, woman warrior
Zeynap—name of prophet mohhamad's child
Zhaisri—victorious, goddess of victory
Zhel—falling of water
Zhiya—pretty, lovely, handsome, graceful name
Ziah—illumination, luminosity, radiance, life, pleasant
Ziana—pretty, lovely, handsome, graceful, blessed, bold
Zia—illumination, luminosity, radiance, illumination, luminosity, radiance tremble
Zila—shadow, bloom, garden stuff

Zil—a river lake
Zinal—loving, pretty, lovely, handsome, graceful, name of place
Zinga—sea food, having long hairs
Zinnat—glamour
Zita—theresa, harvest, seeker, virgin
Zivah—god, illumination, luminosity, radiance of god
Ziva—life, radiantluster, splendour
Ziyana—blessing from heaven, knowledge
Ziyanshi—source of illumination, luminosity, radiance, radiance, body
Ziya—source of illumination, luminosity, radiance, radiance
Zoey—life, responsible, honest, happy
Zohara—pretty, lovely, handsome, graceful, venus, blooming
Zohra—venus, love, pretty, lovely, handsome, graceful
Zora—daybreak, sunrise, dawn
Zoya—shining, life
Zubangi—all rounder
Zubeida—honest, the best one, marigold

Zubira—holy, sanctified, pious, solemn, chaste as spring
Zudora—explore, provider of food
Zueinah—lucky number, stone, metal, colour
Zuha—morning star, illumination, luminosity, radiance, bright
Zuhi—illumination, luminosity, radiance
Zuleika—brilliant, the fair one
Zulema—full of beauty, serenity, calm, calmness, stillness, silence
Zuleyka—pretty, lovely, handsome, graceful
Zurina—white
Zuri—pretty, lovely, handsome, graceful, white, illumination, luminosity, radiance
Zyana—blessing from heaven, knowledge
Zykaraya—smart
Zymal—illumination, luminosity, radiance
Zyna—welcoming

****
******

Made in the USA
Columbia, SC
17 October 2021